THE UNIATE EASTERN CHURCHES

THE UNIATE
EASTERN CHURCHES

THE BYZANTINE RITE
IN ITALY, SICILY, SYRIA AND EGYPT

BY

ADRIAN FORTESCUE, Ph.D., D.D.
LATE PROFESSOR OF ECCLESIASTICAL HISTORY AT ST. EDMUND'S COLLEGE, WARE

EDITED BY

GEORGE D. SMITH, D.D.
PROFESSOR OF DOGMATIC THEOLOGY
AT THE SAME COLLEGE

FREDERICK UNGAR PUBLISHING CO.
NEW YORK

Καὶ ἡμεῖς συναγωγοὶ ἐκ διαφόρων ἐθνῶν
καὶ γλωσσῶν τὰ ἀρνία ὧν ὁ Κύριος ποιμὴν
ὑπῆρξεν

Ap. Const. II, lvi, 3.

Library of Congress Catalog Card Number
57-6424
Printed in the United States of America

EDITOR'S PREFACE

READERS of the two previous volumes of this series[1] will be aware that Dr. Adrian Fortescue intended to complete it by a third.

This volume was to have contained a full treatment of the Uniate Churches corresponding to each of the separated Churches which are treated in his two published works.

The completion of this plan was prevented by that untimely death which, coming as a shock to all who had known Dr. Fortescue, has left in the ranks of Catholic writers a gap which may never be filled.

A few days before he died Dr. Fortescue expressed to me a wish that this work on the Uniate Churches should be published. He said that I might if I chose complete it, or else publish it as it stood; but he left little doubt in my mind which course he would prefer. I am therefore placing before the public his work in its incomplete state as it left the author's hands, with the certainty that in so doing I am fulfilling his wishes. Moreover, I am persuaded, and I think that not a few readers will agree with me, that the unfinished work of Dr. Fortescue himself is preferable to any attempted completion by another hand.

The plan of his projected work is indicated in the prefatory remarks to the introductory chapter (p. xxiii). From these it will be seen that the book was to have had four parts. The first, entitled " The Byzantine Uniates," dealt with the Uniate groups corresponding to the Orthodox Eastern Church. The second and third parts were to have described the Uniate com-

[1] " The Orthodox Eastern Church " (C.T.S., 3rd edition, 1911) and " The Lesser Eastern Churches " (C.T.S., 1913).

munities which correspond to the Lesser Eastern Churches, while the fourth would have treated of the Maronites, who have no similar counterpart.

The present volume contains, besides the chapter on the Uniate Churches in general, the principal portion of Part I. According to the author's intention, about two-thirds of the book were to have been devoted to the description of the Byzantine Uniates. What is now presented is thus about one-half of the proposed work. It includes the interesting study of the Italo-Greeks, a Uniate Church which had a particular fascination for Dr. Fortescue, since in their abbey-church at Grottaferrata[1] he received the inspiration of devoting himself to the study of things Eastern.

Much of the information in the chapter on the Melkites is the fruit of the author's personal investigation during his journeyings in the East. Incidentally it contains several instances of that satirical but not unkindly humour so characteristic of Dr. Fortescue, which even those at whom it is pointed may find difficult to resist.

The book, therefore, must be judged as a fragment. It may be found to lack that finish which it would assuredly have received at the skilful hands of the author. Some inaccuracy may have crept in, which on his revision would have been eliminated. Whatever be its defects, it cannot fail to be of great value to all who are interested in the subject. To ensure that none of the fruits of this study be lost, I have included the author's own copious bibliography for the whole work.

Dr. Fortescue would certainly have wished me to express his thanks to all those—unfortunately I have no record of their names—who have assisted him in collecting material. For even the smallest service he was always most grateful.

My own task in editing the manuscript of one who was a model of neatness and method in his work has been light. It has been rendered still more easy for

[1] See p. 150, n. 4.

me by Dr. Vance, Vice-President of St Edmund's
College, and by Dr. Alfred Herbert, who have been
truly generous with their assistance and advice. What
little labour there has been I am glad to offer as a small
tribute to the memory of my friend. One tribute at
least he would desire of those who have read his work
with interest—a prayer for the repose of his soul.
Opera illorum sequuntur illos.

St Edmund's College,
Feast of SS Peter and Paul, 1923.

NIHIL OBSTAT:

G. H. JOYCE, S.J.,

Censor deputatus

IMPRIMATUR:

EDM. CAN. SURMONT,

Vicarius generalis.

WESTMONASTERII,
die 15ª *Octobris,* 1923.

CONTENTS

	PAGE
EDITOR'S PREFACE - - - - - - -	v
LIST OF BOOKS - - - - - -	xi

INTRODUCTORY CHAPTER

CONCERNING UNIATE CHURCHES IN GENERAL: - - 1

  1. What is a Uniate ? - - - - 1

  2. The Various Uniate Churches - - - 7

  3. Religion, Patriarchate, Rite, Language, Place - 10

  4. Prejudices against the Uniates - - - 21

  5. The Holy See and the Uniates - - - 29

  Summary - - - - - - 43

THE BYZANTINE UNIATES

CHAPTER I

THE ITALO-GREEKS IN THE PAST: - - - - 47

  1. The Greeks of Southern Italy and Sicily - - 47

  2. Christianity in Sicily and Lower Italy to the Eighth Century - - - - - 66

  3. Byzantine Usurpation (Eighth to Eleventh Century) - 80

  4. From the Norman Conquest to the Coming of the Albanians (Eleventh to Fifteenth Century) - 94

  5. The Albanians (Fifteenth to Sixteenth Century) - 115

  6. Byzantine Monasticism in Italy - - - 124

  7. The Greek Colonies at Venice, Ancona, Bibbona, Naples - - - - - - 135

  Summary - - - - - - 145

CONTENTS

CHAPTER II

PAGE

EXISTING BYZANTINE INSTITUTIONS IN ITALY:[1] -   - 146

  1. Grottaferrata -   -   -   -   - 146
  2. The Greek College at Rome -   -   - 151
  3. The Albanian Colonies in Calabria and Sicily - 159
  4. The Greeks of Corsica and Leghorn -   - 169
  5. Italo-Greek Canon Law and Rites -   -   - 176
     Summary -   -   -   -   - 183

CHAPTER III

THE MELKITES: -   -   -   -   -   - 185

  1. Before Cyril VI (1724) -   -   - 185
  2. Union under Cyril VI (1724-1759) - 197
  3. History to Maximos III (1759-1833) - 202
  4. The Monks of St Saviour and the Monks of Shuwair 205
  5. Germanos Adam and the Synod of Ḳarḳafah - 208
  6. Maximos III (1833-1855) -   -   - 210
  7. History after Maximos III (1855-1915) - 221
  8. The Melkite Church at the Present Time[1] - 223
     Summary -   -   -   -   - 233

INDEX -   -   -   -   -   -   -   - 235

---

[1] The author describes the state of things existing in or about the year 1917, when he was engaged on this work.

LIST OF BOOKS

IN this bibliography I have included only those books which, since they appear more prominently in the author's notes, seem to have provided the principal sources for this work. Others, which he consulted incidentally, appear in the footnotes.

Moreover, most of the books on the Uniates treat also of the corresponding schismatical Churches. They therefore form the bibliography for the study of the Lesser Eastern Churches which the author had reserved for this volume.[1]

INTRODUCTORY CHAPTER
ON UNIATES IN GENERAL

J. HERGENRÖTHER: Four articles in *Archiv für kath. Kirchenrecht*, vols vii and viii (New Series, i and ii), Mainz, Kircheim, 1862: *Die Rechtsverhältnisse der verschiedenen Riten innerhalb der kath . Kirche.*

THEINER and MIKLOSCH: *Monumenta spectantia ad unionem ecclesiarum græcæ et romanæ.* (1872.)

A. ARNDT, S.J.: An article in *Archiv für kath. Kirchenrecht*, vol. lxxi (New Series, lxv), Mainz, Kircheim, 1894: *Die gegenseitigen Rechtsverhältnisse der Riten in der kath. Kirche.*

F. KATTENBUSCH: Article *Unierte Orientalen*, in the *Prot. Realencyklopädie.*

Acta et decreta sacr. Conc. recent. Collectio Lacensis (7 tomes; Freiburg, 1870–1890). Vol. ii contains Oriental Councils from 1682 to 1789; also Roman decrees concerning Eastern rites.

S.D.N. Benedicti Pp. XIV Bullarium (4 tom., fol.; Venice, 1778). Especially the Bull *Allatæ sunt*, tom. iv, pp. 123–136.

C. WILL: *Acta et decreta de controuersiis eccl. græcæ et latinæ.* (Leipzig, 1861.)

ADOLPHE D'AVRIL: *Documents relatifs aux églises de l'Orient et à leurs rapports avec Rome.* (Paris, 1885.)

---

[1] See *The Lesser Eastern Churches* (C.T.S., 1913), in the Preface, p. ix.

CHAPTERS I AND II
THE ITALO-GREEKS

PIETRO POMPILIO RODOTÀ: *Dell' origine, progresso, e stato presente del rito greco in Italia.*   (3 vols. 4to, Rome, 1758.)

WETZER U. WELTE: *Kirchenlexicon,* 2 aufl. (Herder, Freiburg, 1886), vi, 1133–1141; article *Italogräci.*

MORONI: *Dizionario di erudizione storico-ecclesiastica* (Venice, 1852), vol. xxxii, 149–153.

J. GAY: *L'Italie méridionale et l'Empire byzantine depuis l'avènement de Basile 1ᵉʳ jusqu' à la prise de Bari par les Normands, 867–1071.* (Paris, 1904.)
  Notes sur la conservation du rite grec dans la Calab. et la terre d'Otrante au XVIᵉ siècle ; listes de monastères basiliens. (*Byz. Zeitschr.,* iv, 1895.)
  Étude sur la décadence du rite grec dans l'Italie merid. à la fin du XVIᵉ siècle. (*Rev. d'histoire et de littérature religieuse,* ii, 1897.)

F. CHALANDON: *Histoire de l'Italie méridionale sous la domination normande.* (Paris, 1908.)
  Histoire de la domination normande en Italie et en Sicile. (Paris, 1907; Picard, 2 vols.)

G. L. SCHLUMBERGER: *L'Épopée byzantine.* (Paris, 3 vols., 1896–1900.)
  Un empéreur byzantin au dixième siècle, Nicéphore Phocas. (Paris, 1890.)

FERDINANDO UGHELLI: *Italia Sacra,* 2nd ed. Nic. Coleti. (Venice, fol., 1717–1722, 10 tom.)

J. S. ASSEMANI: *Italicæ historiæ scriptores : de rebus Neapolitanis et Siculis ab anno 500 ad ann. 1200.* (4 vols. 4to, Romæ, 1751–1753.)

L. DUCHESNE: *Les évêchés de Calabre,* in *Mélanges Paul Fabre.* (Paris, 1902.)

IOS. MORISANI: *De Protopapis et Deutereis Græcorum, et Catholicis eorum ecclesiis Diatriba.* (Naples, 1768.)

S. ZAMPELIOS: Ἰταλοελληνικὰ, ἤτοι κριτικὴ πραγματεία περὶ τῶν ἐν τοῖς ἀρχαίοις Νεαπόλεως ἀνεκδότων ἑλληνικῶν περγαμηνῶν (Athens, 1865.)

GIOV. CAN. MINASI: *Vita di Annibale d' Afflitto, Arcivescovo di Reggio.* (Naples: Lanciano e Pinto, 1895.)
  Le chiese di Calabria. (Naples, 1896.)

MARINUS BARLETIUS: *de Vita moribus ac rebus præcipue aduersus Turcas gestis Georgii Castrioti clarissimi Epirotarum principis.* (Strasburg, 1537.)

ENGENIO: *Napoli sacra di D. Cesare d'Engenio Caracciolo gentilhuomo napolitano.* (Naples: Ottavio Beltrano, 1624.)

MURATORI: *Rerum italicarum scriptores.* (25 vols., Milan, 1723–1751). Supplement by Michele Amari: *Biblioteca Arabo-Sicula.* (1 vol. fol., Turin-Rome: E. Loescher, 1880.)

Rocco Cotroneo: *Il rito greco in Calabria*. (Reggio di Calabria, 1902.)

Raymund Netzhammer (Mgr.), O.S.B.: *Unter den Albanesen Kalabriens* in " *Studien u. Mitteilungen aus dem Ben. u. Cist. Orden.*" (Brünn, 1906.)

Pietro Camodeca de' Coronei: *L'autonomia˞eccl. degli Italo-Albanesi delle Calabrie e della Basilicata.* (Rome, 2nd ed., 1903.)
A S.S. Leone XIII, gli Albanesi delle colonie di Sicilia. (Palermo, 1894.)

Sp ir. Lo Jacono: *Memoria sull' origine e fondazione della comune di Contessa, colonia greco-albanese di Sicilia.* (Palermo, 1851.)

Gustav Parthey: *Hieroclis Synecdemus et Notitæ græcæ Episcopatuum. Accedunt Nili Doxopatrii Notitia Patriarchatuum et locorum nomina immutata.* (Berlin, 1866.)

Ioannes de Ioanne: *De diuinis Siculorum officiis Tractatus.* (Palermo, 1736.)

Francois Lenormant: *La Grande-Grèce : Paysages et histoire.* (Paris: Levy, 3 vols., 1881–1884.)

J. G. Grævius: *Thesaurus Antiquitatum et Historiarum Siciliæ.* (Leiden, 1723.)

Beloudes, J. (Giov. Veludo = Ἰωάν. Βελούδης). Ἑλλήνων [ὀρθοδόξων ἀποικία εν Βενετίαις, ἱστορικὸν ὑπόμνημα (Venice, 1872.)

Oct. Caietanus: *Vitæ Sanctorum Siculorum.* (2 vols. fol.; Palermo 1657.)

Patrice Stephanopoli: *Histoire des Grecs en Corse.* (Paris, 1900.)

F. Tajani: *Le Istorie albanesi.* (Salerno: Fratelli Jovane, 1886.)

Henry Swinburne: *Travels in the Two Sicilies.* (2 vols.; London, 1783–1785.)

J. H. Bartels: *Briefe über Kalabrien u. Sizilien,* 3 parts. (Göttingen, 1787–1792.)

N. Nilles, S.J.: *Kalendarium manuale utriusque ecclesiæ orientalis et occidentalis* (Innsbruck: Rauch, 2nd ed., 1896–7, 2 vols.). For the saints and martyrs of Southern Italy and Sicily.

G. Morin: *La liturgie de Naples au temps de S. Grégoire, d'après deux évangelaires du septième siècle.* (*Rev. Bénédictine*, viii, 1891.)

J. M. Schröckh: *Christliche Kirchengeschichte* (Leipzig, 1804–1812), part ix. For the Greek Church at Venice.

C. F. Staudlin: *Kirchliche Geogr. u. Statistik.* (2 parts, Tübingen, 1804.)

S. Vailhe: *Constantinople (Église de),* in *Dict. de Théol. Cath.,* Vacant-Mangenot, § 11, *L'Italie byzantine, VIIIᵉ–XVIᵉ siècles.*

P. Batiffol: *L'Abbaye de Rossano.* (Paris, 1891.)

Ermanno Aar: *Studj storici in Terra d' Otranto.* (Florence, 1888.)

P. Pisani: *Les chrétiens de rite orientale à Venise . . .* (1439–1791), *Rev. d'histoire et de lit. relig.,* 1896, i, pp. 201–224.

D. G. Lancia di Brolo, O.S.B. (Bp. of Philadelphia, *tit.*): *Storia della Chiesa in Sicilia nei primi secoli del Cristianesimo.* (2 vols.; Palermo, 1880–1884.)

C. KARALEVSKY (CHARON): *Documenti inediti per servire alla storia delle Chiese italo-greche.* (Extract from the review "Bessarione," Anno XIV, Serie 3ᵃ, fasc. 111–112; and Anno XV, Serie 3ᵃ, fasc. 117–118. Rome, 1911–1912.)

A. ROCCHI: *La Badia di Grottaferrata.* (2nd ed.; Rome, 1904.)

D. PLACIDE DE MEESTER, O.S.B.: *Le collège Pontifical Grec de Rome.* (Extract from *La Semaine de Rome*, Rome, Greek College, Via Babuino, 1910.)

F. POMETTI: *Nel Centenario della fondazione della Badia di Grottaferrata. Appunti storici.* (Extract from "Cosmos illustrato," Bergamo, 1903.)

ARSENIO PELLEGRINI: *La Badia di Grottaferrata e l'unione delle Chiese.* (A conference read before Pope Pius X. Rome, Propaganda, 1904.)

Roma e l'Oriente (Rivista Cryptoferratense per l'unione delle Chiese. Began in 1910). Contains much useful information about the Italo-Greeks. See especially: vol. ii, 33–35; iii, 264–270; iv, 181–184; v, 97–117, 159–166; vii, 224–231, 353–364, 272–285, 340–352; viii, 106–119, 339–360; ix, 24–44.

Échos d'Orient (Revue mestrielle de théologie, de droit canonique et de liturgie, d' archéologie et de géographie orientales. Began 1897. Paris: Bonne Presse.) See vol. v, 33; xi, 227; xiv, 146; viii, 55; xvii, 500.

DOMENICO COMPARETTI: *Saggi dei Dialetti greci dell' Italia meridionale.* (Pisa: Frat. Nistri, 1866.)

Journal of Hellenic Studies, x (1889), pp. 11–42. Excellent article by H. F. Tozer: " *The Greek-speaking Population of Southern Italy.*"

CHAPTER III

THE MELKITES

C. CHARON (KARALEVSKIJ): *Histoire des Patriarchats melkites.* (Paris: Picard, 1911 . . .) See p. 185, *note.*

LEQUIEN: *Oriens Christianus in IV patriarchatus digestus.* (Paris, 1740.)

J. BESSON, S.J.: *La Syrie Sainte.* (Paris, 1660.)

P. NACCHI, S.J.: *Lettres édifiantes et curieuses : Mémoires du Levant* (in Bousquet: *Les actes des Apôtres modernes*, Paris, 1852, tom. i).

G. F. HERTZBERG: *Geschichte der Byzantiner* (in Onckel's *Allgem. Gesch.*, Berlin, 1883).

A. RABBATH, S.J.: *Documents inédits pour servir a l'histoire du Christianisme en Orient.* (Paris: Luzac et Cie; London, 1905, etc.)

ALEXIS KATEB: *S.B. Maximos III Mazloum . . . sa vie et ses œuvres.* (Rome, 1902.)

RAPHAEL DE MARTINIS: *Juris Pontificii de Prop. Fide.* (Rome, 1899.)

M. JULLIEN, S.J.: *La nouvelle mission de la Compagnie de Jesus en Syrie* (1831–1895). (Paris, 1899; 2 vols. 8vo.)

GABR. GIBARAT: *Résumé biographique de la vie de Mgr. Mazloum, patr. des Grecs Catholiques de l'Orient.* (Paris, 1853.)

Mich. Rahme: *Livre des divines Liturgies* . . . (in Arabic). (Beirut, 1899.)

Van den Steen de Jehay: *De la situation légale des sujets ottomans non mussulmans.* (Brussels, 1906.)

Revue de l'Église grecque unie, 1885: *Life of Maximos III.*

The following copious Bibliography dealing with other Uniate groups, their rites and Canon Law, is here inserted as being at once of great value to the student and as evidence of the untiring industry of the lamented author.

OTHER BYZANTINE UNIATES

I.—The Ruthenians.

Moroni: *Dizionario* . . . (cf. above, p. xii), article *Ruteni.*

Kirchenlexicon (cf. above, p. xii): vi, 976–979, article *Isidor von Thessalonich. O.S. Basil ;* x, 1418–1420, article on the Ruthenians; vii, 428–446, article *Kiew;* vii, 1724–1731, article *Lemberg*, part ii: *Gr. Kath. Kirchenprovinz.*

Likowski: *Die Union zu Brest.* (Freiburg: Herder, 1904.)

M. Hruszewski: *Geschichte des Ukrainischen (Ruthenischen) Volkes.* (Leipzig: Teubner, 1906.)

Giov. Marcovic: *Gli Slavi ed i Papi.* (Agram, 1897.)

Julian Pelesz: *Geschichte der Union der ruthenischen Kirche mit Rom.* (2 vols.; Vienna, 1878, 1881.)

Wolfsguber (Cölestin), O.S.B.: *Kirchengeschichte Oesterreich-Ungarns.* (1909.)

Roman Sembratowycz: *Le Tsarisme et l'Ukraine.* (Paris, 1907.)

H. Lämmer: *In decreta Concilii Ruthenorum Zamosceniensis animaduersiones theologicæ.* (Freiburg: Herder, 1865.)

J. A. Ginzel: *Gesch. der Slavenapostel Cyr. u. Meth. u. der Slaw. Liturgie.* (Leitmeritz: A. Schnurlein, 1857.)

Bedwin Sands (George Raffalovich): *The Ukraine.* (Franc. Griffiths, 2nd impr., 1914.)

Ios. Sim. Assemani: *Kalendaria Ecclesiæ uniuersæ* (Rome, 1754): *Origines ecclesiæ slavonicæ*, part ii, chap. i.

Ign. Kulczynski (Procurator-Gen. of the O. S. Basil. at Rome): *Specimen Ecclesiæ ruthenicæ ab origine susceptæ fidei ad nostra usque tempora in suis capitibus seu primatibus Russiæ cum S. Sede apostolica romana semper unitæ.* (Rome, 1734; Paris, 1859.)

J. Stilting, S.J.: in *Acta SS. Sept. II*, a criticism of the above: *De conuersione et fide Russorum dissertatio.* (Antwerp, 1748.)

N. Nilles: *Symbolæ ad illustrandam historiam Ecclesiæ Orientalis in terris coronæ S. Stephani.* (Innsbruck: Rauch, 1885.)

J. Mondok: *Breuis historica notitia diœcesis Munkacsiensis.* (Unghvar, 1878.)

Theophile Berengier, O.S.B.: *Les martyrs uniates en Pologne.* (Poitiers: H. Oudin; Paris: Palmé, 1868.)

G. Fejér: *Religionis apud Hungaros initia.* (1846.)

Fr. Snopek: *Konstantinus-Cyrillus u. Methodius die Slavenapostel.* (*Operum Academiæ Velehradensis*, tom. ii; Kremsier, 1911.) See *Roma e l'Oriente*, vol. iii, pp. 45–55.

Jos. Fiedler: *Beiträge zur Gesch. der Union der Ruthenen in Nord-Ungarn.* Sitzungsberichte der Ksl. Akademie der Wissensch. Phil.-hist. Classe (Vienna, 1862), pp. 491–497.

Stanislas Smolka: *Les Ruthènes et les problèmes religieux du monde russien.* (Berne: Ferd. Wyss. 1917.)

Thomæ a Iesu, Carm. discalc.: *De Unione Schismaticorum cum Ecclesia Catholica procuranda* in " Thesaurus Theologicus," tom. vii, part 2 (Venice, 1762, pp. 1517–1720); also in Migne, *Theologiæ Cursus completus*, tom. v, col. 397–710 (Paris, 1841).

Vizzardelli: *De origine Christianæ Religionis in Russia.* (Rome, 1826.)

S. Rudnitsky: *The Ukraine and the Ukrainians*, translated by J. W. Hartman. (Jersey City, N.J.)

Iacobus Susza, O. S. Bas.: *Cursus uitæ et certamen martyrii B. Iosaphat Kuncevicii*, editio noua, emendatior et auctior curante Ioh. Martinov, S.J. (Paris: Palme, 1865.)
Saulus et Paulus Ruthenæ unionis sanguine B. Iosaphat transformatus, siue Meletius Smotriscius. (Rome, 1665. New edition by Martinov. Brussels: Fr. Vromant, 1864.)

Baronii: *Annales Eccl.*, tom. ix, 658–667: *De Ruthenis receptis.*

A. N. Rambaud: *Histoire de la Russie.* (Ed. 6.; Paris, 1914.)

Eugen Lewisky: *Die Ukraine, der Lebensnerv Russlands*, in the series: *Der Deutsche Krieg.* (Stuttgart-Berlin: Ernst Jöckh, No. 33, 1915.)

II

For a schematic treatment of other Byzantine groups, see an article by R. Janin in *Échos d'Orient*, xvii, pp. 497–526.

For each group the author gives the following references to the same periodical:

Uniate Greeks: ix, 335; xv, 171; xv, 64; i, 315; vii, 50; xvii, 497.

Uniate Georgians: viii, 177; ix, 120; xv, 289; xvi, 32, 211; ix, 336; xvii, 525.

Uniate Roumanians: vii, 42; xv, 553; xvi, 188; xvii, 63, 260, 367, 368; vi, 42, 224; vii, 257; viii, 44; x, 49; xvi, 444; xvii, 523.

Uniate Bulgarians: iii, 249; v, 307; xv, 168; vi, 335; vii, 42; xvii, 60, 161, 169, 365, 521, 549; vii, 35, 80; 207; xvi, 68; x, 47.

THE CHALDEES (OR UNIATES FROM NESTORIANISM)

Martin: *La Chaldée.* (Rome, 1867.)

Assemani: *Bibliotheca Orientalis.* (Rome, 1728, tom. iii, part 2: *Dissertatio de Syris Nestorianis.*)

L. Doucin: *Histoire du nestorianisme.* (Paris-Chalons, 1698.)

Barhebrœus: *Chronicon Ecclesiasticum*, ed. Abbeloos and Lamy, 3 vols. (Paris-Louvain, 1872–1877.)

Orientalisches Archiv, herausgeg. von Hugo Gröthe (Leipzig: K. W. Hiersemann, Bd. 1, 1910-11): *Notizen Gröthes uber die Nestorianer.*

Oskar Braun: *Das Buch der Synhados*. (Stuttgart and Vienna, 1900.)

S. Jamil: *Genuinæ relationes inter Sedem apostolicam et Assyriorum orientalium seu Chaldæorum ecclesiam*. (Rome: Loescher, 1902.)

John Hopkins: *Semitic Papers*, 1902, pp. 73–90: Gabriel Oussani: *The Modern Chaldæans and Nestorians, and the Study of Syriac among them*.

J. W. McCrindle's edition of *The Christian Topography of Cosmas, an Egyptian Monk*. (London: Hakluyt Soc. Publications No. xcviii, 1897.)

Aphraatis sapientis Persæ demonstrationes, ed. J. Parisot, O.S.B., tom. i-ii of *Patrologia syriaca*, ed. R. Graffin. (Paris: Firmin-Didot, 1894–1907.)

Fr. Loofs: *Nestoriana*. (Halle, 1905.)

M. Jugie: *Nestorius et la controverse nestorienne*. (Paris, 1912.)

Liturgy of the Holy Apostles Adai and Mari. (S.P.C.K., 1893.)

J. B. Chabot: *Synodicon Orientale* (Notices et extraits des MSS. de la Bibliothèque Nat., xxxvii. Paris, 1902.)
Histoire de Mar Iab-Alaha. (2nd ed.; Paris, 1895.)

Albiruni: *Chronology, or " Traces of Former Generations."* Translated and edited by C. E. Sachau. (London: Oriental Transl. Fund, 1879.)

Shahrastani: *Book of Religious and Philosophical Sects*, ed. in Arabic by W. Cureton (2 vols., London, 1842–1846). In German by T. Haarbrucker: *Schahrastani's Religionspartheien u. Philosophenschulen* (2 vols.; Halle, 1850–1851).

P. Muller-Simonis: *Relation des missions scientifiques de M. H. Hyvernat et P. Muller-Simonis* (1888–1889) *du Caucase au Golfe Persan à travers l'Arménie, le Kurdistan et la Mesopotamie*. (Paris-Lyons, 1892.)

M. Parisot: *Rapport sur une mission scientifique en Turquie d'Asie*. (Paris, 1899.)

Burkitt: *Early Eastern Christianity*. (London: J. Murray, 1904.)

J. Labourt: *Le Christianisme dans l'empire perse*. (Paris, 1897.)
De Timotheo I Nest. Patr. et Christianorum orientalium condicione, sub Chaliphis. (Paris, 1904.)

A. N. Wigram: *History of the Assyrian Church*. (Christian Knowledge Society, 1910.)

Mingana: *Sources syriaques*. (Leipzig, 1907.)

Harnack: *Mission und Ausbreitung des Christentums*. (Leipzig, 1902.)

P. Bejan: *Acta martyrum et sanctorum*. (Leipzig, 1890–1895.)

Thomas of Marga: *The Book of Governors*, ed. by E. A. Wallis Budge. (Kegan Paul, 1893.)

R. Duval: *La littérature syriaque*. (1900.)

Silbernagl: *Verfassung und gegenwärtiger Bestand sämtlicher Kirchen des Orients*. (Regensburg, 1904.)

Alfred v. Kremer: *Culturgeschichte des Orients unter den Chalifen*. (Vienna: Braumuller, 1875–1877.)

Tixeront: *Les origines de l'église d'Odesse*. (Paris, 1888.)

De Lacy O'Leary: *The Syriac Church and Fathers*. (S.P.C.K., 1909.)

UNIATES FROM THE MONOPHYSITE GROUPS.

1. *The Copts.*

EUTYCHIUS (SA'ĪD IBN BAṬRĪḲ): *Contextio Gemmarum*, ed. L. Cheiko, in the *Corp. Script. Christ. Orient.* (1906–1909.)

J. M. VANSLEB: *Histoire de l'Église d'Alexandrie.* (Paris, 1677.)

SEVERUS OF AL-USHMUNAIN: *History of the Patriarchs of Alexandria* (ed. by B. Evetts in the *Patrologia Orientalis*, vols. i and v).

E. RENAUDOT: *Historia Patriarcharum Alexandrinorum.* (Paris, 1713.)

AL-MAḲRĪZĪ: *Maḳrīzī's Geschichte der Copten*, ed. in Arabic and German by F. Wüstenfeld. (Göttingen, 1845.)

AL-MAKIN: *Historia saracenica*, ed. Erpen. (Leiden, 1625.)

JOS. ABUDACNUS: *Historia Iacobitarum sen Coptorum.* (Oxford, 1675.)

A. GAYET: *L'Art Copte.* (Paris: Leroux, 1902.)

G. MACAIRE (afterwards the Uniate Patr. Cyril Macaire): *Histoire de l'Église d'Alexandrie depuis S Marc jusqu'à nos jours.* (Cairo, 1894. Imprimerie gén.)
L'Église Copte, sa foi d'aujourd'hui comparée avec la foi de ses pères. (Cairo, 1893.)

L. BADET, S.J.: *Chants liturgiques des Coptes notés et mis en ordre.* (Cairo: Collège de la S. Famille, Petit Séminaire Copte, 2 parts, lithographed, 1899.)

B. T. A. EVETTS and A. J. BUTLER: *The Churches and Monasteries of Egypt, attributed to Abu Salih, the Armenian.* (Oxford: The Clarendon Press, *Anecdota oxoniensia*, Semitic Series, part vii).

AHMAD ALI IBN ABD AL-KADIR: *Histoire des Sultans.* (1837.)

S. C. MALAN: *Original Documents of the Coptic Church.* (1872.)

BUTE, MARQUIS OF: *Coptic Morning Service for the Lord's Day.* (1882.)

S. LANE POOLE: *A History of Egypt in the Middle Ages.* (Methuen, 1901.)

A. J. BUTLER: *The Arab Conquest of Egypt.* (London, 1902.)
Ancient Coptic Churches of Egypt. (Oxford, 1884.)

SESOSTRIS SIDAROUSS: *Des Patriarchats : Les Patriarchats dans l'Empire ottoman, et spécialement en Egypte.* (Paris, 1907.)

2. *The Abyssinians.*

LUDOLF: *Historia æthiopica siue breuis et succincta descriptio regni Habessinorum.* (Frankfurt, 1681.)
Ad Historiam æthiopicam commentarium. (Frankfurt, 1691.)

JEROME LOBO: *Voyage historique d'Abyssinie du R.P. Jerome Lobo, S.J., traduite du portugais par M. Le Grand.* (Paris, 1728.)

R. BASSET: *Études sur l'histoire de l'Éthiopie.* (Paris, 1882.)
Les apocryphes éthiopiens. (Paris, 1893–1900.)

MORIE: *Histoire de l'Éthiopie.* (Paris, 1904.)

BRUCE: *Travels in Abyssinia.* (London, 1790.)

SALT: *Voyage to Abyssinia.* (London, 1814.)

GLASER: *Die Abessinier in Arabien und Afrika.* (Munich, 1895.)

ISENBERG and KRAPF: *Journal detailing their Proceedings in the Kingdom of Shoa*. (London, 1843.)

ISENBERG: *Abessinien u. die evangelische Mission*. (Bonn, 1844.)

R. P. SKINNER: *Abyssinia of To-day*. (E. Arnold, 1906.)

K. CONTI ROSSINI: *Liber Axumæ* (Chabot: *Corpus Script. Christ. Orient.* (Paris, 1909–10.)

F. E. BRIGHTMAN: *Eastern Liturgies*. (Oxford: Clar. Press, 1896.)

RODWELL: *Ethiopic Liturgy and Hymns*. (London, 1864.)

C. BECCARI, S.J.: *Rerum æthiopicarum scriptores occidentales*. (Rome: Luigi, 1917.) 15 vols. Vol. xv has a good index.

SAMUEL A. MERCER: *The Ethiopic Liturgy*. (Mowbray, 1915.)

3. Syrian Uniates (or Uniates converted from the Jacobites).

J. B. CHABOT: *Chronique de Michel le Syrien, Patriarche Jacobite d'Antioche* (1166–1199), edited and translated by. (Paris: Leroux, 1899–1910.)
Les évêques jacobites du VIIIe au XIIIe siècle, d'après la chronique de Michel le Syrien (in the *Revue de l'Orient chrétien*, 1899, pp. 444–451; and 1900, 605–622).

H. W. CODRINGTON: *The Syrian Liturgies of the Presanctified* (in the *Journal of Theol. Studies*, 1902, pp. 69–82).

GUSTAVE LEBON: *Le Monophysisme Sévérien*. (Louvain, 1909.)

A. SOCIN: *Der neu-aramaische Dialekt des Tur-Abdin*. (Gottingen, 1881.)

M. PEISKER: *Severus von Antiochien*. (Halle, 1903.)

AUGUST F. PFEIFFER: *Joseph Simonius Assemans orientalische Bibliothek, oder Nachrichten von Syrischen Schriftstellern in einen Auszug gebracht*. (Erlangen: Wolfgang Walthers, 2 vols., 1776–1777.)

J. P. N. LAND: *Joannes Bf. von Ephesos, der erste syrische Kirchenhistoriker : Einleitende Studien*. (Leyden: E. J. Brill, 1856.)

BARHEBRŒUS, *o.c.* above, p. xvi.

4. Uniate Armenians.

H. F. B. LYNCH: *Armenia : Travels and Studies*. (Longmans, Green and Co., 1901.)

H. GELZER: *Die Anfänge der armenischen Kirche*, in *Berichte über die Verhandlung der kön. sachsischen Gesell. der Wissenschaften zu Leipzig* (Philolog.-histor. Classe), I, II, Leipzig, 1895, pp. 109–174.

N. TER GREGOR: *History of Armenia*. (London: John Heywood, 1897.)

F. TOURNEBIZE: *Histoire politique et religieuse de l'Arménie*. (Paris, 1910.)

SIR CHARLES ELIOT: *Turkey in Europe*. (E. Arnold, 1908.)

V. LANGLOIS: *Collection des Historiens anciens et modernes de l'Arménie*. (Paris, 1880.)

ALFRED V. GUTSCHMID: *Kleine Schriften.*   (Leipzig: Teubner, 5 vols., 1889.)

S. C. MALAN: *Instruction in the Christian Faith.*   (Rivingtons, 1869.)

M. ORMANIAN: *Le Vatican et les Arméniens.*   (Rome, 1873.)
L'Église arménienne.   (Paris, 1910.)

CL. GALANUS: *Historia Armena ecclesiastica et politica.*   (Cologne, 1686.)
Conciliationis Ecclesiæ armenæ cum romana, ex ipsis Armenorum patrum et doctorum testimoniis, in duas partes, historialem et controuersialem diuisæ.   (3 vols., Armenian and Latin; Rome, 1690.)

L. PETIT: *Arménie* (article in the *Dictionnaire de Théol. Cath.*, vol. i, 1912).

THEOD. ED. DOWLING: *The Armenian Church.*   (Christian Knowledge Society, London, 1910.)

J. ISSAVERDENS: *The Armenian Ritual,* 3 parts.   (Venice: S. Lazzaro, 1873–1888.)

P. BIANCHINI: *Les chants liturgiques de l'Église arménienne.*   (Venice: San Lazzaro, 1877.)

5. Uniates of Malabar.

EDGAR THURSTON: *Castes and Tribes of Southern India,* 7 vols. (Government Press, Madras, 1909.)   Vol. vi especially.

V. NAGAM AIYA: *State Manual of the State of Travancore,* 3 vols. (Trivandrum, 1906.)   Vol. ii, chap. viii, by G. T. Mackenzie.

IO. FACUNDI RAULIN: *Historia Ecclesiæ Malabaricæ cum Diamperitana Synodo apud Indos Nestorianos S Thomæ Christianos nuncupatos coacta ab Alexio de Menezes Augustiniensi An. Dni. MDXCIX . . . cui accedunt cum Liturgia Malabarica tum Dissertationes uariæ.* (Rome, 1745.)   Compiled from

ANTONIO DE GOUVEA, O.S.A.: *Jornado do Arcesbispo de Goa Dom Frey Aleixo de Menezes* (Coimbra, 1606).   A rare work.

JOSEPH DAHLMANN, S.J.: *Die Thomas-Legende u. die ältesten historischen Beziehungen des Christentums zum fernen Osten im Lichte der indischen Altertumskunde.*   (Freiburg: Herder, 1912.)

A. E. MEDLYCOTT (Bp. of Tricomia): *India and the Apostle Thomas,* an Inquiry with a critical analysis of the Acta Thomæ.   (London: D. Nutt, 1905.)

BONNET: *Acta Thomæ.*   (Leipzig, 1883.)

GERMANN: *Die Kirche der Thomaschristen.*   (Gutersloh, 1877.)

CHARLES SWANSTON: *A Memoir of the Primitive Church of Malayala.* (*Journal of the Royal Asiatic Soc.*, 1834, pp. 171–172.)

G. B. HOWARD: *The Christians of St Thomas and their Liturgies.* (Oxford and London: J. H. and J. Parker, 1864.)

MICHAEL GEDDES: *The History of the Church of Malabar.*   (London, 1694.)

E. RENAUDOT: *Anciennes Relations des Indes et de la Chine de deux voyageurs mahometans qui y allèrent dans le neuvième siècle.* (Paris: J. B. Coignard, 1718.)

THE MARONITES

SCHNURRER: *Die Maronitische Kirche*, in *Archiv für alte u. neue Kirchengeschichte.* (Leipzig, 1814.)

NAIRONUS (ANTONIUS FAUSTUS): *Dissertatio de origine, nomine ac religione Maronitarum.* (Rome, 1679.)

LA ROQUE (JEAN DE): *Voyage de Syrie et du Mont-Liban.* (Amsterdam, 1723.)

CANON LAW AND RITES OF THE UNIATES

Codex Iuris Canonici (Rome: Vatican, 1917). Canons: 1; 782; 804; 881; 955; 1004; 1099; 542; 622.

Bullarium Benedicti XIV, ed. cit. See p. xi.

Coll. Lacensis, ed. cit. See p. xi.

LEO ALLATIUS: *De Ecclesiæ occid. et orient. perpetua consensione libri tres.* (Cologne, 1648.)

IOS. PAPP-SZYLAGIY: *Enchiridion iuris ecclesiæ orientalis catholicæ.* (Gross-Wardein, 2nd ed., 1880.)

CARDINAL PITRA: *Iuris ecclesiastici Græcorum historia et monumenta.* (Rome, 1864.)

Des Canons et des collections canoniques de l'Église grecque. (Paris, 1858.)

Analecta. The volume entitled: *Iuris eccl. Græcorum selecta paralipomena.*

CARDINAL BESSARION: *Breve raccolto delle Constitutioni monastiche di Santo Basilio Magno.* (Rome, 1578.)

WERNZ: *Ius Decretalium*, 2nd ed. (Rome, 1906.)

For the Canon Law proper to each group, see the works above quoted.

AUTHOR'S PREFACE

SEVERAL ways of arranging a book about the Uniate Churches suggest themselves, none of them absolutely the best. As far as rank or dignity go, all branches of the one Church of Christ are equal, except that those which use the Roman rite have a certain precedence. The others are absolutely level. Nor does the classification now used at Rome make for clearness, as we shall see. Perhaps the simplest way in this book will be to keep the same order as that of the preceding volumes, since there is a Uniate Church corresponding to each of the schismatical Churches.

So the first part describes the Byzantine Uniates, who correspond to the Orthodox. Part II is about the Chaldees, corresponding to the Nestorians. Part III includes all the Uniates converted from the various Monophysite sects. Lastly, Part IV is about the one Uniate Church which has no schismatical counterpart, the Maronites.

THE
UNIATE EASTERN CHURCHES

INTRODUCTORY CHAPTER
CONCERNING UNIATES IN GENERAL

1. What is a Uniate?

THE now commonly used word " Uniate "[1] may be
defined by taking the idea of " Eastern " as the genus
and Catholicity as the species, or in the reverse order.
So we may say that a Uniate is a member of any Eastern
Church who is in communion with the Holy See, or that he is
a Catholic of any Eastern rite. The name is not a very old
one. Its use began insensibly. In Latin " Orientales uniti
sanctæ sedi," or " Ecclesia unita ecclesiæ romanæ," would
occur naturally as a description, before anyone thought of
" Unitus " as a technical term. From " Unitus " the form
" Uniat " was made, apparently first in Slav languages for the
Ruthenians. So we got it in English. In French, German,
and Italian it has hardly yet become a technical term. They
say " les églises unies," " die unierten Kirchen," " le chiese
unite," using the common word for " united ";[2] though when
used thus alone without further qualification it always means
" united with Rome."

We have, then, under the genus " Catholic," a first great
division into " Roman " and " Uniate." It is hardly necessary
to point out that this division in no way implies two or more
separate Churches. There is only one Catholic Church; the
test of membership in it is to be in communion with all the
other members. In any society the test of unity is the mutual
acknowledgement of all the members. Where there are separate
groups, which do not recognize one another, we have not

---

[1] I prefer " Uniate " to " Uniat " (which sometimes occurs in
English) because it corresponds to the usual English form of such
words (" cognate," " delegate," etc.). " Uniat " looks odd and
foreign in English. There is, of course, no Latin word " Uniatus ";
our form comes from the Russian *Uniyatu*.

[2] German *Uniert* is almost a technical term ; in ordinary
speech we say *Vereinigt*.

one, but several societies.   In this way we speak of separate
Churches, such as the Catholic Church, the Orthodox Church,
the Nestorian Church, and so on.   These are really separate
Churches, because there is no mutual recognition between
their members; they are not in communion with one another.
When we distinguish between the Roman (or Latin) Church
and the Uniate Churches, we make a distinction of quite
another kind.   Really these are all one Church.   All Uniates
are in full and perfect communion with us Latins, with the
Pope, who is their visible head on earth just as much as he
is ours.   But it is an ancient use, and a convenient one to distinguish within this one Church several parts which, although
really parts of the one society, nevertheless have certain
customs, local laws, rites, which justify us in calling each a
" Church," though really it is only a part of the one Church.
So it was once common to speak of the Church of France, the
Church of Spain, although the Catholics of these lands were
in no way separated from their fellow-Catholics in other
countries.   The analogy of an army may make this idea clear.
The French and British armies are really separate; they obey
no common authority, they have even in the past made war on
each other.   But, on the other hand, the French army is one
army; it works together and obeys one common authority.
Yet in the time of Napoleon I it was usual to speak of the
various portions of this one army, each in itself, as an army.
Thus there was the army of Italy, the army of the Rhine,
and so on.   This, then, is the sense in which we may speak of
various Catholic Churches.   Really they are all branches of
the one Church, real branches, in conscious communion with
one another, all joined to the main stem at Rome and so to
the one vine, Christ.   Catholics have no room in their system
for branches cut off from the main stem.   A plant made up
of such dissected fragments would not be one plant at all.
To such branches as are cut off from us we can only apply,
regretfully, our Lord's own word about them, that they shall
wither.[1]   But the one vine has living branches which draw
their life, by real visible communion, from the main stem:
the one body of Christ has many members, not dissected
members, but those which are joined to it, in whom life flows
through the arteries from the one Head.   These branches or
members share the name of the whole.   Each may be spoken
of as a Church, though there is, of course, only one Church
really.

[1] John xiv 6.

What is the counterpart to the Uniate Churches? It might seem simplest to conceive this as the Roman Church, meaning all Catholics who use the Roman rite. That is, at any rate, an intelligible and reasonable use of the term "Roman Catholic." A Roman Catholic is a Catholic who uses the Roman rite, just as an Armenian Catholic is one who uses the Armenian rite. It would then seem obvious to call all Catholics who do not use the Roman rite Uniates. As far as liturgy goes, there is nothing to say against such a classification. In this sense the faithful of Milan and the Mozarabic families in Spain are Uniates. Their rite is not Roman; except for later Romanizing their rites have no more in common with that of the Roman mother-Church than have those of Eastern Catholics. So, also, the old Gallican Catholics, the people before the time of Charles the Great, who used the Gallican rite, were Uniates. But in this case we need not trouble much about them, since, except for its relics at Milan and Toledo, the Gallican rite disappeared long before anyone thought of the word Uniate as a special name.

Yet this is not common use. A Catholic of Milan knows quite well that he is Ambrosian in rite, but he would never think of calling himself a Uniate. He would probably, though foolishly, resent being put in the same category as the Eastern people. Practically in this classification all Western Catholics, all who use Latin as their liturgical language, are put in one class, Eastern Catholics in the other.

Language used in the liturgy is almost the worst possible basis of distinction; yet in this case it comes practically to that. The reason is that liturgy is not really the only, nor even the essential, basis of this distinction. We shall get it better by thinking of the old Patriarchates, which are the reason of the present distinction of rites among Catholics.

Once there were three Patriarchates in all Christendom, those of Rome, Alexandria, Antioch. Now Catholic Canon Law recognises five: Rome, Constantinople, Alexandria, Antioch, Jerusalem. Putting the Roman Patriarchate on one side, we call a member of any of the other four a Uniate. So, since the faithful of Milan and Toledo belong to the Roman Patriarchate, we shall not call them Uniates. We arrive, instead, at the distinction between, not Romans (in the sense of rite), but *Latins* and *Uniates*. Latins include Ambrosians and Mozarabs, as well as the vast majority who have the Roman rite in any language. Uniates are Catholics of the old

Patriarchates of Constantinople, Alexandria, Antioch, and Jerusalem, who have other rites in other languages.

But why is this distinction made at all ? Why do we have one name for members of one Patriarchate and classify all the others together under another name ? Why should one not just as well put the Catholics of any other Patriarchate, for instance, Antioch, on one side and call all the others who are in union with them, Uniates ? There is no special reason why we should not. The distinction between Latins and Uniates comes, first from a certain precedence that the Roman Patriarchate must have, still more perhaps from an accident of history. Certainly, since the Roman Patriarch is the chief of his brethren, it would be strange to begin by considering any other branch of the Church as the standard, and then putting him with all that remain in one group, as being in union with a lesser dignitary than himself. If the Pope is in union with another bishop, it is more natural to call the other bishop the Uniate than the Pope.

But, still more, this distinction between Latins and Uniates is the result of the development of Church History. In the old days when, for instance, the first Council of Nicæa maintained as an " ancient custom " that there should be three chief bishops having jurisdiction over others, those of Rome, Alexandria, and Antioch,[1] then the Roman Pontiff had by no means the best share for his Patriarchate. Alexandria had all the fat land of Egypt, richest and most populous province of the Empire. Antioch had Syria, Asia Minor, Greece—all flourishing lands, full of great cities, the heart of the Empire since Constantine had brought the Eagles back near the Trojan mountains.[2] Rome, besides the old Imperial City itself, had Italy, already threatened, soon to be overrun by barbarians. She had Africa, no mean province, but not to be compared with Egypt (and here, too, the Vandals would come). Then she had only the wild western lands, at that time the haunt of heathen savages, who then were of little use to any bishop. No one in the fourth century could foresee how great a change there would be. This change was mainly the work of the Roman Patriarchs themselves. As distinct from their place as Primates of the whole Church, they held the least enviable of Patriarchates. Without envying their brothers of Alexandria and Antioch the prosperous, civilized territories over which these ruled, the Popes set out to convert the barbarians of their own

[1] Can. 6.   [2] " Paradiso," vi, 1-6.

Patriarchate. So they sent their missionaries to Gaul, Germany, and Britain. Forests were cleared, monasteries and then cities arose, where once wild tribes had barely defended themselves against the wolves; the Western barbarians became the great Christian nations of Europe. So the centre of gravity of civilization gradually shifted to the West. For, while Rome was converting our Fathers, the East was sinking into stagnation.

The Eastern bishops must bear at least a part of the responsibility of this. Except for some late movement on the part of Russia, the East has never shown the missionary zeal which is characteristic of Rome and the West. The Eastern bishops, too, had savage pagans at their doors. There were the Arabs, for instance; but they allowed these to remain pagan, while they quarrelled over abstruse points of theology, and intrigued for the Emperor's favour at the court.[1] That illusion about the unchangeable splendour of the Roman court on the Bosphorus, the typically Eastern idea that nothing could ever alter the position of their Empire as the centre of the world, the complacency with its own state which is so characteristic of Byzantine history, all these things were really mighty causes of the decay of the East, while the despised West was becoming stronger, was educating itself to become the dominant factor in Christian Europe. Then, just when the West had become strong enough to carry on the tradition of Europe, Islam came, and with it the final ruin of Eastern civilization.

Through such causes as these the Roman Patriarchate, from being the least splendid in Christendom, became enormously the most important. As far as Catholics are concerned, another cause greatly helped this development. First the Nestorians, then the various Monophysite sects, lastly the great mass of Christians of the Byzantine rite fell away from the unity of the Church. This fact alters nothing of the canonical position of those who remained; but it helped furthe r to shift the centre of gravity. At one time, indeed, it must have seemed almost as if the Catholic Eastern Patriarchates had finally disappeared, leaving only Latins as the whole Catholic Church. Happily that never quite happened. There have always been a few, though sometimes very few, Catholics of Eastern rites left, and now there are many more. But it is not surprising that within the Catholic Church the vast and

[1] How different the history of the world might have been if the Eastern bishops had built up a strong Christian Church among the Arabs before Mohammed was born, as the Popes had built up churches in Gaul, England, Germany !

enormously more prosperous Latin Patriarchate eventually seemed, if not the whole Church, at least its normal part.

Further, the discovery of new countries added again to the size of the Western half of the Church. Naturally, those countries were added to the Patriarchate to which the men who first colonized them belonged. If Greeks or Egyptians had discovered America, Australia, South Africa, these would have been added to some Eastern Patriarchate. But the people who built up these new lands were, and are, Latins, even if most of them are the rebel Latins we call Protestants. So the Roman Patriarchate received all the new lands too. The final result of all this is then that, considering the gradual stagnation of the East while the West was growing, considering the flood of Islam, the schisms which cut so many Easterns away from the Catholic Church altogether, and the discovery of new countries, the Roman Patriarchate has become so enormously the most important part of the Church that our Canon Law has acquired the habit of considering it as the normal situation for a Catholic to be a Latin. The Eastern rites appear rather as exceptions. It would be a monstrous delusion and the gravest injustice to our fellow-Catholics in the East to look upon them as in any way less Catholic than we are in the West. Nor have we the slightest right to expect them to join our Patriarchate, to accept our specifically Latin ideas or ways of doing things. They are, in every way, on the same plane in the Church as we are. They have just as much right to their customs and liturgies as we have to ours. The chief object of this book will be to show this. But the development of history does now suggest a primary distinction between Catholics of the vastly greater Latin Patriarchate and those of all the Eastern ones put together. Within the Church the Latins alone are about forty times as numerous as all Catholics of Eastern rites together. And this is only part of the general state of things by which the West has prospered while the East has decayed; so that the descendants of the men who thought our fathers contemptible now look to us as their guides in progress, and send their children to schools kept by Latins, to be taught our languages and European civilization.

Thus we have our first main division of Catholics into Latins on the one hand, and Uniates on the other. It ought to be unnecessary to say that this division implies no distinction of faith or of essential Christian law. All Catholics of any rite believe exactly the same faith, all obey the same final authority, that of the united Catholic hierarchy, of which the chief of all is the Pope of Rome. The distinction implies a difference of rites, of points of local Canon Law, of certain customs.

But this distinction is not the final one. We may leave the Latins as one Patriarchate without further subdivision, though, of course, they might be divided again into their various ecclesiastical provinces. However, except for Milan and Toledo, all Latins now use the same rite, all have practically the same rules. But the Uniates must be further subdivided into their various groups. Although we think sometimes of Uniates as one class, distinct from Latins, so that we say of anyone shortly that he is a Uniate, they are not really one group in the sense in which Latins are one.

In the sense in which we speak of the Latin Church there are not one, but several Uniate Churches. A Latin is a Latin; but a Uniate may be a Byzantine, an Armenian, a Chaldean, or a Coptic Uniate. These various people have each their own rite and laws. There is no real unity between Uniates as distinct from Latins. There is always the one unity that really matters, which joins all Uniates, together with Latins, in one Church. Yet, as in the case of Eastern Churches in general, so in the case of the Uniates, we may conceive a kind of bond which joins them all together, as distinct from us. It is not a bond of Canon Law, but rather of habit, of many customs that all have more or less in common. In a word, it is just the bond which joins Eastern Christians together as distinct from those of the West. Even inside the unity of the one Catholic Church it is possible to note this. But now we must see exactly which these various Uniate Churches really are.

2. The Various Uniate Churches.

In this paragraph, besides drawing up a list of the Uniate Churches, we shall explain and justify the name we use for each of them. To anyone who has read the two former books of this series it will not be difficult to understand the grouping of the Uniates. The situation is simple. There is a Uniate Church corresponding to each of the schismatical Churches we have already described; and there is one Uniate Church, that of the Maronites, which has no schismatical counterpart. So we may take these in the same order as the schismatical Churches. There is no order of rank or dignity among them; but this order suggests itself naturally.

First, then, we have the Uniates who correspond to the

great Orthodox Church, people who either remained faithful to Rome when the majority of Byzantine Christians went into schism at the time of Michael Cerularius, or who have been converted back from the Orthodox since. All these use the same Byzantine rite as the Orthodox; all have, except where some moral or really Catholic principle opposes, the same laws and customs as they. In short, this first group of Uniates represents what the Orthodox were before they went into schism. What shall we call these Uniates? They are less uniformly grouped than any other class; indeed, they are grouped in no one body at all, except in the one Catholic Church. This first set of Uniates has no common authority other than the supreme authority of the Pope. Nor is their origin from one source. They represent groups converted at different periods, in different countries, under different circumstances. A few of them have never been in schism, others have come back to the Catholic Church at various times, in countries distant from one another, as the result of different movements. The one connection between this group, separating them from the others, is that all these use the Byzantine rite in various languages. So far they do not seem to have had any common name. Some of them are Ruthenians, some Melkites, some Italo-Greeks.

It might seem convenient to call them all Melkites; but by universal custom, that name is used only for those who speak Arabic, in Syria and Egypt. No one ever calls a Ruthenian a Melkite. " Catholic Orthodox " suggests itself as a name. But this would lead to unnecessary confusion. From people who cannot grasp the principle of using technical terms as such, we should more than ever hear such questions as: " Are not all Catholics orthodox?" Moreover, this name does not proclaim what it means clearly, and it has never been used. It would also seem to suggest such absurdities as " Catholic Nestorians " and " Catholic Monophysites " for the others. Since then the use of the Byzantine rite is the one bond of union that connects these people among themselves and separates them from all others, the name *Byzantine Uniates*[1] seems the most reasonable as a general one for the whole group.

[1] The rite is called Byzantine because it was originally the local rite of the city of Constantinople. For an exactly similar reason our rite, wherever used, is called Roman. A Ruthenian or a Melkite is not, of course, Byzantine by blood or place of dwelling, any more than a German or a Pole is Roman in that sense. Yet each, when we classify ecclesiastical species, takes the name of the rite he uses.

We shall then have to subdivide the Byzantine Uniates into further classes, the Melkites, Ruthenians, and so on.

Next in our order we take the Uniates who have been converted from the Nestorian Church. These form a homogeneous group under one Patriarch. For them we need not seek a new name. By friend and foe they are called universally the *Chaldees*. This name is not a very happy one really. " Chaldee " suggests rather the inhabitants of the second Babylonian Empire, which passed away centuries before there was any Christian Church at all. But here we have at least the advantage of universal use, and of the official language of Rome.

Next comes the small body of Copts who have returned to the Catholic Church. Since " Copt " is merely a national name connoting in itself no theological position, we need have no difficulty in using the common term *Catholic Copts* or *Uniate Copts* for these people. The few *Abyssinian Catholics* are hardly yet a Uniate Church at all. The converts from the Jacobite sect cannot be called " Catholic Jacobites." That is as absurd as " Catholic Nestorians." Nor is it ever used. These are generally called *Catholic Syrians* or *Syrian Uniates*. At Rome they distinguish between the " Ritus antiochenus Syrorum purus," the " Ritus antiochenus Maronitarum," " Ritus Syrorum Malabaricus." This is unnecessary; nor is the idea of a " pure " Syrian rite opposed to, apparently, impure ones, happy. This classification is the remnant of old days when the history of the Eastern rites was but little understood. One rite is not in any real sense more " pure " than another. We shall find simpler and more correct terms for each Uniate Church than these. " Syrian Uniate," then, means the body of Catholics converted from the Jacobites.

Nor is there any difficulty about the name *Malabar Uniates*." *Armenian Uniate* or *Armenian Catholic* is equally plain. Perhaps here the word " Uniate " is better than " Catholic," since there are a few Armenians (by blood) who are Latins.

Lastly, we have the *Maronite Church*. Here, too, there is no discussion about the use of a name applied to them by everyone. But in this case we do not need any further qualification as Uniate. The Maronites are the one Eastern Church which is entirely Uniate. For centuries, surrounded by schismatics and Moslems, they have been the one entirely faithful outpost of Catholic unity in the East. All are in union with Rome; there is no such thing as a schismatical Maronite.

The further organization of these Churches will be described in the course of this book. So far we have noted only the groups themselves in order to understand who they are, and the plan of our arrangement.

3. Religion, Patriarchate, Rite, Language, Place.

Now we come to exceedingly important distinctions, too often confused. These five qualities must be carefully distinguished. The religious body to which a Christian may belong, the Patriarchate of which he is a member, the rite used by him or by his clergy, the language in which that rite is used, and, lastly, the place where he happens to live, are all different ideas; most of them occur in all kinds of different combinations. A man's religion is not implied by the rite he uses. Rite is one thing, union in any given religious body is quite another. Within the Catholic Church all rites occur. It is an unpardonable error, which ought never to be made by educated people, to imagine that all Catholics are Latins, or that there is any inherent reason why a Catholic should use the Roman rite. Nor is there any superiority, any more Catholic quality in the use of the Roman rite than in the use of any other. In this matter we stand exactly where we always have stood. In the days of the great Fathers, would anyone suggest that St Athanasius, St John Chrysostom, St Augustine were imperfect Catholics ? Yet none of these used the Roman rite. The ideal of the Catholic Church has always been perfect unity in the Faith. All Catholics believe exactly the same things, as far as the Faith is concerned. Her ideal has never been uniformity in rite. So little did the Popes care about this, that they were the only Patriarchs who allowed variety of rites within their own Patriarchate. While each Eastern Patriarch enforced uniformity by the use of his own rite throughout his Patriarchate, the Popes let the Gallican rite be used over far the greater part of theirs. When St Augustine wrote to St Gregory asking him what he was to do in the matter of rite in the English Church, it might seem a fine opportunity for the Pope to have the Roman rite adopted, at least by this new Church. Yet so little did St Gregory think this detail mattered that he simply told Augustine to adopt any liturgical customs that he thought suitable, whether from Rome or Gaul or anywhere.[1]

That is always the attitude of the Holy See. The Popes

[1] Greg. I, Ep. xi, 64 (P.L. lxxvii, col. 1187).

understand very well that rite is not of the essence of religion. They tolerate no variety in the Faith, since there can be only one true revelation from God. But in the matter of rite they know that different customs suit different people; they know that God will judge men according to the lives they lead, not according to the rites they use.

So, not only does the Catholic Church allow diversities of rites; as a matter of fact, she is the only religious body that does so. In contemplating the absurd quarrels there have been among Eastern schismatics on the question of rite, in seeing the preposterous way they always seem to think the form of prayers used in a service, even the language in which these prayers are said, to be a vital matter of the Christian faith, in noticing the arrogant tyranny with which Eastern Patriarchs put down any other rite than their own in their spheres of authority, their ridiculous jealousy of foreign rites, in seeing all this, we are always impressed by the different attitude of the Holy See. Rome's calm tolerance, her dignified breadth of outlook in this matter are most significant. She knows how to distinguish between faith and rite; autocratic where she has Christ's commission to teach his faith without ambiguity, she is too secure in her own inapproachable dignity to be jealous if a group of her children prefer to say their prayers in Syriac, or to celebrate the holy mysteries with other ceremonies than hers. It is only the Protestant of the more ignorant kind who can commit so amazing a blunder as to represent the Pope as demanding uniformity of rite.[1] He is the only Head of a Church who does not do so.[2]

So *Rite* is not the same thing as *Religion*. These Eastern Catholics agree in rite with their schismatical cousins; on the other hand, they differ in this from us Latins. Yet in religion, in Faith, and all the essential ideas of Catholicity, they are absolutely one with us, and differ vitally from the schismatics. The situation is curious. A simple Catholic Armenian layman is in union with any Latin priest. He has the same faith, is a member of the same Church. He has no communion with an Armenian schismatic. Yet if he came into a Latin Church to hear Mass, he would understand little or nothing of what was

---

[1] *E.g.*, Mr. P. Dearmer, " Rome and Reunion " (2nd edition, Mowbray, 1911), p. 37: " The Roman Church has rushed to her decline . . . by enforcing uniformity in her borders with an iron hand."

[2] The only other case that could be quoted is a partial toleration now of some of the " Old-Believer " rites within the Russian State Church.

going on. The whole rite and its language would be quite strange to him. But in a schismatical Armenian church every detail of the service would be perfectly familiar to him. Having disposed of this first and greatest confusion, let us consider others less fatal, but still to be avoided.

How does rite stand towards Patriarchate? We have already noted that the idea of Patriarchate is really the basis of that of rite. In the early Church people were divided into Patriarchates according to the geographical position of their races. Putting aside such obvious exceptions as a traveller staying for a time in a foreign country, an ambassador or Legate representing a foreign power, every Christian submitted to the rite of the place where he lived—that is, to the rite of his nation. At first there were diversities of local rite and custom in each country, almost in each diocese or local church. Then gradually, almost insensibly, came the ideal of uniformity *throughout each Patriarchate*. This is merely one special case of the general centralization, not so far under the one chief Patriarch at Rome (that is another matter), but under each Patriarch within his own Patriarchate. As each priest would naturally follow the rite of his bishop, so each bishop followed that of his Metropolitan, and each Metropolitan that of his Patriarch. The principle never went further than that. The Patriarchs themselves were too great, too distant, too much separated by language and custom from Rome, to follow it out to the end, by all adopting the rite of the first Patriarch. So liturgical uniformity throughout the whole Church did not become the ideal at any time. But liturgical uniformity throughout each Patriarchate did.

So we come to the principle that *rite follows Patriarchate*. This does not seem ever to have been laid down formally in so many words; but it became tacitly a principle. Each diocese adopted the rite of its Patriarchal city. The rite used by any bishop became a kind of symbol of his dependence on a certain Patriarch. We have already noted the one significant exception to this, in the case of the Roman Patriarchate. Otherwise, from the fifth or sixth centuries, we may take it that rite followed, was the outward sign of, Patriarchal allegiance.

Patriarchate followed geographical divisions. Each Patriarch had a geographical territory, over whose inhabitants he reigned. Thus the Christians of Egypt obeyed the Patriarch of Alexandria and used the Alexandrine rite; those of Syria obeyed him of Antioch and used his rite, and so on. The situation of strangers in such lands was of course abnormal.

Foreign bishops or priests, residing for a time in the land of a Patriarch who was not their own, would continue to use the rite to which they were accustomed at home. A priest could not use various rites according to the land where he happened to be for a time; he would not know its prayers nor ceremonies.

The simple faithful must, no doubt, in default of a priest of their own rite, have received sacraments according to the use of the place where they happened to be. But in cases of a more or less stable colony of foreigners, there was generally provision made that they should have clergy of their own rite to minister to them. Thus there were, long before the great schism, priests of the Byzantine rite in Southern Italy for the Greeks who had settled there.[1] There were Latin churches at Constantinople for the Western soldiers; the Roman Apocrisarius[2] at the Emperor's court had his own chapel, in which he celebrated according to the Roman rite.

In the case of such fixed colonies of foreigners, the question soon arose which Patriarch they were to obey. Now the reasonable answer to this would seem to be that, if they have settled in a foreign country, they should obey the Patriarch of that country; but that he should provide clergy (brought from their own land) to minister to them.[3] On the one hand, a large group of Christians who disregard the general law of the place where they live will be a cause of disorder and confusion to their neighbours. On the other hand, it would be hard on people, accustomed to attend services to them full of meaning, to make them suddenly forsake these for others, of which they could understand nothing. Nor is there any real difficulty in such an arrangement. The local Patriarch can easily appoint priests, even bishops, for the foreign colony. These will see to the rites, while treating with the local Patriarch about matters of discipline for their own people.[4]

[1] See p. 71, *seq.*   [2] Legate.

[3] The fourth Lateran Council (1215) made very sensible provisions for this case. There are never to be two Catholic Ordinaries in the same city; that would be like a monster with two heads (for a long time this was considered an axiom of Canon Law; it is abolished now). But the Ordinary is to provide priests of other rites, who minister to their own people, but obey him. If necessary he is to appoint Vicars General for the other rites (Cap. ix; Mansi, xxii, col. 998). These provisions are still observed in the case of the Italo-Greeks (see p. 177).

[4] To obey the local Patriarch does not necessarily mean to submit in all things to his normal Canon Law. He can, by his authority, dispense the foreign colonists from special points, and allow them in these to follow their own customs. A reasonable Patriarch would

Yet this arrangement did eventually lead to difficulties, caused, as usual, by the arrogant intolerance of the Patriarchs of Constantinople. First these, and their masters the Emperors, constantly demanded that the South of Italy should belong to the Byzantine Patriarchate, on the strength of the fact that so many people there used the Byzantine rite. So we have the beginning of a new principle. It is no longer that normally rite follows Patriarchate, with exceptions for foreigners, but that in every case *Patriarchate is to follow rite*. Whoever uses a certain rite is to obey the Patriarch of the city where that rite has its original home. This is just a reversal of the old relation of cause and effect. Instead of the lesser, the mere outward symbol, following the thing of prime importance, the primary thing was proposed as a consequence of its natural effect.

But this Byzantine idea was not applied to the East. According to their new principle, the Patriarchs of Constantinople should have ceased to claim any jurisdiction over the Latins in their own Patriarchate. They found, however, a simpler way out of the difficulty.

Michael Cerularius in 1053 opened his campaign against the West by suddenly shutting up all the Latin chapels at Constantinople, and telling the Latins in his power to cease being Azymites and adopt the Byzantine rite. He even had the insolence to do so in the case of the Papal Apocrisarius. Again the contrast between this insolent person and the tolerant Popes is significant. At that time the Popes had Byzantine churches throughout Italy. They claimed the people who used these churches as members of their Patriarchate, since they lived in the heart of it. There was a Byzantine monastery, Grottaferrata, at the very gates of Rome. Yet never once in all that bitter controversy did they think of retorting on Constantinople by shutting up these churches; never once did they suggest to their Byzantine subjects that these should give up being Fermentites and turn Latin.[1]

However, eventually the situation has produced very much the effect desired then by the Greeks. No longer can we say that rite follows Patriarchate so much as that, inversely, Patriarchate follows rite. The cause of this is, first, the

---

naturally do so. The Italo-Greeks, subject not only to Roman Patriarchal authority, but even to the jurisdiction of Latin Ordinaries, yet keeping (by authority of these Ordinaries) their own Byzantine rules, are an example of this. See p. 76, *seq.*

[1] See, *e.g.*, Leo IX's letter to Cerularius, § 29 (Will, "Acta et Scripta de Controversiis eccl. græcæ et latinæ," Leipzig, 1861), p. 81.

breaking up of Eastern Christendom into schismatical sects. In the old days, when East and West were one Church, the situation was different. People then were separated by no difference of faith nor of final obedience. It was easy then to group Patriarchates geographically, and to maintain the principle that, as far as the normal inhabitants of each land were concerned, they should use the rite of the ecclesiastical Head of the land.

But when there were groups of Christians, living mixed together in one city, yet in schism with one another, this could no longer be the case. Each sect or Church naturally still claimed the allegiance of its members, wherever they might live. Already in the fifth century Egyptian Christendom broke up into the rival Churches of Copts and Orthodox; in Syria were Nestorians, Jacobites, and Orthodox.

Since the Moslem conquests of the seventh century the idea of separate communities living side by side in one place has been accentuated. People in the East are accustomed to see groups of Moslems, Jews, and Christians of various kinds in the same town. So the old geographical idea of Patriarchate has broken down completely. Now a man belongs to a certain " nation," in the Turkish sense. He belongs to this by birth and heredity, except in the rare cases of conversion from one "nation" to another. He keeps his membership of his "nation" wherever he may live. The sign of his " nation," at least among Christians, is the rite it uses. The rite has become much more important as a mark of membership than any point of faith. And he is subject ecclesiastically to the Head of his nation, even when that Head lives in a remote land. So the various Patriarchs organize hierarchies for their own people, wherever these people may live. In one town you will find an Orthodox community with an Orthodox priest, dependent ultimately on one of the Orthodox Patriarchs or holy Synods; in another quarter of the same town you will find an Armenian group dependent remotely on Etshmiadzin, a Jacobite group dependent on the Jacobite Patriarch, perhaps a handful of Copts who look to Alexandria as the source of authority to them; then a group of Jews with their Rabbi, and one of Moslems with their Mullah. The geographical distribution exists only as a memory, and as the remote source of the present state of things. There is now an intricate network of various religious bodies interlaced throughout the Levant.

This situation is reflected curiously inside the Catholic Church, in the case of the Uniates.

It would seem most reasonable on the basis of preserving the constitution of Catholic antiquity, that there should be four Catholic Eastern Patriarchs, those of Constantinople, Alexandria, Antioch, and Jerusalem, under the supreme authority of the Chief Patriarch at Rome. Each of these Eastern Patriarchs would then have his own territory and his own rite. Every Catholic native of the territory of a given Patriarch would obey him and follow his rite.

If Eastern Christendom had developed normally without schisms, no doubt this is what would now be the case. It might still be held up as the theoretical ideal. But practical reasons have prevented this ideal from being carried out. Instead we have an involved system, which reflects the state of things among the schismatics. Namely, at various periods certain members of schismatical Churches have returned to the Catholic Church. In each case there was a group coming out of certain surroundings, used to certain rites and customs. These groups, even in becoming Catholic, brought with them their old feeling of being a special " nation." Often they could not easily do away with their inherited prejudices against their old rival " nations."[1] What, then, was the central authority of the Church at Rome to do ? What they did was this: they reformed anything in the rite or custom of the converts which seemed really opposed to any essential point of Catholic faith or practice, otherwise they left them, as far as possible, as they were. In particular, they left the members of each " nation," however little justification there may have been for its original formation, as a special group, forming a Catholic " nation " in each case, to correspond to the schismatical one from which it came. Each of these Catholic groups was given a Catholic Patriarch corresponding to the schismatical Patriarch whose allegiance the converts had thrown off.

This produced a number of Patriarchs within the Catholic Church for which there was no precedent in antiquity. But already, long before the conversion of the Uniate bodies, the old ideal of one Patriarch for each see in the East had disappeared. So we have, as we have seen, a Catholic group or " nation " corresponding to each schismatical group. The many Catholic Patriarchs in the East do not correspond to the old four Eastern Patriarchs, but rather the number of Patriarchs, and alleged Patriarchs, who arose through later schisms and heresies.

[1] For instance, in Syria there is still a good deal of rivalry between Melkites and Maronites, though they are in communion with each other. See p. 202.

So there are now two Catholic Patriarchs of Alexandria. There is a Coptic one for the converted Copts, and a Melkite Patriarch who rules the converts from the Orthodox Church. Antioch is represented by three Catholic Eastern Patriarchs. There is one for the Melkites of the Byzantine rite, one for the Syrian Uniates, corresponding to the Jacobite Patriarch, and one for the Maronites.

This last case is an interesting example of the way Rome, as far as possible, changes nothing of the individuality of Churches in the East which return to her communion. The Maronite Patriarchate began as one more schismatical line. It represents the Monothelete schism of the seventh century. When a body of formerly Orthodox Christians in the Lebanon became a Monothelete sect, it set up a Patriarch for itself. This Patriarch of Antioch had, by common Catholic law, no right to exist. When these Monotheletes came back to the Catholic Church at the time of the Crusades, in theory they should have become Melkites; their Patriarch should have been deposed. But for centuries they were already a " nation " with their own Head. So Rome left them such and recognized the Maronite Patriarch of Antioch as their Head, under the Pope.

So also a Chaldean Patriarch is theoretically an anomaly. When some Nestorians came back to Catholic unity, in theory they should have submitted to the (supposed) one Catholic Patriarch of Antioch. But they had forgotten almost that there was such a person as a Patriarch of Antioch. For many centuries the Nestorians had called their Katholikos Patriarch; so the Uniates from that sect were given a Uniate Patriarch of Babylon, to balance the Nestorian Patriarch and Katholikos of the East.

Then occurs a further complication. Not only are the old Patriarchates divided to correspond to the rival lines outside the Church; portions of them are grouped together, for practical reasons. We have mentioned above the Melkite Patriarch of Alexandria and of Antioch. There is also one of Jerusalem. But these are, for the present, all one and the same person. Namely, there are not at present enough Melkites to justify the appointment of three Patriarchs for their three chief sees. So, until their number grows, the same Prelate is Melkite Patriarch of Alexandria, Antioch, Jerusalem, and all the East.

Thus we have a new grouping of Catholics of Eastern rites, cutting right across the old simple arrangement of Patriarchate by geographical position. One old Patriarchate is divided into

several, and members of several are now joined under one.
The geographical idea is completely lost. A Maronite remains
a Maronite, is still subject to the Maronite hierarchy, wherever
he may dwell. Even in America immigration of Catholics of
Eastern rites has led to the formation of groups there, corresponding to those in their original homes.

In the Levant the various Uniate groups are interlaced all
over the various countries. There are Maronite communities
in Egypt and Cyprus. In Syria especially, you may find
representatives of nearly all the Uniate Churches, often in the
same town. Each has its own hierarchy. The Patriarchs provide priests, and, where necessary, bishops for their own people,
wherever there are enough of these people to make it necessary.
So we find, not only bishops of the various sects as rivals in one
town (that is not surprising), but, what at first does seem
strange, several Catholic bishops bearing the same local title,
residing in the same town. Yet these Catholic sharers of one
title are, of course, not rivals. There is no case of cross-
jurisdiction. No man can be subject to several claimants for his
allegiance at the same time. Each hierarchy exists only for,
rules only, its own " nation." The only modification of the
ancient principle is that the various Patriarchates are no longer
divided geographically. Now, as before, there are various
groups of Catholics, each subject to its own Patriarch. Only
the groups live together in the same cities. It is true that the
groups themselves are no longer quite the same as they were.
The ancient Church, for instance, knew nothing of such distinctions as those between a Copt and a Melkite, a Syrian Uniate
and a Maronite. We have already explained how these came
about.

In view of the controversial capital which people sometimes make out of the presence of several Catholic bishops in
one place, it is important to remember that these do not involve
any kind of cross-jurisdiction or rivalry. Each rules his own
people, as do our bishops in the West. The only difference
is that the subjects of different bishops live side by side in the
same towns.

So, in the Catholic Church too, as far as the East is concerned, we must reverse the old principle, at any rate as a
practical expedient. Instead of saying that rite follows
Patriarchate (with the idea that you obey and use the rite of the
Patriarch in whose territory you live), we must now conceive
the situation that *Patriarchate follows rite*. A man belongs
to a certain rite, wherever he may live. His rite is determined

by his birth and heredity. He obeys the Head of the people of his rite.

Probably the first thing that would strike a stranger who goes into a church would be the language in which the prayers are said and the various chants are sung. Because this is so noticeable a point in the service, it is often given an importance which it by no means deserves.

Really this question of language is the least important note of any rite. In theory any rite may be used in any language, without ceasing to be exactly the same rite. If the Pope were to tell us in England to use our present rite in English, the difference thus made would seem enormous to most people; yet it would still be just as much the Roman rite—that is, in origin, the local rite of the city of Rome—as it is now that we use it in Latin. As a matter of fact, the Roman rite is used in old Slavonic in Dalmatia, and there are a few cases of its use in Greek in Italy; but in both cases it is simply the Roman rite in another language.

It is in no way the language which determines the rite, but the complex of prayers, the order of the service, the ceremonies and so on, which, as long as they remain the same, form the same rite. So all kinds of combinations of these two things, rite and language, have taken place, and still do take place, all over Christendom. The same rite occurs in different languages; on the other hand, totally different rites occur in the same language. In general, we may note that in the West it is rare for a rite to be used in different languages. Rome has no principle of uniformity in rite; the Holy See gladly tolerates a great diversity of rites in the Catholic Church. But she does, as a rule, appear to desire that each rite (at any rate in the West) should be used uniformly in the same language.

The Orthodox Church, on the contrary, has shown herself extremely intolerant of different rites. She has crushed the old rite of Alexandria among her members altogether, and has nearly crushed that of Antioch. Everywhere she imposes the much later and far less venerable rite of Constantinople. But she does not seem to mind in what language that rite is used. The Byzantine rite is now used among the Orthodox in about fourteen different languages. But in each of these it is just as much the Byzantine rite as it is in its original Greek.

From this we see that we can never distinguish rites by the languages in which they are used. We should never talk about a Latin rite, a Greek rite, a Syriac rite. There are now three Latin rites, those of Rome, Milan, and the Mozarabic

rite; there are at least three Greek rites, those of Alexandria,
Antioch, and Constantinople.   Once there were more.   These
are totally different, they represent the first main distinctions
of Eastern rites; yet they are all Greek.   The equally different
Nestorian and Jacobite rites, to say nothing of those of the
Maronites and Malabar Christians, are all in the same language
—Syriac.   Yet in such absolutely different languages as Arabic
and Rumanian we find the same rite of Constantinople.   So
language is no test of rite.   The only real test of a rite is its
order, forms, and arrangements; and the note of each is the
place of its origin.   If people would realize this there would
be less confusion of ideas on the subject.   We should speak
of the Roman, Byzantine, Alexandrine, Antiochene rites.
Then it is clear what we are talking about; and it remains
a very small detail in what language any of these may
be used.

Lastly, in the East at any rate, it makes very little difference
in what place a man may live, as far as his rite or the branch
of the Church to which he belongs is concerned.   Certainly,
originally all depended on this.   A man was not asked to which
Patriarchate he would like to belong.   That was settled for
him by his birth as a native of some land, just as in the West
the Ordinary you must obey is the bishop of the place in which
you were born or now live.   But the dismemberment of the
old Patriarchates by later schisms, the wandering of people
from one place to another, have changed all that in the Catholic
Church too.   There are communities of many different rites
living now side by side in the same towns, each having its own
parish church, sometimes its own bishop.   In Beyrut there are
a Catholic Maronite Archbishop, a Catholic Syrian bishop,
and a Catholic Melkite bishop each ruling his own flock;
while the Latins there obey none of these, but the Latin
Delegate.

A man belongs to his " nation "—that is, to his rite—
wherever he may dwell.   His children inherit this quality from
him, to whatever new city their business may take them.   It
is, indeed, exceedingly difficult for a man to change the rite he
has inherited, both from the point of view of Catholic Canon
Law and that of Turkish State Law.   It clings to him, like his
family name.   So we cannot now adequately define the
flocks ruled by the various Patriarchs of the Catholic Church
by showing maps.   It was so once; it should be so in theory.
In practice we must try to give a statement of the chief places
where members of the various Eastern Churches now happen

to dwell, and in the case of some of them this will include so distant a land as America. There is no reason why there should not be a portion of the Maronite Church, with a Maronite bishop under the Maronite Patriarch, in London. It would be so if a sufficient number of Maronite merchants found it convenient to settle there.

4. Prejudices against the Uniates.

It is now time to say something about that unjust prejudice against the Uniate Churches which one finds, not only among Protestants, but, most strangely, among Western Catholics, who owe them rather the greatest honour and love.

This prejudice seems ingrained in many people who ought to know better. Protestants of all sects constantly make the most absurd statements about them, even otherwise educated Protestants.

The grossest form of error is not even to know that there are any Uniate Churches in the East. One sometimes still hears even this. One reads books in which the writer shows that he really thinks that the only people in union with Rome, the only people who obey the Pope, are those who use the Roman rite in the West.[1] One finds the " East " quoted solidly as a witness against the Roman claims. To such people as those who think this, we can only point out that in no part of the world are there so loyal subjects of the Pope, nowhere are his claims so eagerly defended, as among the most intelligent, the most advanced and civilized portions of Eastern Christendom.

Then, when the Protestant has at last found out that there are such things as Uniate Churches in the East, he often changes his tactics, and now represents them as a contemptible little handful of people who, not very willingly, more or less accept the Papal claims.

They are by no means a handful. There are over $6\frac{1}{2}$ million Uniates. This is a small number compared with the total number of Catholics (over 292 millions),[2] but the Uniates alone

[1] So in Mr. Dearmer's little book. See p. 11, n. 1.

[2] H. A. Krose, " Kirchliches Handbuch," vol. iii (Freiburg i. B., 1911), p. 204, arrives at the total 292,787,085 for all Catholics in the world. His authorities may be seen there. But it should be remembered that the great difficulty against all such figures is that it is almost impossible to define exactly who are members of the Catholic Church or of any religious body. Where exactly can we draw the line between a bad Catholic who neglects all his religious duties, never goes to church, and cares little or nothing about the

often outnumber the whole religious body of the man who speaks of them as a handful.

As for their loyalty to Rome, it is, of course, true that in the past there have been disputes and regrettable incidents among some of them.

Such things have happened in the West too. A man is no more guaranteed against temptation to personal ambition, quarrelling, discontent with the authorities and uncatholic spirit by being a Uniate, than if he were a Latin. We shall, unfortunately, see several examples of such things in our story. But it is absurd to quote one or two regrettable cases, and then to assume that all Uniates groan under the yoke of Rome. Once more, such things happen everywhere. The other Uniates are no more responsible for disloyal conduct on the part of some one bishop than we Latins are all responsible for the shocking behaviour of that Latin bishop who went wrong, Thomas Cranmer.

Let each man bear the responsibility of his own deeds, and do not blame the whole body of Melkite Uniates if an Armenian Uniate bishop is insubordinate. It is true that many Uniates have shown great anxiety about their special organization, their rites, their corporate existence. In view of the inevitable predominance of the Latin part of the Catholic Church, of the fact that the common chief of all, the Pope, is a Latin, in view also of the excessively strong attraction of all Easterns to their particular group or nation, this is not surprising. Nor can we wonder that sometimes the local patriotism of the Easterns, together with the want of appreciation of their point of view among Italian Cardinals, has sometimes produced discussions, protests, and friction. All things considered, it is rather wonderful that there has not been more friction. We must remember that in some points the way in which the West treats the East is galling to the East. We send out missionaries to educate them, we regulate their affairs, tell them what they may do and what they may not do, often teach them their own business,[1] and in general, assume a patronizing attitude towards them. And they are a proud people.

---

faith, and a man who has ceased to be a Catholic at all ? At any rate, friend and foe admit that the Catholic Church is the largest religious body in the world. That does not prevent the fact that it is still only a small minority of the whole human race.

[1] As when the Latin missionary teaches students of Eastern rites how to celebrate their own liturgies.

Such considerations as these will account amply for whatever friction there has been in the past, friction that will cease with a better appreciation of their ideas and attitude (for in as far as the Roman Congregations have ever offended their susceptibilities, it has been from ignorance rather than from malice).

But there is another side to all this. The really wonderful thing about the Uniates is not that occasionally they have grumbled; it is, in spite of that, in spite of blunders made by the West towards them, their magnificent loyalty to the Catholic ideal. It is the right sort of loyalty, to an ideal, not to persons. They have no more personal devotion towards Italian Cardinals and the Monsignori of the Roman congregations than we have in the North. What they care for is the one united Church of Christ throughout the world, and the Holy See as guarding that unity. They see around them the same process of erosion among the schismatics as we see among the Protestants; and they, too, understand that the bond of union among Catholics is our common loyalty to the primate-see. This idea so dominates that, in spite of the occasional friction, the Pope has no more loyal subjects in the world than his brothers and children of Eastern rites. The very fact that they keep and cherish their union with Rome, although the schismatics are never tired of calling them slaves, of boasting of their own liberty, shows how real this ideal must be to the Uniates. It requires some strength of conviction to acknowledge as your chief a bishop of a foreign rite, to submit the rules of your own liturgy to the supervision of men who themselves use another. They draw this strength from their unswerving belief in the Catholic ideal of one universal, united Church of God. It is for the sake of that that they obey a Latin authority, for the sake of that, and because they know that the bishop who holds the succession of Peter rises above all rites and is a foreigner to none of his brethren.

Indeed, from my experience I am inclined to think that the pride of the Uniates in their communion with Rome is sometimes even excessive, that they look with too much scorn on their non-uniate neighbours. Any Latin in the Levant will see with what pride the Uniates he meets remember that they belong to the same body as he does, that they have a right to the same consciousness of citizenship in the great Church as he. They are conscious, too, that they are better educated, more strict in their laws, more edifying in the lives of their clergy than the other Eastern Christians. They feel themselves, as they are, an aristocracy among the others. As the soldiers whom Agricola led in Scotland were conscious of the might of Rome behind them, as they looked to the Imperial City on the Tiber as the centre of their allegiance, and despised the barbarians who had no share in Rome, so do the Uniates look across the Mediterranean to the Patriarchal throne by the Tiber, so do they realize themselves as citizens of no mean kingdom, and rather despise the isolated schismatics who have no share in the great Church.

Lastly, anyone who knows those lands at all will admit that the Uniates are, morally and intellectually, the best of Eastern Christians. The Catholic will not be surprised at this. But even apart from supernatural considerations, the fact can easily be explained. The Uniates are the only Easterns who enjoy what, in this case, is the real advantage of Western ideas. No one will deny that for many centuries the Christian East (except to some extent Russia) has been stagnant. This is not the fault of the Christians. Crushed under the horrible weight of Islam, they could not be expected to live a very active intellectual life; surrounded by the contempt of their barbarous conquerors, with Moslem morals all round them, it is not wonderful that they have not reached very high ethical standards. They learned to cringe, to deceive, to sacrifice principle for money, after the manner of the bribe-taking Turkish Pasha. Who shall blame them if subjection under the Turk has in some points Turkified their manners? It is enough that, in spite of all, they have kept their faith in Christ, Uniates and schismatics alike. For that they deserve all honour from us. But the fact remains that intellectually those poor persecuted Christians have not risen to any great height, and that morally they have become slack in some points.

The lack of education among the schismatical Eastern clergy is the invariable reproach of Western travellers; and the schismatical bishop has too often learned to take bribes, to sell honours and offices, nowhere more scandalously than in the case of the Church of Constantinople. To-day no one would cite a Jacobite parish-priest, a Coptic monk, as a shining example of learning, or as the exponent of a high moral ideal; though often he is sincerely pious. But in these matters the Uniates have the advantage of Western education. There are no theological works produced by modern schismatical Copts or Jacobites; generally, their clergy can hardly read, and do not understand their own liturgical language. Nor is much in this way produced by the Armenians or the Orthodox.

What they do produce is generally a rather naïve reproduction of Western ideas at second-hand.[1]

But the Uniates are taught by Western Latins; their schools and seminaries are conducted on the same lines as ours; they learn their theology from the same textbooks as are used in our colleges in the West. There is no question that the Uniate clergy have had an immeasurably better education than the others. In this matter they have every advantage from their union with the more highly developed West. Even in the detail of language the Uniates have the advantage. Most of them know at least some Latin, many can talk quite good French. This opens to them vast fields of knowledge, closed to the schismatics who know nothing but Arabic. It would be an exaggeration to say that the average Uniate priest is quite up to the level of the average Latin priest. But, at least, he is far in advance of the schismatic. He has received at any rate a fair general education on Western lines,[2] and has gone through a course of theology from Western books. The schismatic generally has had no education, and has learned no theology at all. As a simple test of this, ask priests in the Levant about the great questions which lie beneath their differences, about Nestorianism, Monophysism, the idea of the Church and the Papacy. You will not find one Uniate who is not able to give you a general, fairly accurate, if perhaps rather old-fashioned

[1] There are, of course, degrees in this, and qualifications to be made in so general a statement. The Russian Church has good theological schools and many excellent scholars. Perhaps Greeks and Armenians come second, inasmuch as they have a few scholars who have been to foreign (generally German Protestant) universities. But the average level of their clergy is not high. That of the Jacobites, Copts, Abyssinians, is very low indeed.

[2] It is becoming a commonplace to decry the idea of giving Western education to Eastern people. There is undoubtedly much truth in this protest. A mechanical, unintelligent reproduction of our schools in the East would do more harm than good. On the other hand, there are many things that our schools have, and native Eastern schools lack, which are unmixed advantages in any school. A discipline which is both firm and kind, above all, uniform systematic teaching from well-arranged textbooks, a high tone about truthfulness, honesty, and chastity—these are Western notes; yet they are good for any school. To defend slackness of tone, a discipline which is the arbitrary whim of masters, alternately lax and cruel, desultory teaching with bad textbooks or none in Eastern schools because these things are " Eastern," would be to overdo a principle which has some truth in it. The ideal is to adapt our methods intelligently, being always ready to see and allow for Eastern qualities; and this is what is done in all good Western schools in the Levant, both Catholic and Protestant.

statement on these points, and a defence of what he believes.
You will find few schismatics who know anything about them
at all, who even know what these questions mean.

So also in morals. The Uniate clergy have been brought
up under the rigorously moral eye of Western missionaries;
they have had years of the stern discipline of a seminary, in
which the standard is the same as in ours. The schismatics
have grown up anyhow in villages, in which there was little of
any standard, and have been taken and ordained without any
preparation at all.

Again, among the bishops and authorities of the Uniates,
their union with Rome forces them to apply very much the
same principles of conduct as obtain among us in the West.
Their Canon Law is revised and enforced by the Holy See.
Among the others there are but the loosest principles, and
Canon Law which is often a mere joke.

The disorders among the schismatics are the constant
subject of regret or humour to travellers. You will not find
so great disorders among the Uniates. The state of things
which is almost a matter of course in great parts of the East,
which Eastern people themselves admit and excuse as the result
of their centuries of bondage (quite a fair excuse), is impossible
among those who are in union with Rome. Their bishops
would put it down ruthlessly and at once. If the bishop did
not do so, he would hear from Propaganda. Whatever you
may say about Rome, you cannot say that her discipline is
slack.

Again, we must not exaggerate this. It is true that Uniate
morals, as well as Uniate scholarship, are not always quite
up to the Western standard. In remote parts of the Church
abuses do go on for some time before they are found out and
suppressed. But the point is that such abuses are always liable
to be found out, and that then they certainly will be suppressed
by the authorities at Rome. Among the schismatics there is
no further authority beyond that of the Eastern people themselves, the very people whom long bondage under the Turk
has made less scrupulous. There is no one to find out and
no one to put down the abuses. So in morals, too, we may
claim safely that the Uniates are the best among Eastern
Christians. They have at least that salutary fear of Rome and
what Rome will say, to repress the *animalis homo*.

I think any traveller in those parts will confirm this. As
with the clergy, so it is with the laity. Go into the house of
a Uniate, especially of a Uniate priest. It will perhaps not be

quite as nice as our houses in Western Europe; but it will probably be reasonably clean. You will find in it Western books; your host will be a not altogether uneducated man. He will probably talk French to you. If he is a layman, he will have read papers, and will show an intelligent interest in what is going on in the world, particularly in that West for which he will have an overwhelming secret respect, even if his national loyalty makes him affect to think his own " nation " every bit as good. If he is a priest, he will ask news of Rome, and will discuss theology, liturgy, and the affairs of the Church. In any case, you will feel nothing like that sense of being among a completely different and lower race of people that you cannot help feeling among the other Eastern Christians. I repeat, from every point of view the Uniates are the aristocracy of Eastern Christians. It may not be a very splendid aristocracy, but, compared with the others, it is a real aristocracy, intellectual and moral.

It is much stranger to find sometimes even Catholics who do real injustice to their fellow-Catholics of Eastern rites. One can understand that Protestants are unjust to them. The existence and particularly the superiority of the Uniate Churches is a fact most damaging to their theories of the Papacy as only recognized in the West, to that identification of " Roman Catholic " with " Latin," which is the great point of their branch theory. But of all people we Western Catholics should glory in the Uniate Churches. They are an exceedingly important factor in our concept of the universal Church; they are our great palpable argument that the primacy of Rome is more than Patriarchal rights over part of the Church. Indeed, in some ways, it is just the Uniates who save the whole situation, from our point of view.

To be obliged to reduce the whole Church of Christ to one Patriarchate would be difficult; it would suggest that perhaps our concept is mistaken, that when Patriarchate is divided against Patriarchate there is an internal schism in the Church, which leaves both sides part of the Church, though no longer united.

But this is not the case. On the contrary, within the one united Church all the Patriarchates remain as they did in early days. The fact that vast numbers of the members of the Eastern Patriarchates have gone out of the Church altogether, distressing as it is, does not affect the legal position. In the same way the Latin Patriarchate lost vast quantities of its subjects at the Reformation. In spite of this, in spite of the many heresies and schisms which at various times have robbed each Patriarchate of its members, the constitution of the Catholic Church remains what it has always been, not one Patriarchate with one rite, but the union of East and West, differing in rites, having in many cases different details of Canon Law, but united in the profession of the same faith and in conscious inter-communion. It is just the Uniates who safeguard this position.

Yet so little do many Catholics in the West realize this position, so little conscious have they been of their fellow-Catholics in the East, that one still finds people who make the fatal mistake of confusing our one Patriarchate with the whole Church. When one hears Catholics say that no Catholic priest may be married, that all Catholics have exactly the same Mass all over the world, one sees to what blunders this confusion between our Western Patriarchate and the whole Church of Christ may lead. It is only from ignorance, because in the West we so rarely see a Catholic of an Eastern rite, that our people when they go to the East sometimes make that most injurious mistake of treating the Uniates as if they were in some way rather less perfect Catholics than we are.

Western people get so used to look upon our Roman rite as the only correct one that they are inclined to think a man who does not use it a kind of half-Catholic, better than the schismatics, but not quite so good as we are. Or when they meet a married Catholic priest they look upon his state as a temporary toleration which had better be done away with. Really he is obeying the Canon Law of his Patriarchate, to which he has just as much right as we have to our laws.

Does anyone think St Athanasius, St Basil, St John Chrysostom imperfect Catholics ? The modern Uniate stands exactly where they stood. Like them he is in communion with the chief of all Patriarchs at Rome; like them he acknowledges the primacy of the Pope and obeys him as Primate. But like them he is not bound by local Western Patriarchal laws; like them he thinks his laws and rite and customs just as good as ours. It is really as absurd for us Latins to think our own Patriarchate the whole Church as it would be for a Melkite to think us imperfect Catholics because we do not use the Byzantine rite.

And from every point of view we Latins owe all possible honour to our brothers the Uniates. They not only save the situation canonically, they are the most splendid example of Catholic loyalty in the world. For the Pope's cause is in some measure our cause. He is a Western bishop, a Latin as we are, and our own Patriarch. It is not difficult for us to be loyal. The fact that the constitution of the Church gives the first place to our Patriarch is no doubt an honour for us; but it would ill beseem us to boast of this before Uniates. Let us rather understand that their loyalty is all the more splendid just because it is less easy for them. We take up the long quarrel between East and West, on the Western side, without difficulty, because we are Westerns. The Uniates are on our side, although they themselves are Easterns. They honour us, and are in communion with us, rather than with their schismatical countrymen, although externally we are further from them than the schismatics. They do this because of their loyalty to the Catholic ideal. Of all people, we who profit by their loyalty should be the first to appreciate it.

So let this be clear. We have no reason to reproach the Uniates, no right to the faintest sense of superiority over them, no right to suggest that they would be in any way better or more Catholic if they turned Latin. They might just as well invite us to turn Uniate of some rite. Let us realize that we all stand on exactly the same footing as fellow-citizens of the same kingdom of God on earth, and let us revere with special honour those who stand by this ideal under the greatest difficulties.

5. The Holy See and the Uniates.

In order now to show that if there has been any prejudice against the Uniates among Latins it is not the fault of the Holy See, in order to establish that the ideas described above are those of the chief authority of the Catholic Church, we will quote some general pronouncements of Popes about the Uniate Churches.

That our fellow-Catholics of Eastern rites deserve all honour; that their position is absolutely correct and unassailable; that all Latins have to do is to honour, and, if necessary, protect their venerable rites, this has been declared in the plainest language, over and over again, by the Popes.

The attitude of the Holy See that nothing need be, nothing should be, changed in the rites which Eastern Christians inherit from their fathers, so long as in all essential points of faith and morals they agree with the Catholic Church, is shown at the very outset of the great schism. Before the schism of Photius, during the Iconoclast persecution in the East (eighth and ninth centuries), a great number of image-worshippers, particularly monks, fled to Italy. Here they were received with all honour as confessors of the faith, and no one dreamed of suggesting that their Byzantine rite was in any way inferior, or that it would be an advantage to them to become Latins.[1]

Just when the trouble began, in 862, Pope Nicholas I (858–867) writes to Photius to explain that he has no kind of objection to the fact that the people have different rites, as long as there be nothing in these opposed to the holy canons.[2]

Then, in the next quarrel, when Michael Cerularius was cursing Latins because we use unleavened bread for the holy Eucharist, and with characteristic Byzantine indecency was calling the Blessed Sacrament, as consecrated by Latins, " dry mud,"[3] Dominic, Patriarch of Gradus and Aquileia,[4] wrote to Peter of Antioch in a way which is equally typical of the Latin attitude in this deplorable quarrel. He not only recognizes entirely that either use, of azyme or fermented bread, is in itself lawful; he tries to find parallel reasons to justify both customs. " We have heard that the holy Roman Church is abused by the clergy of Constantinople. They blame the most holy azyme which we sanctify and receive in the Body of Christ, and they say that because of this we are deprived of that Body, and they judge us to be separated from the unity of the Church because we offer the sacrifice without the mixture of leaven. But we, wishing to keep the unity of the Church without any kind of schism, hold the custom of azyme by the tradition, not only of the Apostles, but of the Lord himself. Yet since we know that the sacred mixture of leaven is accepted and lawfully used by the most holy and orthodox fathers of the Eastern Churches, we understand both customs faithfully, and confirm both by a spiritual meaning. For the mixture of leaven and flour, which the Churches of the East use, shows forth the substance of the Incarnate Word; but the simple azyme kept by the Roman Church, without controversy, may

[1] So Leo IX writes to Cerularius in 1053: " Since both in and outside Rome many monasteries and churches of the Greeks are found, none of them has been disturbed or hindered in the tradition of their fathers, or their customs; but rather, they are advised and encouraged to keep these " (Will, op. cit., p. 81).

[2] Nic. I ep. ad Photium, Ep. xii (P.L. cxix, 789).

[3] Will, op. cit., p. 105.

[4] The Patriarchs of Gradus and Aquileia were not finally merged into the title Patriarch of Venice till 1751. See the article " Patriarch, Patriarchate," in the Cath. Encycl.

represent the purity of the human flesh which it pleased the Divinity to unite with itself."[1]

It would be impossible to urge too strongly that this discussion represents exactly the invariable habit of the two sides in this controversy. The Byzantine Christians have never ceased impudently to quarrel with our customs, have never ceased calling us offensive names because of mere trifles of rite in which we differ from them; on our side there has always been the most complete, the most generous recognition that custom and rite are not in themselves essential things; that it is quite natural that East and West should each have their own practices; that both are equally lawful, both may be defended equally well by mystical interpretations; that the only duty on either side is to keep its own uses, and not to quarrel with the other, not to call other people silly rude names, because they differ in such a matter as this.

The idea that the Popes have demanded uniformity is about as gross a misrepresentation as an ignorant controversialist could make. They have never done so. It is always the other side, the insolent Patriarchs of Constantinople, who cannot tolerate any custom different from their own, who curse us for being Latins (we have never cursed them for being Byzantine), call us heretics, and deny the validity of our sacraments because of differences of mere ritual; who have forced their own late derived rite on the whole Orthodox Church, and destroyed the far more venerable uses of Alexandria and Antioch.

The Fourth Lateran Council (1215) assured the Greeks that it intends " to cherish and honour them, maintaining their customs and rites, as much as, with the help of the Lord, we are able."[2]

In 1222 Pope Honorius III writes to the King of Cyprus (Henry I de'Lusignan, 1218–1253): " We wish to favour and honour the Greeks who come back to the obedience of the Apostolic See, maintaining the customs and rites of the Greeks as much as we can, with God's help."[3]

In 1247 Basilicus, King of Lodomeria, wrote to the Pope, asking to be restored to communion with him. Innocent IV (1243–1254) answers: " We admit that the bishops and priests of Russia shall be allowed to consecrate in leavened bread,

---

[1] Dominici Ptr. Veneti ep. ad Petrum Antiochen. (in Will, *op. cit.*, p. 207).
[2] Cap. iv; Mansi, xxii, 989.
[3] Raynaldus, " Annales eccl.," i (Baronius, xx), p. 501.

according to their use, and that they shall observe their other rites which are not opposed to the Catholic faith, which the Roman Church holds."[1]

After the union of Lyons, in 1278, Nicholas III writes to Bartholomew, Bishop of Grosseto, then his legate at Constantinople, that the now united Greeks are to say the *Filioque* in the Creed;[2] " but concerning the other rites of the Greeks, you are to answer that the Roman Church intends the Greeks to follow them, as far as they can under the favour of God; and that they are to keep these rites, concerning which it appears to the Apostolic See that the Catholic faith is not offended, nor the laws of the sacred canons disobeyed."[3]

Our next example shall be the Council of Florence (1439). It is significant that this Council, after centuries of wild abuse of our Latin use of azyme on the part of the Byzantines, so far from any attempt to retort, should again solemnly defend the equal rights of either custom, and disclaim any idea of imposing one only on the whole Church. " So also, whether in azyme or in leavened bread, the Body of Christ is truly present; and priests must consecrate the Body of the Lord in either, each according to the use of his Church, whether Western or Eastern."[4]   At the time of the fall of Constantinople many Greeks fled to Italy.   Here they were received with the most generous hospitality; the Popes again never thought of changing or blaming the rites they used, as we shall see when we come to the Italo-Greeks (p. 136).

From this time, we have a large number of documents, Bulls and Briefs, by which one Pope after another defends the use of the Byzantine rite in Italy, and forbids any attempt at latinizing the Greek colonies there.

Leo X (1513–1521) and Clement VII (1523–1574) blame Latins who despise the Byzantine rite.   Pius IV (1555–1559) proclaims the inviolability of that rite; Gregory XIII (1572–1585) founds the Greek college at Rome in 1577, and orders that its students shall be carefully instructed in their own rite.   Clement VIII (1592–1605) and Paul V (1605–1621) defend the Ruthenians of Poland against the Latin government. Benedict XIII (1724–1730), in approving the Synod of Zamoisk, inserted a special clause that nothing was to be allowed

[1] Raynaldus ii (Baronius, xxi), p. 378.
[2] Concerning this Roman legislation has varied considerably at different times.
[3] Raynaldus, iii (Baronius, xxii), p. 447.
[4] Mansi, xxxi, 1031.

which could injure the rite of the Ruthenians.[1]   Most of all,
the great Pope Benedict XIV (1740–1758) stands out as the
champion of the Eastern rites.   A great part of his legislation
is concerned with their defence.   We shall often have to refer
to it.   Meanwhile we may note his laws that the Byzantine
monks in Italy are to know the Greek language and observe
their rite exactly, that no Latin is to attack this.[2]   His three
chief Bulls on the subject are *Etsi pastoralis*, *Demandatam
cælitus*, and especially *Allatæ sunt*.

All these contain much Canon Law for Uniates of various
rites.   As specimens of the attitude of the Holy See towards
Catholics of other rites, these quotations will serve here.

In *Etsi pastoralis*[3] the Pope says that many Christians of the
Byzantine rite have come to live in Italy; that " they and their
children are to keep studiously and carefully the habits, institutions, rites, and customs which they have received from
their Greek fathers, only to show to the Roman Church due
obedience and reverence."[4]   He says that before God there
is neither Greek nor Jew, nor Barbarian nor Scythian, for all are
one in Christ; so the Pope, too, wishes rather to grant special
favours and graces to these strangers, as his predecessors have
always done.   He renews all privileges, immunities, exemp-
tions, indults, and so on, which the Greeks have ever enjoyed.[5]
Then he lays down careful rules for the Byzantine rite in Italy,
to which we shall return, always with the greatest care not to
modify or latinize any of its ancient principles.   " Our
predecessors, the Roman Pontiffs, considered it more proper
to approve and permit these rites, which in no way are opposed
to the Catholic faith, nor cause danger to souls, nor diminish
the honour of the Church, rather than to bring them to the
standard of the Roman ceremonies."[6]   " Nor do we allow
any Latin Ordinary to molest or to disturb these or any of
them.   And we inhibit all and any prelates or persons from
blaspheming, reproving, or blaming the rites of the Greeks,
which were approved in the Council of Florence or elsewhere."[7]

[1] For all these see Benedict XIV, *Allatæ sunt*, §§ 13-16
(Bullarium Benedicti XIV, ed. Venet., 1778, t. iv, pp. 12-1363,
No. xlvii).

[2] Constit.: *Etsi persuasum*, April 20, 1751 (*op. cit.*, t. iii, p. 163,
No. xliv).

[3] May 26, 1742, for the Italo-Greeks (*op. cit.*, t. i,p p. 75-83,
No. lvii).

[4] In the introduction.   [5] *Ibid.*

[6] § ix, n. 1.   [7] *Ibid.*

So anxious is the Pope that there should be no idea of superiority on the part of the Latins, that he draws up elaborate rules of precedence between the clergy of both rites in public functions. In this there is to be no question of the rite either follows, but only of their dignity in their own rite; and among those of equal rank, precedence is to go by date of ordination.[1]

It is sometimes said that all the Roman legislation in favour of the Eastern rites is not sincere, that it is really only a trap to attract the schismatics, and make them believe that Rome does not want to destroy their rites.

At any rate, in the case of these Italo-Greeks, there can be no such idea. They were absolutely helpless in the midst of a solidly Latin population. They had not even their own bishops. The Pope had only to let things alone, and they would all have turned Latin centuries ago, automatically. But the Pope did not want this. It is a childish idea that the mighty Roman rite could be jealous of any other. Benedict XIV, and many other Popes, had a genuine desire that the other ancient rites of the Church should not die out; so, at considerable trouble to themselves, by constant severe legislation, they kept them alive; in some cases, as we shall see, almost in spite of the people of these rites themselves.

On December 24, 1743, Benedict XIV published the decree *Demandatam cælitus*.[2] This is addressed to the Melkite Patriarch of Antioch, Cyril VI,[3] and the bishops of his Patriarchate. In this he answers various questions that had arisen regarding rites and customs of the Melkites, always with the idea of preserving their rite in its purity, of restoring genuine Byzantine practices, abolishing later abuses, especially insisting on uniformity within each rite, and forbidding either a mixture of rites or attempts to persuade the faithful of one rite to leave it for another. " Concerning rites and customs of the Greek Church in general, we decree in the first place that no one, whatever his rank may be, even Patriarchal or episcopal, may innovate or introduce anything that diminishes their complete and exact observance."[4] But bishops may allow harmless practices within the limits of what is essential to the rite. Certain obvious abuses and superstitious ideas are forbidden, as, for instance, the absurd idea that, if a priest uses vestments already used by someone else that day, he thereby breaks his fast.[5] The Pope forbids Maronites to mix themselves in the affairs of Melkites, or to try to persuade

---

[1] § ix, n. 17.   [2] *Op. cit.*, t. i, p. 129, No. lxxxvii.
[3] See p. 197 for this Patriarch.   [4] § 3.   [5] § 8.

Melkites to turn Maronite.[1] The same law, even more severely, applies to Latin missionaries. " Moreover, we expressly forbid all and each of the Catholic Melkites who use the Greek rite, to pass over to the Latin rite. We command severely that all missionaries, under pains named below, and under others to be inflicted according to our pleasure, shall not dare to persuade anyone of these to pass from the Greek to the Latin rite, or shall even allow them to do so, if they wish it, without having first consulted the Apostolic See."[2] The pains are deprivation of active and passive voice in elections, and inability for any office or degree in their Order or Congregation.[3]

There were, then, ambiguous people, who followed both rites, Roman and Byzantine, on various occasions. This must stop. Such persons are to make a final statement as to the rite to which they wish to belong, without further delay, and then to keep to it exclusively as long as they live.[4] The decree contains many other wise and tolerant rules about the children of mixed marriages,[5] children of Melkite parents who by accident have been baptized by a Latin priest, and so on. The Pope ends: " We do not doubt but that you will recognize that we have no other intention but that the venerable rites of the Greek Church and its customs shall persist in all their force; and that the due obedience of your people and your authority and jurisdiction over them shall be kept whole and entire."[6] And again: " We wish all the rights, privileges, and free jurisdiction of your Fraternities[7] to remain intact, that you may rule the sheep committed to your care, and may direct them by the paths of the laws of God, with the help of his grace, to the goal of eternal salvation."[8]

But the most important legislation of Benedict XIV on this subject is contained in the Encyclical *Allatæ sunt* of July 26, 1755.[9]

This is addressed to missionaries in the " East," meaning chiefly in Syria and Asia Minor. It is a long document. First, the Pope explains at length the care his predecessors have always had to preserve the Eastern rites unchanged and unhurt.

He sums this up accurately by saying that hitherto union with the Eastern Churches has always been arranged so that " errors opposed to the Catholic faith were rooted out; but it

---

[1] § 12.   [2] § xv.   [3] § xix.   [4] § xvi.
[5] Mixed, that is, between Catholics of different rites.
[6] § xxvi.   [7] The Uniate Patriarchs and bishops.
[8] § xxvi.
[9] Bullarium Bened. XIV, *ed. cit.*, t. iv, pp. 123-136, No. xlvii.

has never been attempted to do any injury to the venerable Eastern rite."[1]   Examples and proofs of this follow, beginning with the tolerance of Leo IX towards Byzantine churches in Italy, at the very time when Cerularius was shutting up Latin churches at Constantinople.   Then comes a long list of Popes who, in various ways, have protected Eastern rites; so that from this Bull alone a good idea of the position may be obtained.[2]

The missionaries are to convert Eastern schismatics to the Catholic faith; to fight against errors; but in no way to try to make their converts Latins.   In order to show the respect which the Holy See has for Eastern rites, the Pope quotes a number of cases in which liturgical practices from the East have been introduced into the Roman rite, such as the use of the Nicene Creed at Mass, and so on.[3]

There are sharp laws against mixing rites; priests of Eastern rites may celebrate in Latin churches, but they must, in that case too, follow their own rite exactly.

The Pope sees that there is a greater advantage for the Catholic faith in maintaining Eastern rites than in abolishing them: " As for the arguments that missionaries should use, since Eastern people greatly adhere to their own ancient fathers, the works of the diligent Leo Allatius and of other illustrious theologians should be studied carefully, in which it is shown that the ancient and venerable Greek Fathers and those of the Western Church agree entirely among themselves in all things that affect dogma, and that they confute equally the errors in which the Eastern people, and particularly the Greeks, are now unhappily involved.   Hence without doubt the study of their works will be of the greatest use."[4]

So he concludes: " We have explained these things in this our Encyclical letter, not only to make the principles clear by which we have answered the questions of the missionaries, but also that all may see the goodwill with which the Apostolic See embraces Eastern Catholics, since it orders that by all means their ancient rites are to be preserved, as opposed neither to the Catholic faith nor to morals.   Nor do we demand that schismatics who return to Catholic unity should forsake their rites; but only that they should renounce and detest their heresies.   We desire vehemently that their various nations should be preserved, not destroyed; that, to say all in one word, they should be Catholics, not that they should become Latins."[5]

[1] § vi.   [2] §§ vii–xviii.   [3] § xxviii.
[4] § xix.   [5] § xlviii.

This Encyclical contains full details about all the points of Canon Law which affect the Uniates, so that it has become the standard precedent for Papal legislation ever since. Here, so far, we are only concerned with the attitude of the Holy See in general. This attitude could not be better expressed than it is by the closing words of *Allatæ sunt*, quoted above: " Exoptans vehementer ut omnes Catholici sint, non ut omnes Latini fiant."

The great mind of Benedict XIV, the Canonist-Pope, hereby set a standard which his successors have observed faithfully. He made many other rules about details of Eastern rites, always in the same spirit.[1] Indeed, the tone of the Holy See towards the Uniates is set by the laws and declarations of Benedict XIV. His successors have taken back nothing of his large-minded toleration; they have only urged the same principles more strongly.

Pius VI and Clement XII fostered the Byzantine rite in lower Italy and Sicily.[2]

Pius IX (1846-1878) distinguished himself as a Pope who favoured Uniates. In his Encyclical of the Epiphany, 1848,[3] while inviting Eastern Christians to come back to unity with Rome, he repeats that the universal Church will always respect the rites and customs of her Eastern parts. He says: " We will consider your special Catholic liturgies as entirely safe and protected; we think much of them, although in some points they differ from the liturgies of the Latin Churches. Indeed, your liturgies were valued by our predecessors, as recommended by the venerable antiquity of their origin, written in languages which the Apostles and Fathers used, containing rites celebrated with splendid and magnificent pomp, so that the piety and reverence of the faithful towards the divine mysteries are thereby fostered."[4]

In his allocution of December 19, 1853, Pius IX said:

---

[1] Besides these three Constitutions, the Bullarium of Benedict XIV contains a mass of legislation about Uniates.

[2] See pp. 161-162.

[3] *In suprema* (Pii. XI, P.M. Acta—Typ. Bon. Art.), part i, p. 78.

[4] *Ibid.*, p. 81: "Omnino autem sartas tectas habebimus peculiares uestras Liturgias; quas plurimi sane facimus, licet illæ nonnullis in rebus a Liturgia Ecclesiarum Latinarum diuersæ sint. Enimuero Liturgiæ ipsæ uestræ in pretio pariter habitæ fuerunt a Prædecessoribus nostris; utpote quæ et commendantur uenerabili antiquitate suæ originis, et conscriptæ sunt linguis, quas Apostoli aut Patres adhibuerant, et ritus continent splendido quodam ac magnifico apparatu celebrandos, quibus fidelium erga diuina mysteria pietas et reuerentia foueantur."

" Our predecessors declared not only that nothing is to be blamed in the sacred rites of the Eastern Church, that nothing in them is opposed to the true faith; but also that these rites must be kept and reverenced, being worthy of all respect by the antiquity of their origin, coming as they do, in great part, from the holy fathers. Particular constitutions have forbidden those who follow these rites to abandon them without special permission of the Supreme Pontiff. Our predecessors knew that the spotless bride of Christ presents in these external notes an admirable variety, which in no way alters her unity. The Church, spreading beyond the frontiers of States, embraces all peoples and all nations, which she unites in the profession of the same faith, in spite of diversity of customs, language, and rites; these differences being approved by the Roman Church, mother and chief of all."[1]

So, on the Epiphany, 1862, Pius IX founded a special Congregation for Eastern rites. It was perhaps less happy that this was made a subdivision of Propaganda, with the title " S. Congregatio de propaganda Fide pro ritibus orientalibus "; but in founding it the Pope used again the same language of respect for the Eastern rites, made again the same assurances that he had no wish to destroy these:

" Our predecessors not only never had the intention to bring Eastern people to the Latin rite, but, every time they thought it expedient, they have declared in clear and precise terms that the Holy See does not ask Eastern Christians to abandon their own rites, venerable by their antiquity and by the witness of the holy fathers. The Holy See demands one thing only, that in these rites nothing be introduced which would be contrary to the Catholic faith, dangerous for souls, or opposed to virtue; as one of our predecessors, Benedict XIV of happy memory, shows in his Encyclical *Allatæ sunt*, of July 5, 1755, addressed to missionaries in the East. If, then, any harm has ever been done to the rites of the East, it is not to the Holy See that it can be ascribed."[2]

Pope Leo XIII (1878-1903) was perhaps even more eager in his zeal for the Eastern Churches and their rites. Almost as soon as he became Pope, on April 1, 1879, he said: " How dear to us are the Churches of the East ! How we admire

---

[1] Acta *loc. cit.*, p. 553.
[2] Constit.: *Romani Pontifices*, Acta, iii, p. 402. But see " Codex Iuris Canonici," Can. 257. The Pope himself is now the head of this Congregation, which was separated from that of Propaganda by Bened. XV, *motu proprio, Dei Prouidentis*, May 1, 1917. [*Editor's note.*]

their ancient glories, and how happy we should be to see them return to the splendour of their first greatness !"

In September, 1880, he published the Encyclical *Grande Munus*, whereby he extended the cult of the Apostles of the Slavs, St. Cyril and St. Methodius, to the whole Church.[1]

In a Consistory of December 13, 1880, he said: " At the beginning of our Pontificate we hastened to occupy ourselves with the people of the East. There, indeed, was the cradle of the salvation of the whole human race, and the first fruits of Christianity; thence, as a mighty river, all the blessings of the Gospel came to the West."[2]

In 1882 Leo XIII did a graceful and friendly thing towards the schismatical Eastern Christians. Till then it had been the custom to give to Latin auxiliary bishops titles of old dioceses in the East, which no longer had Catholic Ordinaries. There are many such which have fallen into the hands of the Moslems; in some there were no longer any Christians at all. Since a bishop must have some title, the titles of these were used for non-diocesan bishops in the West. To these titles was added the form " in partibus infidelium." But during the nineteenth century many of these places have been restored to Christian hands, though not to those of Catholics. Still, there is a great difference between Christians of any Church and people who are not Christians at all. It would naturally be offensive to Greeks, for instance, to know that we spoke of the cities of their kingdom as being " in partibus infidelium." So the Pope abolished this form altogether, and substituted for it the harmless description " sedes titulares."

In August, 1892, Leo XIII sent Cardinal Langénieux as his legate to the Eucharistic Congress at Jerusalem. The Cardinal says in his letter on this occasion: " Shall not the Greeks, our brothers, be met by a glance of Jesus, whom they love, as was the Apostle Peter ?" And in his inaugural address: " I come as a pacifier; I come in the name of him whom history calls the chief pacifier of modern times. It is he who sends me, to give a new proof of his sympathy and admiration for the Eastern Churches, which are the first-born daughters of the Church of God."

In 1894 Leo instituted at the Vatican conferences for the union of Churches. The Uniate Patriarchs were invited to attend these as well as theologians and others who would be interested in the question. It is true that not much came of

[1] Leonis XIII, P.M. Acta (Rome, Vat., 1882), vol. ii, p. 125.
[2] *Ibid.*, p. 179.

the conferences; but their foundation again shows the Pope's zeal for the Christian East. It was also during his Pontificate that a number of journals and reviews were founded by Catholics, under his auspices, for the study of Eastern Christendom.[1]

On November 30, 1894, Leo XIII published his famous Constitution *Orientalium Dignitas*,[2] which takes a place second only to those of Benedict XIV.

In this he enforces even more strongly the old principles of the Holy See; that Latins are in no way to disparage Eastern rites, nor to try to persuade Eastern Christians to become Latins. He begins by explaining again that the ancient Eastern rites are a witness to the Apostolicity of the Catholic Church, that their diversity, consistent with unity of the faith, is itself a witness to the unity of the Church, that they add to her dignity and honour. He says that the Catholic Church does not possess one rite only, but that she embraces all the ancient rites of Christendom; her unity consists not in a mechanical uniformity of all her parts, but on the contrary, in their variety, according in one principle and vivified by it.

So he continues: " It is therefore more than ever the duty of our office to watch strictly that no injury be done to them (Eastern rites) by the imprudence of ministers of the Gospel from Western lands, whom zeal for the teaching of Christ sends towards Eastern nations." He repeats the statement of Benedict XIV, that Western missionaries are sent to the East only to be helpers and supports to the Eastern Catholic Patriarchs and bishops, not in any way to prejudice the rights of Eastern Churches. He sanctions this principle by a penalty: " Any Latin missionary, whether regular or secular, who by his advice or influence shall have persuaded an Eastern Christian to adopt the Latin rite, shall incur *ipso facto* suspension *a diuinis* and all other pains threatened in the Constitution *Demandatam*."[3]

In order to give greater force to this penalty the Pope orders that it shall be put up publicly in the sacristy of all Latin Churches in the East. It may still be seen there. I have found it in sacristies of Latin Churches in the Levant. When I went to say Mass the first time in the Latin church at

---

[1] *Revue de l'Orient chrétien, Revue des Églises d'Orient, Echos d'Orient*, Bessarione, *Oriens christianus*, Ἁρμονία, Χριστιανικὴ Ἀνατολή, Καθολικὴ ἐπιθεώρησις, etc.

[2] Leonis XIII, Acta, vol. xiv, p. 358.

[3] See above, p. 35.

Damascus, I saw this clause from *Orientalium dignitas*, framed over the place where I was to vest. It was further pointed out to me by the rector of the church; I shuddered to think of what would happen to me if I hinted to one of my Uniate friends that I consider it better to be a Latin than a Melkite.

This Constitution contains laws in protection of the Eastern rites which go further than any Pope had gone before. For instance, in spite of the dislike which the Roman authorities have for any vagueness or change of rite, a Uniate who has adopted the Latin rite because of the impossibility of finding clergy of his own where he lives, must return to it as soon as the cause of his latinization is removed. A woman who has followed the Latin rite after marrying a Latin husband, may return to her own use after the husband's death. Any Eastern Catholic who has turned Latin, even by virtue of a Papal rescript, is now free to go back to his original rite. Schismatics who become Catholics are not to become Latins, but are to keep their rite. The greatest possible difficulties against their turning Latin are made.

In colleges where students of the Roman and Eastern rites study together, the Pope abolishes all privileges by which, for the time of their studies, the Easterns are allowed to follow the Roman rite. On the contrary, the superiors of such colleges are bound to make provision that each may follow his own. Eastern students are to be taught the use of their rites carefully, because, says the Pope: " There is more importance in the conservation of the Eastern rites than might appear at first sight."

Two years later, in March, 1896, he returns to the same subject, and enforces again all the rules of *Orientalium dignitas*.[1]

Moreover, Leo XIII showed practically his care for Eastern rites. In 1883 he founded the Armenian college at Rome; in 1897 he established a Coptic Uniate college at Cairo. In 1895 he sent the French Assumptionists to Chalcedon, with the mission to study the Greeks; and he founded through them colleges at Philippopolis and Adrianople for the Bulgars. He opened the college of St. Anne at Jerusalem, under the White Fathers, for the Melkites. He founded a Greek Catholic Lyceum at Athens in 1889. He separated the Ruthenians from the Greek college at Rome, and gave them a college of

[1] *Motu proprio, Auspicia rerum secunda*, March 19, 1896; *op. cit.*, vol. xvi, p. 74.

their own in 1896; then he reorganized the Greek college, introducing a number of obvious improvements. He reformed the famous Greek monastery of Grottaferrata, and insisted that in it the Byzantine rite should be followed in a more correct form; at the monastery he founded a college for the Italo-Greeks. During the Turkish-Greek War of 1897 the Turkish Government ordered that all Greeks in the Empire should be expelled. It was Leo XIII who intervened and prevented this harsh order from being carried out, thereby saving both Uniates and Orthodox from misery.

Lastly, towards the end of his long reign, this great Pope, who had already given so many proofs of his care for Eastern Christians of all rites, wrote his Encyclical *Præclara gratulationis* (June 29, 1894).[1] In this he addresses first Catholics, then other Christians. So he comes to the Orthodox:[2] " First of all," he says, " we turn a look of great affection to the East whence came salvation to the world. We have glad hope that the Eastern Churches, illustrious by their ancient faith and glories, will return whence they have departed. This we hope especially because of the no great distance which separates them from us; so that, when little is removed, in the rest they agree with us; so much that for the defence of Catholic doctrines we take arguments and proofs from the rites, the teaching and practices of Eastern Christians." And he assures them again that " for all their rites and practices we will provide without narrowness."[3] He did not expect to see reunion with the Eastern Churches in his own lifetime. " Because of our great age," he said, in 1893, " we do not expect that it will be granted to us to see the happy event; but we salute it from afar and try to hasten it by our prayers."[4]

Pope Pius X followed in the steps of his predecessors. To show this it may be enough to remember the thirteenth centenary of the death of St. John Chrysostom at Rome. The chief ceremony of this was the Byzantine liturgy, sung with every possible solemnity in the Hall of Beatifications of the Vatican on February 12, 1908. The liturgy was celebrated by the Melkite Patriarch, Lord Cyril VIII, with a great number of con-celebrants in the presence of twenty-four Cardinals, the Syrian Catholic Patriarch, Ignatius Ephrem II, and the Pope himself. Pius X assisted in state, and as a

---

[1] *Op. cit.*, vol. xiv, p. 195.
[2] *Ibid.*, p. 199.   [3] *Ibid.*, p. 201.
[4] P. de Meester, " Leone XIII e la chiesa greca " (Rome, 1904), pp. 53-54.

compliment to his fellow-Catholics of Eastern rites, pronounced certain blessings, chanting them in Greek. It must have been a long time since a Roman Pope publicly officiated according to any other rite than his own.[1]

So we see that, down to our own day, the attitude of the Holy See has not varied in this point. That attitude is always one of entire approval of and respect for those other rites, which have just as legitimate a place in the Catholic Church as the Roman rite. No Pope has ever wanted to force the Roman rite on all Catholics. In faith and morals we all have one standard; in rites, different races have their own customs.

It is true that not all Papal legislation for the Uniates has been happy; moreover, it has varied occasionally in detail. But, as a general principle, no greater mistake could be made than to think that Rome has anything against other rites. She always acknowledges their complete justification in the Catholic Church, she respects and honours them sincerely, and wishes them to be maintained and carried out correctly, just as much as she wishes this in the case of her own rite.

The Catholic who desires to conform his ideal to that of the Holy See will find in this matter, too, that he has a very definite standard set by the Popes. To disparage Eastern rites, to think them less Catholic than ours, to look upon Uniates as a kind of compromise between us and schismatical sects, is not only a gross injustice to them, it is also in clear contradiction to the attitude of the Holy See.

Summary.

In this chapter we have seen what a Uniate is. The name is used for a Catholic of any other rite than the Roman rite, or, rather, in practice, for a Catholic of some Eastern rite. There is no essential reason why all Catholics except those of one rite should be classed under a general name; yet the preponderance of the Roman rite, and certain qualities common to Eastern Christians, and special to them, are no doubt sufficient justification for the usual term.

However, Uniates are in no sense one body as distinct from Latins. They are, of course, all members of the one Catholic Church, together with us Westerns; but under that genus there is no one Uniate species. Each Uniate Church is independent of the others; all are equally dependent on the central authority of the whole Church at Rome.

[1] See the full account of this liturgy in the *Echos d'Orient*, xi, 131.

All the old rites of Christendom are still represented within the Catholic Church; there is a Uniate Church corresponding to each schismatical body, and one entirely Uniate Church, that of the Maronites.

The connecting link in each is now, practically, the rite. Originally, and still, in theory, it is their common obedience to their Patriarch. From this obedience follows the common use of his rite. Yet now it is perhaps more according to the circumstances to say that each Church obeys a certain Patriarch because it uses his rite, rather than to say that it uses its rite because it obeys him.

In any case, language makes no difference to rite. Nor does the place where a man may be born or live.

Nothing is more to be denounced than any attitude of superiority on the part of Latins towards their Uniate fellow-Catholics. The Uniates have exactly as much right to their venerable liturgies and customs as we have to ours. They are in no sense a compromise or an accidental adjunct to the Catholic Church. They form integral and important parts of it. They represent the old Catholic Eastern Churches, as they were before later schisms cut off so many of their members. Their position is exactly that of the great Eastern Fathers, Catholic, but not Roman. Indeed, in principle, they are the people who save the situation of a universal Church, for which we too stand.

We have no more right to think less of them than they have to despise us. This has always been most clearly the attitude of the Holy See, best summed up in the immortal words of Benedict XIV: " Eastern Christians should be Catholics; they have no need to become Latins." For our Lord gave his followers most explicit commands that they should belong to the one Catholic Church he founded; he never commanded them all to say their prayers in Latin or to use the Roman rite.

THE BYZANTINE UNIATES

CHAPTER I

THE ITALO-GREEKS IN THE PAST

THE name Italo-Greek (Italo-Græcus) is a convenient one now commonly used for the inhabitants of Italy or its islands (Sicily, Sardinia, Corsica), who use the Byzantine rite in Greek. It denotes, therefore, a liturgical distinction, not one of race. As a matter of fact, the Italo-Greeks consist of three different races. There are the original Greek-speaking inhabitants of Lower Italy and Sicily. These had nearly become latinized by the fifteenth century, when their rite was much fortified, almost, one might say, revived, by an immigration of Albanians. Lastly, there are later immigrations and colonies of Levantines in these parts, though many of these people are Orthodox, and so do not enter into our scheme.

1. The Greeks in Southern Italy and Sicily.

It would perhaps surprise anyone, who heard of the fact for the first time, that for centuries there were large districts in Italy and Sicily where the Byzantine rite in Greek was used. Since the Roman rite has become so prevalent throughout all the West, since even in distant Norway, Greenland, and America Catholics are Latins, it may seem strange that here so near Rome itself there were, and still are, these Catholics who, in rite, are not Roman. The fact is explained by the political history of Southern Italy and Sicily.

This history begins with that of the Greek colonies, long before Christianity. There was, of course, a native population still earlier; but we know little about it. The original people of Sicily and Southern Italy, the barbarians whom the first Greek colonists found there, spoke some forms of the common Italian group of languages, not Latin.[1]

---

[1] Mommsen calls them " Iapygians." They were Aryans, but not the same race as the Latins or Samnites. They were easily hellenized by the Greek colonists (" History of Rome," Eng. trans.

47

Since about the ninth century B.C. the Greeks began to wander forth from Hellas and to plant colonies all round the Mediterranean. So they came to Sicily and the lower part of Italy. Cumæ (Κύμη) is said to be the earliest Greek colony on Italian soil; this seems to have existed already by the year 800 B.C. It was colonized by the people of Chalkis in Euboea.[1] In 735 B.C. Theokles of Chalkis founded the city of Naxos[2] in Sicily, and there set up an altar to Apollo the Guide. Then came the Dorians under Archias of Corinth and laid the first foundation of what was to become the great Greek city Syracuse, in 736. Messana was founded soon afterwards, and gradually all the sea-coast of Sicily was covered with Greek cities. Tarentum, Locri, and Rhegium followed on the main coast. Calabria and Apulia became so much a centre of Greek life that they were *Greater Greece*. The same process was taking place all round the Mediterranean. The Greeks never wandered very far from the coast; they planted their colonies in barbarian lands near the sea, and so made centres of Greek influence for the country behind them.

These Greek cities round the Mediterranean were not politically united to the Motherland. Each was an independent state; but they were always conscious of their union with all other Greeks in race, language, and religion. All looked upon themselves as one people. The Greek states in Sicily and Lower Italy took their part in the quarrels of the Greeks at home in Hellas. The famous story of the siege of Syracuse marks the end of the power of Athens. Syracuse had taken the Spartan side in the Peloponnesian war. Alcibiades made the fatal mistake of sending a fleet to subdue the distant city when Athens needed all her resources nearer home. They besieged Syracuse in 414–413 B.C., and the siege ended in the most disastrous defeat for them. The Syracusans put the Athenian generals, Nikias and Demosthenes, to death, and shut up the Athenian prisoners in the quarries still shown on the hillside of Epipolai, till they died of want and disease. All of which may be read in Thucydides.[3]

During the centuries that followed the establishment of these Greek colonies they hellenized the barbarians around

---

by W. P. Dickson, Macmillan, 1908, vol. i, pp. 11-13). For the few remnants of these peoples' languages see R. S. Conway, " The Italic Dialects," Cambridge, 2 vols., 1897.

[1] So it is the "Euboean Cumæ," "Et tandem Euboicis Cumarum allabitur oris " (Æn. vi, 2).

[2] Just south of Taormina.   [3] " Hist.," Bk. vi-vii.

them.[1] It is difficult to say how far this hellenization went. Perhaps to the end, till all were swamped in a common Italian nationality and language (if indeed Sicily even now can be called Italian), there were remote inland districts where the inhabitants had remained free from Greek influence. But of these history knows nothing. From a time long before Christianity the Sicily and Southern Italy we know were *Greek;* Greek is the language of these parts, at least as far as our records tell us anything; the people looked to Rome and the north of the peninsula as foreign countries, and to the Athenians, Spartans, and later the Byzantines as their fellow-countrymen.

Nor is there anything surprising in this from the point of view of geography. We are so accustomed to look on Italy as one land that perhaps we forget what any map of Europe will show —namely, how near the south of Italy is to the Greek lands across the water. The cities of the east coast of Italy, at any rate, are much nearer to Macedonia and Epirus than they are to Rome. Greeks from Hellas could come to these parts sooner and more easily than they could go to Crete; Sicily is nearer to Athens than is Cyprus. Indeed, Magna Græcia and Sicily were just as really parts of Hellas as Attica and the Peloponnesus. For at no time was Greece united as one political state till Alexander united it, with Asia and Egypt, in his great empire. What joined Greeks together was their blood; or, since blood is a difficult factor to estimate, their language, religion, civilization. In this Magna Græcia had the same share as the other Greek states. There was no bond between Athens and Sparta which did not equally bind Athens to Syracuse.

Many of the Greek writers and heroes we remember were Greeks of Italy or Sicily. Pythagoras, though a Samian by birth, lived in Calabria; Empedocles, Theocritus, Archimedes were Sicilians. When the Athenians besieged Syracuse, it was not a war of Greek against foreigners—Greeks fought Greeks. There were indeed foreigners in Sicily: the Carthaginians, who also had their colonies to the west of the island. With these the Greeks fought with varying success, till the Romans came and conquered both. Otherwise we must conceive Magna Græcia and Sicily as Greek lands; the Greek element in them is the first in our period. It remains the original element till far into the Middle Ages. But into these Greek lands came a series of invaders of different races. The Romans, Lombards, Saracens, Normans, in turn brought their

---

[1] Diodorus Siculus, " Hist.," Bk. v, ch. vi (" Scrip. Gr. et Rom.," Teubner, vol. ii, pp. 11-12).

various civilizations to this part of the world.   It is the meeting
of so varied elements in the same place which makes the history
of Lower Italy and Sicily more involved, and at the same time
more romantic, than that of any country we know.   But always
beneath the invasions of such different races we must conceive
the old Greek or hellenized population and the Greek language
as (practically) the lowest stratum.

First came the Romans.   Rome spread her power over the
whole peninsula by the third century B.C.; she was mistress
of all Sicily at the end of the first Punic war (241 B.C.).   From
this time till far into the Middle Ages these lands formed part
of the Roman Empire.   But that does not mean that all their
inhabitants became Romans.   The Empire included men of
every kind of race; as a rule, Rome left them to continue their
own civilizations with the use of their own languages.   Undoubtedly now the Latin element enters Southern Italy, but
only so far as that Roman governors were appointed and Latin
was the language of the Government.   In some cases we know
of deliberate Latin colonization, though it was not the common
practice.   Augustus (31 B.C. to A.D. 14) sent Roman colonists
to Sicily; then for the first time Latin was spoken in the island.
But these Latin colonies were minorities.   There were such
at Syracuse, Panormus (Palermo), and Messana.   Only in the
case of Tauromenium (Taormina) do we read that all Greeks
were expelled to make room for a Latin colony.[1]   But we know
that long after the Roman power was firmly established here
the people remained Greek.   Diodore says of Sicilians that
the Greek language was commonly spoken among them.[2]   In
Cicero's time the Syracusan Senate spoke and even wrote to
Rome in Greek.[3]

Both the Greek and Latin of Sicily were looked upon as
provincial, less elegant than the languages of Athens and Rome.
So Cicero again says that Q. Cæcilius would have done better
if he had learned " Greek letters at Athens, not at Lilybæum,
Roman letters at Rome, not in Sicily."[4]   During the first
Christian centuries the chief writers of Sicily and Southern

---

[1] Augustus colonized Syracuse, Panormus, Messana, Tauromenium.   From Tauromenium (Ταυρομένιον, Taormina) he expelled
the Greeks to make room for his Roman colonists (Diodor. Sic.,
'' Bibl. Hist.,'' Lib. xvi, § 7; ed. Teubner, vol. iv, p. 14).

[2] Diodor. Sic., v, 6 (Teubner, vol. ii, pp. 11-12).

[3] Cicero, " In C. Verrem," Act. ii, L. v, cap. 57 (=§§ 148-149):
'' ἐδικαιώθησαν, hoc est, ut Siculi locuntur, supplicio adfecti ac
necati sunt.''

[4] Cicero, Orat. '' In Q. Cæcilium Diuinatio,'' cap. 12 (=§ 39).

Italy wrote Greek.[1] Strabo († *c.* A.D. 24) says that the people
of Calabria are Greek in language, but in other things
Roman.[2] Yet, from the time of Augustus and so during the
first six Christian centuries, there was undoubtedly a considerable Latin element in Southern Italy and Sicily and
growing latinization. Morisani says that he has found many
Latin, but no Greek Christian inscriptions in Bruttii (Calabria).[3]
The Latin element was advancing; but the Greek element
never died out. It was reinforced by later events.

When the centre of the Empire was moved to Constantinople
this made no change to the Greeks of Lower Italy, or, rather,
it confirmed their hellenism. These people looked to Constantinople as easily as to Rome for the centre of government.
Only the change was the beginning of a gradual hellenization
of the Roman Government itself, so that when that change had
taken place the Greeks of Lower Italy found themselves under
the rule of men of their own language. Now the governors
sent to rule them from the capital were Greeks like themselves.
The transfer of the seat of government to Constantinople did
not mean to the people of Lower Italy any of that loss of influence, that sense of being subject to a foreign power that in
time it meant to those of the North and of Rome. The Italian
and Sicilian Greeks were zealously loyal to the Byzantine
Government, more so than they had been to the rule of Latins
in Rome; they felt themselves of one race with their rulers, all
the more when barbarians, neither Greeks nor Romans in
any sense, began to invade and plunder their land.

The first of these invasions was that of the Goths.[4]
Theodoric brought his East Goths into Italy in 489; in 493
he defeated and slew Odouaker, and became the supreme
authority over the whole peninsula and Sicily. But this did

[1] There are some of less importance who wrote Latin, such as
Julius Firmicus Maternus (fourth century in Sicily). John di Giovanni,
Canon of Palermo (see p. 73, n. 1), is anxious to make out that all
Sicily was Latin till the eighth century, though he admits that Greek
was used also, in private life. See his work, " De diuinis Siculorum
Officiis " (Palermo, 1736), cap. iv, pp. 23-33.

[2] Strabonis " Geographica," L. vi, cap. i, § 2 (ed. Teubner,
vol. i, p. 348).

[3] Morisani, " De Protopapis " (Naples, 1768), p. 158, n. 42.

[4] The Vandals plundered Sicily in 439-440, and again in 455 and
461. They devastated the country and persecuted the Catholics;
but they made no permanent occupation. B. Pace, " I Barbari e i
Bizantini in Sicilia " (Rome, 1911), pp. 5-16. Lancia di Brolo,
" Storia della Chiesa in Sicilia " (Palermo, 2 vols., 1880-1884), i,
cap. xii, pp. 257-287.

not mean in theory any change in the political state of the
Romans of Italy. They would have been very much surprised
to hear that the Roman Empire had come to an end. Theodoric
never called himself King of Italy. He was only King of his
own Goths. In theory the Romans remained subject to the
Emperor at Constantinople. The two Roman Consuls were
still regularly appointed, one nominated by the Emperor
and one by Theodoric himself. Nor did the Gothic King
tamper with the language, religion, or institutions of the
Romans. Especially in the South and in Sicily the Gothic
power made little difference, except that practically they were
now subject to a foreign King. The defeat of the Goths by
the generals of Justinian (527–565), first Belisarius, then Narses,
put an end to this, and incidentally fortified the Greek element
in the South. Belisarius landed in Sicily from Africa in 535.
A war of eighteen years against the Goths follows, during which
the people suffer the usual evils of war. Totila succeeded
Theodoric as Gothic King. Rome was taken and retaken
altogether six times; in 549 the Goths devastate Sicily. The
end of the war was when Totila was defeated and killed in
battle in 553. So, after being subject to the barbarians for
sixty years, all Italy and Sicily again obey the Basileus at
Constantinople.

The Gothic occupation of Italy left hardly any traces
among the Greeks of the South;[1] though in the strange medley
of descent of modern Southern Italians there may be some
particles of what was once Gothic blood. But hardly had
Italy returned to the obedience of her lawful sovereign when
a new race of Teutonic barbarians appear, who are destined
to have enormously more influence on her history, particularly
on the history of the South. These are the Lombards.

The Lombards invaded Italy under their King Alboin in
568, just fifteen years after the final defeat of the Goths. At
first they, like the Goths, were Arian heretics. Chiefly by the
work of St Gregory I (590–604) they were converted to the
Catholic Church in the course of the sixth and seventh centuries.
By the time they appear in the South they are all Catholics.
The great Lombard kingdom had its centre in the North.
The Lombard King reigned at Pavia. But they spread over
a great part of the whole peninsula.

During the seventh and eighth centuries Italy was divided

[1] For the Goths in Sicily see Lancia di Brolo, " Storia della
Chiesa in Sicilia " (Palermo, 2 vols., 1880-1884), i, cap. xv, pp. 320-
329.

between the authority of the Imperial Exarch[1] at Ravenna and that of the Lombard king. In the South the Lombards formed the great Duchy of Beneventum, which left to the empire only the extreme South, one or two cities, and Sicily. Nor was this merely a matter of political allegiance. The Lombards were a numerous race, which profoundly affected the descent (by blood) of Italians all over the country. Their kingdom and Duchies were not merely so much territory inhabited by Romans, but subject to Lombard authority; these lands were peopled by Lombards; though, of course, Romans remained in them as well.

The Romans seem to have hated the Lombards even more than they had hated the Goths. When Charles the Great was going to marry the daughter of the last Lombard King Desiderius, Pope Stephen III (768–772) cannot understand that a Frankish gentleman should think of taking a wife from the " perfidious, unspeakable, most stinking nation of the Lombards," who first introduced leprosy to the world.[2] For all that, the Lombards soon became completely latinized, as the Goths had never been. Against the Lombards the Frankish Kings came to Italy. They fought and defeated them, and so, in the North, opened a new chapter of Italian history, in which Italy is severed finally from the old Empire at Constantinople, the Papal States are founded, and the new Western Empire begins.

But this did not affect the South. After the destruction of the Lombard kingdom, the Lombard Duchy of Beneventum continues. When Charles the Great defeated King Desiderius,[3] Duke Arichis II of Beneventum remained to represent the power of his nation in the South. He made a nominal submission to Charles, but remained really independent. In 774 he took the title Prince. So Arichis II reigned over all Southern Italy, except the cities by the coast, which remained faithful to the Emperor at Constantinople. After Arichis II the Principality of Beneventum broke up into three Lombard states—Beneventum, Salernum, and Capua. To the North

---

[1] The Exarch (ἔξαρχος) ruled Italy for the Emperor at Constantinople from the end of the sixth to the end of the eighth century. The first Exarch whose name we know is Smaragdus in 584 (*ep.* Pelagii II. ad Eliam et eppos Istriae; P.L. lxxii, 707, B). Narses was not called Exarch, but Patricius. The last Exarch was when the Lombards conquered Ravenna in 751.

[2] Ep. Steph. III, no. L, ad Carolum (P.L. xcviii, col. 256, C).

[3] Desiderius, the last Lombard king, was defeated in 774 at Pavia and shut up in a monastery.

of these was a fourth, the Duchy of Spoletum. At Capua a great Lombard prince, Duke Pandulf Iron-Head, was invested by the Western Emperor Otto I (936–973) in 966, as Duke of Capua and Spoletum. He imposed his own son on the Duchy of Beneventum, became Lord of Caieta (Gaeta) and Prince of Salernum, and so again formed a great Lombard state in the South. But after his death (981) this also broke up; Caieta, Salernum, and Beneventum became independent under other Lombard princes; Pandulf's descendants kept only Capua.

From the eighth century to the coming of the Normans in the eleventh, the Lombards are a great factor in Southern Italy. They formed a powerful aristocracy and spread, beyond the borders of their states, all over the South. But they had completely lost all trace of their Teutonic descent, except in their laws and customs. They were Latin Catholics, and spoke, or at any rate wrote, always Latin. Their laws and system of administration had a profound effect even on the cities which remained Imperial. Under the Lombard dukes were lesser lords, the *Gastalds*, whom the Romans call counts. The Lombard laws were perhaps their chief contribution to Italy. One hears a good deal of these laws, the " consuetudines gentis nostræ Langobardorum." They are followed in many cases by the Greek cities. Bari, Amalfi, and Caieta, for instance, even when Caieta was Imperial, are ruled by the Lombard law. Also the Lombards introduce for the first time a considerable Latin element in the South of Italy. So many of the Greek cities begin to write Latin, as they follow Lombard law, and call in the help of the Lombard Gastalds in times of disturbance. Yet they still date their documents by the reign of the Emperor at Constantinople, and recognize him as their sovereign. In one word, the Lombards are the first whom we can already call Italians, as opposed to Greeks, in the South.

But the Empire, already so despoiled in Lower Italy by the Lombards, was destined to suffer equally disastrous losses from another, a still stranger and fiercer foe.

In the seventh century the Saracens had conquered Egypt and then all North Africa. Sicily is temptingly near the African coast. Already in 652 Saracens from Syria had landed at Syracuse and had devastated the city. In 669 another band again made a sudden descent and plundered Syracuse. In 704 descents from the African coast began. In that year the Emir Mūsā (Moses) ibn Nusair made a raid on Sicily; in 705

Syracuse was again devastated. Then, from 827 to 965, the Saracens gradually seize the whole island. In 827 Ziyādatullah ibn Aġlab, Emir of Africa under the Khalif Abdullah al Ma'mūn (at Bagdad), sent his general, Asad ibn Furāt, Ḳādi of Kairowān, with an army to Sicily. In 827 Asad took Agrigentum, in 831 Panormus, in 842 Messana, in 869 Malta, in 878 Syracuse. Finally, by 963, the Saracens have taken Tauromenium and occupy the whole of Sicily.

Meanwhile their fleets attack the coast of Italy. In 846 they sail up the Tiber and lay waste the suburbs of Rome. In 848 they seize Tarentum, then Bari and other places on the mainland. But they did not stay long in Italy. The two Emperors, Basil I (867–886), in the East, and Louis II (855–875), in the West, for once made an alliance against the common foe. Basil supplied a fleet, and Lewis an army. In 872 the Moslems are defeated in a great sea battle; in 875 Bari is taken from them, and so they lose all their conquests in Italy. In the eleventh century a valiant Greek general, George Maniakes, conquered back Messana, Syracuse, and the eastern part of Sicily. However, these were again lost. When the Normans came in the end of the eleventh century Sicily was in Moslem hands, though they had lost all they ever held in Italy.

But meanwhile these savage enemies of Christendom had become in Sicily fairly inoffensive neighbours. Since the year 969 Egypt had been conquered by a new line of Khalifs, the Fatimides. The Emirs of Sicily renounced the Fatimide authority and so became practically independent princes; though I suppose they admitted a nominal authority of the Abbaside Khalif at Bagdad and prayed for him in their mosques.

The Moslems of Sicily then became peaceful traders between Italy and Africa. They were tolerant to Christians, bartered on friendly terms with the Christians of the mainland, and evolved a very splendid civilization in Sicily, so that their capital Palermo[1] rivalled Cordova. When the Normans came, the Moslems were no longer a danger to their neighbours.

Now we must see what the Empire was doing while it was losing so many provinces. In the first place, we must remember that Southern Italy and Sicily, before the Norman conquest, in as far as these parts were not lost to the Lombards or Saracens, remained part of the Roman Empire of the East.

---

[1] Palermo (Panormus) in Arabic is Balaram; Girgenti (Ακράγας Agrigentum) is Ġurġunt; Messana (Messina) is Massīn; Syracuse is Sarakūsa; Tarentum (Taranto) is Tārant. From now on we may perhaps best call these places by their modern Italian names.

The Western Empire never extended into the South of Italy; it stopped at the frontier of the Papal States. It is true that once or twice a Western Emperor claimed jurisdiction in the South, as when Arichis II of Beneventum paid homage to Charles the Great, or Pandulf I, Iron-Head of Capua, was invested by Otto I. But these are isolated cases, in which someone seeks an appearance of legality by applying to the Western Emperor. He never had any real power down here. When Basil I and Lewis II joined forces to drive the Saracens from Bari, although Lewis would have liked to claim some reward for his trouble, as a matter of fact, all that was recovered came back to the allegiance of Constantinople. These lands were never part of the Western Empire. Even under the Normans they were considered independent of the Empire. The first who seriously disputed the authority of the Basileus here was not the Western Emperor, but the Pope, when he gave authority to the Norman conquerors.

The Lombards, together with a gradual latinization, already begun in Calabria and Apulia, might have done away with all that was left of Greek language and influence, but for a contrary movement, fostered by the Government at Constantinople since the seventh century. At that time there was again constant communication between Italy and the East. After the Moslem conquest of Egypt and Syria great colonies of Christians from those lands, fleeing from persecution and famine, came to Sicily and Rome. Thus the Popes Theodore I (642–649) and John V (685–686) were Levantines of the Eastern colony at Rome. Sergius I (687–701) was " by nation a Syrian of the land of Antioch, but born of Tiberius at Panormus in Sicily."[1] These colonies made a great revival, almost a new beginning of Greek population in Italy and Sicily. The Emperor Constans II (641–668), fleeing from Constantinople in 662, came to Rome with the idea of reigning there. Then, finding that he could do little against the Lombards on the mainland, he came to Syracuse and lived there for six years, till he was murdered in 668. Those years represent a new hellenization of Sicily, when the Byzantine court had its centre on the island. It was this Constans II who reformed the administration of the Imperial provinces.[2]

Since the seventh century the former wave of latinization in Calabria was met by this new spread of hellenization, coming in the first place from Sicily. Except for the Lombards, Calabria

[1] " Liber Pontificalis," lxxxvi (ed. Duchesne, Paris, 1886, vol. i, p. 371).   [2] See pp. 58, 59.

appears to have been systematically re-hellenized. Then in the ninth century, when the Moslems conquered Sicily, another wave of Greeks poured over Southern Italy; enormous numbers of them, notably crowds of monks, came from Sicily to Calabria, and so made that land again a " Greater Greece," again a centre of Greek ideas and language, Greek piety, Byzantine rite, Greek monasticism.

We may then date, as it were, a second Greek conquest of Sicily and Lower Italy from the seventh to the ninth centuries. It forms part of the great revival of power of the Roman Empire in the East, roughly from Justinian I to Basil I (527–886). It accounts for the easy ecclesiastical conquest of these dioceses by the See of Constantinople in the eighth century (pp. 80 *ff*).[1]

The administration of the Imperial lands in Italy and Sicily naturally varied with the fortune of war. The Greek element had been fortified by the invasion of Belisarius and Narses against the Goths. Then the Empire kept whatever the Lombards had not conquered. The Greek element was strongest in the extreme South of Italy, around the gulf of Terentos,[2] and in the heel of the peninsula (South of the original Calabria, now Apulia); it was almost indisputed throughout Sicily till the Saracens came. The height of Greek power in Italy was under the Emperor Basil II (976–1025); it reached then to the gates of Rome.

The Empire was divided into Themes ($\theta \acute{\epsilon} \mu a \tau a$). There was a Theme of Italy and a Theme of Sicily. The original Theme of Italy went up to the River Aufidus (now the Ofanto). About the year 1000 the Romans conquered back the land north of the Aufidus as far as the Fertorius (Fortore). This became a separate province, the *Capitanata*. At one time, just after the formation of the Lombard Duchy of Beneventum, the Empire in Italy was reduced to the mere peninsula of Tarenton. Then it got back a fairly large tract of the country, up to the Aufidus and eventually to the Fertorius. So after the Moslems had been expelled, Apulia and Calabria were again Imperial lands.

There is a curious point to notice about the name *Calabria*. Originally Calabria had been the heel of Italy, as any classical

---

[1] For this political hellenization, closely involved with the ecclesiastical movement, to which we shall come, see especially G. Schlumberger, " L'Épopée byzantine " (Paris, 2 vols., 1896-1900); J. Gay, " L'Italie méridionale et L'Empire byzantin " (Paris, 1904); P. Batiffol, " L'Abbaye de Rossano " (Paris, 1901); L. di Brolo," Storia della Chiesa in Sicilia," ii, 16-23.

[2] Tarentum, Taranto.

atlas will show. Then, under Constans II (641–668), there was a new administrative division of the Empire. According to this, the old provinces of Calabria, Apulia, and Bruttii (the toe of Italy) were united as " Calabria." Soon after 671 Romuald, Duke of Beneventum, seized the greater part of this land, leaving the Empire not much more than Bruttii. So this remained as Calabria. It is so still. In this way the name Calabria has changed from the heel of Italy to the toe.[1]

Even before the conquests of Basil II the old Theme of Italy had become the two Themes of Lombardy (capital Barium) and Calabria (capital Rhegium).[2] The Theme of Lombardy (not to be confused with the Lombardy of the North)[3] remained as a memory of the long Lombard occupation of that province. Besides these Themes three cities, Naples, Caieta, and Amalfi, were outlying imperial territory.

After Barium had been conquered back from the Saracens, Basil II fixed this city as the centre of the whole government in Italy. Here the *Catapan*[4] ruled in his master's name.

---

[1] The present Calabria was first " Calabria Bruttia," then simply " Calabria." The story of this change of name is told at length by M. Schipa, " La Migrazione del nome Calabria " in the *Archivio storico per le provincie napoletane*, Naples, 1895, p. 23 *seq*.

[2] This is so from the time of Nikephoros Phokas (963-969). The Theme of Lombardy kept the name Italy. Its inhabitants were mostly Latins (including the Lombards). Distinct from " Italy " was Calabria, including Sicily, where the people were mostly Greek. So we hear of " Italy and Calabria " (*e.g.*, in the " Life of St Neilos," 45 (P.G. cxx, col. 85). At first each Theme was governed by an Imperial Strategos. Then, from the end of the tenth century, the Catapan governs both. See Gustave Schlumberger, " Un Empereur byzantin au dixième siècle, Nicéphore Phocas " (Paris, 1890), p. 591 *seq*. The frontispiece of his other work, " L'Épopée byzantine à la fin du dixième siècle " (Paris, 3 vols., 1896-1905), is a map of the Empire, showing the Themes of Lombardy and Calabria.

[3] The Greeks distinguished between Λομβαρδία (the old Northern kingdom of Lombardy) and Λογγιβαρδία (their Theme in the South); see Freeman, " Historical Geography of Europe " (3rd edition by J. B. Bury, Longmans, 1903), p. 371, note. Nilos Doxopatres (p. 93) calls the Southern Theme ἡ Λομβαρδία καὶ ἡ νῦν λεγομένη Λογγιβαρδία (ed. Parthey, p. 270).

[4] The title *Catapan* (Catapanus) is a curious one, which has caused some discussion. Formerly it was said that it meant κατὰ πᾶν (" for all "). So Rodotà, " Rito greco in Italia," i, 32. It seems, however, to be ὁ κατ' ἐπάνω (" the one above ") (J. Gay, " L'Italie mérid. et L'Emp. byz.," p. 348). William of Apulia (*c.* 1085) defines the name, " Quod Catapan Græci, nos ' iuxta ' dicimus ' omne ' " (" Histor. Poema de rebus Norman."; Muratori, " Rerum Ital. Script.," v, 254, B.). This office came to an end at the Norman Conquest. The last Catapan was Exaugustus, expelled from Bari by the Normans

As long as there was an Exarch at Ravenna the Catapan in the South was subordinate to his authority. After the disappearance of the Exarchate the Catapan remained the supreme Imperial authority for all Italy. Under the Catapan were inferior governors of districts called *Turmarchs*.[1]

The development of the cities of the Empire in Lower Italy was much the same as the later development of Italian cities in the North, nominally subject to the Western Empire. Just as Florence, Genoa, Pisa, and so on, became really self-governing republics; as in many cases this self-government of the cities ended in the hereditary rule of princes, although all the time they were supposed to belong to the Emperor's domains, so was it in the South. Here, too, the Greek cities soon governed themselves, giving only a nominal obedience to the Catapan and paying tribute, not very regularly, to Constantinople.

The chief Greek city in Italy was *Naples*. Under Constans II (641–668) Naples became a Duchy of the Empire (661). From that time it ruled itself. Its governor was the Duke of Naples, " Magister militum."[2] He had a council of " Nobiliores." So it became an aristocratic republic, not unlike Venice. At first the dukes were nominated by the Exarch; then a hereditary line began. The Duke of Naples with his council ruled a fairly large stretch of country behind

---

in 1042. Popular etymology confused " Catapanus " with " Capitaneus," " Capitano." So the district in Apulia, between the rivers Ofanto and Fortore (where Monte Gargano is), reconquered by the Empire in the eleventh century (above, p. 57), was, and still is, called " Capitanata," after this title. See Card. Leo of Ostia († *c.* 1115), " Chron. s. monast. Casinensis," L. ii, cap. 50; " Rer. It. Scrip.," iv· 371, and Muratori's note, *ibid.* The province *Basilicata* is a parallel case. There was a Byzantine official called the Βασιλικός, or rather, this title seems to cover several offices. In the Conc. Nic. II (787) at the beginning of its second Actio, they send for a person called first Βασιλικὸς ἄνθρωπος, then βασιλικὸς μανδάτωρ (=mandator; Mansi, xii, col. 1051, D-E). St Neilos the Younger († 1004) has dealings in Calabria with Eupraxios, who is ὁ βασιλικός (" Vita S. Nili," viii; P.G. cxx, 96, A-B). Basilicata, covering most of the old Lucania, takes its name from this title. " Basilicata " occurs first in documents of 1134, where Roger II of Sicily writes of " Iustitiarii nostri Basilicatæ." In 1161 William I mentions " Philippus de Gussone regius Iustitiarius Basilicatæ " (Homunculus, *op. cit.*, p. 46). See Homunculus (pseudonym of Racioppi), " Storia della denominazione di Basilicata " (Rome, 1874), and Giacomo Racioppi, " Storia dei popoli della Lucania e della Basilicata " (Rome, 1889), vol. ii, cap. ii, pp. 13-26.

[1] Τουρμάρχαι. Τόρμα, τοῦρμα (*turma*) means a region.
[2] Στρατηγός.

the city. But the authority of the Emperor at Constantinople was acknowledged, at least in theory, till 1138, when the Normans added Naples to their kingdom.[1]

The case of *Amalfi* was much the same. Here there were Imperial " Prefects "; in 958 these Prefects become hereditary dukes, and reign till the Norman conquest in 1073. In the tenth and eleventh centuries Amalfi was a mighty power. Its fleet sailed all over the Mediterranean; it became a kind of emporium where the merchandise of Italy, Sicily, and Africa was bartered. The Amalfitans obtained special privileges at Constantinople; they had a large colony there.

Caieta[2] was another famous Greek city. It had " Consuls " since the early part of the ninth century, and it also became, practically, a self-governing republic.

In these and the other Greek Imperial cities there were councils, the " Boni homines " (καλοὶ ἄνθρωποι), who settled their internal affairs. The Code of Justinian was their law, though it was often crossed by the Lombard customs. They dated their acts by the reign of the Great Basileus at Constantinople. They were, at any rate, supposed to send him tribute and to consider the views of the Catapan on any important matter. But the Empire was conscious that it had but a loose hold on its Italian Themes. Its policy was to leave the Italian cities alone as much as possible, to keep them in good temper by showering titles and honours on their chief citizens, and to be content with nominal recognition and such occasional tribute as could be raised without exciting bad feeling. The Catapan had a difficult place to fill; he would need to be a person of considerable tact—but that is naturally a Greek quality. The titles given by the Emperor to various leaders of the South Italian cities are curious. At Salernum the governor was the Στρατηγός; there was a Πρωτοσπαθάριος of Bruttii, a " Patritius " at Amalfi, a Protoscriba of the Salentini. I have seen the title " Protonobilissimus " for one of these people.[3]

---

[1] The last Imperial Duke of Naples was Sergius VI (the thirty-third). He died in battle at Salerno in 1138. The Neapolitan republic had lasted 480 years. After the death of Sergius the people, making the best of things, elected the eldest son of Roger II as their Duke. So the city became part of the Norman state. But it still kept the forms of its Republican government, went on electing Consuls, and so on. Venice in the North followed the same course. It was not part of the Western Empire. It became a self-governing republic under the suzerainty of the Eastern Emperor. A. F. Gfrörer, " Byzantinische Geschichten," vol. i (Graz, 1872).   [2] Gaeta.

[3] " Magister militum " in Greek takes the odd form Μαστρομίλιος.

Meanwhile, though the cities treated with their neighbours and the Lombards as independent powers, they seem always to have had a certain corporate consciousness as parts of the Empire and as Greeks among barbarians. Occasionally they act together; when the Imperial Government takes some step to defend what is left of its Themes, as for instance when George Maniakes comes to fight the Saracens, the Greek cities all look upon this as their cause.

As far as language goes, the Lombards spoke that Latin which was on its way to become Italian; but Greek remained the language of most of the Imperial Themes. Greek was commonly spoken in the South of Apulia and Calabria till long after the Norman conquest; it was, with Arabic, the common language of Sicily during the reign of the Norman Kings, and was heard in the streets of Naples till far into the Middle Ages.

To unite these different elements, Greek, Lombard, and Saracen, first into one political State, and then, gradually, into one people, was the work of the Norman conquerors.

The Normans first appear in the South of Italy as pilgrims, then as mercenaries, fighting for pay under either the Lombard princes or the Greek cities, in the early eleventh century. From the beginning they seem irresistible. As the news of the pleasant Southern land came to Normandy, more and more adventurers come South to join their cousins in Italy, so that a great number of Norman warriors are found in these parts. They came, as true adventurers, bringing nothing with them but a horse and a sword, ready to take whatever they could get. They got so much that after a time some of them became the strongest kings in Europe. Soon they began to see that it would pay them better to fight for their own sake than for Lombard or Greek paymasters. They become the terror of the South of Italy. Lombards and Greeks unite to oust these strangers, but in vain. The Normans at first had no shadow of right to be in Italy at all. From the point of view of legal right they form one of the worst cases of lawless usurpation in European history, quite as much so as the old Goths and Lombards. But they had that foundation of so many rights, successful conquest. Later they tried to obtain some colour of legal right by grants from the Pope.

There were two lines of Norman conquerors in Southern Italy. The first in the field, destined to disappear before its successful rival, was the line of Aversa and Capua. In 1030 a Norman adventurer, Rainulf, becomes Count of Aversa[1]

---

[1] Aversa is a town about five miles due North of Naples.

under the Duke of Naples. This is the first Norman state, as distinct from groups of mercenaries who fought for a master. At that time Pandulf V, a Lombard, reigned as Duke of Capua. He died in 1057; then Richard of Aversa, Rainulf's nephew, besieged Capua, took it in 1058, and so, in 1062, began the line of Norman Dukes of Capua. The Pope, Alexander II (1061-1073), confirmed his title and made him independent of either Empire. This is significant. The Norman states in Italy from the beginning claimed absolute independence of any Emperor at all.

Meanwhile a mightier line of conquerors was arriving from Normandy. Eight miles north-east of Coutances stood the castle of Hauteville-la-Guichard. Here lived a Norman knight, Tancred de Hauteville.[1] He was quite a small knight; he had only one manor. He was destined to be the father of one of the greatest conquerors and the grandfather of one of the greatest kings of Europe. Old Tancred had twelve sons, fine young men all of them, three of them very great men indeed. They were of the classical type of Norman adventurers. At home they could not look for much inheritance; but they had their swords, their horses, their Norman valour, and, I suppose one must say, their Norman unscrupulousness. They were ready to go forth with these and see what they could pick up in the great world beyond Coutances. William, Drogo, Humfrey, Robert, and Roger picked up quite a lot.

One after another the de Hautevilles came South to Italy. William came first. About the year 1032 he took service under Pandulf of Capua; then he fought for George Maniakes in Sicily. In 1042 he founded the county of Apulia, with Melfi as its capital. He is William Iron-arm. Melfi is the first of the de Hauteville settlements in Italy. In 1053 Pope Leo IX (1048–1054) headed an alliance of Lombards and all inhabitants of Southern Italy against the Normans. Even the Western Emperor (Henry III, 1039–1056) sent a small contingent. This army was going to efface even the Norman name. Instead, it was utterly defeated. The Pope himself fell into the hands of the Normans, but they knelt at his feet and escorted him back to Benevento with all respect. Then the Pope made the political mistake of investing his former enemies with all they could conquer. This gave them a pretence of right, though they hardly needed that.

---

[1] De Hauteville—Az. a bend counter-gobony, gu. and arg., which arms may now be seen triumphant all over the Cappella Palatina at Palermo.

Meanwhile other sons of Tancred de Hauteville were arriving, one after another. Drogo and Humfrey did well for themselves and became Dukes. In 1045 the greatest of all arrived, Robert, surnamed the Wizard.[1] He was in the fight of 1053, and did great things there. Eventually Robert Guiscard gathered up all the Norman conquests and became the chief Norman conqueror of Southern Italy. In 1059 he was Duke of Apulia; in 1077 he held all Apulia. The Lombard states were destroyed, Benevento became part of the Patrimony of St Peter, the Eastern Empire held only Naples.

The news of the successes of his brothers at last brought the youngest of the de Hautevilles, Roger, to Italy in 1057. While he was looking out for something to do, Robert called his attention to Sicily. In 1061 Roger took Messina. Then he and Robert joined forces; between them they seized Palermo in 1072, and so most of the island. Robert, as Duke of Apulia, was considered Roger's suzerain. He kept for himself Palermo, the Val Demone, and half Messina. Roger, Count of Sicily under his brother, had the rest. During the following years Roger gradually seized all that was left of the Saracen possessions in the island. In 1079 he took Taormina; so that the Moslems held only Girgenti, Syracuse, and Castrogiovanni[2] in the middle. By 1091 they had lost these places too. The last Moslem Emir, Hāmud, submitted himself, turned Christian, and was rewarded with a fine property in Calabria. Meanwhile Robert Guiscard was completing the conquest of the mainland. In 1071 he took Bari; in 1077 he occupied Salerno and deposed the last Lombard prince in Italy, Gisulf. Then he carried war against the Empire to Kerkyra and Dyrrhachion. He died in Kerkyra; they brought his body home to Venosa, near Melfi, and buried him there, and put on his grave: " Hic terror mundi Guiscardus."

In 1099 Richard II of Capua, of the other Norman line, was obliged to recognize the suzerainty of the Dukes of Apulia.

In 1098 a Concordat was made between Roger of Sicily and Pope Urban II (1088-1099), by which Roger became Apostolic Legate[3] for Sicily. He now takes the title " Magnus

[1] Robert Guiscard. The name means rather a clever, sharp fellow, *callidus*.

[2] Castrogiovanni was originally Enna. The Moslems called it Ḳasr Yannī; then the Christians translated this back into Castrogiovanni.

[3] Based upon this concession are all the endless claims of Neapolitan kings to some kind of canonical authority in Church matters. Roger and his first successors made many Church laws on the strength of it.

Comes Siciliæ." He died in 1101. He was succeeded by his son Simon, a child, under the Regency of his widow Adelaide. Simon reigned only four years (1101–1105), then he died, and was succeeded by his brother, Roger II. This Roger II finally gathered up all Southern Italy and Sicily into a great kingdom. One by one the other Norman possessions are first made dependent, then amalgamated into his territory. Naples, the last imperial possession, was taken in 1138. Roger II also sent across the water and added part of North Africa to his domain. It was time that so great a prince should have a prouder title than that of Great Count. In 1130 a Bull of the Antipope Anacletus II (1130–1138) makes Roger king. After swearing fealty and homage to the Holy See,[1] he was crowned at his capital Palermo, on Christmas Day, 1130. Cardinal Conti, the Antipope's nephew, anointed him, and Robert II, Prince of Capua, as first of his vassals, put the crown on his head. So begins the kingdom of the two Sicilies. From now all Southern Italy is one state, under Norman kings. Its further history no longer concerns us.[2]

But we must note something about the people. To be one state does not at all mean that all the people in these parts became one race. It was still many centuries before that final amalgamation took place.

The government of Roger II and of his successors gives a unique example of mediæval toleration. The Norman conquerors of Sicily, beginning with Roger I, found themselves reigning over people of two races, two languages, and two religions. There were Greek Christians and Moslem Saracens. To these we may add the Latin Lombards of the mainland. Meanwhile the kings were Norman Latins. From the beginning the Norman kings made no attempt to impose one language, one religion or civilization on their subjects. They, at least the two Rogers and the first William, were men of sceptical views and of immoral lives. They granted entire toleration to all races and religions. So the Norman kingdom

---

[1] This oath of fealty should be noted. Because of it, all through the history of the kingdom of Naples and the two Sicilies, the Popes consider that state as dependent politically on the Holy See. The only legal claim the Norman kings had was the grant by the Pope; their kingdom was founded as a fief of the Papacy.

[2] An excellent Life of Roger II and of the Norman state in Italy and Sicily is E. Curtis, " Roger of Sicily and the Normans in Lower Italy," Putnam (" Heroes of the Nations "), 1912; also A. H. Johnson, " The Normans in Europe" (Longmans, 1880); Gibbon, chap. lvi, Rodotà, *op. cit.*, i, cap. viii.

of Sicily presents an astonishing state of things in the Middle
Ages, a complex society of Moslems, Byzantines, and Latins.
All these had their share. The Moslems had real affection
and loyalty to their Christian King. At the beginning of the
reign of Roger II, Palermo was still much more a Moslem
than a Christian city. The Moslems call Roger the " great
Sultan "; his armies are composed chiefly of Moslems. Indeed,
they believed that he himself had joined their religion. He
kept a harem like a Moslem emir; he adopted many Moslem
customs. At least his successors understood Arabic. He
employed Saracen architects, enjoyed the society of their learned
men, which he was said to prefer to that of priests and monks.
Under his rule Islam produced great writers in Sicily, such as
the famous geographer Abū 'Abdillah Muhammad alIdrīsī.

The Byzantine Christians also enjoyed his favour. He
used their artists to make mosaics in his churches; he was
surrounded by them also at his court. His admirals, Eugenios,
Christodulos, and George of Antioch, were Greeks. He had
a Greek court preacher,[1] and Byzantine polemists writing against
the Papacy at his court dedicated their works to him.[2] Meanwhile Roger II was himself, as far as he had any religion at all,
a Latin Catholic. He was Apostolic Legate for Sicily; he set
up Latin bishops in the cities. When he said any prayers at
all, he said them in Latin.

This curious combination of races and civilizations lasted
a long time in Sicily. Under Frederick II[3] we still find Moslem

---

[1] Theophanes Kerameus (ὁ Κεραμεύς), Metropolitan of Rossano.
His fifty-fifth homily was preached in Roger's presence in the Cappella Palatina; it describes its mosaics (P.G. cxxxii, 952-956).

[2] So Nilos Doxapatres (see p. 93).

[3] Frederick II, King of Sicily from 1198 to 1250 (Emperor, 1220-
1250), inherited the kingdom through his mother Constance, daughter
of Roger II. This is the lady whom Dante puts in the heaven of the
moon ("Par." iii, 118). Before him had reigned William I, "the
Bad " (1154-1166), son of Roger II; then William II, " the Good "
(1166-1189), son of William I. William II died *s.p.*; so ended the
direct main line of the de Hauteville kings. There remained Constance, William II's aunt, who had married the Emperor, Henry VI
(1190-1197). William II, by his will, left the crown to Henry VI;
at his death (1197) it came to his son, Frederick II. When Frederick II
died (1250) his illegitimate son Manfred first administered the kingdom
for his nephew Conradin, then made himself king (1258-1266). But
the Pope (Alexander IV, 1254-1261) gave the kingdom to Charles of
Anjou, brother of St Lewis IX of France. At Benevento, in 1266,
Charles defeated and slew Manfred; so the kingdom passed to the
French House of Anjou. In 1282 a revolution in Sicily (the Sicilian
Vespers) expelled the French. Peter III of Aragon, son-in-law of

favourites at his court.   The Greek influence lasted still longer.
The Moslem religion did gradually die out.   Though there
must be a good deal of Moorish blood among the Sicilians,
they have all long become Christians.[1]   The Greeks of Sicily
and Southern Italy have left, besides traces of their blood
and character, their rite, too, as a memory of the days when
they were the dominant element of those parts.   The first
stratum, if one may so call it, of the Byzantine rite in Italy
is the remnant of the old Greeks of Calabria, Apulia, and Sicily.

We must now see how Christianity was introduced here, and
in what form the first Christians of Lower Italy said their
prayers.

2. Christianity in Sicily and Lower Italy to the Eighth Century.

The Italians of the South count their Churches as Apostolic
foundations.   That is so common an attitude in the case of any
relatively old Church that we should not be much impressed
by it.   But in this case there are undoubted facts which supply
at least a good foundation for their belief.

Both St Peter and St Paul came to Lower Italy.   In
St Paul's first journey to Rome, after he had appealed to
Cæsar, he came, after the shipwreck at Malta, in an Alexandrine
ship first to Syracuse.   Here he remained three days.   Then he
sailed to Rhegium, stayed there one day, went on to Puteoli,
where he stayed among the brethren seven days (there were

Manfred, united Sicily to his kingdom; Charles of Anjou kept Naples.
The " Two Sicilies " were the island and the mainland opposite.
The lighthouse at Messina divided them.   Southern Italy was
" Sicilia citra Pharum," the island " Sicilia ultra Pharum."   The
king was " King of Naples and the two Sicilies."   Roger II called
himself " Rogerius Dei gratia Siciliæ, Apuliæ et Calabriæ rex,
adiutor Christianorum et clypeus."   The form " Rex Siciliæ citra
et ultra Pharum " also occurs.   See Carlo Nardi, " Dei titoli del Rè
delle due Sicilie " (Naples, 1747).   In Arabic the king was alMalik or
asSultan; in Greek he was 'Ρήξ or 'Ρίξ. Βασιλεύς always means
" emperor."   Roger II described himself as 'Ρογέριος ἐν Χριστῷ τῷ
θεῷ εὐσεβὴς κραταιὸς ῥὴξ καὶ τῶν χριστιανῶν βοηθός. Frederick II
was: Βασιλεύς τῶν 'Ρωμαίων, τῆς 'Ιερουσαλὴμ καὶ Σικελίας 'Ρήξ.

[1] The Royal charters of Norman Sicily, written in three languages,
Latin, Greek, and Arabic; the inscriptions in these languages on
churches and monuments at Palermo remain as witnesses of the three
elements of the Norman kingdom.   Best of all is this represented by the
gorgeous chapel of the King's palace (the Cappella Palatina) at Palermo.
This was built for Roger II in 1129-1140.   Its Romanesque doors,
Byzantine cupola and mosaics, Saracen arches, Arabic, Greek, and
Latin inscriptions, give exactly a picture of the state of Roger's court.

already Christians at Puteoli), and so at last came to Rome.[1]
We are not told in the Acts anything about missionary work
done by the Apostle at Syracuse and Rhegium; but it would
have been unlike Paul not to preach the Gospel during the three
days at Syracuse and the one at Rhegium. As soon as he got
to Rome he made an appointment with the Jews and " bore
witness of the Kingdom of God, and persuading them about
Jesus from the Law of Moses and the Prophets from morning
till evening."[2] We may no doubt suppose that he did the
same at Syracuse and Rhegium.

St Peter, too, must have been in these parts. We have
nothing from the Acts about his coming to Rome at all; but
when he did, he could hardly have come except by passing
through Lower Italy, if not through Sicily. So the Sicilians
and Italo-Greeks have some reason when they ascribe the
foundation of their Churches to St Peter and St Paul.

Naturally they have more detailed traditions as to how
this happened. When St Paul was at Rhegium, they say, he
made a certain Stephen, born at Nicæa, first bishop of that
city. St Stephen died a martyr in 74. The Sicilians count
their lines of bishops rather from St Peter. They believe that
he passed through the island on his way to Rome, and everywhere ordained bishops for the cities. So we hear of a
St Marcian, " Bishop of Sicily,"[3] St Pancras, Bishop of Tauromenium, and others, all disciples of St Peter. At Naples
St Peter is believed to have founded a flourishing Church, to
have baptized St Candida, to have turned a heathen temple
into a church in which he celebrated the holy liturgy (S.
Petri ad aram), to have converted, baptized, and ordained
St Aspren, whom he then left as the first bishop.[4]

We have further details about the Churches of Southern

---

[1] Acts xxviii, 11-16. On St Peter and St Paul in Sicily see the
excellent work of D. G. Lancia di Brolo, O.S.B. (now Archb. of Monreale), " Storia della Chiesa in Sicilia nei dieci primi secoli del Cristianesimo " (2 vols., Palermo, 1880-1884), i, pp. 32-34.

[2] Acts xxviii, 23.

[3] St Marcian, or Marcellus, and St Pancras occur in the Byzantine
Menologion on February 9. In the Roman Martyrology we have,
on June 14, " Syracusis S. Marciani ep., qui a b. Petro ordinatus ep.
post euangelii prædicationem a Iudæis occisus est "; on April 3,
" Tauromenii in Sicilia S. Pancratii ep. qui christi euangelium, quod
a S. Petro ap. illuc missus prædicauerat, martyrii sanguine consig-
nauit."

[4] In the Rom. Mart. September 4, St Candida, August 3, St
Aspren. On the local cult of St Aspren see C. d'Engenio Caracciolo,
" Napoli Sacra " (Naples, 1624), p. 12.

Italy and Sicily. There were great colonies of Jews here, among whom, as usual, the Gospel would first be preached. At the Nicene Council (325) there was present a bishop, Mark of Calabria.[1] We have still earlier evidence of Christianity in Sicily. The Roman presbyters and deacons, during the vacancy of the See after the martyrdom of St Fabian (250), write to St Cyprian: " You will have received the letter we wrote to Sicily."[2] There are Christian catacombs in the island, which appear to date from the second century. At Naples, too, are catacombs of the same time.[3]

Then for Southern Italy and Sicily we have a number of acts of martyrs. There are the acts of St Euplius (Εὔπλος) at Catana[4] in the year 304. The " Acta S. Felicis " (Bishop of Tubuza in Africa, † 303) mention Christian communities in Agrigentum, Catana, Messana, and Tauromenium.[5] The " Acta Petri et Pauli " (second or third century) speak of Christians at Messana.[6] The book " Prœdestinatus " (fifth century) mentions the Bishops Eustachius of Lilybæum and Theodorus of Panormus,[7] from which Harnack concludes that it is probable that there were bishops in these cities about the year 300.[8] The most famous Sicilian saints of the Roman persecution are St Agatha at Catana,[9] who was martyred in 251 under Decius, and St Lucy of Syracuse[10] under Diocletian (284–305). On

---

[1] Hefele-Leclercq, " Hist. des Conciles," i, p. 411.

[2] Inter ep. Cypr. xxx, 5; ed. Hartel, ii, 553.

[3] Harnack, " Mission u. Ausbreitung," 501-502.

[4] In the " Acta Sanctorum," Aug., vol. ii, pp. 721-722; Ruinart, " Acta Martyrum " (Regensburg, 1859, pp. 437-439); L. di Brolo, " Storia d. Chiesa in Sicilia," i, 150-154.

[5] R. Knopf, " Ausgewählte Märtyreracten " (in Krüger's " Sammlung ausgew. Quellenschriften "), Tübingen and Leipzig, Mohr, 1901, pp. 85-86.

[6] Ed. R. A. Lipsius and M. Bonnet, " Acta Apost. apocr." (Leipzig, 1891), Pt. I, p. 182.

[7] " Prædestinatus," Lib. i, cap. 16 (P.L. liii, col. 592, B); cf. L. di Brolo, op. cit., i, 64-69.

[8] " Mission u. Ausbreitung des Christertums " (Leipzig, 1902), p. 503, n. 1.

[9] February 5, " Acta Sctor." February 1, pp. 621-629. There are three versions of the acts of St Agatha; the last is by Simeon Metaphrastes. L. di Brolo, op. cit., i, 89-95.

[10] Her acts are in Oct. Caietanus, S.J. " Vitæ Sanctorum Siculorum " (Palermo, 2 vols., fol. 1657), i, 116-118, and the " Animaduersiones," pp. 87-102. Here is the poem about her by Sigebert of Gembloux († 1112). The acts are not very authentic; so Ruinart did not include them in his collection. The prayers of her Mass and office (December 13) are in the Gregorian Sacramentary and Liber Responsalis (P.L., lxxviii, cols. 151-152; 819). See Ioh. de

March 23 both the Roman Martyrology and the Byzantine Menaia commemorate St Nikon, bishop, and his companions. He was a Neapolitan, said to be martyred with 199 companions, all monks, in Sicily in the year 250. St Vitus, a child, martyred, with St Modestus his tutor and St Crescentia his nurse, in Sicily, under Diocletian, occurs in the Roman Martyrology on June 15.[1] At Acis Xynophonia (Acireale, north of Catana), they have a famous martyr, St Parasceve (Παρασκευή, so called because she was born on a Friday). She is believed to have died under Antoninus Pius (138–161). The Byzantine Menaia keep her memory on July 26. But when her name was to be translated into Latin and they made " St Friday " into " Scta Venera," the Pope (Pius VI, 1775–1799) thought that was not a proper name for a Christian saint to have; so he changed it into " Veneranda," in which form she occurs in the Roman Martyrology on November 14, with Gaul as the place of her death ![2]

There are saints of the Roman persecution on the mainland of Southern Italy too, as St January at Naples, who, although there seems to be the greatest possible uncertainty as to who he was or when he suffered, still does astonishing things with his blood.[3]

In short, from about the second century there were flourishing Christian communities all over Southern Italy and in Sicily. By about the middle of the third century, at latest, we have evidence of regularly established Churches with lines of bishops. Nor is there any doubt in what language the Gospel was preached here during that time, or in what language the holy Mysteries were celebrated. Greek was the language of the country, and we know that the first Christians said their prayers in their native tongue. Indeed, even in Rome, Greek was the liturgical language, at least till about the middle of the third century. All the more was it so in the South, where few spoke anything else. The acts of martyrs and other fragments of Christian literature from these lands are Greek. There was constant intercourse with Greece, and then with Constantinople. Bishops from Sicily receive sees in Greece

---

Iohanne, " De diu. Siculorum officiis," pp. 47-50; L. di Brolo, *op. cit.*, i, 159-166.

[1] " Acta Sanct.," Iun. III, pp. 499-501; L. di Brolo, *op. cit.*, i, 154-158.

[2] See Nilles, " Kalendarium Manuale " (2nd edition, Innsbruck, 1896), pp. 223-225.

[3] For the local cult of St January (Ianuarius, Gennaro) see C. d'Engenio Caracciolo, " Napoli Sacra " (Naples, 1624), pp. 6-10.

and the Greek islands, and Greeks send bishops to Sicily, Calabria, and Apulia. It does not seem to have made any difference whether a man was a Greek from Syracuse or a Greek from Athens or Constantinople. Moreover, the reasons which caused the use of Latin in church at Rome did not obtain in the South. There was no need to adopt another language than Greek for use in church here, because Greek was still the vulgar tongue.

Yet there are difficulties about the ecclesiology of Southern Italy and Sicily during the first seven centuries. For one thing, it is curious, and to the liturgical student disastrous, that writers of the early Christian centuries disregard these questions of rite, liturgical language, and custom. They, naturally, think matters of faith and unity of great importance. They give us plenty of information about these; so that we have no difficulty in finding out which bishops were Arians, Pelagians, and so on. We can also tell easily if any bishop was in schism with the rest of Christendom. These matters are noted in an abundance of letters and contemporary documents. But, supposing a bishop was a good Catholic, no one seems to think it worth while to note what rite he used, how he said his prayers. This is disappointing to the modern student of liturgy. If early bishops had written down exact accounts of their services, it would have been a great benefit to us. But it is, in itself, natural. To them these were matters of very little importance. Liturgiology as a science was not yet born. They knew that it matters very much whether a man is a Catholic or not, very little in what language he says his prayers.

The difficulty, then, is this: we know that in Sicily and Southern Italy at the beginning Greek was the ecclesiastical language. We know, too, that when the Normans came in the eleventh century they found a flourishing Greek Church in possession here. It would then seem natural to suppose that there had never been anything else, that the first Latin influence was that of the Normans. Yet we have evidence that it was not so. On the contrary, there had been, centuries before the Norman conquest, much Latin influence in the Church of Lower Italy, and there had been a deliberate introduction of Greek customs and language imposed on the people, in spite of opposition, in the eighth century. When the Normans began spreading Latin uses among the clergy, they were not so much introducing a new element as rather restoring what the Emperors at Constantinople had destroyed.

We cannot say how or when this earlier Latin influence began. It is tempting to ascribe it to the Lombards. Yet it was there before the Lombards arrived. The Latin influence was less in Sicily. There were Romans in Sicily who spoke Latin before Christianity was preached there. There were Latin priests and bishops in the island who celebrated their rites in Latin from a very early date; yet, on the whole, Sicily was more Greek than the mainland. Its connection with the East and with Constantinople was closer. Till the Moslems came and swept nearly all the Christian Church away, we may take it that Christianity in Sicily was mainly Greek.

In the time of St Leo I (440–461) the Sicilian bishops, though they had been ordained at Rome, follow the custom of Constantinople and the East in at least one important detail. They baptize, not at Easter, according to the Roman rule, but at the Epiphany. St Leo reproaches them for this and says: " You would not have fallen into this fault if you had taken the rule of your observance from that place where you received the honour of consecration; if the See of blessed Peter, which is the mother of your sacerdotal dignity, had been the teacher of your ecclesiastical custom."[1] Some writers see evidence here of the Roman rite in Sicily at that time.[2] It seems to me proof that, at least in this point, the Roman custom was not followed. St Gelasius I (492–496) writes a letter[3] to the bishops of Lucania, Bruttii,[4] and Sicily. In this are twenty-eight " capita "—that is, rules of Canon law which they are to observe. Many of these rules are about liturgical matters. As far as they go, they show the wish of the Pope that the bishops should conform to Roman customs. But they do not really prove much either way; and again they may perhaps be taken as evidence that hitherto such customs have not been observed. Cap. 10 says that the bishops are to baptize only at Easter and Pentecost, except in case of necessity.[5] Cap. 11 that priests and deacons are to be ordained at the Ember days, and it supposes the Saturday fast.[6] These two letters (of Leo and Gelasius) were written to repair the damages to the Church of Lower Italy and Sicily done by the Vandals. St Gregory I (590–604) showed great zeal in arranging the affairs of these Churches. Many of his letters are directed to

---

[1] Leonis I, Ep. 16, ad uniu. eppos per Siciliam constitutos (P.L., liv, 695–704; *cf.* 696).   [2] See p. 73, n. 1.

[3] Gelasii I, Ep. 9 (P.L., lix, 47–57).

[4] Bruttii is the present Calabria, Lucania the province immediately north of it.   [5] P.L., lix, 52.   [6] *Ibid.*

bishops of Sicily and Lower Italy.[1]   His famous letter to John
of Syracuse,[2] in which he defends the Roman Church from
the accusation of having imitated Constantinople, begins by
saying that he has heard of these accusations from Sicilians,
" either Greeks or Latins "[3] (so both were in Sicily then).
In the course of it he asks: " Have your Churches received a
tradition from the Greeks ?   Why then do the subdeacons to
this day wear linen tunics, except that they have received this
custom from their mother the Roman Church ?"[4]

Then, after the second hellenization of Sicily and Calabria
in the seventh century (when Constans II came to Syracuse
in 662, p. 58), we find evidence of a considerable Greek
element in Sicily.   St Maximos the Confessor (ὁ ὁμολογητής,
† 662)[5] preached in Greek " in Africa and the islands near "[6]
(clearly including Sicily), and all the people and bishops came
to hear him.   While he was on the island he wrote a letter, in
Greek, to the " holy fathers, hegumenoi, monks, and orthodox
people of Sicily."[7]   Gregory, the Hymnograph in the seventh
century, who wrote a Greek Kontakion in honour of St Marcian,[8]
was certainly a Sicilian, probably Bishop of Syracuse.[9]   St
Gregory of Akragas (Girgenti, in Sicily), author of a Com-
mentary on Ecclesiastes,[10] was a bishop of the Byzantine rite.[11]
His date is difficult to determine exactly; he was probably of the
seventh century.[12]   Our St Theodore of Canterbury (668–690),

[1] See L. di Brolo, " Storia d. Chiesa in Sicilia," i, cap. xx (pp. 382–
400).
[2] Greg. I, Ep. ix, 12 (P.L., lxxvii, 955-958).
[3] *Ibid.*, 955.   [4] *Ibid.*, 956.
[5] The famous monk of Constantinople and opponent of the
Monotheletes.
[6] " Vita S. Maximi Conf.," § 14 (P.G., xc, 84).
[7] P.G., xci, 112-132.   That he wrote the letter in Sicily is shown
by his reference to " this Christ-loving island of the Sicilians "
(*ibid.*, 112).
[8] Published by Card. Pitra, "Analecta Sacra" (Paris, 1876), i,
p. 273.
[9] He refers to " this our island of the Sicilians " (*ibid.*).   See
L. di Brolo, " Storia d. Chiesa in Sicilia," ii, 17-21.
[10] P.G., xcviii, 741-1181.
[11] He writes in Greek, quotes only Greek fathers and the LXX,
quotes the Eucharistic words of Institution according to the Byzantine
form (*e.g.*, ii, 12; P.G., xcviii, 837).
[12] Gregory's Life, by Leontios, monk of St Sabas at Rome (P.G.,
xcviii, 549-716), does not give the name of a single Pope or Patriarch
as clue.   We only discover that he came once to Rome (col. 653).
Stephen Morcellus conjectures his date as 548-*c.* 630 (*ibid.*, 543-
544).   Baronius thinks he is the Gregorius Agrigentinus of the Letters
of St Gregory I (590-604; *e.g.*, Ep. i, 72; P.L., lxxvii, 526).   Lancia

originally from Tarsus in Cilicia, and his companion the
Archimandrite Adrian, were Greek monks of Calabria sent to
England by Pope Vitalian (657–672). Tarasios, Patriarch of
Constantinople (784–806), was a Greek of Sicily. During
Iconoclast times, at the second Council of Nicæa (787), and
then at the time of Photius' schism, Sicily seems solidly Greek
and Byzantine. Gregory Asbestas of Syracuse ordained
Photius. But this already brings us to the period after the
Byzantine usurpation in Lower Italy and Sicily in the eighth
century.[1]

---

di Brolo denies this, and fixes his date only as somewhere between
680 and 730 (" St. d. Ch. in Sicilia," ii, cap. ii, pp. 38-57). In
P.G., xcviii, 1181-1228, is a dissertation on his date by John Lancea
of Palermo. Krumbacher says, " At any rate, he must not be considered later than the seventh century " (" Byzantinische Litteratur,"
2nd edition, Munich, 1897, pp. 128-129).

[1] There has been considerable controversy about the rites used
in Magna Græcia, and still more about those of Sicily in the period
before the Byzantine aggression in the eighth century. The controversy is complicated by the fact that writers on all sides speak of
two rites, " Latin " and " Greek," supposing always that " Latin "
means Roman, and " Greek " Byzantine. In the eighteenth century
John di Giovanni, Canon of Palermo, wrote a book to defend the
theory that in Sicily Latin was the common language from the time
of the apostles, the Roman rite being used almost exclusively from
the fifth to the eighth century. He calls himself Iohannes de Iohanne,
" De diuinis Siculorum officiis Tractatus," Palermo, 1736 (see
especially chaps. iv-vii, pp. 23-47). He argues from Innocent I's
letter to Decentius and those of Leo I and Gregory I (quoted above).
Joseph Morisani, Canon of Reggio, " De Protopapis et Deutereis
Græcorum et Catholicis eorum ecclesiis Diatriba " (Naples, 1768),
holds the same view, admitting only occasional " Greek " liturgies
in some cities, for the Byzantine officials (pp. 157-164). J. S. Assemani, " Italicæ hist. Scriptores," vol. iv, cap. iii, pp. 102-111, agrees,
on the whole, with this. Mgr. Lancia di Brolo believes that the
Sicilian rite was exactly that of Rome, on the strength of Leo I and
Gregory I's letters (" Storia della Chiesa in Sicilia," i, 398). On the
other hand, Ottavio Caetano maintains that everything in Sicily,
language and rite, was always Greek (" Isagoge ad hist. s. Sic.,"
cap. xlii; in J. G. Grævius, " Thesaurus Antiq. et Hist. Siciliæ,"
vol. ii, Leiden, 1723, cols. 210-218). In § xi (cols. 215-216) he quotes
many witnesses. P. P. Rodotà refutes di Giovanni's arguments, I
think, successfully. He quotes many texts, showing that the Popes
tolerated other rites in their Patriarchate, as, for instance, in Illyricum
and Thessalonica. He thinks that the earliest liturgical use in Sicily
was Greek, that there was then considerable Latin infiltration, that
from 553, when the Greeks took over again the rule of the island,
Greek language and rite " took again their ancient vigour " (" dell'
Origine, Progresso e Stato presente del Rito greco in Italia," 3 vols.,
Rome, 1758-1763, vol. i, cap. iii, §§ 12-18, pp. 74-87). For my part,

It is chiefly on the mainland that there was a considerable Latin body of Christians, Latin influence and Latin uses in Church, coming presumably from the North.   The best proof of this is that, as we shall see, when the court of Constantinople tried to enforce its own rite throughout its possessions in Italy, there was much opposition, many bishops preferring to go on using the Latin rite to which they were accustomed.[1]

Yet this Latin use, these Latin rites, were not necessarily Roman.   One of the few fragments of liturgical use in Southern Italy that remain, the lectionaries of Naples at the time of St Gregory I (590–604),[2] are Latin, but not Roman.   They show rather the type of liturgy common in Gaul, Spain, and other parts of Italy before the spread of the Roman rite. There is Roman influence, as would be natural because of the nearness of Rome; but there are marked non-Roman features, signs of Eastern influence, such as we find in most of these local Churches since their more frequent relations with the East in the fourth century.   For instance, Baptism is administered at the Epiphany, during a special midnight Mass.   Baptism at the Epiphany is a markedly un-Roman custom, which St Leo I (440–461) had tried to put down in Sicily (p. 71). Perhaps another proof of Latin influence is in the Latin names

---

having read all these arguments, I agree, on the whole, with Rodotà. It seems certain that Christianity in Lower Italy and Sicily was at first Greek.   Then, gradually, a considerable Latin element was introduced, Latin language, Latin rites, and Roman influence.   The bishops were ordained in Rome; the Pope occasionally demanded conformity to Roman use in certain particulars.   But the Greek language and rites never disappeared, and already in the sixth century there was a great revival of them.   From the eighth to the eleventh century they dominated these parts; then they went back and almost disappeared under the Normans and their successors.   Certainly the idea of R. Cotroneo, G. Minasi and other Calabrian writers (see, for instance, "Roma e l'Oriente," vii, 275), that there was no Byzantine rite in Italy till the Emperors imposed it in the eighth century, is a mistake.   [1] See p. 85.

[2] Published by Dom G. Morin, "La Liturgie de Naples au temps de S. Grégoire" (Revue Bénédictine, viii, 1891, pp. 481–493; 529–537), reprinted at the end of his "Liber Comicus" (Anecdota Maredsolana, I), 1893, pp. 426–435.   They are two Calendars or quasi-Capitularia, one in the "Euang. S. Cuthberti" (Cotton MS., Nero, D. iv) and one in the "Cod. Reg., I, B. viii."   Morin shows that both are Neapolitan in the beginning of the seventh century.   They were brought to England by Adrian, Abbot of a monastery near Naples, then a companion of St Theodore of Canterbury, in 668.   They contain the feast of St January with a vigil and the dedication of the basilica of St Stephen (the cathedral church of Naples).

of bishops in Southern Italy. It is not safe to make much depend on this. We know, for instance, of Patriarchs of Constantinople named Maximus and Flavian. Latin and Greek names seem to have been exchanged freely. Still, when we find a number of Southern Italian bishops called by such names as Sergius, Maximus, Innocent, Benedict, it is difficult not to see in this a sign of Latinity.

We have, then, as the situation before the eighth century, a background of Greek Christianity already considerably overlaid by Latin uses in Southern Italy, less so in Sicily. But the Latin rites used here were not Roman. As for the rites followed by the Greeks, it is still more difficult to say exactly what they were. They could not have been Byzantine in the first four or five centuries, because the Byzantine rite was not yet formed. They must have been forms of the many rites in Greek, presumably akin to that of Antioch, of which the Byzantine rite itself is one. Because of the close connection of Greater Greece with Constantinople, no doubt these rites developed in much the same direction as that of Constantinople. There would naturally be constant Byzantine influence over bishops who had so much to do with the capital. But the formal imposition of the Byzantine rite is part of the work of the Emperors from the eighth century. The Gothic invasion had little effect on the ecclesiastical situation. The Goths were Arians, but tolerant towards the Catholic Romans. For their own people they had one Arian Church, which disappeared from Italy when their kingdom broke up. But this sect, out of communion with the Catholic Church, did not affect any of the Catholic institutions. The case of the Lombards is different. By the time they came to Southern Italy they were Catholics, therefore in communion with the Romans. We know little of their organization in Church matters, except the names of some Lombard bishops.[1] We can only suppose that they used the rites they brought with them from the North of Italy, presumably rites of that vague class generally called " Gallican " (as at Milan). In matters of jurisdiction there is no sign that they had any exceptional position. Probably in time the Lombards conformed in rite to the Latin uses of the South. At any rate, I do not know of any evidence of special Lombard rites down here.

Altogether distinct from the question of rite is that of

---

[1] Thus, in the tenth century, a Bishop of Cosenza, Itelgrimus, negotiates with the Abbot of St Vincent at Volturno (Gay, " L'Italie méridionale," pp. 187-188). By his name he must be a Lombard.

hierarchical jurisdiction. In modern times we are accustomed to think of these as connected. Among the Uniates they go together. It was not so in the first eight centuries. Then groups of people in a foreign land kept their own rite, but were subject to the jurisdiction of the local bishops. So in Lower Italy, all the bishops, whatever rite they may have used, were subject to the Pope, *not only as Patriarch, but also as Metropolitan.*

In the first place there was no question of being subject to any authority of the Patriarch of Constantinople. Till the first Council of Constantinople (381) the Bishop of Constantinople had no claim to any jurisdiction beyond his own diocese at all. Even then he only got an honorary position which involved no jurisdiction. It is not till Chalcedon (451) that we find the beginning of what can be called a Byzantine Patriarchate; and then it was defined clearly as covering the provinces of Asia and Thrace. There was no suggestion of jurisdiction in Italy. As far as Patriarchal jurisdiction goes, as soon as the concept of Patriarchal jurisdiction was evolved, all Italy, including the South, without distinction of rite, looked to Rome. The Pope's legate at Nicæa (325), Hosius of Cordova, signs in the name of " the Church of Rome and the Churches of Italy, Spain, and all the West."[1] Indeed, as we shall see, when the usurpation of the Byzantine Patriarch in Lower Italy began (in the eighth century), his defenders admitted frankly that this was a new claim, and they tried to find excuses why these dioceses should be taken from the jurisdiction of Rome and handed over to that of Constantinople.[2]

But, more than this, the Pope was head of the Sees of Southern Italy and Sicily, not only as Patriarch, but as their immediate Metropolitan. There is an important point to realize about this. It was certainly rare that any Metropolitan province should be so great. However, it was so; all Southern Italy and even Sicily was included in the Roman *province* during the first seven centuries. This explains a point often misunderstood. Some Anglican writers have conceived the idea that the Roman Patriarchate extended only throughout Southern Italy, and did not include Gaul or even North Italy, in spite of the clear witness of Hosius at Nicæa.[3] Their

---

[1] Mansi, ii, 882, 927.   [2] P. 82.

[3] So Mr. E. Denny, " Papalism " (Rivingtons, 1912), note 24, pp. 626-629. He refers to Rufinus, " Hist. Eccl.," i, 6, referring to Migne, P.L., xi, 473 [*sic*, should be xxi, 473], saying, " Rufinus . . . describes the limits of the jurisdiction of the Roman Bishop as con-

mistake is that they confuse the Metropolitan province with the Patriarchate. The texts they quote defining the Pope's jurisdiction to the Sees close to Rome and to the South of Italy mean his authority, not as Patriarch, still less his universal authority as Pope. They describe his Metropolitan province.

The proof of this, that Southern Italy and Sicily had the Pope himself for Metropolitan, is first the fact that there was no Archbishop there till the Byzantine usurpation of the eighth century. This is curious and significant.

The earliest Archbishopric in these parts is Naples in the eighth century, made so by the government and Patriarch at Constantinople; and this is just one of the examples of the change made by their usurpation at that time.[1] Then the Emperor made Sicily a province under an Archbishop of Syracuse, again a new dignity, and set up Rhegium and Sancta Severina (ἡ ἁγία Σεβερίνη) as Metropolitan Sees in the same way. Before that there was no Archbishop in Southern Italy and Sicily, or rather there was one only, the Pope himself.

Another proof of the Metropolitical authority of the Popes in these parts is that all the bishops in them had to come to Rome to be ordained. Thus Pope Celestine I (422–432), writing to complain of the candidates for episcopal ordination sent to him from Apulia and Calabria, shows clearly that he himself ordains all these bishops; " they think," he says, " that we can consecrate such people "; and again, " they think very ill of us since they believe that we can do this."[2] Leo I says the same (p. 71). Gregory I (590–604) writes to Peter, Bishop of Hydruntum (Otranto), giving him delegate jurisdiction to visit neighbouring sees, and he insists that the bishops " must come to us to be consecrated."[3] Nearly three centuries later, in 860, when the Holy See was first beginning to admit the title of archbishop in what had been its own

---

sisting of the ' Suburbicarian Churches.' " What Rufinus really says is, " Hic suburbicariarum ecclesiarum sollicitudinem gerit " (*loc. cit.*). There is no question of describing the limits of jurisdiction; he says merely that the Pope has care of those Churches, and he means the special " sollicitudo " of a Metropolitan. As for the Patriarchal jurisdiction of the Bishop of Rome, at about the same time as Rufinus wrote this paraphrase of the sixth canon of Nicæa, St Jerome (Ep. 17 ad Marcum; P.L., xxii, 360) describes it simply as " the West." That has been the conviction of antiquity ever since there was a clear idea of Patriarchates. *Cf.* Hefele-Leclercq, " Hist. des Conciles " (Paris, 1907), vol. i, pp. 562-566.

[1] P. 85.   [2] Cœl. I, Ep. 5, ad Eppos Ap. et Cal. (P.L., l, 436).
[3] Greg. I, Ep. vi, 21, ad Petrum eppum (P.L., lxxvi, 812).

province, Nicholas I (858–867), though he calls the Ordinary of Syracuse Archbishop, still insists that the ancient custom be maintained, according to which he must come to Rome to be ordained: " We require that the consecration of the Archbishop of Syracuse be performed by our See; that the tradition founded by the Apostles in no way be abandoned in our time "[1]

So, as far as I know, all authors of repute agree that the ordination of bishops in the Campagna, Bruttii, Apulia, and Sicily were performed by the Roman Pontiffs.[2] Now, for a long time in the West, as still in the East, the right of ordaining bishops was considered a mark of immediate jurisdiction over them. The Popes never attempted to ordain all the bishops of their vast Patriarchate. It is all the more significant that they ordained those of Southern Italy and Sicily.

Another proof that these dioceses were part of the Roman province is that their bishops attended the Roman provincial synods. They were summoned to these and attended them regularly. St Leo I (440–461) insists that the Sicilian bishops must attend the Roman synods every year.[3] As late as 680, when Pope Agatho (678–681) held a provincial synod at Rome to arrange about the Legates he was to send to the sixth general council (Constantinople, III, 680), all the bishops of Calabria and Sicily attend it.[4] Even after the Byzantine usurpation had begun, the more conservative bishops, who would not accept the new state of things, still go to the Roman provincial synods. Thus the Bishops of Tarentum, Cosentiæ, Bisinianum, Luceræ, Beneventum, and Capua are present at the Roman Synod of 743.[5]

Moreover, in all this earlier period we find the Popes legislating for details of Church government in the South in a way that argues not only supreme Papal or Patriarchal authority, but the more intimate supervision of a Metropolitan. Gregory I's letters contain many examples of this. He

---

[1] Nic. I, Ep. 4, ad Michaelem Imp. (P.L., cxix, 779).

[2] For instance, Peter de Marca, Archbp. of Paris, " de Concordia Sacerdotii et Imperii " (Paris, 1641), Lib. i, cap. i, § 4 (pp. 7-8); Lequien, " Oriens Christianus " (Paris, 1740), Tom. i, cap. 14, § 2 (col. 96); Iohannes de Iohanne, " de Divinis Siculorum Officiis " (Palermo, 1736), cap. v (pp. 33-41); Assemani, " Italicæ hist. scriptores " (Rome, 1751-1753), iii, pp. 472-473; Rodotà, " del Rito greco in Italia " (Rome, 1758), i, cap. ii, pp. 49-60. See Rocco Pirri (quoted here, p. 80, n. 1).

[3] Ep. 16 (P.L., liv, 702).

[4] Their signatures are in Mansi, xi, 299-306.

[5] Mansi, xii, 367. Cf. J. Gay, " L'Italie mérid. et L'Emp. byz.," pp. 187, 190.

writes to Honorius of Tarentum giving him faculties to build and consecrate a parish church with a font.[1]   When the See of Naples was torn by local quarrels, he appoints the subdeacon Peter to arrange the election of a bishop.[2]   He himself then ordains the bishop (Fortunatus) so chosen.[3]   He delegates this same Fortunatus to visit other dioceses in the Campagna.[4] He deposes Demetrius of Naples and makes a certain Paul Vicar Capitular of the diocese, till a new bishop shall be elected.[5] He makes laws for the rites of Sicily, and insists that these should, in certain points, conform to those of Rome.[6]   A special point was that no bishop might consecrate a new church without special delegation from the Pope.   So Gelasius I (492–496) says of the Southern Italian bishops: " They may not venture to dedicate new basilicas, without having received again faculties according to custom," and he reproaches those who had presumed to " consecrate holy churches or oratories without the command of the Apostolic See."[7]   Martène says: " In Italy the diocesan bishops did not presume to do this [consecrate churches] until they had first obtained faculty from the Sovereign Pontiff."[8]   In Sicily, too, the bishops were ordained by the Pope; they received from him leave to consecrate churches; they, too, had to attend the yearly provincial synods at Rome; when their sees were vacant they were administered by vicars appointed by the Pope, till the new bishop was elected.[9]

All this means more than Patriarchal jurisdiction.   The Pope was Patriarch of all the West; yet we do not find him arranging these more intimate matters in the North of Italy, in Gaul, or Spain.[10]   They were regulated by the Metropolitans of those places.   When we see the Popes thus using local Metropolitical jurisdiction in the South of Italy and

---

[1] Greg. I, Ep. xiii, 20 (P.L., lxxvii, 1274-1275).
[2] Ep. iii, 35 (P.L., lxxvii, 631-632).   [3] *Ibid.* (P.L., lxxvii, 632).
[4] Ep. ix, 75, 76 (P.L., lxxvii, 1009-1010).
[5] Ep. ii, 6, 10 (P.L., lxxvii, 542-543; 546-547).
[6] Ep. ix, 12 (P.L., lxxvii, 956); L. di Brolo, " Storia d. Chiesa in Sic.," i, cap. xx (pp. 382-400).
[7] Gel. I, Ep. ix, ad Eppos per Lucaniam, etc., caps. 9 and 25 (P.L., lix, 50, 55).
[8] E. Martène, " de antiquis Eccl. ritibus " (2nd edition, Antwerp, 1736), vol. ii, lib. ii, cap. xiii, § 7 (col. 673); see the whole paragraph.
[9] See the quotations in Rodotà, " Rito greco in Italia," i, 58-60.
[10] Notably it was only in his metropolitical province that the Pope confirmed the election of the bishops and himself ordained them.   In the first eight centuries this was the special right of the Metropolitan (Hefele-Leclercq, " Hist. des Conciles," i, 566).

Sicily, we conclude again that this was part of his own province. So Rodotà: " The Pope, therefore, not only as Head of the Church and Patriarch, but also as Metropolitan, used his authority over the lands contained in that district which is now known as the kingdom of Naples and Sicily; it knew no other Metropolitan during the first seven centuries of the Church than the Bishop of Rome."[1] Perhaps the simplest proof of this is the fact that, when Constantinople in the eighth century first began to tear these dioceses away from Rome, to set up local Metropolitans in these parts, it was admitted by the Greeks themselves, it is indeed manifest from the whole proceeding that this was then an innovation (see p. 90).

3. Byzantine Usurpation (Eighth to Eleventh Century).

In the eighth century the use of the Byzantine rite began to spread throughout Lower Italy at the cost of the Roman rite, and for the first time the Christians of these parts were brought into subjection to the Patriarch of Constantinople. We have seen the second hellenization of the old Greater Greece from the seventh century.[2] The eighth set a seal on this movement by hellenizing ecclesiastical affairs as well. So we come to the last great wave of Greek influence here. It lasted till the Norman conquest of the eleventh century finally turned the tide towards Rome.

The aggression of the Patriarchate of Constantinople in what had been the Roman ecclesiastical province began at the time of the Iconoclast troubles. When the Emperor Leo III, the Isaurian (717–741), began his campaign against the holy images, he came into conflict with the Pope (Gregory II, 715–731). Unless the Pope obeyed his Iconoclast law, he threatened to send an army to Rome, break up the statue of St Peter there and take the Pope prisoner.[3] He could

---

[1] Rodotà, *op. cit.*, i, 53. See all his chap ii. (pp. 49-60) for further evidences and authorities. Harnack holds this as " probable," and says, " I cannot prove it here " (" Mission u. Ausbreitung des Christentums," Leipzig, 1902, p. 500). Morisani brings evidences to prove it (" de Protopapis," 155-157). See also especially the two dissertations of Rocco Pirri (Abbot of Noto in Southern Sicily), " Disquisitiones de Patriarcha Siciliæ," and " de Metropolita Siciliæ " in I. G. Grævius, " Thesaurus Antiq. et Histor. Siciliæ," tom. ii (Leiden, 1723), where there is abundance of evidence.

[2] Above, p. 56. L. di Brolo dates the second hellenization of these Churches from the coming of Constans II to Syracuse in 668 (" Storia d. Chiesa in Sicilia," ii, 16-23).

[3] Greg. II, Ep. 12, ad Leonem Imp. (P.L., lxxxix, col. 519, B).

not carry out this plan; but he could annoy the Pope throughout the territory of Italy which was still in possession of the Empire. At that time Ravenna and the Exarchate, Rome itself (in theory) and Naples with their duchies, Calabria, Sicily, and some maritime cities of Apulia, were still imperial. The Emperor wrote to enforce his Iconoclast decrees in these provinces. This led to rebellion throughout most of Italy. " The wickedness of the Emperor being known, all Italy took counsel to choose a new Emperor and to lead him to Constantinople; but the Pontiff repressed this plan, hoping for the Prince's conversion."[1] At Rome the Government of Constantinople could do nothing. There was a great rebellion against it at Naples, where the people were particularly Roman in feeling.[2] It was this quarrel which resulted eventually in the loss to the Empire of Ravenna with the Exarchate, and of Rome, when Gregory called in Charles Martel and his Franks.

Meanwhile, in Sicily and the South, where the Emperor had more power, he began a campaign against the Pope. In this campaign we must distinguish three objects. The Emperor tried first to force the people and the clergy to accept his Iconoclasm; secondly, he confiscated the territorial possessions of the Holy See in the South;[3] thirdly, he tried to detach all the dioceses of the South and of Sicily from their allegiance to Rome, and to unite them to the Patriarchate of Constantinople. There is a difference in the importance of these three policies. The first was a matter of heresy which, if it had succeeded, would, of course, have involved schism. On this point there could be no question of compromise. The confiscation of the property of the Holy See was robbery and spoliation; but it did not involve any point of faith or Church order. The third, the annexation of dioceses to the

---

[1] " *Liber Pontificalis*, xci, Greg. II " (ed. Duchesne, Paris, 1886-1892, vol. i, pp. 404-405). *Cf.* Theophanes, " Chron.," ad ann. M. 6221 (P.G., cviii, col. 825, B). For the relations of the Pope, Emperor, and people of Italy after the first Iconoclast law, see J. S. Assemani, " Italicæ historiæ scriptores " (Rome, 1751-1753), vol. iii, pp. 215-227, and Hefele-Leclercq, " Hist. des Conciles " (Paris, 1910, iii), pp. 647-675.   [2] See p. 85.

[3] The Holy See at that time had vast properties in the Campagna, Calabria, Sicily, Tuscany, Corsica, Sardinia, Dalmatia, Gaul, Africa. See Assemani, " Ital. hist. script.," vol. iii, cap. v, pp. 297-339; L. A. Muratori, " Antiq. Ital.," v, Diss. 69, cols. 797-908; L. di Brolo, " Storia d. Chiesa in Sicilia," i, cap. xxii, pp. 445-485; K. Schwarzlose, " Die Patrimonien der röm. Kirche bis zur Gründung des Kirchenstaates " (Berlin, 1887).

Patriarchate of Constantinople, was an injury to the Holy See, and one more case of lawless interference by the civil Government in ecclesiastical affairs. But it did not necessarily involve schism. The Holy See could tolerate that certain dioceses in Italy should become part of the Byzantine Patriarchate. Probably, for the sake of peace, it would have done so; but just at the time when this question was being most discussed, there came the great schism, first under Photius (867), then under Cerularius (1054), which put an end to negotiations. Then the Normans conquered the South of Italy and Sicily. Under their rule the Byzantine element gradually receded till it almost disappeared.

Anastasius Bibliothecarius tells of the confiscation of property and the beginning of the attempt to snatch the Southern dioceses from the Roman Patriarchate. He says that when the Iconoclast quarrel began: " Then they who are now called Emperors of the Greeks . . . since they could not otherwise injure the Roman Pontiffs, seized their ancient inherited territories, violated the rights of the Apostolic See, and took away nearly all the rights of the Pope in the dioceses of which they [the Emperors] could dispose, giving these to their own friends and followers. So they usurped the right which the Apostolic See had in these places, because they were situated near it, and they wickedly handed them over to the diocese of Constantinople."[1]

The Emperors carried out the same policy in Illyricum, which till then had been part of the Roman Patriarchate. All through this story Illyricum and the old Magna Græcia in the South of Italy go together. The same policy of the Emperors wanted to detach both from Rome, to join both to Constantinople. In the South of Italy and Sicily their policy could be carried out the more easily because of the considerable revival of Greek language in those parts since the sixth century (p. 57). Their excuse was that the people were Greeks, attached to the Empire; whereas Rome itself was falling under the power of Barbarians, Lombards, and Franks.[2] Therefore it was right that the Church in Sicily and Greater Greece should depend rather on the imperial and Greek See of Constantinople.

Sicily was more Greek than the mainland. Here the Greek element had always been the stronger.[3] So the

---

[1] In his preface to the acts of the fourth Council of Const., Mansi, xvi, col. 10, C. See Pagi's note in Baronius, " Annales Eccl.," ad ann. 730 (Lucca, 1742, vol. xii, pp. 391-392).

[2] See pp. 52, 53.   [3] P. 57.

Emperor began with Sicily. Already before the second Council of Nicæa (787), which put an end to Iconoclasm, he had made the See of Syracuse into an Archbishopric, as the Metropolitan See of the island.[1] Tauromenion was also made an Archbishopric, but without suffragans. These two Archbishops were to be ordained at Constantinople. At the synod the Sicilian bishops sign as subject to the Patriarch of Constantinople; John of Tauromenion calls Tarasios of Constantinople (784–806) " our Œcumenical Patriarch."[2] But there was still some ambiguity about the position of these bishops. Pope Nicholas I, as we have seen (p. 78) in 860, admits the title of Archbishop of Syracuse, but requires that he come to Rome to be ordained. Yet in 787 the Papal Legates do not refuse to acknowledge Sicilian bishops ordained at Constantinople. At the fourth Council of Constantinople (869) Gregory Asbestas of Syracuse is called Archbishop in the Greek acts, but only bishop in the Latin text.[3] However, by this time the dependence of Sicily on Constantinople seems to be admitted. The Patriarch Ignatius sends Theodore of Syracuse to Rome as his Legate;[4] and Nicholas I complains that Gregory Asbestas, in ordaining Photius, had rebelled against " his Patriarch," Ignatius.[5]

Just at the time of the schism of Photius Sicily seems more Greek, its connection in various ways with Constantinople is more evident than ever. Methodios I of Constantinople (842–846), Ignatius' predecessor, was a Greek of Sicily. The originator of the trouble, Gregory Asbestas, who had already a quarrel with Ignatius and then ordained Photius, himself a Greek, was Archbishop of Syracuse.

After Sicily the Emperor began in the same way to detach Apulia and Calabria from Rome, and to join them to Constantinople. This further development seems to have some

[1] For the date of the Byzantine Archbishopric of Syracuse see Rodotà, " Rito greco in Italia," i, 155-158.

[2] In the Acts of Nicæa II, Mansi, xii, col. 1095, Tarasios writes encyclical letters to the Sicilian bishops, treating them as his own subjects. Gay sees in the fact that Tarasios addresses these bishops as συλλειτουργοί evidence that they used the Byzantine rite (" L'Italie méridionale," p. 14, n. 2). I do not think there is much argument in this. One bishop constantly addresses another as συλλειτουργός. It means no more than " fellow-minister."

[3] Mansi, xvi; Greek acts, 381, D; Latin acts, 106, E, 133, C.

[4] Ep. Nicholai I, 86, ad Michaelem Imp. (P.L., cxix, 936, B). The Pope counts Theodore of Syracuse among the Archbishops sent by Ignatius.

[5] Ep. 98, ad Mich. Imp. (P.L., cxix, 1030-1031).

connection with the Moslem conquest of Sicily. By that conquest the Empire lost the island; on the other hand, a great number of Sicilian Greeks, particularly monks, fled to the mainland opposite. This was a further Greek impulse to Calabria and Apulia. Under the Emperors, Leo VI (the Wise, 886–911) and Nikephoros Phokas (963–969), two Byzantine provinces were formed in Calabria, Rhegium and St Severina, and one, Hydruntum, in Apulia. In Apulia the Greek element was less strong; parts of the province, in the North, remained Latin throughout this period.

Luitprand of Cremona, Ambassador at Constantinople in 949 and 968,[1] has this account of the policy of Nikephoros Phokas: " Nikephoros, being an impious man to all Churches, because of his hatred of us, commanded the Patriarch Polyeuktos, of Constantinople,[2] to raise the Church of Hydruntum to the honour of an archbishopric, and not to allow that the divine mysteries throughout Apulia and Calabria be celebrated any longer in Latin, but in Greek. . . . Therefore, Polyeuktos, Patriarch of Constantinople, sent to the Bishop of Hydruntum the privilege that, by his (Polyeuktos') authority, he should have leave to consecrate bishops in Acirentia, Turcicum, Gravina, Materia, Tricaricum,[3] whose consecration belonged to the Apostolicus."[4] With regard to this evidence we should note that, though the main fact he tells is undoubted—namely, the erection of Hydruntum to be the Metropolis of a new Byzantine province in Apulia—there may be reason to doubt the accuracy

[1] Luitprand (Liutprand) was a Lombard of Pavia. He was sent to Constantinople, as a deacon, by Lothar, son of Hugh of Arles, and King of Italy (947-950). This first embassy was in 949. Luitprand became Bishop of Cremona in 962. In 968 the Emperor, Otto I (936-973), sent him a second time to Constantinople to negotiate the marriage between Otto's son, afterwards Otto II (973-983) and Theophania, daughter of the Emperor in the East, Romanos II (959-963). He died, probably, in 971. Luitprand's chief historical work is " Historia gestorum Regum et Imperatorum sive Antapodosis," in six books, from the reign of Charles III (the Fat, 881-887) to 949. During his embassies he had good opportunity of knowing the Greeks. He is bitter against them, as a Lombard naturally would be. There is an amusing account of Luitprand's life and his embassies in G. Schlumberger, " Un Empéreur byzantin au dixième siècle, Nicéphore Phocas " (Paris, 1890), chap. xiii, pp. 577-694. His works are in " Mon. Germ. Hist.," tom. v (*Scriptorum*, tom. iii, Hanover, 1839), pp. 273-363, and P.L., cxxxvi, 769-938.

[2] Polyeuktos of C.P., 956-970.

[3] These cities are now Acerenza, Tursi, Gravina, Matera, Tricarico in Basilicata and North Apulia.

[4] *De Legat. C.P.*, 62 (P.L., cxxxvi, 934, C.)

of his other statement that the use of Latin was forbidden throughout so large a region.[1] Certainly, during the whole of this period of Byzantine aggression, the use of Latin rites, at least in Apulia, never entirely ceased.

The policy of the Emperors, then, was to set up Metropolitans with provinces all over Lower Italy, to see that these were ordained at Constantinople, that they were Greeks, either Greeks from the East or Greeks of Italy or Sicily, to insist that they use the Byzantine rite, and so to detach all this part of the Church from its ancient immediate dependence on Rome. As soon as the Great Schism began the Byzantine Government and Patriarch naturally tried to drag these Greek bishops in Italy with them into schism. Fortunately the Norman conquest, which happened just at that time, prevented the formation of anything like an organized schismatical Church in Italy. At the time of that conquest, however, there are many of these Greek bishops who sympathize with the schismatics at Constantinople and show every disposition to share their schism. The object of the policy of hellenizing the Church was naturally to attach the people the more to the Byzantine Government, and so to fortify Byzantine rule against Lombards, Saracens, and Normans.[2]

But an irreconcilable Latin element remained in the Lombards themselves. They had no tendency to adopt the Byzantine rite or to send their bishops to Constantinople to be ordained. At least, in the Lombards there remained a Latin and Catholic element all the time. In 743 Pope Zachary (741–752) held a provincial synod at Rome. While at this time, as the acts of the second Nicene Synod show, the bishops of Calabria and (in great part) Apulia were reckoned among those of the Byzantine Patriarchate, the Bishops of Tarentum and Cusentia (Cosenza) attended this Roman Synod.[3] These were still Lombard cities.

Nor had the Greek propaganda any success at Naples. Naples was always particularly Roman and Latin in feeling.

---

[1] J. Gay, for instance, doubts Luitprand's accuracy in this point (" L'Italie mérid.," pp. 351-352).

[2] In justice to the Government at Constantinople we must remember that the loyalty of Southern Italy and Sicily was of great political importance. It kept the Eastern Mediterranean open to the Imperial fleet and prevented hostile incursions on the coast of Greece. This point is well brought out by S. Zampelios, Βυζαντῖναι Μελέται (Athens, 1858), pp. 505-506.

[3] Other bishops from Apulia and Calabria attended the Roman Synod of 743 also; see p. 78.

When Leo the Isaurian promulgated his Iconoclast law, the Duke of Naples, Exhilaratus, tried to enforce it in his city. He also made plans to have Pope Gregory II murdered. But the Neapolitans revolted against the edict, and it was Exhilaratus himself who was murdered (728). Then the Patriarch of Constantinople, Anastasios (730–754), offered to make the Bishop of Naples, Sergius (715–c. 744), an Archbishop. He accepted the title; but when the Pope (Gregory III) reproached him for this, he laid it down again and begged pardon.[1] In 763 Pope Paul I (757–767) himself ordained a certain deacon, Paul, to be Bishop of Naples. For fear of the persecution of the Government, Paul had to enter his city secretly at night.[2] When Paul died, the Duke Stephen was elected bishop, with Pope Stephen III's consent, who himself ordained him. Stephen ruled the Church of Naples nearly thirty-three years (767–799). He was a zealous propagator of Latinism.[3] From his time Naples, both in Church and in political matters, remained steadfastly Latin; though the city was always full of Greek strangers.

There were other places, too, where the Byzantine propaganda had no success. We have seen that in 743 a considerable number of bishops from Calabria and Apulia attend a Roman provincial Synod (p. 78). During the reign of Pope Stephen V (885–891) there was an agitation at Tarentum because the Byzantine governor (the " Patritius ") tried to prevent the lawfully elected bishop from going to Rome to be ordained, and to force on the people a Byzantine priest, who should be ordained bishop at Constantinople.[4] When Nikephoros Phokas

---

[1] " Gesta Eppor. Neapol.," i, § 36 (" Mon. Germ. Hist." *Script. rerum Langob. et Ital.*, Hanover, 1878, p. 422). See also L. A. Muratori's note on this text, " Rerum Ital. Script.," tom. i, pt. ii (Milan, 1725), p. 307; Ughelli, " Italia sacra," 2nd edition, vol. vi, 59-60; Assemani, " Italicæ hist. script." (Rome, 1751-1753), iii, 243-244.

[2] " Gesta Episcoporum Neapol.," *op. cit.*, pp. 422-424.

[3] This is Stephen II, Bishop and Duke of Naples. When he became bishop he secured for his sons, Gregory and Cesar, the rank of duke. When Cesar died, Stephen composed an epitaph, which expresses well the attitude of Naples, now practically an independent state, towards the Lombards and the Empire: " Sic blandus Bardis eras ut fœdera Graiis seruares." " Bardi " for Langobardi. J. Gay, " L'Italie mérid.," pp. 18-20. Ughelli quotes the lines in the form: " Sic blandus Bardis erat, ut sua fœdera gratis seruaret sapiens inuiolata tamen " (" Italia sacra," 2nd edition, vi, col. 63; see cols. 62-66 for an account of this Stephen II of Naples).

[4] Jaffé, " Regesta Pont. Rom." (ed. II, Leipzig, 1885-1888), nos. 3436-3437, vol. i, p. 431.

and the Patriarch Polyeuktos tried to bring these Italian bishops under Constantinople and to make them use the Byzantine rite, John of Barum (951–978) refused to submit and kept a Latin (possibly the Roman) rite, recognizing the Pope as his Patriarch.[1] Altogether the Byzantines had less success in Apulia than in Sicily and Calabria. Many of the inland cities of both Apulia and Calabria remained Latin, in some cases because they were held by the Lombards. Cusentia, Bisinianum, Cassanum, Anglona seem never to have used the Byzantine rite, nor to have acknowledged Constantinople as their Patriarchate. It was chiefly in the sea-board towns that the bishops became Byzantine. Rossanum had a Greek chapter and bishop, also Tricaricum.[2]

The plan of the Byzantine Government was to erect archbishoprics and to shower honours on the clergy of Southern Italy and Sicily. In return it demanded that they should look to Constantinople as their Patriarchate and adopt its rite. The reason they give for this is always the same: the Pope is now in the hands of Barbarians; therefore he has lost his rights over these dioceses.

There are a number of Greek lists of provinces and sees (called τακτικά) drawn up between the reigns of Leo VI (the Wise, 886–911) and Andronikos II (Palaiologos, 1282–1328), which show the claim made by Constantinople during this time. It is difficult to date any of these exactly, because additions were made to them at various times. The first is dated 883, under Leo the Wise and Photius Patriarch.[3] Among other provinces it names those of Illyricum, Sicily, and Calabria. " From the Roman diocese detached and now subject to the throne of Constantinople are these Metropolitans with the bishops under them: He of Thessalonica, he of Syracuse, he of Corinth, he of Rhegium, he of Nikopolis

---

[1] See Ughelli, " Italia sacra," vii, 601.

[2] See Rodotà, " Rito greco in Italia," p. 198.

[3] This is the *Notitia I* in Gustav Parthey, " Hierodis Synecdemus et Notitiæ græcæ episcopatuum. Accedunt Nili Doxopatrii Notitia Patriarchatuum et Locorum nomina immutata," Berlin, 1866. H. Gelzer has shown that it is composed from two sources, a description of the civil world by a certain George of Cyprus, in the seventh century, and a list of dioceses compiled by an Armenian monk, Basil, about 840. See Gelzer, " Georgii Cyprii descriptio orbis romani " (Leipzig: Teubner, " Bibl. Script. Gr. et Rom.," 1890), pp. xiii–xv, and his article, " Zur Zeitbestimmung der griech. Notitiæ Episcopatuum " in the *Jahrbücher für Prot. Theol.*, xii (1886), pp. 337–372; 529–575.

(St Severina),[1] he of Athens, he of Patras, he of New Patras. These are added to the Synod and Church of Constantinople, since the Pope of ancient Rome is held by gentiles."[2]   Another of these lists counts under the Byzantine Patriarchate, " the Eparchy of the island of Sicily (Metropolis Catana); Eparchy of Calabria (Rhegium)."[3]   Sicily has at this time fourteen sees: Syracuse, Catana, Tauromenion, Messana, Cephalœdium (Κεφαλούδιον, Cefalù), Thermæ,[4] Panormus, Lilybæum, Trikala,[5] Akragas (Girgenti), Tyndaris,[6] Leontinoi,[7] Alesa,[8] the island Malta. All these are counted as Byzantine sees. In the beginning of the ninth century the Armenian monk Basil writes: " These Metropolitans with their bishops were taken from the Roman diocese and subjected to the throne of Constantinople: Thessalonica, Syracuse, Corinth, Rhegium, Nikopolis (St Severina), Athens, Patras; because the Pope of old Rome is in the hands of Barbarians."[9]

After the Norman conquest the Greek Archimandrite Neilos Doxopatres[10] at Palermo, in his account of the division of Christendom between the five Patriarchates, admits that originally " Apulia, Calabria, and all the Campagna " were under the Roman Patriarch, also " Pannonia and all Illyricum, Macedonia and Thrace, whereas Byzantium and all the rest of the West in the same way belonged to the Roman."[11]   His view is that Rome obtained her position because she was the Imperial city.   " But when she ceased to be the Empress, because she was enslaved by foreigners and barbarous people and Goths, and being still under these as one who had lost the Empire, then she lost both her privileges and her Primacy."[12] So Neilos thinks that Constantinople has inherited the rights

---

[1] The Greeks began to call Sancta Severina (ἡ ἀγία Σεβερίνη) Νικόπολις after Nikephoros Phokas had conquered it from the Moslems (886).   [2] Parthey, op. cit., p. 74 (P.G., cvii, 340).

[3] The eighth Notitia in Parthey (op. cit., p. 162). Catana as metropolis of Sicily is puzzling. Otherwise the Metropolis is always Syracuse.

[4] Thermæ Himerenses, now Termini Imerese, on the coast between Palermo and Cefalù.

[5] Τροκαλείς = Τριόκαλα, Τρίκαλα, between Sciacca and Porto Empedocle, on the south-west coast. There is nothing now left of this city.

[6] There is now only a Capo Tindaro, on the North coast, by Patti.

[7] Now Lentini, between Catania and Syracuse.

[8] Ἄλεσα = Ἄλαισα, Halesa, on the North coast, East of Cefalù; only ruins now remain.

[9] Gelzer, " Georgii Cypr. descr.," p. 27.   [10] See p. 93.

[11] Ed. Parthey, p. 271.   [12] Ibid., p. 289.

of Rome.[1] In the list he draws up of sees under the Patriarch of Constantinople he counts " from the Western land two Exarchs who have now submitted themselves to him of Constantinople "—namely, the Bishops of Thessalonica and of Corinth. " But also Sicily, after this, and Calabria, came under him of Constantinople, and St Severina, which is also called Nikopolis. All Sicily had one Metropolitan, him of Syracuse. . . . Calabria also has one Metropolitan, him of Rhegium."[2] Yet Neilos counts St Severina as a Metropolis, having sees under it.[3] He adds: " These Churches are described in the lists (τακτικά) of the Nomocanon under the throne of Constantinople. . . . Therefore the sees of Sicily, Calabria, and of St Severina have been taken away from the Roman and added to the Byzantine throne, when the Barbarians, having seized the Pope, made Rome their spoil and turned it to their own use."[4] " Nevertheless," he says, " the Pope is found to retain some mean places and certain bishoprics in Sicily and Calabria; but the Byzantine possessed the Metropolitan cities and the more famous and illustrious ones, till the Franks (Normans) came. So also in Langobardia[5] and Apulia, and in all those parts, Constantinople once held the chief cities, Rome the others."[6] He says that " Langobardy," " which was old Greece, was once under the Emperor (namely, before the Lombards came). The Pope lived apart under other nations; therefore the Patriarch obtained these Churches. For Brundisium and Tarentum received their bishops from Constantinople; no one is ignorant of this. But when the Franks occupied this Duchy, then the Roman held ordinations in all these Churches. In all those regions which the Emperor at Constantinople held, or afterwards conquered from foreign races, the Constantinopolitan ordained by right, while Rome, alien from Constantinople in every way, subjected others to herself."[7] Neilos then draws up a long list of sees subject to Constantinople. Among these are " Rhegium of Calabria, having thirteen sees," " Syracuse of Sicily, having twenty-one sees," " Catana, being an episcopate under Syracuse, has

---

[1] Ed. Parthey, p. 289.   [2] *Ibid.*, pp. 293-294.

[3] *Ibid.*, p. 294. He seems to distinguish the province of St Severina from Calabria.

[4] *Ibid.*, p. 294.

[5] For this " Langobardia " (not our Lombardy), see p. 58.

[6] *Ibid.*, p. 295.

[7] Neilos Doxopatres, Τάξις τῶν πατρ. θρόνων, ed. Parthey, p. 295.

been honoured because of St Leo."[1] " St Severina of Calabria[2] has five sees."[3]

In all this we have a good example of the Byzantine attitude of that time. There is, first, frank acknowledgement that originally the sees of Southern Italy and Sicily were under the Pope (whether as Patriarch or as Metropolitan); but, because he is no longer in the Roman Empire (of the East, the Empire whose capital was Constantinople), therefore he has lost all his rights. He is in the hands of Lombards, Goths, or Normans, whom the Byzantines pleasantly dismiss as Barbarians. We see also the typically Byzantine idea that politics must settle the whole question of ecclesiastical order. Wherever the Emperor holds territory the bishops in that territory must depend on the Emperor's Patriarch. Neilos did not foresee that three hundred years later his principles would fall with much greater force on the Patriarch in whose favour he writes. If to be in the hands of Barbarians be a reason for taking away a Patriarch's jurisdiction, what would become of that of Constantinople after 1453 ? It is a curious point, worth noticing, how the unchanging Byzantine habit of making Church affairs depend on those of the state, their invariable practice of founding ecclesiastical rights on the splendour of the Emperor would react against themselves, as soon as there was no longer an Emperor. But Constantinople has never thought of applying its principles to its own case since the Turks came.

We have, then, as the general situation, that from the time of the first Iconoclast persecution, under the Emperor Leo III (717–741), till the Norman conquest of Southern Italy (beginning about 1030), there was a determined attempt on the part of the Emperors and Patriarchs at Constantinople to detach Sicily, Calabria and Apulia from their ancient obedience to the Roman Pontiff, and to make the Church in these parts dependent on the See of Constantinople. With this dependence, shown mainly in the ordination of the bishops at Constantinople, went naturally the use of the Byzantine rite. The object of this movement was to unite these provinces more closely to the capital. Its chief moments were Leo III's

---

[1] St Leo, Bishop of Catana, † c. 780. His feast, in the Byz. Menaia and the Roman Martyrology, is February 20. See Nilles, " Kalendarium manuale," i, 108; L. di Brolo, " Storia d. Chiesa in Sicilia," ii, cap. vi, pp. 121-135. St Leo of Catana's Life is in the *Acta Sanctorum*, February III, pp. 227-229.

[2] ʽΗ ἁγία Σεβερίνη τῆς Καλαβρίας.

[3] Neilos, ed. Parthey, pp. 300, 303.

attempt after he promulgated his first Iconoclast edict (*c.* 732), and Basil I's attempt further to carry out the same plan in Calabria and Apulia, after he had reconquered these from the Saracens (875); whereas, meanwhile, the Saracens had seized all Sicily (827–965). Through this a great number of Sicilian Greeks, especially monks, came to the mainland and so fortified the Greek element there. Then we have a further Hellenization under Nikephoros Phokas (963–969).

The Popes Adrian I (772–795)[1] and Nicholas I (858–867)[2] protested against this spoliation of their province. But their protests are rather against the robbery of the patrimony of the Holy See in Sicily and Calabria. They do not seem to have done much to prevent the change of jurisdiction. Only from this time they begin to establish Latin provinces, as an answer to those set up by Constantinople. John XIII (965–972) made archbishoprics at Naples, Amalfi, Capua, Benevento, Salerno, with suffragans.[3] From now the Latin bishops are no longer immediate suffragans of the Pope; they, too, have their own provinces. These Latin provinces were chiefly for the Lombards; but there are curious cases of cross jurisdiction between them and the Byzantine bishops, and cases of an understanding between the two hierarchies.[4]

This usurpation of Constantinople did not of itself lead to a schism. Schism is breach of communion. As long as there is no such breach there is no schism; though there may be acts which would naturally lead to one. The usurpation of Constantinople, though obviously a gross injury to the Holy See, did not itself affect any essential point of faith or morals. One cannot say that there is any essential reason why bishops in any part of the Church should obey one Patriarch rather than another. These are matters of ecclesiastical discipline which may, and often do, change. So the Popes seem to have been willing, in order to avoid greater evils, to tolerate the new arrangements made by the Emperors, in what was politically imperial territory.

Just about the time of this Byzantine aggression in Italy

[1] Jaffé, "Regesta Pont. Rom." (2nd edition, Leipzig, 1885-1888), tom. i, no. 2448.

[2] P.L., cxix, 779, B.

[3] Gay, "L'Italie méridionale et l'Empire byzantin," pp. 353-354.

[4] Gay, *op. cit.*, pp. 188-190. He suggests, for instance, that the Bishops of Cusentia and Bisinianum were elected by the local Lombard (Latin) clergy, went to Rhegium to be ordained (according to the Byzantine rite) by the Greek Metropolitan, but used the Roman rite themselves when they came back home.

came the beginning of the great schism between Constantinople
and Rome.   No doubt, had it not been for the Norman conquest, which reversed the whole development, these Greek
bishops in Italy would have fallen into schism with their new
Patriarch.   As it was, the Normans prevented that.   I do not
think we can charge the Greeks in Italy at this time with
schism, though we see that many of them were on the high road
to it.   It is generally difficult to say exactly at what moment
an outlying province of the Church becomes schismatical.
There is usually a period in which the schism is forming at
headquarters, while the provinces hardly, if at all, realize what
is happening.   At any rate, we can never charge a man with
schism till he has broken, and knows he has broken, communion
with the Holy See.   That does not seem to have happened in
Italy or Sicily.   In fact, the beginning of the great schism is
particularly hard to define in the case of the dependent
Byzantine bishoprics.

Did the first schism, of Photius, affect them at all ?   Certainly, when the synod of 869 deposed Photius, the other
Eastern Patriarchs and bishops then declared that they had had
no idea of going into schism against the Pope.   If they at the
time had not also condemned Photius, it was only because they
considered that the Pope's sentence alone was enough.[1]

It is even more difficult to define a moment at which the
Church in the East became schismatical in the second schism,
that of Michael Cerularius in the eleventh century.   No Pope
has ever excommunicated the Eastern or the Byzantine Church
as such.   The excommunication of the year 1054 was directed
carefully only against Cerularius and his followers.   If other
bishops in the East have also incurred this excommunication,
it is only because, deliberately, they made themselves supporters
of the schismatical party at Constantinople.[2]   The Patriarch
of Antioch, Peter III (1053), though he was in sympathy with
Cerularius, certainly did not intend to go into schism with the
Pope, nor did he ever do so.[3]   In much the same way we may
say that the Greeks of Lower Italy and Sicily, though their
sympathies were with Constantinople, though many of them
had views which would easily have led them into schism, though
no doubt they would have been so led in time had the Normans
not come, nevertheless were never actually schismatics.   They
did not, as a matter of fact, break communion with the Holy
See.   As an example how far some of them went along the

---

[1] " Orth. Eastern Church," pp. 157-158.
[2] Ibid., p. 185.   [3] Ibid., pp. 188-192.

road which would have led them into schism eventually, we may see the ideas of Neilos Doxapatres,[1] whom I have already quoted.

This worthy was Archimandrite at Palermo at the time of the Norman conquest. Afterwards he went to Constantinople, where he became Notary and Nomophylax of the Great Church.[2] While he was still at Palermo he wrote a book about the Patriarchates, which he calls " The Order of the Patriarchal Thrones."[3] His views on the Papacy are distinctly heretical. It is significant of the attitude of the first Norman kings of Sicily that he wrote this work by command of King Roger II. It was written in the year 1143. We have already seen what Neilos Doxapatres has to say about Byzantine sees in Italy and Sicily.[4] Here I add his ideas on the question of Church government in general. He knows that originally there were only three Patriarchates, Rome, Alexandria, and Antioch. He thinks that these three were in every way equal. No one of the Patriarchs " dared to put his foot into the diocese of another, nor to ordain in it, nor to arrange any sacred matter."[5] He thinks that when Jerusalem was made a Patriarchate it was taken from Alexandria.[6] He counts the Churches of Cyprus and Bulgaria as autocephalous.[7] But, he says, five Patriarchates were necessary, because our body has five senses.[8] Therefore the Synods of Constantinople I and Chalcedon erected a Patriarchate at Constantinople.[9] He denies absolutely that the Pope inherits any rights from St Peter. The Pope's position was due solely to the fact that Rome was the Imperial city. So when it ceased to be that, when it fell into the hands of Barbarians, all the Pope's privileges and his Primacy fell with it. Constantinople is the new Rome; it has all the rights of old Rome, therefore the Patriarch of Constantinople " obtained the privileges and Primacy of Rome."

---

[1] The printed editions of his work call him Doxopatrios. Other forms that occur are Doxapatros, Doxapatrì, Doxopater, τοῦ δόξα πατρί. Krumbacher says his name should be Νεῖλος Δοξαπατρῆς (" Byzantinische Litteraturgeschichte," 2nd edition, Munich, 1897, pp. 462-463). I am not quite convinced by his reasons; but one cannot do better than follow Krumbacher in such a matter.

[2] For his career see Krumbacher, *op. cit.*, p. 415.

[3] Τάξις τῶν πατριαρχικῶν θρόνων, in P.G., cxxxii, cols. 1083-1114 and Parthey, " Hieroclis Synecdemus," etc. (Berlin, 1866), pp. 256-308.

[4] Pp. 88-90.   [5] Ed. Parthey, p. 278.   [6] P. 281.

[7] P. 285.

[8] This is a favourite Byzantine idea at that time; see " Orth. Eastern Church," p. 46, n. 2.   [9] *Op. cit.*, pp. 286-287.

That is why he is called Œcumenical.[1] Once Rome had received appellations. Now that Constantinople has obtained the rights of Rome, that Patriarch has jurisdiction over the other Patriarchs.[2] It is easy to see on which side Neilos would have been, had he been conscious of schism between old and new Rome. As a matter of fact, in the latter part of his life, when he was at Constantinople, he was conscious of this. He certainly ended as a schismatic.[3] His views, in those earlier days, when he was at Palermo, show the tendency of the Greek clergy of Sicily.

4. From the Norman Conquest to the Coming of the Albanians (Eleventh to Fifteenth Century).

The first Norman kings and princes in Southern Italy and Sicily found established here a powerful body of Greek bishops, clergy, and people, who used the Byzantine rite and looked to Constantinople as their centre. They found, indeed, three religious establishments, those of the Latins (Lombards and others), Greeks, and Moslems. The Latins and Greeks were not yet two Churches; but they were becoming so. The Normans, however, turned back the tide towards Rome, so that from the time of their coming the Byzantine rite gradually retired. It had almost disappeared in Italy and Sicily, when in the fifteenth century the Albanians came and caused its great revival.

The Norman kings did not begin by forbidding or in any way persecuting the Byzantine rite. They found these three forms of religion in possession; and they, alone among mediæval sovereigns, followed a policy of absolute toleration for all. In their hearts the first Normans probably cared very little about any religious rite. They continued to maintain all institutions as they found them; the cynical Roger II much preferred the conversation of learned Moslem divines to that of a lot of monks.[4] He had Moslem men of letters, Byzantine preachers, and Latin chaplains at his court. There are even cases in which the Normans restored Byzantine institutions which were disappearing.[5] But, in spite of their tolerance, under them the tide turned finally towards Rome. The Normans themselves were Latins of the Roman rite. Their

---

[1] Ed. Parthey, pp. 289-292.   [2] P. 292.

[3] Morisani calls poor Neilos Doxopatres " this schismatical sycophant " (" de Protopapis," p. 191).

[4] So says Ibnu-lAthīr alGazarī, " Kāmilu-tTawārīkh," in M. Amari, " Biblioteca arabo-sicula " (Turin and Rome, 1880), i, p. 118.

[5] See p. 65.

alliance with the Papacy was their chief asset; whatever right they had in these parts came to them only from a Papal grant. So under these kings the Pope easily recovered his ancient rights in Southern Italy and Sicily. As far as the jurisdiction of the Patriarch of Constantinople went, that disappeared with the civil power of the Emperor. The Normans allowed no traffic with Constantinople. Then, since the great schism was just beginning, they also prevented the people of their territories from drifting into that. From the time of the Norman conquest, whatever use of the Byzantine rite may remain, all the Christians are Catholics in communion with the Pope.

Already before the Norman conquest the Western Emperor Otto I (936–973) had promised to restore the Patrimony of the Holy See in Lower Italy and Sicily, if he should have the power.[1] The Norman kings, in their treaties and arrangements with the Popes, came to a friendly agreement about these possessions. Further, under the Normans the Pope used again his ancient right of ordaining the bishops of their kingdom. Paschal II (1099–1118) says that Robert Wiscard and his brother Roger I arranged this.[2] Roger I himself bears witness that the Pope ordains the bishops.[3] Gregory VII (1073–1085) refers to the fact that in his time the bishops of Sicily come to Rome to be ordained.[4] Romuald of Salerno[5] says of the year 1150: " King Roger (II) ordered that the archbishops and bishops of his land be consecrated by Pope Eugene " (III, 1145–1153).[6] But William II of Sicily (1166–1189) wanted the Archbishop of Palermo, Walter (1170–c. 1187), to be ordained by his own suffragans, after the manner of an autocephalous bishop. Pope Alexander III (1159–1181) at first protested, but eventually agreed to this.[7] Indeed, from this time the old

[1] Baronius, ad ann. 962 (tom. xvi, p. 121).

[2] The text is quoted in Rodotà, " del Rito greco," i, 300.

[3] " The Bishop of the Apostolic See himself approving, granting, and consecrating the bishops." Ibid., p. 301.

[4] Ep. ix, 24, ad Robertum Com. (P.L., cxlviii, 625-626). Although the Archb. of Reggio should ordain the Bp. of Mileto, Gregory himself will ordain him of Traiana (Troina in Sicily).

[5] Romuald Guarna, a Lombard, Archbishop of Salerno (1153-1181) wrote a " Chronicon seu Annales." Like so many of the mediæval chronicles, it tells the history of the world, more or less, from the Creation; but it has value for the history of Italy in his own time. It ends with the year 1178. Romuald's " Chronicon " is printed in Muratori, " Rerum Italic. Scriptores," vii, cols. 7-224.

[6] Ad annum 1145, " Rer. It. Scrip.," vii, col. 193, B.

[7] See the quotation in F. Scorsa's Preface to the homilies of Theophanes Kerameus, ii, § 7 (P.G., cxxxii, 107).

custom that the bishops of these parts should go to Rome to be ordained gradually dies out. Neilos Doxapatres says that the Pope ordained all the bishops after the Norman conquest;[1] yet Gregory VII refused to ordain the Bishop of Mileto in 1081, explaining that this is the right of the Archbishop of Reggio.[2]

Instead of the old state of things, according to which all Southern Italy and Sicily were part of the Roman Metropolitan province, we come now to the establishment of Latin archbishops with their separate provinces in these parts. The country remains part of the Roman Patriarchate; it is no longer part of the Roman province. The Normans also brought back the Roman rite to those Churches which had been made Byzantine by the Eastern Emperors. They built many new churches and monasteries; in most cases, they arranged that the services in these should be carried out according to the Roman rite.

One famous example of this is the monastery built by Roger I in 1090 at Messina. He made this subject to the monastery S Maria de Latina at Jerusalem; the monastery at Messina was also S Maria de Latina.[3] Roger also subjected the Byzantine clergy of his domain to the Roman Ordinaries. Rodotà quotes a number of his diplomas to this effect.[4] He did away with the privilege by which many Byzantine monasteries had been *Stauropegia*—that is, independent of diocesan authority, subject directly to the Patriarch of Constantinople—and put all the Byzantine monasteries under the Latin bishops. This seems rather a hardship, since there were many Latin monasteries independent of the ordinary, directly subject to the Pope. However, it was difficult to do anything else. The Byzantine monasteries could not remain subject to the Patriarch now that the Patriarch had become a schismatic. They might, perhaps, have been made immediately subject to the Holy See, like the Latin ones.

The Synod of Melfi in 1059 was a considerable factor in the restoration of the Roman rite after the Norman conquest. Melfi is a city on a hill between Benevento and Venoso. The Normans in 1042 made this their first capital in Apulia, and

---

[1] Ed. Parthey, p. 296, " Since the Franks occupy this duchy [Longobardia] the Roman holds ordinations in all these churches."

[2] See above, p. 95, n. 4.

[3] For the history of this monastery see Rodotà, " del Rito greco," i, 309-310.　　　　　　　　　　　[4] *Ibid.*, i, 317-318.

they built a most beautiful fortified city with a rampart and gates, a church, and a strong citadel at the highest point of the hill.[1] Here Pope Nicholas II (1058–1061) held a synod, soon after the Norman conquest, to arrange the new state of things. The Pope arrived in July, 1059, with the subdeacon Hildebrand (afterwards Gregory VII), three Cardinals, and a large retinue. Robert Wiscard met him here, with Richard Count of Aversa and Capua,[2] and many soldiers. There were two objects in this synod. The first was to restore ecclesiastical discipline, especially in the matter of clerical celibacy. It is a case of the application of the principles of Cluny, of which later Gregory VII was to be the great champion, to Southern Italy, where celibacy was in a particularly dangerous state. Side by side with the Roman priests were those of the Byzantine rite, who could lawfully be married. Their example was always felt to be dangerous for the Latins. The other object of the synod was to arrange the treaty between the Normans and the Holy See. The Pope made severe laws in favour of clerical celibacy among the Latins; he then determined the limits of the Norman territories; invested Robert Wiscard with these lands; while he, for his part, took an oath of fidelity to the Pope, recognized that he held his lands as a fief of the Holy See, and promised various privileges to the clergy.[3]

But not all the bishoprics at once became Latin. *Gerace* (Hieracium) in Calabria, for instance, kept Byzantine bishops for some time after the Norman conquest.[4] Roger I of Sicily restored the See of *Rossano* to the Pope's jurisdiction and appointed a Latin bishop. Then, in 1092, he gave way to the feeling of the people and allowed them to have a Byzantine Metropolitan, too. By 1293 the Latin see had become an archbishopric; there remained two Ordinaries, the Latin Archbishop and the Byzantine Metropolitan, till the fifteenth century (p. 109).

St Severina had been made a Metropolis during the time of the Byzantine power. The Normans reduced it again to a simple bishopric; but the bishop remained a Greek till after

[1] There is a picture of Norman Melfi in Curtis, " Roger of Sicily " (Putnam, 1912), p. 46.

[2] This Richard was the chief of the other line of Norman adventurers, eventually crushed by the de Hautevilles; see p. 62.

[3] The Synod of Melfi in 1059 is one of the important Italian synods of the eleventh century. Its acts are in Mansi, xix, 919–922; See also Hefele-Leclercq, " Histoire des Conciles," iv (Pt. ii), pp. 1180–1189.

[4] See below, p. 98.

the twelfth century.[1]   *Bova* in Calabria had Byzantine bishops till the sixteenth century (p, 109), *Oppido* (p. 108) and Gerace till the fifteenth (p. 108).   In Sicily, too, there remained Byzantine diocesan bishops for some time after the Normans came.   Under the Normans there was a Nicodemus, Archbishop of Palermo, who was a Greek.   Leo Allatius says: " In the time of Roger there were many Greek bishops in Sicily, as can be proved by the Ectypus of Roger. . . .   No one can doubt that at that time there remained many Greeks in Sicily, or that the Greek bishops were not yet replaced by Latin ones."[2]

But these cases were the exception.   The general trend after the Norman conquest was that the Byzantine bishops were succeeded by Latins.   The See of *Otranto* became Latin in the eleventh century.   It remained an archbishopric and had new Latin suffragans.[3]   At *Gallipoli* there were alternately Latin and Byzantine bishops.[4]   Roger I changed the See of *Reggio* from Byzantine to Roman; Gregory VII confirmed its rank as an archiepiscopal see (but a Latin one) in 1081.[5]   At *Squillace* (Scyllatium) Roger I built a new cathedral; when its Byzantine bishop, Theodore Mesmer, died in 1096, he appointed a Latin successor, John de Nicephoro.[6]   The See of *Tropea* became Latin in 1094, under the Bishop Iustego.[7]   In Sicily, although Roger I expressly said he would tolerate the Byzantine rite, yet he used influence to make the people accept that of Rome.   In short, the policy of the first Norman kings seems to have been to avoid anything like open hostility to the rite of Constantinople; while prudently, where they could, they introduced that of Rome.

Meanwhile the Patriarchs of Constantinople went on count-

---

[1] It is not known at what date the See of St Severina became Latin.   There is a letter of Innocent III (1198-1216) in which he says that the Canons of St Severina are not bound to observe celibacy, " cum sint Græci " (Regest. xiv, Ep. 99.   Migne, P.L., ccxvi, 462, D ann. 1211).   In the thirteenth century the see again became an archbishopric; possibly then it adopted the Roman rite.   At any rate, in the sixteenth century Card. Santoro, Archbishop of St Severina (p. 113) was a Latin, though he had Byzantine clergy in his diocese. For this see, *cf.* Ughelli, " Italia sacra " (2nd edition), vol. ix (Venice, 1721), cols. 473-493.

[2] " De Symeonum scriptis diatriba " (P.G., cxiv, 60, B-C).

[3] Rodotà, " del Rito greco," i, 374-379; Ughelli, " Italia sacra " (2nd edition), ix, 51-67.

[4] Rodotà, i, 386-388; Ughelli, ix, 98-110.

[5] Rodotà, i, 402-411; Ughelli, ix, 315-338.

[6] Rodotà, i, 411-413; Ughelli, ix, 422-448.

[7] Rodotà, i, 413; Ughelli, ix, 448-472.

ing the Sees of Sicily and Italy as part of their Patriarchate, keeping up a futile theoretic claim to them for centuries after they had lost all authority there.[1] But, when a diocese received a Latin bishop, it did not follow that all the clergy of the diocese were Latins. Under the Latin bishops there remained Byzantine churches, Byzantine priests, monasteries, and institutions of various kinds, all through the Middle Ages. At first, large numbers of the people continued to worship God according to the Byzantine rite. These Greek institutions (in many cases) came to an end at last; but some of them lasted on till the coming of the Albanians in the fifteenth century, thus forming a link between the older Greek churches here and the new wave of the Byzantine rite. Indeed, there are still in Italy one monastery and many curious relics of the old Byzantine influence, apart from the new Albanian settlers who now form the main Byzantine element.

At *Naples* in the thirteenth century there were still six parish churches of the Byzantine rite;[2] a document of the year 1305 speaks of the " assembly of priests, Greek and Latin," of the church of St January ad Diaconiam, " in regione Furcillense."[3]

In the thirteenth century *Altamura* was a tiny village. The Emperor Frederick II (1215–1250) in 1232 restored this place, and made it an asylum for many Greeks dispersed throughout the province of Lecce. They used the Byzantine rite and built three churches for it.[4] *Reggio* was particularly tenacious of its Byzantine use. After the Metropolitan see had become Latin,[5] it still had Byzantine suffragans. Alexander III (1159–1181) in 1165, in confirming the use of the Pallium by Roger, Archbishop of Reggio (*c.* 1146–*c.* 1165), expressly gave him the right of ordaining suffragans " both Latin and Greek."[6] So the Third Lateran Council in 1179 names among the bishops who attended it two: " Philippus Crotonias (*al.* Crotomas) græcus, Leratinus (*al.* Eterantinus), Episcopus græcus,"

---

[1] The names of the sees in Italy and Sicily do not disappear from the Byzantine τακτικά till the fall of Constantinople in 1453.

[2] Cesare d'Engenio Caracciolo, "Napoli sacra" (Naples, 1624), gives their names (p. 14). He thinks all were built by Constantine. The clergy of these churches had the duty of chanting the Greek lessons at the Cathedral (alternate with Latin) on Holy Saturday, and the Creed in Greek on Easter Day.

[3] *Ibid.*, p. 339. For Naples see Ughelli, vi, 7-216; Rodotà, i, 329-354.

[4] Rodotà, i, 368-372. [5] See above, p. 98.

[6] Ughelli, " Italia sacra " (2nd edition), ix, 325.

both of the province of Reggio.[1]   For the " Greek " canons of
St Severina in the thirteenth century, see above (p. 98, n. 1).

In Sicily, too, long after the bishops had become Latins,
there remained under them Byzantine clergy.   In 1082 Count
Roger I submits to the Bishop of *Traina* " all the priests of his
diocese, both Latin and Greek."   In 1093 the Archbishop of
Syracuse has under him " priests and clerks, both Greek and
Latin."[2]   At Palermo and Messina the Byzantine rite remained a long time.   At *Palermo* there were under the Norman
kings two Greek chapters, ruled by a " Protopapas."   There
are documents naming these of the years 1164 and 1190.[3]   The
famous church S Maria dell' Ammiraglio at Palermo[4] was
served by eight canons of the Byzantine rite, at least till the
thirteenth century.   Pope Honorius III (1216-1227), in 1221,
says that " this church is to be served only by the Rector and
Greek clergy."   *Messina* kept the Byzantine rite in some
churches till the seventeenth century (p. 111).

M. Jules Gay has found in the Vatican archives two lists
of contributions, to be paid to the Holy See from Calabria
and the extreme South of Apulia (the " Terra d' Otranto "),
dated 1326-1328 and 1373.[5]   Although these lists are incomplete, they give a good idea of the extension of the Byzantine
rite at that time.   As one would expect, it is found, then,
chiefly in the Basilian monasteries.[6]   Yet there are still a
number of institutions, chapters, and " Protopapatus."[7]   In
the diocese of Reggio there are twenty-nine clerks (in the city
itself) of the Roman rite, and thirty-seven " Greek clerks of the
city of Reggio "; in the rest of the diocese are thirty-two Latin
canons and clerks and thirty-nine Byzantines; also ten
Byzantine monasteries and three convents of nuns.   In the
diocese of Tropea there are twenty-six Byzantine clerks.   At
Oppido is one monastery;[8] at Gerace two Greek canons, four

[1] Mansi, xxii, 462, A; *cf*. Harduin, vi (Pt. 2), 2057, D.   " Crotonias " apparently means Bishop of Crotone.
[2] Rodotà, i, 454.
[3] *Ibid*.
[4] The " Martorana " church, built in 1143 by George of Antioch,
Admiral of the Fleet to Roger I.   From 1433 it was the chapel of a
convent founded by Aloisia Martorana.
[5] Published by him in the *Byzantinische Zeitschrift*, iv (1895),
pp. 59-66, " Notes sur la conservation du rite grec dans la Calabre et
dans la terre d'Otrante au XIVe siècle."   [6] See pp. 124 *seq*.
[7] The title " Protopapa " does not prove that the Byzantine rite was
still used.   These Greek titles often remain after the Roman rite has
been introduced.
[8] I count the Byzantine institutions only.

Protopapæ; and eleven monasteries in the diocese. At Catanzaro are twenty-nine Greek priests, three Protopapæ, two monasteries. At Nicastro two Protopapæ, five monasteries. At Squillace sixteen priests, four Protopapæ, five monasteries. At Cotrone are priests of the Byzantine rite. Nothing is said of the rite in the dioceses of St Severina, Belcastro, Cosenza, Cassano, Bisignano. But the notices of these are short. At Rossano are the two monasteries, S Maria del Patire (p. 127) and St Adrian. The Byzantine rite in the fourteenth century seems to have maintained itself most of all at Reggio. It had not yet in any way given place to that of Rome here. Outside the province of Reggio, where the Byzantine rite still remains in Calabria, it has already become an exception, rather than the rule. Thus, among the numerous clergy of the diocese of Cassano there is but one Greek priest. The other list, for the land of Otranto in 1373, notes eight Protopapæ and one Byzantine monastery in the diocese of Otranto. In that of Nardo " Greek and Latin " clergy are named. There are ten Protopapæ and eleven monasteries. For the other dioceses of the land of Otranto the indications are vague.

During the Middle Ages Sicily, Calabria, and Apulia were channels of Greek learning for the West. Thus, Roger Bacon (1214–1294), in his *Compendium studii philosophici*, writes concerning the interpretation of the Greek Bible: " There are many in England and France who are sufficiently instructed; nor would it be a great thing, for the sake of so useful a work, to go to Italy, where the clergy and people in many places are purely Greek. Bishops and Archbishops, and rich people and elders, could send there for books, and for one or more men who know Greek, as Lord Robert, the holy Bishop of Lincoln,[1] was accustomed to do. Of these some are still alive in England at this time."[2]

After the fourteenth century the decadence of the Byzantine rite in Italy went on apace; so that only few remnants of it were left when, in the fifteenth, the Albanian colonists brought it back. We shall return to these Albanians later (pp. 115-124). Meanwhile, it will be convenient first to trace the gradual disappearance of the older Greek element, which had existed

[1] Robert Grosseteste (1235-1253).
[2] " Fr. Rogeri Bacon Opus Tertium," etc., ed. J. S. Brewer (" Rerum Britan. medii æui Scriptores," London, 1859), p. 434; *cf. Ibid.*, p. 33 (in the " Opus Tertium "), " Italy was Greater Greece and still traces remain; for in Calabria and Apulia and Sicily and elsewhere there are many Greek churches and people belonging to them."

here since the days of Leo the Isaurian, or even from the earliest period of Christianity in Italy.

After the Albanians had come the distinction between them and the older Byzantine element was still clear. Thus the Archdeacon of Spoleto writes to Cardinal Santoro in 1577: " You know that there are, in the diocese of Otranto, several lands and villages, which from time immemorial have always been Greek. These are called Italo-Greeks; they are natives of the land, going back to Minos and Diomede. They are not a collection of vagabonds, Albanians, Slavs, or schismatics. They are faithful, since the earliest times, to their special religion, which is considerably different from that of the East."[1] Mgr. Giuseppe Schirò, former Archbishop of Durazzo, in his notice about the Italo-Greeks sent to Rome in 1742,[2] makes the same distinction.

It is not surprising that the Byzantine rite in Italy should gradually die out. For one thing there were no bishops of this rite. Those who followed it were subject to Latin Ordinaries. It was not till the need became pressing, through the coming of the Albanians, that the Holy See established ordaining bishops for the Italo-Greeks. Even then, as we shall see, these had no jurisdiction (p. 123). Before that, sometimes a wandering Greek bishop from the Levant was invited to ordain, sometimes such travelling prelates usurped jurisdiction over those of their rite in Italy; generally, in spite of the canons, the Italo-Greek clergy were ordained according to the Latin rite by the Ordinaries. Naturally these Ordinaries preferred their own rite, and tried to put down what seemed so startling an exception to the uniformity of their dioceses.

Then the neighbours of the Italo-Greeks neither understood nor liked their ways. Nearly all Christians of the Byzantine rite were schismatics and bitter opponents of the Papacy. It is not surprising that there should be suspicion of those in Italy who

---

[1] Quoted by Jules Gay in the *Revue d'hist. et de lit. relig.*, ii (1897), p. 491.

[2] In the archives of the Greek college at Rome, printed by Cyril Karalevsky (Charon), " Documenti inediti per servire alla storia delle chiese italo-greche " (Rome, Bretschneider, 1911), fasc. i, pp. 5-15, and in the review *Roma e l'Oriente* (Grottaferrata), vii (1914), pp. 282-285; 340-349. This notice, sent in answer to questions by an unknown person (probably a Cardinal of Propaganda) shortly before the publication of Benedict XIV's Constitution *Etsi pastoralis* (May 26, 1742), gives a valuable account of the state of the Italo-Greeks in the first half of the eighteenth century. There are MS. copies of it at Grottaferrata and in the archive of the church at Piana dei Greci (see p. 165). For Schirò see p. 117, n. 3.

used a rite now associated with schism. The Italo-Greeks were looked upon as an inferior caste, tainted with schism; they were always suspect of sharing the heretical views of the East on such questions as that of Purgatory and the Papacy. One of the great disputes between Catholics and Orthodox was whether the use of azyme bread for the Eucharist be lawful. The Italo-Greeks were suspect from the very fact that their bread was leavened; though, of course, this does not really imply any wrong view about azyme.

Lastly, the preponderance of the surrounding Roman rite had a tendency to overwhelm that of Constantinople. The Byzantine parishes were few and scattered. It was difficult and annoying for the Italo-Greeks to have to seek a priest of their own rite, or to abstain from receiving Sacraments. It was so much simpler to conform to the common use of the country. So we find always the same story. The bishops put down the Byzantine rite in one place; in another the Latin neighbours protest against it, and suspect its users of all kinds of heresies; in yet another the Italo-Greeks themselves, weary of annoyance and suspicion, petition the Holy See that they may turn Latin. The really curious point to notice in the whole story is how extremely unwilling the Popes were to let these people do so. They could have crushed the whole Byzantine rite in Italy, over and over again, with the greatest possible ease, making all Italy Latin. That is what most Protestants think Popes always want to do. The truth is the exact contrary. In this case, too, Rome was faithful to its traditional policy. The Popes have never made the slightest attempt to Romanize people of other rites.[1] They show always the most complete indifference to the rite a man uses. Indeed, if anything, it would seem as if Popes rather disliked a man turning Latin. At any rate, they keep to the principle that a man should remain faithful to his own rite, not lightly changing it. It is true that there are a few cases in which a Pope confirms what some local bishop has done in abolishing the Byzantine rite in his diocese, or concedes the petition of the people to become Latins. But, on the whole, the situation is the reverse of this. Constantly the Pope, in spite of the local bishop, in spite of the wish of the Italo-Greeks themselves, refuses to allow them to change their

---

[1] I believe this is strictly true; that all cases of the change from another rite to that of Rome have come from persistent demands of the people themselves or, at any rate, from other Latins, not from the Pope. The purifying of the Roman rite from late mediæval accretions is another matter.

rite. That it remained so long in spite of all obstacles is due to the persistent way in which Rome maintains it.

We may now see some typical examples, showing how the older tradition of the Byzantine rite in Italy gradually disappeared.

In the diocese of *Policastro* the Byzantine rite remained till at least the year 1567. At Rivello in this diocese were two collegiate churches, S Maria del Poggio of the Byzantine rite, and S Niccolò of the Roman rite. Between them there was an old rivalry as to which should have precedence of the other. This situation occurs frequently in such cases. About the year 1572 the clergy of S Maria del Poggio petitioned Pius V that they might adopt the Roman rite. This time the Pope granted their request. Later, having reconsidered the matter, they wanted to go back to the Byzantine rite. But the bishop, Mgr. Spinelli, who had welcomed the opportunity of getting rid of the foreign use in his diocese, was now able to prevent this. Although both colleges were now Latin, the canons of S Maria still claimed that they had precedence over those of S Niccolò. They said their church was the " Matrice " of the town and a " Collegiata insigne."[1] There was a lawsuit about this in 1746. Such quarrels about precedence between churches, originating in the difference of rite, but continuing long after all had become Roman, are very common in the South of Italy.

At *Brindisi* the Byzantine rite declined under the Normans. It was revived by colonists from Crete in the seventeenth century. Meanwhile a vestige of the older Byzantinism remained in a ceremony once a year. On Palm Sunday the procession went to a church called " Sannà." Here the Epistle and Gospel were sung in Greek. But for a long time there were no more clerks of the Byzantine rite to sing; so the subdeacon and deacon were Latins. In 1659 the Archbishop, Denis Odriscol,[2] wanted to put down this ceremony. The zeal of many of these bishops is very strange. One would not have thought that there was any danger in this interesting little relic of the past. Fortunately the Pope (Alexander VII, 1655–1667) protected the ceremony and snubbed the Archbishop.[3] Now all trace even of this has disappeared. At Brindisi only some tombs with Greek inscriptions remain. At *Messagne* there is a memory of the old rite in a church still called " S Maria della Greca "; but it is now Latin in rite.

[1] Rodotà, " del Rito greco," i, 356-359.
[2] He must have been an Irishman.
[3] Rodotà, i, 362-363.

At *Altamura*, since Frederick II (1215–1250), the Byzantine rite had remained (p. 99). In the sixteenth century the (Latin) Archpriest of Altamura was scandalized because the Byzantine clergy were married. He wanted to prevent them from administering Sacraments, especially Penance, to Latins. Cardinal William Sirlet (p. 113, n. 2), then prefect of the Congregation for Eastern rites, to whom the Archpriest applied, told him to leave things as they were.

In 1602 Clement VIII (1592–1605) substituted Latins for Byzantine clerks in one of the three Byzantine churches at Altamura.[1] Since then the Byzantine rite has disappeared here too.

It was in the two extreme ends of Italy, the toe and the heel —that is, the peninsula in the South of Calabria jutting out towards Sicily, and on the other side the bottom of Apulia, the ' Terra d' Otranto "—that the older Byzantine rite survived longest. This is natural. These two are the remotest parts of Italy. Strangest of all is the fact that in both there are villages where the peasants still speak Greek. The Byzantine rite has now disappeared from both provinces; but this Greek dialect still living in them is a wonderful relic of the old days when they were Greater Greece.[2]

In Southern Calabria the chief town is *Reggio*. We have seen that at the Third Lateran Council (1179), though the Archbishop of Reggio was of the Roman rite, he still had two Greek suffragans (p. 99). At that time there were eleven Byzantine parish churches in the city. The most famous of these, indeed the chief church of this rite in all Italy, was S Maria della Cattolica.[3] This was long considered the Mother-Church, the " Matrice " of all Byzantines in

---

[1] Rodotà, i, 369–372.   [2] See p. 48 *seq.*

[3] ἡ καθολική, name for the chief church of a place in the Byzantine rite. The earliest use of it for a building that I know is when the second synod in Trullo (692) orders that baptism is not to be administered in private oratories of houses, but in the " Catholic " (*i.e.*, parish) churches (Can. 59; Mansi, xi, 969, C). Ducange thinks that public churches were called " catholic " (in the normal sense of " universal ") because both men and women went to them; whereas chapels of monasteries or convents were for one sex only. For the same reason the large public church of a monastery was so called because women, as well as men, were admitted to it. The name is still commonly used in the rite. Thus the central Orthodox part of the Anastasis at Jerusalem is τὸ καθολικόν, and in Italy and Sicily " La Cattolica," as a name for certain large churches, survives in memory of the old Byzantine rite. Morisani goes into the whole question, and quotes many examples of the use of the word; " de Protopapis," cap. xiv, pp. 265–276.

the peninsula. It had a chapter of Byzantine canons, who celebrated their rite with great pomp. The head of this chapter was the Protopapa. Down to about the seventeenth century the Protopapa of Reggio had quasi-episcopal jurisdiction over those of his rite throughout the diocese. Second to him was the " Ditereo " (δευτερεύων).[1] This church and chapter were said to have been founded by Count Roger I (1072–1101). The canons kept his anniversary and sang πρεσβείας for the repose of his soul every year.[2] There was also a church " d' Osanna," whither they went on Palm Sunday to bless the palms, according to their rite. In 1595 a canonical visitation of the diocese reports nine Greek priests in the city and fifty more in other parts.[3] But already the rite was decadent. The report says that many of these heroes did not know the elements of Greek grammar. So the Archbishop appointed a sub-deacon to teach them. But he, Hannibal d'Afflitto,[4] was a determined enemy of the Byzantine rite. As Rodotà says: " He, abusing the exercise of his sacred ministry, artfully suppressed the Greek ceremonies, and introduced Latin ones in this church [S Maria della Cattolica], in order that, when no vestige of the old rite should remain, he could so open for himself by this path a free field to exercise jurisdiction over it and its clergy."[5] It was, in fact, jealousy of the exempt position of the Byzantine canons and of the jurisdiction of their Protopapa that made d'Afflitto so great an enemy of their rite. Not only in this church, but throughout his diocese, he sup-

---

[1] These titles, " Protopapa " and " Ditereo," still remain in many places of Southern Italy as memories of the old rite. Joseph Morisani, Canon of Reggio, wrote a whole book about them, " de Protopapis et Deutereis Græcorum et Catholicis eorum ecclesiis Diatriba " (Naples, 1768). In this he traces the history and meaning of the titles (πρωτοπαππᾶς = ἀρχιερεύς), and gives much valuable information about the Italo-Greeks in general.

[2] Schirò, in his report of 1742, says that the Collegiate Chapter of the Cattolica at Reggio is already incorporated with the Cathedral Chapter (Karalevsky, " Documenti inediti," i, 7).

[3] Quoted by J. Gay, " Étude sur la décadence du rite grec " (*Rev. d'hist. et de lit. rel.*, vol. ii, 1897, p. 489).

[4] D'Afflitto (1594-1638) was in most ways a very zealous and praiseworthy bishop. His one fault was the mistaken idea of procuring uniformity in his diocese by making everyone a Latin. His Life has been written by Canon G. Minasi, " Vita di Annibale d'Afflitto, Arcivescovo di Reggio " (Naples, Lanciano e Pinto, 1898); see also " Roma e l'Oriente," viii (1914), 106-111. Morisani tries vainly to maintain that d'Afflitto was not really opposed to the Byzantine rite (" de Protopapis," 294).

[5] Rodotà, i, 406.

pressed it. In this he was encouraged by an absurd person named John Baptist Catanziriti, who in Latin called himself Catumsyritus. Although himself an Albanian of Reggio, he was a bitter enemy of the Byzantine rite. Jealous of Peter Arcudius' famous book on the Sacraments,[1] in 1632 he published a foolish rival work, in which he made a violent attack on the Byzantine manner of administering them.[2] According to him Byzantine rites are gravely defective and mostly invalid.[3] Because of its impudent attack on venerable forms always approved by the Church this book was promptly put on the Index. The Orthodox in the East were much surprised to see the Pope thus defend their rite. Their surprise was superfluous. The Holy See is as concerned to defend all Catholic rites as its own.[4] By the year 1628 it appears from the report of d'Afflitto's visitation that " the Greek rite had breathed its last breath in the lands of the diocese of Reggio."[5] In that year Adam Flocari, the last Byzantine priest of the diocese, obtained leave to pass to the Roman rite; so that he " completes and crowns the number of Greek priests."[6]

Yet a great dispute arose later as a remnant of the old rite. The Protopapa of Reggio, though he was now a Latin, still kept his old title; and he wanted still to keep his old state of exemption and to use the jurisdiction his Greek predecessor had enjoyed. There was a lawsuit before the courts of Naples[7] about this in 1726. The " Cappellano maggiore " of the King of Naples heard the case. Rodotà, who was living at the time, notes its " strepito forense."[8] Sentence was pronounced in favour of the Protopapa, and all his rights were confirmed.

[1] P. Arcudius, " Libri VII de Concordia ecclesiæ occid. et orient. in VII Sacramentorum administratione " (Paris, 1626).

[2] J. B. Catumsyritus, " Vera utriusque ecclesiæ Sacramentorum concordia " (Venice, 1632).

[3] He thinks all Byzantine ordinations invalid ! This was at a time when scores of Byzantinely ordained Catholic priests were celebrating the holy Mysteries all round him. See Goar, " Euchologion " (2nd edition, Venice, 1730), p. 246.

[4] Rodotà, i, 408-409; Morisani, " de Protopapis," pp. 291-293.

[5] Ibid., i, 410.

[6] Ibid. Rodotà's statement is, no doubt, true of the older Byzantine element at Reggio. But we know now that there was an Albanian colony in the diocese which kept the rite later than 1628.

[7] To understand how it was that so many ecclesiastical questions in the kingdom of Naples and the two Sicilies came before the civil courts, we must remember that the king always claimed to be Legatus of the Holy See, as successor of Roger II of Sicily (p. 64). This would give him ecclesiastical jurisdiction.

[8] Rodotà, i, 407.

But, while Rodotà was writing his book, the " strepito forense " had not yet died out. The Vicar General of the diocese was writing books against the Protopapa.[1]

Near Reggio, at *Oppido*, the Byzantine rite remained till the fifteenth century. Then the bishop, Jerome di Napoli, an Augustinian friar (1449–1472), introduced that of Rome.[2] After his death Sixtus IV (1471–1482) united the Sees of Oppido and Gerace.

Gerace had the Byzantine rite till the fifteenth century. Here the bishops, too, were of this rite (p. 98). The most famous Bishop of Gerace was Barlaam, the anti-Hesychast. He was a Greek of Calabria. He came to Constantinople in the early fourteenth century, in the reign of Andronikos III (1328–1341); and there, having turned Orthodox, wrote books against the Catholics. Andronikos sent him on an embassy to the Pope at Avignon (Benedict XII, 1334–1342), to try to arrange reunion. Nothing came of this; but already he had distinguished himself as an opponent of the Hesychast movement,[3] then just beginning. As the Orthodox Church accepted Hesychasm, Barlaam was condemned by it in a synod in 1341. Then he came back to Italy, returned to the Catholic Church, and was made Bishop of Gerace. Barlaam had some reputation as a Greek scholar. He taught Greek to Boccaccio, Petrarca, Paolo Perugino. Boccaccio thought much of his learning.[4] Leo Allatius refutes his anti-

---

[1] In 1730 and 1735 (Rodotà, i, 407).

[2] Rodotà, i, 413–415; Ughelli, " Italia sacra," ix, 417–421.

[3] *Hesychasm* (ἡσυχαμός) is a very curious system of mysticism, half pantheist, which tore the Orthodox Church by controversy in the fourteenth century, till it was finally recognized, in the sixth Hesychast synod, in 1351. Its founder was Gregory Palamas, first monk at Athos, then Metropolitan of Thessalonica († *c.* 1360); Barlaam was its chief opponent. The theory is, first, that by following an elaborate system of ascetic training a man may see a mystic light, which is the light that appeared at our Lord's Transfiguration, and is none other than the uncreated light of God. Secondly, this light, and all divine operation (ἐνέργεια), although divine and uncreated, is really distinct from the divine essence (οὐσία). Quietist contemplation of this " Light of Tabor " is the highest and best occupation for man; by it he becomes absorbed in God. See *Hesychasm* in the " Cath. Encyclopædia."

[4] " Barlaam, a monk of Basil of Cæsarea, a Calabrian, small in body but very great in knowledge, so learned in Greek that he has testimonies from Greek emperors and princes and doctors. There has not been in our time, nor for many centuries past, any Greek filled with such famous or such great knowledge." Boccaccio, " Genealogiæ deorum," lib. xv, cap. 6 (ed. Paris 1511, fol. cxii, b.).

Catholic writings.[1] At the time of the Council of Florence (1439) Athanasius Kalkeophilos was Abbot of the Monastery of S Maria del Patire. At the council he argued vigorously against the schismatics of Constantinople. Then, apparently, wishing not even to share their rite, when as reward for his services he was made Bishop of Gerace, he turned Latin (1467).[2]

At *Bova* the first Latin bishop was Julius Staurieno, a Cypriote who obtained the see from Pius V in 1571. At once he began to undermine the Byzantine rite in his diocese; he himself celebrated a Roman Mass for the first time in his cathedral in January, 1573. The people revolted and sent a petition to Rome. But this time the Pope (Gregory XIII, 1572–1585) confirmed the change of rite. There remain vestiges of the older order in the title of the cathedral of Bova, S Maria dell' Isodia,[3] of other Churches such as that of " della Teotoco," of St Constantine the Emperor equal-to-the-Apostles, and others.[4] Bova is one of the chief places in Italy where Greek is still spoken (p. 105).

Going North from Bova we come to the famous city of *Rossano*, once a great centre of Byzantinism in Italy. Here was the monastery of S Maria del Patire;[5] from Rossano came St Neilos of Grottaferrata.[6] We have seen how there came to be both a Latin archbishop and a Byzantine Metropolitan of Rossano (p. 97). In 1265 Pope Clement IV (1265–1268) received a petition to grant bulls to a Greek bishop, signed by " the Chapter of Greek Canons of the Church of Rossano in Calabria." The archbishop so elected signs " Ego Angelus, Rossanensis archiepiscopus græcus."[7] After the Council of Florence (1439) the Byzantine see came to an end, and with it the rite. Matthew Saraceni, O.F.M., was made Archbishop.[8] In 1461 he abolished the Byzantine rite, as the inscription on his tomb testifies.[9] There remained only the ceremony

---

[1] " de Consensu," ii, cap. 17 (cols. 824-840); an account of Barlaam's life also; see further Krumbacher, " Byzant. Liter." (2nd edition), pp. 100, 102.

[2] Rodotà, " del Rito greco," i, 418-419; Ughelli, " Italia sacra " (2nd edition), ix, 393-399.

[3] " Isodia " is for τὰ εἰσόδια (τῆς θεοτόκου εἰς τὸν ναὸν), the Presentation of our Lady in the Temple.

[4] Rodotà, i, 419-423; Ughelli, ix, 338-342.   [5] P. 127.

[6] P. 146.   [7] Ughelli, ix, 300-301.

[8] He seems to have been an absurd person, according to Rodotà's account (i, 426-428).

[9] " Hanc quam cernis ille cuius laus est perennis
  Transtulit in Latinum, ecclesiam, de græco ad cultum diuinum."

of reading the lessons of Palm Sunday in Greek on a hill by the city.[1]

Across the water, *Messina* was long a great centre of Byzantinism. There is here a famous collegiate church, S Maria del Grafeo,[2] also called the Cattolica, which had a Byzantine chapter under a Protopapa.

In the fifteenth century the Byzantine rite was still flourishing at Messina. It was used in the Cattolica, several parish churches, and by the monks in the great monastery of St Saviour (p. 125), and others. In 1418 there were altogether fifty Byzantine churches in the diocese. But there was already lack of priests to serve them. In that year the Protopapa of the Cattolica, Nicholas di Benedetto, petitions the Archbishop that one priest be allowed to serve three, four, or even five churches.[3] A century later five Byzantine parishes are incorporated into one, St Nicholas.[4] After the Council of Trent five diocesan synods were held at Messina, in 1588, 1621, 1648, 1681, 1725. All make laws " pro Græcis orientalibus." In the case of the later synods these " Greeks " are Albanians. The Archbishop, Antony Lombardi (1585–1597), wrote to Cardinal Santoro, after the Synod of 1588, asking for instructions about the " Greeks " of his diocese. They are, apparently, new refugees from the Levant, and have clearly a schismatical spirit. They refuse to make a profession of faith in the terms of Gregory XIII's form; they will not accept Lombardi's chrism, but have their own from the East (probably from a schismatical bishop); their clergy go off to the East to be ordained without dimissorial letters; their priests confirm immediately after baptism, they will not fast on Saturday, and, in mixed marriages, they make all the children " Greeks." Some of Lombardi's questions are about matters of mere rite; yet from the whole letter one can see that these people are a great nuisance to him. Santoro's answer is admirable. He explains all the questions of rite with judgement and learning, quoting Fathers and liturgical authorities. This letter alone is enough to show

---

[1] Ughelli, ix, 285-314; Rodotà, i, 424-430.

[2] " Grafeo " for γραφεῖον or γραφή. The local legend is that our Lady sent a letter to the people of Messina, by St Paul, promising them her protection. This letter is kept in the archive of the cathedral. Really, it was the name of the church that suggested to Constantine Laskaris to forge this letter in 1467, when he was professor of Greek at Messina. Its text will be found in Henry Swinburne, " Travels in the Two Sicilies " (London, 1783-1785), ii, 391. It is a poor forgery. The real reason of the name " Grafeo " seems unknown.

[3] " Roma e l'Oriente," viii (1914), 341-342.   [4] *Ibid.*, n. 2.

that he was a most serious student of the Byzantine rite.[1]　He will not allow the Greeks to be worried about their rites.　Only in the matter of faith is he, of course, uncompromising.　Their clergy must make a Catholic profession of faith.　Yet even here he is tolerant.　He says they are very ignorant; the best thing will be to get a learned man of their own race to explain the position to them.　Then they are to be " warned mildly," " instructed gently," " invited kindly."　Then there are to be " sermons, repeated warnings, and threats."　If it is all no good, they are to be removed from the care of souls; and if they are still obstinate they are to be delated to the office of the Holy Inquisition.　Santoro does not say what will happen to them after that; but I imagine it would be something excessively unpleasant.[2]

By the seventeenth century the Greeks of Messina had modified their rite into one of those curious mixtures that are sometimes called " Italo-Greek " rites (p. 178).　In 1613 the Archbishop of Messina petitioned the Holy Office to abolish this mixed rite, on the plea that the clergy were so ignorant of the Greek language that they could not even pronounce the words properly: " Because of the crass ignorance of the Greek language which they ought to pronounce, they hesitate in reading, and do not understand a word of what they say."　Once more Rome took up the defence of old custom, and refused to allow the Italo-Greeks to be latinized.　The Holy Office merely answered that, if they are so ignorant, it is the business of the Archbishop to see that in future they should be better instructed.[3]　Besides the Cattolica, Rodotà names four other Byzantine churches in Messina, dependent on it.[4]　Since his time all have abandoned the Uniate Byzantine rite.[5]

Turning now to the other extreme corner of Italy, the land of Otranto, we find here, too, the Byzantine rite continued till after the sixteenth century.　In the diocese of *Otranto* itself, a synod of the year 1583 was attended by 200 Byzantine priests.[6] But later the rite died out gradually; though in some villages of the diocese it lasted till far into the seventeenth century.　At

---

[1] For Card. Santoro, see p. 113, n. 1.

[2] Lombardi's letter and Santoro's answer are printed in " Roma e l'Oriente," viii, 347-360.

[3] Rodotà, i, 459.

[4] For Messina, see Rodotà, i, 455-461.

[5] The old Uniate Church is now Orthodox (see p. 168).　The Collegiate Chapter of the Cattolica at Messina was still flourishing in 1742, when Joseph Schirò wrote his report (Karalevsky, " Documenti inediti," i, 6-7).　　　　[6] Rodotà, i, 378.

one village, Calimera, it was used as late as 1663; at another, Zollino, in 1688.[1] These are two of the places where Greek is still spoken by the peasants; but their rite is now Roman.

At *Galatina* till 1507 practically the whole population was Byzantine. But the Franciscans had a church there, in which they used to romanize the people. A chronicle of the order in these parts tells us that the intention of the founder of this church " was solely to introduce the Latin rite, since all then lived in the Greek rite. . . . Here the Fathers administered to those few Latins who were mixed with the Greeks; they administered Sacraments, practised the Gregorian chant, and sang according to the rite of the Roman Church, while their Superior acted as parish priest." So after 1507 they managed to latinize all the people.[2]

At *Corigliano d'Otranto* there was a revival of the Byzantine rite in the fifteenth century. Carlantonio de'Monti, Lord of Corigliano in the time of Ferdinand I of Naples (1458–1494), protected it, established schools for Greek, and so on. A Greek lady, Maria Bucali, then founded a monastery for Basilian monks and left property to it, on condition that it should always be occupied by them. In spite of that, her grandson handed it over to the Capuchins in 1587. Still the Byzantine rite was used in the parish church till 1600. In that year the last Byzantine parish priest, Sergio de Paulis, died. His successor, Damasceno Comi, was a Latin. A few other priests remained. The last of them, Antony Indrini, died in 1683. " With him," says Rodotà, " the Greek rite was buried in perpetual oblivion."[3]

At *Gallipoli* till the end of the fourteenth century the bishops were alternately Byzantine and Roman. The Byzantine rite was extinct here by 1513.[4] At *Nardò* the old see was abolished by Pope Paul I (757–767) in 761. The Bishop of Brindisi, who thereby became the ordinary, appointed an archpriest (Protopapa) of the Byzantine rite for Nardò. The revenues of the see were given to a Basilian monastery. Urban II (1088–1099) replaced the Basilian monks by Latin Benedictines. There remained two archpriests, one for each rite. The public rites in the monastery church were mixed. The lessons were read in Latin and Greek. A ritual of the year 1348 describes how they sang: " Meanwhile, the Greek and Latin choirs alternating, the Responsale is sung."[5] In 1402 Philip, Archbishop of Otranto

---

[1] J. Gay, " Étude sur la décadence du rite grec " (*Rev. d'hist. et de lit. rel.*, ii, p. 490).   [2] Rodotà, i, 380-381.   [3] *Ibid.*, i, 381-386.   [4] *Ibid.*, i, 386-388.   [5] Quoted by Rodotà, i, 392.

and Metropolitan of the province, wanted to latinize the Church of Nardò completely; but the Pope would not let him. The See of Nardò, after many vicissitudes, was restored finally in 1413. In the sixteenth century Fabio Fornari again made an effort to abolish the Byzantine, or mixed, rite in his diocese. But the Byzantine canons appealed to the Congregation for Eastern rites. At that time the prefect of this Congregation was Cardinal Santoro, Archbishop of St Severina.[1] He was himself of the Roman rite; but he deserves to be remembered as, with Cardinal Sirlet,[2] the great protector of the Byzantine rite in Italy in the sixteenth century. His answer is quoted in full by Rodotà. He refuses to allow the latinization of those

[1] Cardinal Julius Antony Santoro (in Latin sometimes " Sanctorius," 1532-1602) was a famous person of great merit. He was Archb. of S Severina, Cardinal in 1570, and a member of the Holy Office. In 1577 he became one of the five first protectors of the Greek College at Rome. In 1585 he succeeded Sirlet as protector of the reformed Order of St Basil (p. 132). In the same year he became president of the Congregation for Eastern rites. It was Santoro who composed Clement VIII's Instruction for the Italo-Greeks in 1595. He also arranged a Roman " Rituale seu Sacerdotale," printed at Rome in 1586, but never published. This is the chief source of our present Ritual (published by Paul V in 1614). In the Constitution *Apost. sedis* in the preface of our Ritual, is a reference to this work of Santoro, " Iulius Antonius S.R.E. Card. S Seuerinæ nuncupatus."

[2] William Sirlet (Sirletus, Sirleto, 1514-1585) is the other, even greater, friend and protector of the Italo-Greeks in the sixteenth century. He was a Calabrian, very learned in Greek, but himself of the Roman rite. He was one of the chief consultors of the Council of Trent (1545-1563), one of the editors of the Sixtine Vulgate, president of the Commissions for the reform of the Calendar (1582), for the new editions of the Missal, Breviary, and Martyrology, one of the " Correctores romani " of the C.I. Can., and author of many treatises, chiefly on liturgical matters. He was a member of the Commission for " the reform of the Greeks," one of the first protectors of the Greek College at Rome, chief author of the reform of the Basilian monks in Italy, and first protector of the new Congregation (p. 132), Vatican Librarian from 1570 to his death. In 1565 Sirlet was made a Cardinal with the title of St Lawrence in Panisperna. In 1566 he was ordained Bishop of San Marco in Calabria by Pope Pius V himself; two years later he was transferred to Squillace; but he did not reside much in his diocese. He lived at Rome, consulted by learned men all over Europe, while his nephew, Marcellus Sirlet, administered his diocese in his name. At the Conclave of 1585 he nearly became Pope. He was a friend of St Charles Borromeo; his death-bed (October 6, 1585) was attended by St Philip Neri. He is buried in his titular church, San Lorenzo in Panisperna, at Rome.

First Sirlet, then Santoro were consulted, and had a decisive voice in all the affairs of the Italo-Greeks in their time.

places where the people are accustomed to the Byzantine rite. He declares that Byzantine ceremonies, such as the blessing of the water at the Epiphany, and the lessons in both languages, are to be maintained. The Byzantine clergy may keep their wives, according to their own Canon Law; but Latins must not be ordained in this rite for the sake of being married. There was, at Nardò, too, the difficulty of finding clerks sufficiently instructed in Greek to sing lessons in that language correctly; so he allows Latins to do this, " that the ancient right be not lost."[1]   This want of people sufficiently instructed to carry on the Byzantine rite eventually led to its disappearance at Nardò.[2] *Galatone* had a Byzantine Protopapa, Nicholas Theodoros, who was present at Florence in 1439.   There were two chapters here, one of each rite, and mixed ceremonies. But the Franciscans worked against the Byzantine rite, and it disappeared by 1510.[3]   At *Alessano* a synod in 1587 shows that there were then still Byzantine priests there.[4]

About 1560 the Byzantine clergy of *Taranto* sent an account of their rite to Rome,[5] which shows that it still survived there.   Jules Gay found in the Brancaccio library at Naples a manuscript from the collection of Cardinal Santoro.   It contains a list of monasteries sent by him to Sirlet, several treatises about the Italo-Greeks sent to Santoro in the years 1572, 1580, etc., and some polemic works against the errors of the " Greeks."   From this manuscript Gay has compiled a statement about the condition of the Byzantine rite in Italy at the end of the sixteenth century.[6] The Albanians had already arrived.   They form a special class, to which we shall come in the next paragraph.   There were also colonies of people of the Byzantine rite who had fled from the Turks. But, apart from these, there still remained vestiges of the old Italo-Greeks, who had kept their rite since the eighth century. Their language and rite were gradually disappearing; but they were not yet extinct.   They remained in the two extremities, the South of Calabria and the land of Otranto.   There were also still a good number of Basilian monasteries; though these

---

[1] See the decree quoted by Rodotà, " del Rito greco," i, 396-397, n. 1.

[2] For Nardò see Ughelli, " Italia sacra," i, 1035-1063; Rodotà, *op. cit.*, i, 388-396.

[3] Rodotà, i, 397-400.   [4] *Ibid.*, i, 400.

[5] Published in " Roma e l'Oriente," vol. ii, pp. 33-35.

[6] " Étude sur la décadence du rite grec dans l'Italie méridionale à la fin du XVIe siècle," in the *Rev. d'hist. et de lit. rel.*, ii (1897), pp. 481-495.

were then in a state of great decadence (p. 129). And in many churches otherwise latinized there remained certain Byzantine ceremonies, such as the blessing of the water at the Epiphany, the reading of the Epistle and Gospel on certain days, notably on Palm Sunday. Among the older generation of Italo-Greeks certain admixtures of the Roman rite had crept into the Byzantine offices; so they had what is sometimes counted as a special " Italo-Greek " rite.[1]

5. The Coming of the Albanians (Fifteenth to Sixteenth Century).

In the fifteenth century, just as the Byzantine rite in Italy seemed to be at its last gasp, it received new life from colonies of Eastern Christians who sought refuge in the West. The chief of these colonies were those of the Albanians.

The Turkish invasion of the Balkans drove numbers of Christians to the West into exile. Among these were Christian Albanians. In our time the Albanians are either Catholics of the Roman rite, Orthodox (of course, of the Byzantine rite), or Moslems. But in the fifteenth century there were many who were Uniates of the Byzantine rite. At any rate, when they came to Italy they professed to be Catholics, in union with Rome. It is not easy to be sure whether they had already been so or whether they became Uniates, perhaps found it politic to profess their union with the Pope when they arrived in Italy. Yet there is, I think, reasonable probability that at any rate many of them were already Catholics before they fled from the Turks. The most serene Republic had held large parts of their country for some time before the Turks conquered it; we know that she was not tolerant of schism. It is then quite likely that many, if not all, these Albanians had already returned to union with the Holy See before they came to Italy. There are, indeed, Albanians who protest that their nation was always Catholic, that their forbears had never lost communion with Rome. This is presumably only one more case of the pleasant illusion in which Uniates of many groups now live. Rodotà accepts this view, persuaded by the Albanian priest Don Paolo Maria Parrino.[2]

[1] See below, pp. 178-179.

[2] Parrino wrote a large work in two MS. volumes, " Perpetuæ Albanensis Ecclesiæ consensionis cum Romana Libri VII." The MS. is at the Greek-Albanian seminary at Palermo. It has never been published. Rodotà quotes from it at some length (" del Rito greco," iii, 1-11). The Grottaferrata monks are very anxious that Parrino's work should, at last, see the light (*e.g.*, " Roma e l'Oriente," iv, 1914, pp. 346, n. 1; 340, n. 1).

" I should say," he tells us, " that the pure dove of the Holy Ghost, after it had been outraged by the Greeks, gathered its feathers and wings and took flight to rest its foot among the Albanians, inspiring them with greater courage than they had had before, and illuminating their minds, so that they should keep far from the wiles and traps of false prophets."[1] I doubt very much, however, whether this beautiful language corresponds to the fact. Indeed, among the Albanian refugees in Italy we shall hear of some who, even after they had arrived, remained in schism (p. 119). However, there seems a reasonable probability that many Albanians, before they fled the Turk, were already Uniates. In any case, when they came to Italy, by far the greater number accepted that position, and protested that they always had been in union with Rome. In those days it would have been difficult for a community to settle down in peace in the kingdom of Naples, unless it were Catholic.

In the fifteenth century, during the disorders of the Turkish conquest of the Balkans, an Albanian chief, George Alexander Castriota, called Scanderbeg,[2] succeeded in making a great part of his country, for a time, independent. He had been given by his father as a hostage to the Sultan; he was brought up as a Moslem and was at first a favourite of Murad II (1421–1451). Then he rebelled against the Turks, fought not only against them, but against Venice too, and became the great hero of the independence of his people. He established himself at Croia.[3] In his lifelong war against the Turks he had varying success; but eventually the Sultan was forced to recognize him as a semi-independent prince, on condition that he paid tribute. Meanwhile Scanderbeg became known all over Europe as the great enemy of the Turk, so he had the sympathy of Christendom. He came to Italy several times. In 1461, leaving for a time his war against the Turks, he came with an army and restored King Ferdinand I of Naples, who had been deposed by his subjects. In 1465 he came to Rome, to ask the help of Pope Pius II (1458–1464) against the common enemy. He was received with great honour. His negotiations with the Pope had to do with Pius II's attempt to organize a

---

[1] Rodotà, iii, p. 11.

[2] Scanderbeg is his Turkish name. They make " Alexander " into " Aliskandar," then (treating the first syllable as the Arabic article) " Iskandar." " Scanderbeg " is " Iskandar Bey."

[3] Croia is about thirty miles South of Scutari, in the mountains, about nine miles from the coast.

crusade. Scanderbeg died fighting at Alessio in 1467. During his long war against the Turks he became a Christian, presumably a Catholic. At any rate, he was treated as such by the Popes.[1] He is said to have received the last Sacraments before his death; he is buried in the cathedral of Alessio.[2] From his time dates the connection between Albania and Italy, never since forgotten, of which we have heard much lately.

There are other cases of alliance between Italian princes and the valiant Albanian warriors. In the sixteenth century there was an Albanian regiment in the service of Naples. They fought for Spain, too. In short, as their own land was gradually lost to the Turks, the Christian Albanians formed companies of mercenaries at the service of any Christian prince, particularly at the service of those who were fighting against their old enemies. Then came the period of the refugees. Horribly persecuted by the Turks, they began to flee to lands where they could practise their religion under a Christian government. The region Chimara[3] in Albania has long been a centre of Catholicism there; already in the fifteenth century Chimara sent out a number of Catholic refugees. Many Albanian exiles fled to Cattaro and other Venetian possessions;

[1] Calixtus III (1455-1458) writes to him as a Pope would hardly write to a Moslem or schismatic; Pius II (1458-1464) and Paul II (1464-1471) both call him " mighty warrior of Christ." See the texts in Rodotà, " del Rito greco," iii, 23-24.

[2] Alessio (Lissus, Alise, near the coast, in the Gulf of Drin) has long been a centre of Catholicism in Albania. It is still a Catholic (Latin) bishopric. The classical Life of Scanderbeg is that of his countryman and contemporary, Marinus Barlettius, " de Vita moribus ac rebus præcipue aduersus Turcas gestis Georgii Castrioti clarissimi Epirotarum principis," Argentorati (Strassburg), 1537; Portuguese version by F. Dandrade (Lisbon, 1567); German version Frankfurt, 1577, Italian by P. Rocha, Venice, 1580. A good and amusing modern Life is A. Zoncada, " Scanderbeg, Storia albanese del sec. XV " (Milan, 2nd edition, 1882).

[3] Chimara (Italian Cimarra) is a town and region on the coast between Avlona and Delvinon, where are the 'Ακροκεραύνια mountains, Horace's " infames scopulos Acroceraunia " (Od. i, 3). In the eighteenth century Catholic Albanian monks from Sicily had a flourishing mission there. Most of the people seem to have been Byzantine Uniates. Joseph Schirò, born in 1690, an Albanian of Piana dei Greci (p. 165), student of the Greek College at Rome, then monk at Grottaferrata, finally Archbishop of Durazzo and Vic. Ap. of Chimara, worked here for twenty-four years. A report about the people of Chimara, sent by him to Propaganda in 1729, is printed in " Roma e l'Oriente," v (1912), 97-117; 159-166. See other reports in C. Karalevsky, " Documenti inediti," ii (Rome, 1911-1912). For Schiro's Life see " Roma e l'Oriente," v, 103.

but the main stream was towards the nearest Christian land, Sicily, and the mainland of the kingdom of Naples. It is difficult to fix the exact date of the first arrival of the Albanian colonists in these parts. The first date I have found for certain, so far, is 1448. In that year Alphonsus I of Aragon, in return for services rendered by Albanian soldiers in his pay against the French, granted them lands in Sicily with a certain measure of autonomy under their Captains George and Basil Reres.[1]

In 1456 there was a great earthquake throughout Calabria and Apulia. After this the Neapolitan Government granted large districts of the country laid waste to Albanian colonists, in order that they might reclaim it. When Scanderbeg had fought for Ferdinand I of Naples, he was rewarded by the grant of land at S Pietro in Galatina. He did not himself occupy his new estate; but his son and many of his countrymen came. Other Albanians came in 1467 after Scanderbeg's death, many more during the Pontificate of Paul II (1468–1471); others, again, after the year 1478, when the Sultan finally subjected all Albania to his rule. The town of Korone (Κόρωνη) in the Peloponnesos had surrendered freely to the Venetians in 1204. Later many Albanians came to settle here.[2] In 1498 Bayazed II seized the town. In 1532 Charles II sent a fleet under Andrew Doria to retake it. The Christian Albanians rose against the Turks and helped the Imperial fleet. But soon after the Turks recaptured the place. Then, fearing their vengeance, the Albanians fled to Italy. There were more than 200 ships full of them; their bishop Benedict[3] came too. So they arrived in the kingdom of Naples. The Government gave them grants of land and money. The Albanians of Korone spread throughout the kingdom. Some joined Greek refugees in the city of Naples, and there formed a community of the Byzantine rite, under Prince Thomas Palaiologos. The name " dei Coronei " remains as a memory of this immigration.[4]

[1] These were the sons of Demetrios Reres, who had led the Albanian forces for Alphonsus. His diploma is printed by Rodotà, iii, 52-53. The name Reres occurs constantly among the Albanians in Italy.

[2] There are still large colonies of Albanians in the kingdom of Greece.

[3] It is strange that an Albanian bishop of the Byzantine rite should have a Latin name. Perhaps he took it after he had arrived in Italy. Or was his name Εὐλογητός?

[4] So the Archimandrite Pietro Camodeca de Nobili Coronei in Calabria now. For the story of Korone see Rodotà, iii, 54-57.

The village S Demetrio Corone (p. 162) also keeps the name. In short, during all the second half of the fifteenth century, and in the sixteenth, there was a stream of these refugees to the kingdom of Naples. They were kindly received by the Government and were granted considerable tracts of land, to be held by them and their descendants. There was, naturally, much sympathy for the victims of Turkish barbarity; moreover, a great part of Southern Italy and Sicily was then sparsely peopled (as indeed it still is). The king was very willing to grant such tracts of land to people who would cultivate them, and then pay him taxes, the more since the Italians soon found that their new guests were exceedingly industrious, thrifty, and respectable folk. All over the kingdom the new colonists watered the waste places and made wild districts flourish.

The largest Albanian colonies were in the kingdom of Naples and the two Sicilies; but there were others in most parts of Italy, Tuscany, Venice, Rimini, the Papal States, and so on. The descendants of these have long been italianized, and have adopted the Roman rite. In the Papal states there was a great family of Albanian origin—namely, the descendants of Michael de'Lazii. They kept the name Albani. Pope Clement XI (John Francis Albani, 1700–1721) was of this family; so there has been one Pope of Albanian blood.[1]

The Albanians in Italy kept, of course, their own language and customs. They were a foreign colony among the Italians.[2] What is strange is that fragments of these colonies still remain, are still not absorbed into the Italian race. They were allowed a large measure of self-government under their own chiefs, acknowledging the supreme authority of the King of Naples and paying taxes to his Government. They spoke, of course, the Albanian language; but their rites were Byzantine in Greek.

Among these first settlers were some schismatics, some who had adopted the Paulician heresy and even some Moslems.[3] But the greater number, at any rate when they arrived in Italy,

[1] For the history of the Lazii-Albani family see Rodotà, iii, 30-34.

[2] The Italians were quite conscious of the difference between the Albanians and others who had the same Byzantine rite, whether old Italo-Greeks or new Greek refugees. Thus they called the district of Apulia between Taranto and Lecce, where Albanians settled, *Albania*; but the country south of that, where the old Italo-Greeks still kept their rite, was called *Grecia*. The original Albania, in the Balkans, covers the old province Epirus; hence the Albanians are often called " Epiroti."

[3] For these see Rodotà, iii, 57-58.

maintained that they were Catholics in union with Rome, though not of the Roman rite. In the case of many of these we have perhaps an example of the ease with which union with Rome can be brought about, so long as there is no interference with local rites. Even if they had been schismatics before, the acceptance of the position of Uniates would not make much visible change to these simple people. The Albanians had no great theologians among them. Probably they understood very little of the change of principle involved by their reunion. It would indeed have been hardly possible to remain in schism at that time in Italy. Meanwhile they went to the new churches they built in Calabria and Sicily, and followed in them the services to which they were accustomed.[1] The Holy See applied to them its invariable policy of not interfering with their rite, only taking care that their clergy should be brought up in the Catholic Church, and taking certain precautions to put down customs that were really superstitious or immoral.

So the Albanians brought new life to the expiring Byzantine rite in Italy. Yet from the beginning there were difficulties about their position. For one thing they had no bishops. Till the eighteenth century they had no bishop at all. They were, according to the normal Catholic rule, subject to the diocesan Ordinaries of the places where they settled. These Ordinaries were all Latins. There was the greatest possible difficulty about the ordaining of their clergy. Occasionally a wandering bishop of the Byzantine rite is sent down to Calabria to ordain. Sometimes the Albanians begin to dispute their ecclesiastical position, and to claim that they are exempt from the jurisdiction of the Latin Ordinaries. Some bishop of the rite, who happened to be in the South of Italy or Sicily, would begin to use jurisdiction over them, to the great annoyance of the Latin Ordinary. There was a famous case of this in the diocese of Messina. In 1556 a Levantine bishop, Pamphylios,

---

[1] That is, supposing they had been Orthodox before they came to Italy. There is, however, good reason to suppose that, at any rate, many Albanians were Uniates already in their own country (p. 116). Another factor to realize is that at that time, in face of the overwhelming disaster of the Turkish invasion, there was less opposition between Catholics and Orthodox than at any other since the great schism. Indeed, fear and hatred of the common enemy drew all Eastern Christians together for a time and made them well-disposed towards the West, from which they hoped so eagerly for help. I know several curious examples of this, even Patriarchs agreeing that their subjects should unite with Rome.

arrived at Messina, and began to behave as the Ordinary of the Albanians and other Byzantine Christians in the diocese. He ordained, visited their churches, made rules for them, reformed their rite, and so on. Gian Andrea Mercurio, Archbishop of Messina, sent an angry protest against him to Rome, and he was put down.[1] The same kind of thing happened at Benevento and in various places in Calabria. Because of these disorders the Holy See laid down definite rules about the position of the Albanians and other Italo-Greeks.[2]

Then, although at first the Albanians were warmly welcomed by the Government of Naples, as Christian heroes who had suffered much from the Turk, it seems that in time they were no longer popular among their Italian neighbours. There was always a certain suspicion of their strange rites. Frequently they are accused of various bad habits, some of which are nothing really but the lawful custom of their rite, while others are certainly things that ought to be put down, if the accusations were true. Thus they were accused of not observing the fasts and feasts of the Roman rite, of giving holy Communion to children just baptized, and so on. But they are also accused of despising the authority of the Holy See, of scorning the censures of the Latin bishops, of sharing the errors of the schismatics with regard to purgatory and azyme bread, of digging up dead bodies and burning them.[3] In the reign of Pope Paul III (1534–1549) the Albanians from Korone, now in Sicily, sent their bishop Benedict (p. 118) to Rome to protest against these accusations. The Pope received him most graciously, and in answer to his petition wrote a Brief to the Sicilian bishops, in which he praises the Coronei for their valour and fidelity to the Catholic faith, severely forbids any bishop to interfere with their rite or annoy them because they are not Latins, renews former Papal laws to that effect, and threatens grave censures against anyone who does so. There are many constitutions of Popes to the same effect. The attitude of the Holy See was always, first that the Albanians are to be subject to the ordinary jurisdiction of the Latin bishops; but, on the other hand, that nothing is to be done to alienate them from their own rite. So, after a long quarrel between the Albanians of the province of Benevento and their neighbours, Pius IV (1559–1565) published a Constitution

---

[1] Rodotà tells the whole story, iii, 139-140.
[2] See below, pp. 122, 123.
[3] For examples of these accusations see Rodotà, iii, 139-146. He discusses each, and defends the Albanians.

(February 16, 1564) declaring again that the Albanians are to obey the diocesan authority of the local bishop; " but by this we do not mean that the Greeks themselves are to be taken from their Greek rite, or that they are to be in any way hindered by the Ordinaries or by others."[1] However, in spite of constant Papal legislation, there are many cases of bishops who do try to make the Albanians of their diocese turn Latin. For instance, in 1616 Mgr. Buonincontro, Bishop of Girgenti, made a determined but an unsuccessful effort to persuade those of the great colony of Contessa,[2] in his diocese, to adopt the Latin rite.[3] In 1622 Cardinal Gaetano, Archbishop of Taranto, forbade the Byzantine rite to the Albanians between Lecce and Taranto (the district called Albania).[4] Through such efforts as these, and through the prejudice of the Italians around them, which made their rite burdensome, during the course of time a great number of Albanians did finally give up their own peculiarities. This happened in various ways. Sometimes they kept their language, but adopted the Roman rite; sometimes, on the other hand, they lost their language, learnt to speak only Italian, but still preserved the Byzantine rite in Greek. It is not wonderful that among a minority, surrounded by suspicious Italian neighbours, many should eventually have become italianized. The wonderful thing is rather that, in spite of all, so many still keep their own language and rite.

In arranging their position the Holy See at first required that, where there were colonies of the Byzantine rite in the diocese, the Latin Ordinary should have a special Byzantine Vicar General to look after their affairs. But this did not really solve the difficulty. Without a bishop of their rite it was impossible that their state should be satisfactory. During the sixteenth and seventeenth centuries there are all kinds of confusion of rite. Byzantine clergy are ordained by Latin bishops, according to the Roman rite, and then themselves use that of Constantinople. The faithful frequent Sacraments according to the Roman rite when they cannot find a priest of their own; and conversely many Latins living in places where the majority is Byzantine go to the Byzantine churches

---

[1] Const. *Romanus Pontifex*, cf. Bull. Rom. (Rome, 1745, tom. iv, Part II, p. 169).   [2] See p. 167 for Contessa.

[3] The story is told in Rodotà, iii, 114-115.

[4] His excuse, or opportunity, was the arrival of a swindler who called himself Archbishop of Corinth, and ordained priests; but then turned out to be not a bishop at all. Rodotà, iii, 103.

for Sacraments without scruple.[1] So at last Clement XII (1730–1740) decides to provide a bishop of the Byzantine rite for the Italo-Greeks. He was not to be a diocesan bishop with jurisdiction. This would have offended against the principle, once considered most important, that there should not be two ordinaries in one place.[2] So the difficulty was solved by appointing an " ordaining bishop "[3] of the Byzantine rite. This bishop was to consider himself the vicar of the Ordinaries of those dioceses in which there were Albanians. He was to have no ordinary jurisdiction, only the right of visiting their churches and looking after them as delegate of the Ordinaries. In the diocese of Bisignano there was a disused Benedictine monastery, S Benedetto d'Ullano (p. 161). In the same place was a large Albanian colony. They had already three churches of their rite. Clement XII turned the monastery into a seminary for the Byzantine clergy, and determined that its rector should be the ordaining Byzantine bishop. The Bull of this foundation is dated 1735.[4] The ordaining bishop was to be a bishop *in partibus*, as it was then still called, with a title conveying no jurisdiction. And the first of these was Felix Samuel Rodotà, the uncle of Pietro Pompilio Rodotà, who wrote the history of his rite in Italy. Clement XII's successor, Benedict XIV (1740–1758) issued many laws for the Italo-Greeks. He arranged all kinds of matters concerning their marriages with Latins, their Sacraments, and so on.[5] There are two other Byzantine lines of bishops on the same terms, one at Rome, and one in Sicily; so that now there are three.[6]

An important factor in the preservation of the Byzantine rite among the Sicilian Albanians was the *Congregation of the Oratory of the Greek rite* (Congr. Orat. rit. græci). This was

---

[1] Rodotà mentions places where, still in his time, this happened; for instance, San Benedetto d'Ullano (" del Rito greco," iii, 71).

[2] The fourth Lateran Council (1215) had set up this idea as a principle, " We forbid altogether that one and the same city or diocese should have several Pontiffs, like one body with several heads, which would be a monster " (Mansi, xxii, 998). For a long time this was considered essential. Benedict XIV (1740-1758) explains and defends it (" de Synodo diœcesano," lib. ii, cap. 12; ed. Rom., 1767, pp. 46-50). It is now quite obsolete. Throughout the East, in Austria-Hungary, etc., wherever there are communities of various Uniate rites, there are several Catholic bishops, each for his own rite. Lwow has three; there are four Catholic Patriarchs of Antioch, three Bishops of Beinit, and so on.

[3] For further details and the present arrangement see pp. 177-178.

[4] There was already a Byzantine bishop at Rome, since 1595; see p. 177.   [5] See pp. 33-37.   [6] Pp. 177-178.

founded by Fr. George Guzzetta. He was a Latin priest of
the Oratory at Palermo, distinguished for learning and piety.
He conceived the idea of forming a Congregation of priests,
under the patronage of St Philip Neri and following his con-
stitution,[1] but for the Byzantine (that is, Albanian) clergy in
Sicily. He persuaded a number of these to join him. This
Oratory was approved in 1725. It had no organic connection
with the other Oratories. It possessed one house at Piana dei
Greci (p. 165). By the end of the eighteenth century Guzzetta's
Congregation was already decadent. It could not find subjects among the Albanian clergy because it maintained the
Roman principle of celibacy. In 1801 Pius VII allowed the
Congregation to receive Roman priests, on condition that they
should use the Byzantine rite only as long as they remained in
it—an early and at that time rare exception to the rule against
change of rite.[2] During the nineteenth century this Oratory
of the Byzantine rite died out. During its century and a half
of existence it had done much to raise the tone of the Albanian
clergy and people in Sicily. Guzzetta also founded a Congregation of religious women called the Institution of the Holy
Family, to educate Albanian girls in what he called "Schools
of Mary."[3] One convent and school remain, at Piana dei
Greci, in Sicily (p. 165).

Besides the Albanians there are, or were, other groups of
Byzantine Uniates in Italy dating from the same time. It
was not only Albanians who fled the Turk in the fifteenth
century. So there were colonies of Greeks at Venice, Ancona,
Leghorn, Bibbona, Trieste, in Corsica, and Malta. We shall
come back to some of these (pp. 135-145; 169-175).

6. Byzantine Monasticism in Italy.

The monks of the Byzantine rite have had so great an
influence on the development of the Italo-Greeks that we
must say something about them before we come to the present
state of things.

It is difficult to say when first the rule of St Basil was introduced into Italy. Nor does it follow that everyone who

---

[1] The Constitution of the Oratorian Congregations was drawn up
from St Philip's ideas by Cæsar Baronius, approved by Paul V on
February 24, 1612.

[2] Pii VII, Const. 59 (" Bull. Rom. Cont.," Rome, 1846, tom. xi,
p. 165).

[3] For the life of Guzzetta see Giov. d'Angelo, " Vita del servo
di Dio P. Giorgio Guzzetta," Palermo, 1798, where curious information about the Albanians of Sicily in the early eighteenth century will
be found (Rodotà, " del Rito greco," iii, 119).

followed this rule at the beginning used the Byzantine rite. There is no necessary inherent connection between a monastic rule and a rite. Rufinus translated the rule into Latin.[1] Already in Arian times there were, however, communities of Eastern clergy and, presumably, monks at Rome.[2] In the Lateran Synod of 649 there is evidence of Greek and Armenian monasteries at Rome.[3] But it was chiefly during the Iconoclast persecution that great numbers of Byzantine monks came to Italy. That persecution was directed almost as much against monks as against the images. So from that time we hear of innumerable monasteries of Greek monks, who kept the rule of St Basil and used the Byzantine rite, especially in the South and in Sicily.[4] There were Greek convents of nuns, too.[5] The Norman kings rebuilt and endowed many Greek monasteries that had been devastated by the Saracens. Under their government Calabria became like a second Thebais, full of monks. The chief Byzantine monastery was *St Saviour* at Messina. Count Roger I founded it in 1059; St Bartholomew became its first Archimandrite. The Archimandrite of St Saviour at Messina had enormous privileges all through the Middle Ages. He had forty-four dependent monasteries under him; he summoned synods of monks from all parts of Sicily and Calabria. He had also episcopal jurisdiction and a considerable amount of civil authority over territory around the monastery. So he was a great Prince of the Church; there were constant quarrels and lawsuits between him and the Archbishop of Messina. From the year 1504 begins the series of Commendatory Archimandrites[6] of

---

[1] In Migne, P.L., xxi, 35-37.

[2] Julius I, Ep. ad Ant. (342), § 18 (P.L., viii, 902, B); Cœlestinus I, Ep. xiv, ad clerum et pop. C.P., § 7 (P.L., l, 496, C). *Cf.* St Jerome, Ep. 127 (P.L., xxii, 1090).

[3] Actio II. The archimandrites of Greek and Armenian monasteries at Rome present themselves (Mansi, 903, B-C).

[4] For Sicilian monasticism see L. di Brolo, " Storia d. Chiesa in Sicilia," i, cap. xxi, pp. 401-444; ii, cap. xv, pp. 364-378.

[5] See Rodotà, " del Rito greco," ii, 57-61. Some of these communities, both monks and nuns, turned Latin and adopted the rite of St Benedict.

[6] A Commendatory Abbot was a man, not a member of the order, generally a Cardinal or even a lay prince, who received the abbey " in commendam "—that is, took possession of its revenue for his own use, but was supposed to consider it as recommended (*commendare*) to his care and protection. Meanwhile quite another person was appointed acting superior. Friedrich Vering defines *Commenda* as " the grant of the revenue of an ecclesiastical office without demanding the corresponding obligations " (" Lehrbuch des Kirchenrechts,"

Messina. This abuse was common at that time. Often the Commendatory Archimandrites[1] were laymen. They were nominated by the King of Naples, the benefice being presented by the Pope. They had various curious privileges of dress and rank, even at Papal functions.[2]

In 1738 the Congregation of the Council established a concordat between the Archbishop and the Archimandrite of Messina which at last put an end to their continual disagreement.[3] But the monastery lost all importance; the only thing that remained of it was the title " Archimandrite of St Saviour," given to prelates who had no connection with the place, and rights and privileges attached to this title which no longer had any reasonable justification. So, at last, in 1883 the Holy See ended the process of dissolution by uniting the office of Archimandrite to the Archbishopric. All that remains now of this once famous monastery is that the Archbishop of Messina also has the title " Archimandrita SS Saluatoris Messanæ "; certain rights which would otherwise belong normally to the ordinary come to him in this capacity, as holding the jurisdiction of the exempt monastery. It is an odd situation, that privileges of independence of the bishop of the diocese should be held by the bishop himself; but undoubtedly it prevents troublesome litigation. The Archbishop of Messina can hardly quarrel with himself about the limits of his own independence of himself.

There were other famous monasteries of the Byzantine rite

Freiburg, 3rd edition, 1893, p. 453). For a supposed serious definition this is as humorous a thing as you will find. The whole system was an outrageous abuse. It was, of course, really a trick by which the revenue of a rich monastery could be given to some outsider who wanted money. So the promise of an abbey *in commendam* became a valuable bribe. Francis Delfau, O.S.B. (1637-1676), one of the most learned and pious of the Benedictines of St Maur, wrote a scathing attack on the abuse, " L'abbé commendataire " (Köhn, 1673), for which he was banished by Louis XIV. " Neither nomination by the King, nor Bulls and dispensations by the Pope, nor common use can justify it."

[1] I say " Archimandrite " since we are in the Byzantine rite. As a matter of fact, the heads of Italo-Greek monasteries were constantly called, and called themselves Abbots, which means the same thing. The head of a large and important monastery in the Byzantine rite is an Archimandrite (ἀρχιμανδρίτης), the head of a smaller one a Hegumenos (ἡγούμενος). There is not much difference in practice.   [2] See Rodotà, ii, 86-87.

[3] A full account of the disputes and their settlement will be found in Rodotà, ii, 87-88. The decision is in the *Thesaurus Resolutionum Concilii* (Urbino, 1739), ad annum 1738, p. 117.

all over Southern Italy and Sicily. The Norman kings easily gave the wilder and more desert parts of their kingdom to monks to cultivate.[1] It was, however, the general rule that Byzantine monasteries were subject to the jurisdiction of the Ordinaries.[2] There were no *Stauropegia* in Italy after the Norman conquest.

One of the great centres of Italo-Greek monasticism was *Rossano* in Calabria. St Neilos the Younger, founder of Grottaferrata, came from Rossano. About a century later another St Neilos founded the famous monastery *S Maria del Patire* outside the city (on a mountain by the road to Corigliano) in 1090. Count Roger I of Sicily (1072–1101) built a great part of the church, cloisters, and so on, and gave rich presents, ornaments and endowments.[3] Then Constance, daughter of Roger II and wife of the Emperor Henry VI, took it under her protection.[4] In 1198 Innocent III (1198–1216) in a Bull counts up its domains and riches.[5] So it became one of the most powerful and splendid religious houses in all Italy. The Archimandrite of S Maria del Patire was almost as great a person as his brother of Messina. But after the Council of Florence (1439), as part of the general latinizing policy of the Archbishop Matthew Saraceni (p. 109), the monastery became Roman and Benedictine. Its name is curious. What does " del Patire " mean? In the first documents it is called " S Maria *Hodegetria.*"[6] This title of our Lady occurs often in the Byzantine rite. It means " Guide of the Way."[7] It is first the name of a famous picture of her at Constantinople, painted, naturally, by St Luke. This picture was placed in a church at Constantinople by the Empress Pulcheria (450–457). The usual explanation of the title is that generals, before setting out to war, went to pray before this picture, asking the blessed Virgin to guide them on their journey.[8] In imitation of this

---

[1] A long list of Italo-Greek monasteries, with an account of their foundation and history, is in Rodotà, vol. ii, chap. xi, pp. 176-224.

[2] Rodotà, ii, p. 90, where documents and proofs are quoted.

[3] Ughelli, " Italia sacra," ix, 291-292, quotes two diplomas of Roger II, 1104 and 1122.   [4] *Ibid.*, ix, 295.

[5] *Ibid.*, ix, 295-297.   [6] So in Roger II's diplomas.

[7] 'Οδηγήτρια, from ὁδηγός. In Italian this is abbreviated into " S. Maria de Itria." For an account of the philological process by which this form is attained see " Roma e l'Oriente," ix (1915), 31, n. 1.

[8] See Nilles, " Kalend. Man." (2nd edition, Innsbruck, 1897), ii, 163-164; Ducange, " Glossarium ad Script. med. et inf. Lat." *s.v. Hodegitria* (ed. Henschel-Lavre, Niort, 1885, iv, 211) attributes the word to the return of Michael VIII to Constantinople in 1261, after the expulsion of the Franks.

picture many others received the same name, and it became a favourite title of our Lady.[1]   There are several Hodegetria pictures and churches with this dedication among the Italo-Greeks.   Perhaps, as wandering foreigners in a strange land, they saw how appropriate is the title " Guide of the Way." The monks at Rossano, fleeing from the Saracens in Sicily, set up a shrine of our Lady Hodegetria.   The Albanians from Korone, arriving at Messina in 1533, brought with them a picture of the B.V.M. Hodegetria and set it up in the church of St Nicholas.[2]   There was another Hodegetria picture at Messina in the church of St Marina; this was brought from Rhodes in 1512.[3]   The Sicilians have a national church (of the Roman rite) at Rome, " S Maria Odigetria."[4]

The other name of the monastery at Rossano is *del Patire*. This occurs first in the form " de Patirio " in the Bull of Innocent III (1198).[5]   The meaning of the word has been much discussed.   The most probable opinion seems to be that of Montfaucon, that this, too, is Greek: " τοῦ πατρός ," that the " Father " is the founder, St Neilos, that originally it was merely an addition to " Hodegetria."   Our Lady was " Guide of the Way of the Father (Neilos)."   Then " de Patirio," " del Patire " became the only name.[6]

Since the eleventh century Grottaferrata has always been one of the most important centres of Byzantine monasticism in Italy; and now it is the only survivor of so many once famous houses.[7]

The Byzantine monks naturally followed the rule of St Basil.   In Italy, especially, they are always called *Basilians*. The first official use of the expression " Ordo S Basilii " occurs in 1382.[8]   It is not really a correct form.   In the

---

[1] The Byzantine rite keeps the feast, ἡ παναγία Μαρία τῆς ὁδηγητρίας.   The Italo-Greeks on the third day after Pentecost (Nilles, ii, 548); the Orthodox in Russia on July 28 (*cf.* A. v. Maltzew, " Menologion," Berlin, 1901, ii, 621-633).

[2] Rodotà, " del Rito greco," iii, 116.   [3] *Ibid.*

[4] S Maria d'Itria, in the Via del Tritone.   Agnoletti, " Compendio storico della chiesa e dell' ospedale di S Maria d'Itria di Constantinopoli della nazione siciliana in Roma " (Rome, 1889).

[5] Ughelli, ix, 295.

[6] B. de Montfaucon, " Palæographia græca " (Paris, 1708), lib. vii, pp. 382-384, quoting the diploma of Roger II (1130), νέας ὁδηγητρίας τοῦ πατρός.   *Cf.* p. 398.

[7] See pp. 146-151.

[8] This is, at any rate, the first case Rodotà knows.   In 1382 Cyprian, Archimandrite of the monastery of St John Theristes in the diocese of Squillace, appoints a procurator at Rome.   He signs the

Byzantine Church there are no distinctions of religious orders. A monk is a monk, just as a deacon is a deacon. No further qualification is needed or is used in the East.[1] But it was natural that a special name should be given to the Byzantine monks in Italy. Here people were accustomed to distinguish various religious orders. As they spoke of Benedictines, Dominicans, Franciscans, so they spoke of Basilians. Moreover, there were monks of this rule who were Latins; they at least would need a special name. Since, then, the name Basilian became official in Italy, we need have no hesitation in using it.

Undoubtedly the Basilian monks were the chief factor in preserving the Byzantine rite in Italy. During the later Middle Ages, before the Albanians arrived, while the rite was dying out in the parish churches, it was kept alive in the Basilian monasteries. There was much less danger of its extinction here. The parish clergy, under a Latin bishop, easily forsook the foreign rite for his; but the monasteries were closed corporations, much less liable to such influence. The Byzantine rite was, as it were, part of their rule. It was easier for the monks to get recruits for their rite than for the Byzantine diocesan clergy. Among secular priests there were great difficulties in ordaining a man born of Latin parents as a Byzantine priest; but anyone might join a Basilian monastery as easily as he might go to the Benedictines. If he did so, he became a user of the Byzantine rite, as part of the institution of his order.

Already in the thirteenth century we hear of decadence of the Basilian monks in Italy. This decadence went on, in spite of repeated attempts by Popes to reform the monks, all through the later Middle Ages, and so on, till we come to the all but extinction of Byzantine monasticism in our own time. The reason of the decadence was always the same; it is indeed the same reason which brought about the gradual disappearance of the rite (except for the Albanians). The Greek element was dying out; the descendants of the original Italo-Greeks were becoming italianized. This applied to the monks, too. They were becoming practically Italians, to whom, if Latin offered no great difficulty, Greek did. So the constant complaint is of the ignorance of the monks, which means that they

---

document, " Cyprian Archimandrite of the monastery of St John Theristes, *of the Order of St Basil* " (Rodotà quotes the whole text, ii, 38-39).

[1] See " Orth. Eastern Church," 354-355.

did not understand the Greek language.   They did not know enough Greek to be able to read their rule or understand their office.   In 1221 Pope Honorius III (1216–1227) heard that the Basilian monks of Calabria and Apulia were in a parlous state; they were ignorant, lazy, and a scandal to the people. So he sent the Bishop of Cotrone and the Archimandrite of Grottaferrata as visitors, to see about reforming them[1] Urban V (1362–1370) in 1370 made the Archbishop of Otranto visitor to all the Basilian monasteries in the South.   He was to see to it that their liturgical books contained no errors. Their ignorance of Greek was believed to have allowed various errors of the schismatics to creep into their prayers.[2]   In 1424 Martin V (1417–1431) again sent a visitor, Laurence Carella, Archdeacon of Ascoli.[3]   The civil Government also tried to improve the condition of these monks.   Alphonsus I (1442–1458), established schools of the Greek language for them, and threatened that, if they would not learn, he would take away their monasteries and give them to Latins.[4]   Pope Eugene IV (1431–1447) summoned a synod of the monks to Rome in 1446, appointed regular visitors for their monasteries and Greek teachers, whom the monasteries had to pay out of their revenues. But the monks would not pay to be taught Greek, and there were further difficulties.[5]   In 1461 the Town Council of Messina set up a school where its monks were to be taught their liturgical language.[6]

Cardinal Bessarion was Commendatory Archimandrite of St Saviour at Messina, then of Grottaferrata.   As he was one of the chief protectors of the Byzantine rite in Italy in his time, so he took a special interest in the Byzantine monasteries.[7] Since the monks knew so little Greek, he translated the rule of St Basil into Italian for them.   In the Preface of this translation he says: " Some men, following the monastic life, especially in Italy and Sicily, pretend to keep the laws and rules of that life, yet, ignorant of the Greek language, being born of Latin parents, cannot read Greek, or if they can read it,

[1] Ughelli, " Italia sacra," ix, 385.
[2] The Brief is quoted in full by Rodotà, ii, 133.
[3] Rodotà, ii, 135.   The instructions given to these visitors all insist on the need of radical reform.
[4] Rodotà, ii, 135-136.
[5] Ibid., 136.
[6] Ibid., 137.
[7] R. Rocholl, " Bessarion, Studie zur Gesch. der Renaissance " (Leipzig, 1904), "Die Basilianer," pp. 79-85.   In 1446 Bessarion was appointed Protector of the O.S. Bas. in Italy.

nevertheless often make mistakes and do not understand the words.''[1] Then he brought masters from the East to teach the monks, first Andronikos Gallinatos, then Constantine Laskaris. He founded a chair of Greek at Messina at the cost of the monks. Gallinatos, then another Greek of Constantinople, Glykas, then Laskaris held this chair in turn.[2] Bessarion was also concerned to reform the life of the monks. In 1466 he summoned a synod of Basilians to Rome to consider various points of reform.[3]

But the disorders went on. In the sixteenth century, Rodotà says: " Degenerate from their institution, they had nothing of monks but the name. They observed no rule of life but that which was suggested by their own will, without any command of superiors. They wandered from town to town. Many lived in the houses of their relations, without any restraint, and far from all pious practices. With pride and arrogance they interfered in worldly affairs; there was no business of the people in which they did not wish to have their say."[4] Julius II (1503-1513) named Cardinal Dominic Grimani Protector of the Basilians. He at once sent two visitors to reform them.[5] But later, Cardinal Santoro says of them: " The rule of St Basil lies in darkness and dirt . . . the monasteries, filled with a mass of men, are looked upon as a joke. In them is no pious habit of life, no order, no discipline. The monks wander everywhere without a rector, and ruin the dignity of the ordinaries . . . though they say their office in Greek they can neither read nor write Greek properly, and they spoil the rites. . . . Cruel shipwreck of discipline, most lamentable fall and certain death of the ancient order established by the most holy and learned Father, which has lasted so many centuries."[6] In Santoro's time the Basilians in Italy nearly came to an end. Philip II of Spain (1556-1598) was so annoyed by the scandals of the monks that he determined to abolish them altogether. It was Santoro who persuaded him not to do so.[7] Though Santoro was so conscious of the disorders of these monks, yet he did not want to see the old order done away with.

Meanwhile a curious side-issue to our subject is the establishment of a branch of the Basilian order in Spain. But these

[1] " Prologus in Asceticarum s. Basiliicom pendium " in P.G. clxi, 528, B.
[2] Rocholl, *op. cit.*, p. 83.
[3] Rodotà, ii, 141.
[4] *Ibid.*, 143-144.
[5] *Ibid.*, 144.
[6] Quoted by Rodotà, ii, 135.
[7] *Ibid.*, 145.

Spanish Basilians were Latins, using the Roman rite; so they do not concern us here.[1]

To remedy so many evils, at last Gregory XIII (1572–1585) decided to form the Basilians of Italy, Sicily, and Spain into one Congregation under one general, after the manner of so many Western religious orders. This is pure Latinism. Nothing could be, in principle, more alien from the ideal of Byzantine monasticism than this organization as one Congregation. Yet, no doubt, it was the best way of remedying their disorders. If the purist regrets this case of latinizing a Byzantine institution, he should remember that the monks brought it on themselves. They could have kept their ancient system unchallenged if they had led decent lives. It is better for a monk to obey even a latinized rule than none at all. Cardinal Sirlet persuaded the Pope to take this step. In 1579 Gregory issued his Constitution for the Order of St Basil in Italy, Sicily, Spain. Other Uniate Byzantine monks, for instance, those of Ruthenia, Hungary, Transylvania, though they had the same rule, were not to belong to this Congregation. The Pope abolished the abuse of the Commendatory Archimandrites, who were not monks at all. The monks are to be exempt from the jurisdiction of the Ordinaries. The Congregation is to hold a General Chapter every three years, to watch over discipline and reform abuses. This chapter is to elect a *Minister generalis*, visitors for the monasteries, and a procurator general. All monasteries of the Basilians in Italy, Sicily, Spain, are subject to the general. The first General

---

[1] The Basilian order spread into Spain at the time when the Spanish king also ruled Naples and the two Sicilies. The founder of the Spanish branch was a certain Fr. Bernard della Cruz in Andalusia, who obtained a Brief from Pius IV (1559-1565) in 1561. He went to Grottaferrata to learn the rule and made his own profession there. There were seven monasteries in Andalusia and six in Castile. But great disputes arose in Spain between a reformed and the unreformed branches of the order. Finally Gregory XIII united all Basilians of Italy, Sicily, and Spain in one Congregation (see above). Those of Spain were always Latins of the Roman rite. Gregory XIII, in his Constitution of 1577, says that, although the Holy See had required them, after a certain number of years, to adopt the Byzantine rite, " the time appointed is now past, and they, frightened by the labour of learning Greek, neglect the Greek rite and keep the Latin one in which they have been brought up " (see the text quoted by Allatius, " de Consensu," lib. iii, chap. ii, § 8, cols. 1092-1093, and Rodotà, " del Rito greco," ii, p. 154, n.). There are now no longer any Spanish or other Latin Basilians. For their history see Rodotà, *op. cit.*, ii, cap. ix, pp. 146-159; Moroni, " Diz. di Erud.," iv, 183-185; Hergenröther in *Archiv. f. Kath. Kirchenrecht*, N.F. ii (1862), p. 82.

Chapter was held in the monastery of St Philaret, in the diocese of Mileto in the same year (1579 . It elected Nicholas Antony Ruffo, Archimandrite of St Nicholas at Butramo, in Sicily, as first general. The reformed rule was published in 1678.[1] The general of the Basilians had and has the same privileges at Papal functions as the generals of other orders. Though this congregation is now reduced to one monastery, it is still bound by the rule of 1678.

Meanwhile, during all this period, the rule of St Basil lost many subjects. Just as the other Italo-Greeks, harried by their neighbours, asked and obtained permission to turn Latin, so numbers of Basilian monasteries, weary of the difficulty of keeping up this foreign rule with its Greek office and services in a Latin land, tired, too, of the greater strictness of their rule,[2] got leave to drop the whole thing, to become Latins and follow the rule of St Benedict. Thus Abbot Ferdinand Ughelli, writing about 1640, says of the great monastery " del Patire " at Rossano (p. 127): " This church a few years ago became Latin. Formerly it used the Greek language and rite."[3] Others, while keeping their rule and rite, nevertheless modified it in various ways by adopting Latin customs.[4] Very many Basilian monasteries disappeared altogether, for lack of subjects. In the eighteenth century the rule of St Basil again nearly disappeared in Italy. This time it was two of their own generals who tried to turn the Congregation into a Latin order. They are Peter Menniti in 1709 and Joseph del Pozzo in 1746. Both presented petitions to the Pope that the Italo-Greek rite might be finally abolished.

[1] " Constitutiones monachorum ordinis S Basilii congregationis Italiæ," Rome, 1678.

[2] The comparative severity of the Roman and Byzantine rites is a curious point. In one point at least, the celibacy of secular clergy, the Byzantine rite is notably more lax. In almost all others it is more severe. The laity have many more, and more severe, fast-days. For monks it is much severer. Byzantine monks have perpetual abstinence from flesh-meat, all their lives, a huge amount of fasting and enormously long office. Another rule from which many Basilian monks often wished to escape is the obligation of wearing the beard and long hair. This, it seems, exposed them to derision (though, as far as the beard is concerned, there have always been plenty of Capuchins in Italy).

[3] " Italia sacra," ix, col. 286.

[4] For instance, by shaving the beard, wearing the close-fitting Italian cassock instead of the ample ῥάσον, eating flesh-meat, shortening the Canonical Hours and adapting them, more or less, to the Roman order, and so on. Grottaferrata, I regret to say, was a bad offender in such ways as this (see p. 150).

Neither was successful. Rodotà argues indignantly against the reasons they give.[1]

Rodotà laments the diminution of the ancient order in Italy. He says that, whereas once there were about a thousand monasteries of this rule, in his time they are reduced to " the mean number of only forty-three."[2] Since his time the process has gone on apace. At the present moment all that is left of the rule is one single monastery, Grottaferrata. If ever that disappears, or is turned into a Benedictine house, then all Italo-Greek monasticism will be a mere memory. Fortunately, though reduced to this one house, it still remains, heir to so many glorious memories (pp. 146-151).

There were once many convents of Basilian nuns in Calabria and Sicily. Rodotà gives a list of those that once existed in Calabria.[3] Already in his time all were extinct. Some had disappeared, some had adopted the rule of a Latin order. When he wrote a few remained in Sicily. But here, too, they were disappearing.[4] One of the greatest was the convent of St Saviour Philanthropos (Filatropo) at Messina, founded by Roger I of Sicily. " Down to our own time," says Rodotà, " they sang the divine praises in Greek."[5] But then the usual difficulty arose. It was perhaps even more difficult to find ladies in Sicily who knew Greek than to find such men. So they were allowed to adopt the Roman rite and the Benedictine rule. Only the Blessing of Waters at the Epiphany, the lessons on Palm Sunday, and the Liturgy and Hesperinon on the feasts of St Basil and his sister St Makrine were still Byzantine, in Greek.[6] At Palermo there was still a convent, St Saviour, founded by Robert Wiscard. Bessarion arranged their rule for them.[7] All these have now disappeared. But there is a Byzantine convent of nuns belonging to the Albanian colonies (p. 166).

---

[1] See the text of their *suppliche* and the whole story in Rodotà, ii, chap. xiii (pp. 234-265).

[2] II, " argomento " at the beginning (not paged; but it is p. 2). Joseph Schirò in his report (1742) gives a list of the then extant monasteries (Karalevsky, " Documenti inediti," i, p. 6).

[3] ii, 269.　　　　　　　　　　[4] Rodotà, ii, 269-271.

[5] *Ibid.*, 270.　　　　　　　　　[6] *Ibid.*, 270-271.

[7] *Ibid.*, 271. Schirò in 1742 mentions the two convents of Palermo and Messina. He says that the nuns at Messina were Byzantine to the reign of Clement XI (1700-1721); he knows of many others at Naples and Rome which had already become Latin (Karalevsky, *op. cit.*, i, 6).

7. The Greek Colonies at Venice, Ancona, Bibbona, Naples.

At the end of this chapter I add a note about colonies of Uniates now extinct. The most important of these was at Venice. The most Serene Republic, by her conquests in the Levant, had a great number of Christians of the Byzantine rite under her authority. Ever since the fourth crusade she had interests and possessions in Greek lands. At the fourth crusade (1204) Venice obtained Crete, then the land of Methone and Korone, at the bottom of the Peloponnesus. Soon after she occupied Chalkis in Euboia. By the fifteenth century Venice held, besides these, all Euboia, Kerkyra, and most of the land that is now Dalmatia. In the wars of the seventeenth century she conquered the Peloponnesus. The Peace of Karlowitz (1699) left this to her. The Peace of Passarowitz (1718) restored the Peloponnesus to the Turks, but left Dalmatia with its islands to Venice. The long centuries of Venetian occupation have left a marked impression in these countries. In all the coast towns of Dalmatia Italian is still talked. Kerkyra has a large Catholic-Latin population; there are Latin Catholics in great numbers in many Greek islands.[1] Meanwhile, after the fall of Constantinople (1453) a number of Greek merchants fled to Venice and there formed an established Greek colony.

Now the policy of the Republic was curiously different with regard to the Greeks in her conquered territories and those at the city itself. In the conquered lands the Government was not tolerant of schism. Latin bishops were set up throughout Dalmatia, Albania, the Peloponnesus. These had authority from the Government to visit the Greek clergy and schools, and to impose on them Catholic professions of faith. They did not make the people Latins, but they did all they could to make them Uniates. Those who would not accept union with Rome were punished severely. Large numbers were sent to the galleys; others managed to flee to Trieste or to other Italian cities, where Venice had no power.[2] There was, indeed, a regular persecution of the Orthodox by the Venetian Government in its Levantine colonies; a fact that is the more curious since the Government itself was constantly in a state of interdict. The meaning of this policy is, of course, obvious. It was to

---

[1] Notably in Syra and Tenos.

[2] J. M. Schröckh, " Christliche Kirchengeschichte " (Leipzig, 1804-1812), Theil. ix, pp. 43-52, and Diomede Kyriakos, Ἐκκλησια-στικὴ Ἱστορία (Athens, 1898), iii, 118-123, give lurid accounts of this persecution.

unite the people, as so many states have tried to do, in one religion. The Doge might have his own disagreements with the Holy See; but he would not tolerate strange religions in his state.

But, in the case of the Greek colony at Venice itself, the policy of the Government was quite different. It appreciated the advantage of having these prosperous Greek merchants at the capital;[1] it wanted others to come. So it was careful to respect their religious convictions. Even when there were laws requiring that these Greeks, too, should be Catholics, the Government studiously winked at their non-observance. So we have the curious situation that, while the Council of Ten was persecuting the Orthodox in Dalmatia for not being Catholics, it ignored the repeated demand of the Pope that it should begin at home by converting these obstinate schismatics at its very gates. All of which shows how little religion had to do with the matter either way.

When the first Greek exiles from Constantinople arrived in Venice, in 1453, it was Cardinal Isidore of Kiev, then in the city, who arranged with the Government for their reception. They were given a chapel in the Church of St Blasius[2] for their rites. Here, in 1498, they set up a confraternity,[3] with the provision that no one should be a member of it who was not in union with the Holy See. They had not yet begun their movement towards schism. At first, indeed, the Greeks made a great parade of their union with Rome.[4] The Ten allowed them to build a church for themselves in 1511, and Leo X published a brief to this effect in 1514. The church was built between 1539 and 1592, and was dedicated to St George. It was not large, but elegant and well fitted for the Byzantine rite. It was served by two chaplains.[5] The Government ordered that

---

[1] Besides merchants the Greek colony consisted of fishermen and daring sailors. The Republic was able to form from it a company of soldiers in its pay, called *Estradiote* (στρατιῶται).

[2] San Biagio di Castello, near the Arsenal.

[3] Confraternity of St Nicholas of the Greeks. The Government insisted that it was not to have more than 250 members.

[4] In 1456 the Pope (Calixtus III, 1455-1458), writing in their favour to the Patriarch of Venice, says that they live " as Catholics under the obedience of the holy Roman Church." In 1511 they assure the Government that they are " true and Catholic Christians " (Pisani in the *Rev. d'hist. et de lit. relig.*, i, 205). They knew of course, what such language meant at Venice.

[5] The second chaplain was not allowed till 1534. He was to be nominated by the Latin (Venetian) Bishop of Monembasia in the Peloponnesus.

these should make a Catholic profession of faith in the terms
of the Council of Florence, and should be approved by the
Papal Nunzio or by the Patriarch of Venice. These chaplains
were then paid by the State.[1]

But among the Greek community there were some who
had no sympathy with the idea of being Uniates, who rather
turned longing eyes towards the Patriarch of Constantinople,
now again a schismatic. It is not difficult to understand this.
The colony was being continually reinforced by new arrivals
from the East; these brought with them the ideas of their homes.
Then, surrounded by Venetian Latins, the exiled Greeks all
the more clung to their own nationality; of this nationality
the Patriarch of Constantinople, whether he be a Uniate or
not, is always the great representative. Meanwhile, the
colony having grown, the Greeks thought they ought to have
not merely two priests to minister to them, but a bishop. They
petitioned the Government to allow this, and obtained what
they wanted. The Holy See allowed it willingly enough.
It was time to do away with the anomalous condition of Italo-
Greeks without bishops. Naturally, the Byzantine bishop at
Venice was to be a Uniate, to satisfy the same conditions as the
chaplains. Nor was he to have jurisdiction. This is, in fact,
the first case of a titular Byzantine bishop in Italy. The
Council of Ten kept to itself the chief influence in the election
of this bishop; he was to be the auxiliary of the Patriarch of
Venice for the Greek colony. The first so chosen was
Pachomios, exiled Metropolitan of Zakynthos and Kephallenia.
He made a Catholic profession of faith, was approved by the
local Patriarch, and began his work at Venice in 1557. At first
there was no difficulty about the ordination of these Greek
bishops; there were plenty of exiled Metropolitans from the
Levant who were glad to get the post. They were paid
generously by the Government. It was the second of this
line who did the mischief. This was no less a person than
Gabriel Seberos,[2] formerly of Philadelphia. This Seberos

---

[1] Rodotà, " del Rito greco," iii, 220; Schröckh, " Christl. Kirchengesch.," ix, 43; P. Pisani, " Les Chrétiens de rite orientale à Venise "
in the *Rev. d'hist. et de lit. relig.*, i (1896), pp. 201-224; Kyriakos
'Εκκλ. 'Ιστ.,, iii, 118-119.

[2] Σεβῆρος. He had been chaplain in Venice, came in 1577 to
Constantinople, where he was ordained Metropolitan of Philadelphia,
and then back to Venice as bishop in 1582. He never resided at
Philadelphia; ordained in schism and always at heart in union with
the Œcumenical Patriarch, it was, nevertheless, against the Patriarch's
will that he went back to Venice. Later he received from the Patri-

was a determined enemy of union with Rome all his life. He was appointed in 1582. Towards the Government and the Patriarch of Venice he concealed his feelings, and professed to be converted to union with the Holy See. But to his own community he preached the usual Orthodox things about the horns of Roman pride, the chains of Latin slavery now imposed by proud barbarians on the descendants of Achilles and Agamemnon. So from his time it seems that by far the greater part of the Greek Venetian community was schismatic at heart. It accepted the position of Uniates only as an unpleasant necessity. From the time of Seberos[1] the Greek bishop at Venice always kept the title of Philadelphia.[2] Then the Venetian Government began to connive at the breaking of its own law. It ignored the rule that the bishop should make a Catholic profession of faith. He began openly to pray in his church for the Patriarch of Constantinople; when he was not already a bishop he went to Constantinople to be ordained. The Greek community had become schismatical. More and

---

arch the office of 'Επίτροπος (Vicar) for the vacant see of Monembasia, which apparently means authority over all the Orthodox in the Venetian states. It is clear then that, all the time, he was really a schismatic. He published his views so openly that the Venetian Government must have known them and connived at them. At Venice he came into conflict with Maximos Margunios (who also lived there; † 1602). Margunios was a friend of union with Rome; Seberos opposed him in a number of books and pamphlets. Seberos wrote a book with a long title in defence of the adoration of the Holy Gifts at the Great Entrance in the Liturgy (Venice, 1604), a treatise on the Sacraments (*ibid.*, 1600), a defence of the Orthodox Church against the charge of schism (his chief work, unpublished; it is against Bellarmin), and many short theological treatises, mostly against the Latins. See E. Legrand, " Bibliographie Hellénique " (Paris, 1885), ii, pp. 144-151; Richard Simon, " Fides Eccl. Orient. seu Gabrielis Metr. Phil. opuscula " (Paris, 1671); Ph. Meyer, " Die theolog. Litter. der griech. Kirche im XVI Jahrht." (Leipzig, 1899) pp. 78-85.

[1] Seberos died in 1616 and is buried in the Greek church at Venice.

[2] It is curious that, although the Venetian Greeks were still supposed officially to be Uniates, the Patriarch of Constantinople always legislates for them as if they were his people—so ambiguous was their position. In 1644 the Patriarch Parthenios II (1644-1645, 1648-1651) decrees that the See of Philadelphia has been transferred to Venice " from ancient times," and that its occupant shall be Exarch of the Patriarch for all Greeks under the Venetian Government. In 1651 Ioannikios II (1646-1648, 1651-1652, 1653-1654, 1655-1656; these Patriarchs are constantly being deposed and restored) grants further privileges. The titular Metropolitan of Philadelphia is to ordain the

more Greeks arrived in Venice; they became a most prosperous and wealthy community. They established a great school, the Phlangineion, destined to be one of the chief Greek schools abroad, when there were none under the Turk. And the Œcumenical Patriarch wrote strong letters to them, fortifying them in their resolution not to bow to the horns of Roman pride.

In 1700 the Government seems suddenly to have realized how this community was slipping away from its influence. It was not so much the question of faith as that of the Government's rights that brought about a crisis. While the bishop was now frankly a schismatic, he was even nominated at Constantinople. So all the rights of the state in his election were ignored. When the bishop Gerasimos died, in 1679, the Council of Ten resolved to make itself felt in the nomination of his successor. The Venetian Patriarch, Peter Barbarigo, seized this opportunity to restore the old state of communion with Rome. Between them they arranged for the election of Meletios Typaldos in 1680. He was a Greek from the island Kephallenia, presumably formerly a schismatic. But he became a Uniate, made a Catholic profession of faith, satisfied all the conditions set by the authorities at Rome, and so was ordained in the church of St George as Catholic auxiliary of the Patriarch of Venice for the Greek community. Typaldos held this office thirty-seven years (1681–1718), during which he remained always a zealous supporter of the Government and of union. He insisted that all his clergy should make a Catholic profession of faith, would not allow any wandering Greek priest to officiate in his church till he, too, had done so, and used every means to put an end to the spirit of schism among his people. He was on excellent terms with the Venetian Government, obtained further privileges for his people from it, and helped it to put down and punish any attempt at schism.

Naturally there is difference of opinion as to the character of Typaldos. The Orthodox Kyriakos and the Protestant Schröckh cannot bear him. Kyriakos says he was corrupted by Roman gold and betrayed the Orthodox by himself helping the Government to carry out its persecuting laws.[1] Schörckh

---

Metropolitan of Zakynthos and Kephallenia (then Venetian territory); he may himself be ordained by any bishop, at the choice of the Venetian Government (Pisani, *loc. cit.*, p. 210).

[1] 'Εκκλ. 'Ιστ., iii, 120.

says he did all this in the hope of being made a Cardinal.[1] On the other hand, the Catholic Rodotà is charmed with him. " The regularity of his life, his wisdom in the most difficult questions, his learning both sacred and profane, and his love of the truth made him the object of universal admiration. Admitted to the Pontifical rank he became the model of prelates; nor was a more exemplary ecclesiastic known among the Greeks."[2]   At his death Pope Clement XI (1700–1720) wrote a letter of condolence to the Doge, full of his praise.

After the death of Typaldos, the Government would not allow the Greek community to elect a successor for forty-four years.[3]   The reason of this was, partly that it still feared that a bishop might the more easily lead the people again into schism, partly that it feared lest the Greeks of Illyricum might also want a bishop of their own, and then, under him, make difficulties.   The Venetian Greeks were allowed to choose an episcopal Vicar, who was to be a priest with some episcopal rights; he must make a Catholic profession of faith and guarantee that all the clergy be Catholics too.   One of these vicars, Gerasimos Phokas, was openly a schismatic.   He removed the Pope's name from the liturgical diptychs and inserted that of the Patriarch of Constantinople.   So he was removed by the Government, which declared that the Greeks must pray for the Pope.   Now it began to take severe measures against schism.   Two Catholic vicars followed, an Archimandrite Moazzo in 1751, then a man named Milia[4] in 1760. At last, in 1762, the Chapter of St George had leave to proceed to the election of a bishop.   He must be a native of the Venetian state, a Catholic, and must profess the faith of the Council of Florence.   The man so chosen was the monk George Facéa.[5]   But meanwhile all the old tendency towards

---

[1] " Christl. Kirchengesch.," ix, p. 44.

[2] " del Rito greco," iii, 224.

[3] Altogether there were eight bishops from Seberos to Typaldos (1582-1718).   A list of them is given by Rodotà, iii, 223-225, and by Pisani, *loc. cit.*, p. 209.

[4] That is how Rodotà spells their names.   Presumably Mu'āzz (=" cherished ") an Arab, and Μηλιάς (or some such name), a Greek.

[5] The Italians call him Facéa, the Greeks φατσέας.   In the case of the later Italo-Greeks it is often difficult to say which form of their name is original.   Probably they used both themselves.   But here " Facéa " seems obviously the original form.   The Greeks' documents call him sometimes George and sometimes Gregory, the Latin ones always George.   I suppose he was baptized George, and became Gregory as a monk.

schism had reappeared in the community. For one thing, their national feeling encouraged this; for another, there was a continual influx of Greeks from the Levant, who brought with them all the ideas of the Orthodox Church at that time. So the people were again, in the majority, schismatics at heart. The Council of Ten approved of Facéa's election; so far, outwardly at least, he was a Uniate.

But now he begins to play a double game. He tries to satisfy both the Orthodox at Constantinople and the Catholics at Rome; he hedges with both, and, as one might expect, ends by being excommunicated by both the Pope and the Œcumenical Patriarch. First he went to Kerkyra and was there ordained by two Orthodox bishops, Chrysanthos of Leukas and Sophronios of Zakynthos and Kephallenia. It would seem as if this meant so definite a breach with Rome that he had better frankly throw in his lot with the Orthodox and take his chance of the inevitable quarrel with the Pope and the Venetian Government. However, Facéa now begins to hedge. Ioannikios II of Constantinople, delighted to hear of his ordination by Orthodox bishops, sent him an Orthodox profession of faith to sign. But Facéa refused to do so, saying that he was a Catholic. Now come a series of fulminations on Facéa from both sides. The Pope then was Clement XIII (1758–1769). He wrote three Briefs; in the first he says that Facéa is a schismatic, unlawfully ordained, who has received the imposition of hands outside the Church; in the second, the Pope forbids all Catholic Greeks to communicate with " the Pseudo-bishop Facéa "; in the third, he repeats that he is a schismatic, and orders that he be expelled from the Church of St George.

Meanwhile the Œcumenical Patriarch was just as angry. He, too, wrote three synodical letters against Facéa. In the first, he complains that Facéa was ordained without having received the Patriarchal and Synodal Bull, and without having made a profession of the Orthodox faith. So the Patriarch also deposes him, forbids all the Orthodox to attend his services, and excommunicates all who " shall kiss his not-sacred hand." In the second letter the Patriarch excommunicates the two Orthodox bishops who had ordained him. In the third, he explains, justifies, and repeats the excommunication of " the monk George Facéa." Eventually the Venetian Government persuaded Facéa to make up his mind one way or the other. It seemed simpler to be reconciled with Rome. So he submitted, made profuse apologies and explanations of his conduct so far, signed the decree of Florence, and so at the end was recognized by the Pope.[1]

But the harm he had done was not appeased thereby. By this time the majority of the Greek community was definitely schismatical. Facéa, after his lurid career, kept the allegiance of but few. He died not long after, and it seems that what was left of a Uniate party among the Greeks of Venice died with him. From now all the community is Orthodox. In 1781 they got the Orthodox Metropolitan of Kerkyra and Zakynthos to come and minister to them. He was the last Greek bishop at Venice. But the people ever since have been in union with the Œcumenical Patriarch. When Napoleon conquered Venice (1797) he proclaimed entire liberty of conscience for all the Orthodox in its territory. In 1808 he ordered that the Orthodox of Dalmatia should elect a bishop, and should have a chapter and a seminary for the education of their clergy. There was to be a synod to consider future arrangements. By the Treaty of Pressburg (1805) Austria obtained Venice. The Austrian Government also allowed full liberty to the Orthodox; so does the Italian Government (since 1866). There is still a flourishing Greek community in the city; but it is entirely Orthodox.[2] The Church of St George[3] is now an Orthodox church.[4]

In the sixteenth century there was also a community of Greek merchants and exiles at *Ancona*. They, too, on their arrival in Italy, professed to be Uniates in communion with the Pope. Probably, as in the case of all these Greeks in Italy, they did not really care much about the matter one way or the other; but they foresaw that it would be impossible to maintain a schismatical community in Italy (all the more since Ancona was in the Papal states), so they accepted union with Rome, caring only to keep their rite and

---

[1] The case of Facéa is told in full, with the documents (six excommunications, three by the Pope and three by the Œcumenical Patriarch), in a curious little work, M. J. F. le Bret, " Acta ecclesiæ græcæ annorum 1762 et 1763, siue de schismate recentissimo in eccl. gr. subnato commentatio," Stuttgard, 1764.

[2] Till 1904, or thereabouts, the official press which printed all Orthodox liturgical books was the τυπογραφία ὁ φοῖνιξ at Venice. Now it has been removed to Patras.

[3] " S Giorgio dei Greci," in the Rio dei Greci between St Mark and the Arsenal. It is a very fine specimen of a Byzantine church with a handsome Ikonostasion. It has a leaning tower.

[4] For the Greek community at Venice, besides the works quoted, see the history of Ἰωάννης Βελοῦδος (Giovanni Veludo): Ἑλλήνων ὀρθοδόξων ἀποικία ἐν Βενετίαις (Venice, 1872).

customs. Clement VII (1523–1534) gave them the Church of St Anne in 1524; and in order to prevent quarrels between them and the Ordinary, he exempted them from local jurisdiction, reserving to himself all authority over their church, their clergy, and a confraternity they formed. In return they were to make an offering of candles to the Pope every year at Candlemas. All went well for about two centuries. The Greeks at Ancona had their chaplain, who was proud of his immediate dependence on the Holy See. But in the time of Benedict XIV (1740–1758) there were disputes between them and the Bishop of Ancona. No diocesan bishop much likes exempt communities in his diocese; in this case (as usually happens) he complained that the Greeks were exceeding the limit of their just exemption and were defying his authority, making it contemptible throughout the diocese. So Benedict XIV in 1750 abolished the exemption. At Ancona, too, the Greeks seem to have borne union unwillingly, at least in the later period. They, too, turned longing eyes to Constantinople, where reigned the great head of their nation.

But, as long as they were in the Papal states, it was vain to hope to be allowed to go into schism. They showed their minds when the French proclaimed the Cisalpine Republic in 1797. At once they broke their communion with Rome and turned Orthodox. The result of this was that in 1822, after a long lawsuit, the bishop was able to claim the Church of St Anne and to turn them out of it. Since then the church is restored to the Latin rite. There is still a small Orthodox community at Ancona, consisting of Greek merchants. They have now built themselves a new church.[1]

In 1671 a number of Greeks from Maina in the Peloponnesus came to Tuscany. They were well received by the Grand Duke (Cosimo III, 1670–1723), and settled about Volterra. They, too, declared that they were Uniates. They were given a church at *Bibbona*.[2] In 1674 the Bishop of Volterra, profiting by the accidental presence of the Byzantine Uniate Bishop of Samos in Tuscany, sent him to Bibbona as delegate and visitor of the Greek community there. The

---

[1] Rodotà, iii, 228-229; Moroni, " Dizionario di erudizione storico-ecclesiastica " (Venice), vol. xxxii (1845), p. 150; J. Hergenröther, " Die Rechtsverhältnisse der verschiedenen Riten innerhalb der Kath. Kirche " (in the *Archiv für Kath. Kirchenrecht*, Mainz, vol. vii, 1862), p. 181. The only connection between St Anne's Church and the Greeks now remaining is that its parish priest is bound, at least once a week, to preach against the Eastern schism.

[2] Bibbona is a small place in the Maremma toscana, South of Pisa.

Greeks then had five priests. The bishop was cordially
received by the people. On May 3, 1674, he called them together in their church and spoke to them at length on the
Catholic faith and the necessity of union with the Holy See.
The five priests made a public profession of faith in the form
of Florence, and all the people declared their hatred of schism.
Then the bishop solemnly kept the *Hesperinon* office according
to the Byzantine rite. The next morning he conceived a pretty
way of symbolizing their union with the Latins. He brought
from the neighbouring Latin church holy water blessed in our
rite, sprinkled the people with it, and celebrated the holy
Liturgy according to theirs. He then held a service for the
repose of the souls of their dead, gave them further instructions
in the Catholic faith, and told them how to be on good terms
with their Latin neighbours. Altogether this visit of the
Bishop of Samos seems to have been the ideal of such a visitation to people of one rite in a land of another.

But the Greeks of Bibbona still had some taint of schismatical
infection. In 1675 there were complaints that they allowed
divorce on the terms of the Orthodox. So the Pope sent a
Benedictine, Dom Oderisio Maria Pieri, who had been missionary in the island of Chios. Rodotà says: " He made them
conceive a horror of solution of matrimony, and prevented them
from contracting it in the forbidden degrees. He abolished the
cult of certain schismatics whom they had honoured as saints,
and persuaded them to conform to the Gregorian Calendar."[1]
So this visitation, too, seems to have been eminently satisfactory. There are now no Byzantine Uniates at Bibbona.
They kept their rite till 1693, then they all turned Latin,
" yielding to the insinuations of a certain missionary Gregorii."[2]

There was a Uniate Byzantine church at *Naples* from
1518 till the Italian Revolution. Thomas Asan Palælogos, of
the House of the Despots of Mistra, fleeing to Italy from the
Turk, arrived in Naples, with many other Greeks, at the end
of the fifteenth century. Here, in 1518, he built a chapel
in honour of St Peter and St Paul for the use of his rite. Then
a larger church was built in 1544. It was always Uniate,
the chaplain being nominated by the Archbishop of Naples.
Later, many of the Albanians from Korone joined this congregation (p. 118). But here, too, a schismatical party appeared. When the Italian Government was set up in Naples
(1860) this party obtained its permission to keep the church

[1] Rodotà, iii, 232.
[2] *Ibid.*; for the Byzantine community at Bibbona see pp. 231-232.

as an Orthodox one. Since then the Uniates (now all Albanians) have tried in vain to reclaim it.[1] The Byzantine Uniate communities at Leghorn and in Corsica still exist, and will be discussed below (pp. 169-175).

Summary.

There have been Greeks in the South of Italy and in Sicily since the days, long before Christianity, when colonists from Hellas made these parts Greater Greece. There has been Christianity of a Greek type, using Greek as its liturgical language, ever since the Gospel was first preached in Calabria, Apulia, and Sicily. During the first six centuries there was a gradual but incomplete process of latinization of the Southern Italians and Sicilians, both in ordinary life and in religious matters. In the seventh century, fresh influence from Constantinople fortified the Greek element. In the eighth, the Lombards came, bringing with them the Latin language and Latin rites, but as a foreign element, in their case. Meanwhile the Roman citizens looked to Constantinople as their capital, and remained for the chief part Greek. Yet the Church of Southern Italy and Sicily all the time was closely dependent on Rome. The Pope ordained all its bishops; it had no other Metropolitan than him. In the eighth century, as part of the Iconoclast persecution, the Emperors at Constantinople made a determined attempt to hellenize all that was left of their empire in Italy and Sicily. They affected to withdraw the bishops from dependence on the Pope, to join them to the Patriarchate of Constantinople, to make them use only the Byzantine rite. This process was going on when the Great Schism broke out. But then, in the eleventh century, the Norman conquerors again turned the tide towards Rome. From their time the Byzantine rite declined steadily till the fifteenth century. It had almost expired, when it received new life from the Albanian refugees. Now it is represented here by the descendants of these; though there remain curious traces of the older Greek element. During all this period, from the fourth century at latest, Byzantine monasticism has been a great factor in the preservation of the rite in Italy.

[1] Rodotà, iii, 97-99; Kyriakos, Ἐκκλ. Ἱστορία, Γ′, 118; V. Vannutelli, O.P., " Le Colonie Italo-greche " (Rome, 1890), 37-38.

CHAPTER II

EXISTING BYZANTINE INSTITUTIONS IN ITALY

WE come now to the remains of what was once so great an element in the ecclesiastical life of Southern Italy and Sicily. The Byzantine rite is still used here; there are still Italo-Greeks, though now they are all Albanians. In describing their institutions we must go back, to trace the origin of each in particular.

1. Grottaferrata.

First among all Italo-Greek institutions I place the dear monastery of the Mother of God at Grottaferrata.[1] It is the oldest Greek centre now existing in Italy; it has a glorious history covering ten centuries; it has always been, it still is, the chief centre of their rite, to which all Italo-Greeks look. To the man who thinks that Popes want to turn everyone into a Latin the best answer is this venerable sanctuary, where under the very walls of Rome, protected, blessed, and favoured by a long series of Popes, Greek monks for over 900 years have never ceased to worship God according to an Eastern rite. How easily during all these centuries, time after time, might Grottaferrata have been turned into a Latin monastery! Who would have noticed or cared? The Pope himself would have cared. It is the Popes who have maintained here, in the heart of the Papal states, a rite foreign to them, yet no less Catholic than their own; so little have they ever thought that all Catholics must be Latins.

About the year 910 Nicholas, said to belong to the family

---

[1] Ἡ ἱερὰ Μονὴ τῆς Θεοτόκου ἡ ἐν Κρυπτοφέρρῃ, La Badia di Grottaferrata. Grottaferrata (Latin: Crypta Ferrata) is an old name of the place, probably older than the time of St Neilos. The local tradition is that there was an ancient picture and shrine of our Lady here in a grotto or crypt behind an iron grating (ferrata). The Roman place Lucus ferentinæ was here, between Tusculum (Frascati) and Castrimœnium (Marino). The country round was Tusculanum.

of Malena, was born at Rossanum. He was a Greek of Calabria. He married and had a child, then, both wife and child dying early, he went to be a monk. He entered the monastery of St Nazarios, near Palmi in Calabria, and at his profession took the name Neilos,[1] in memory of St Neilos of Sinai, who had also become a monk after the death of his wife.[2] He then moved to several monasteries, and became Hegumenos of St Adrian near San Demetrio Corone. But at that time the Saracens from Sicily were devastating Calabria; so at last, about 981, Neilos with his monks, fleeing from them, went north to the Campagna. They came first to the great Benedictine monastery of Monte Cassino. The Abbot of Monte Cassino gave them a dependent house, Vallelucio, then the Greek monks moved again to Serperi, near Gaeta. Then Neilos went to Rome.

There had just been a revolution at Rome and an Antipope. The family of Crescentius had driven out the lawful Pope, Gregory V (996–999), and had set up a Calabrian, John Phila-gathos (Bishop of Piacenza), as Antipope, with the title John XVI. The Emperor Otto III (993–1002), coming to Rome in 998, had deposed Philagathos and put him in prison.

It was to beg for the life of his countryman that Neilos first came to Rome. He was received with great honour by Otto and Gregory. But, in spite of his efforts, Philagathos was murdered by the people (998). Then Neilos went back to Serperi. He was back in Rome four years later, and then set out for another Greek monastery, St Agatha, south of Tusculum. He was now a very old man. On his way he fell sick on the slopes of the Alban hills. Lying sick here at the place where Cicero had once had a villa and had written his " Quæstiones tusculanæ," Neilos had a vision, from which he learned that here at last his wandering monks were to find rest. He obtained a grant of the land from the Count of Tusculum, sent for his monks from Serperi, told them that they were to build a monastery here, and died on September 26, 1004.[3] He was

---

[1] Nilus, Nilo. It seems unreasonable to call a tenth-century Greek by a modern Italian name; nor, since he was a Greek, does there seem any reason to call him by a Latin name, when writing English.

[2] St Neilos of Sinai († 430) a follower of St John Chrysostom, monk at Sinai and writer (his works, many of which, however, are spurious, are in P.G., lxxix) is Neilos the Elder. Our Neilos, of Rossanum, is the Younger (Νεῖλος ὁ Νεώτερος).

[3] I have given some account of the life of St Neilos the Younger and of Grottaferrata in " Orthodox Eastern Church," pp. 168-170.

succeeded by his disciple Paul, then came Cyril, then Bartholomew of Rossanum († 1065), who wrote his Life.   Meanwhile
the monks had begun to build their monastery and church
at the place where their founder died.   The church was consecrated by Pope John XIX (1024–1033) in 1024.   Benedict
IX (1033–1048) confirmed the possessions of the monastery,
made it exempt from diocesan jurisdiction, and placed it under
the immediate protection of the Holy See.

At this time there was the wildest disorder at Rome and continual strife between the party of the Counts of Tusculum, the
people, and the Emperor.   Benedict IX himself was made Pope
by his father, Alberich, Count of Tusculum, at the age of twelve
years.   Bartholomew of Grottaferrata persuaded him to resign
the Papacy; so that he then came as a simple monk to Grottaferrata, ended his days there, and is there buried.   From now
the monastery plays an important part in the history of the
Papal states.   Robert Wiscard and his Normans camped under
its walls in 1084.   Then it acquired vast territories, and so
came into conflict with the Count and Bishop of Tusculum.
William I of Sicily (the Bad, 1154–1166), making war on Pope
Adrian IV (1154–1159), sacked Grottaferrata.   Innocent III
(1198–1216) and Gregory IX (1227–1241) protected and
enriched it; Frederick II (1215–1250) came and sacked it.   It
was again besieged and sacked during the Western Schism
by the soldiers of the Avignon Pope.   In the fifteenth century
the Orsini and the Caetani made it a fortress, from which
they went out to fight.   The King of Naples, Ladislaus (1400–
1414), occupied it with his soldiers when he invaded the Papal
states in 1408.   Martin V (1417–1431) made efforts to repair
the damages done by so many wars.   Pius II (1458–1464)
was a constant visitor at Grottaferrata.   It was with the
idea of restoring its former prosperity that he applied to
Grottaferrata the system of giving monasteries *in commendam*,
making Cardinal Bessarion († 1472) its first Commendatory
Archimandrite.   Bessarion did much for Grottaferrata; he

The Life of the saint by his disciple and successor, St Bartholomew
of Rossanum, is a characteristic example of Greek hagiography of
that period, interesting, edifying, and full of incidental information
about the Italo-Greek monasteries of Calabria.   Unfortunately want
of space makes it impossible to quote more of it here.   It is printed
in P.G., cxx, 16-165; in an Italian version by A. Rocchi, " Vita di
San Nilo Abate " (Rome, 1904).   St Bartholomew's own Life was
written by Luke I, the seventh Archimandrite (*c.* 1085); it is in P.G.,
cxxvii, 476-497.

restored the buildings, gave gifts of valuable books and church plate.[1]

But the system of commendatory abbots is wrong radically. In this case, too, it led to all kinds of abuses; the revenues of the monastery were used by Cardinals who did nothing for it. In 1473 one of these Commendatary Archimandrites, Cardinal Julian della Rovere,[2] gave orders to Bramante to transform the monastic buildings into a fortress. It is chiefly from this transformation that Grottaferrata has still so much the appearance of an ancient castle, with ramparts, bastions, moat, and portcullis. In 1608 the Commenda was happily abolished, and the community returned to the old principle, under a real acting Archimandrite.

The church has been restored and rebuilt many times. The outside West front is fourteenth-century, with a superb Lombard tower of the twelfth century. But the inside was completely re-formed in the year 1754, with deplorable results. Already in 1665 there had been a far-reaching restoration. In 1754 an altar, quite on the Latin model of that time, had been erected, with an elaborate reredos of marbles. But in 1881, with a better appreciation of the rite, several successful changes were made. The reredos of the altar was turned into an Ikonostasion, with the royal doors where the altar had been, and a good Byzantine altar, with a ciborium, was erected behind it. In spite of later changes much remains to be seen in the church. One of the best-known sights is the series of frescoes illustrating the life of the saint by Domenichino (1610) in the chapel of St Neilos. The West door of the church in carved wood is of the eleventh century, with a mosaic over it. In the middle of the Ikonostasion is a picture of our Lady, originally Latin, said to have been given by Pope Gregory IX (1227–1241). There are many paintings of Byzantine and Basilian saints, dating from the last restoration in 1881. Outside the West front is a fountain, used liturgically, with a good canopy of pointed arches over it, and around this is the " Paradise " of trees, that ought to be at every monastery of the rite.

The monks of Grottaferrata have always had a reputation for their studies. They produced the Typikon which is still the official book for all Italo-Greeks (p. 179). In the twelfth

---

[1] For Bessarion's relations with Grottaferrata see R. Rocholl, " Bessarion, Studie zur Gesch. der Renaissance " (Leipzig, 1904), pp. 79-85.

[2] Afterwards Pope Julius II (1503-1513).

century they formed quite a school of Greek hymn-writers.[1]
In their splendid library they have valuable manuscripts.
Now they continue their tradition of learning by publishing a
good review[2] and valuable documents.[3]   In the twelfth century
they had a famous hospital and a Xenodochion for pilgrims.

The great reform of the monastery was under Leo XIII
(1878–1903).   Formerly there had been considerable Latin-
Roman infiltrations in the rite used by the monks.   We shall
come to these later, since they affected all the Italo-Greeks.
Here I note the fact that, when we say that Grottaferrata has
never been latinized, we mean that it has always kept the
Byzantine rite in Greek.   But there was much Latin infiltration
in that rite.   This came about naturally, in an age when no one
cared much about ritual purity, from the influence of their
Roman neighbours.   But it is all done away with now.   In
August, 1881, Leo XIII ordered the restoration of the Byzantine
rite to its pure form.   So it is observed here now.   I doubt
if anywhere else in the world the Byzantine rite is now celebrated with such punctilious exactness.   There is no trace of
latinization or of " mixed rite."   Indeed, the monks are almost
nervously anxious to avoid such a suspicion.   It would hardly
be possible to find an accusation that would offend them more,
or be more unjust, than to say that they are not purest of the
pure Byzantines, in their rites, habits, rule, and everything.
At the same time Leo XIII founded, in the monastery, a college
for Italo-Greeks, youths who are to become priests of their rite.
These boys serve the church and sing the offices with the monks
most beautifully.   Any traveller who goes out from Rome on
a Sunday morning may assist here at the Byzantine Liturgy,
celebrated perfectly and sung exquisitely.[4]   The monks are
now Albanians from the Italian colonies.   The present

[1] Krumbacher, " Byzantinische Litteratur " (2nd edition, Munich,
1897), p. 678.

[2] " Roma e l'Oriente, Rivista Criptoferratense per l'Unione delle
chiese," published at Grottaferrata, monthly since November, 1910.

[3] " Studi liturgici," since 1912.   They have a printing press,
" Tipografia italo-orientale: S Nilo."

[4] In noting this I hope to be excused for adding a personal remark.
Years ago, when I was a student at Rome, it was at Grottaferrata
that I first learned to be interested in the Byzantine liturgy.   It was
from a Grottaferrata monk that I learned to speak Greek.   After
nineteen years, on Sunday, February 9, 1913, I stood again in that
church and heard the heavenly music of the Trisagion, the Cheru-
bikon, Εἶς ἅγιος, εἶς κύριος, Ἰησοῦς χριστὸς εἰς δόξαν θεοῦ Πατρός,
before the Ikonostasion.   So I thought of the days when I had stood
there, a boy in my purple cassock, and I thanked God for all Grottaferrata had given me.

Archimandrite is Arsenois II (Pellegrini), the seventy-ninth in direct succession from St Neilos (not counting the bad period of the Commendatory Archimandrites).[1] In the first period (till the fifteenth century) this monastery was not the most important of its rite in Italy. St Saviour at Messina eclipsed it easily. Then it became the chief. Now it is the only one left. The whole Italo-Greek Basilian Congregation is reduced to this one house.

Grottaferrata, with its wonderful traditions, its strange rite out there in the middle of the Roman Campagna, its splendid library, and the amazing picturesqueness of its old ramparts and towers, among the vineyards and olive orchards, on the slopes of the Alban hills, is one of the most fascinating places in Italy. Greek and Catholic, it should form a bond between the East and the West. It is always a standing witness that to be a Catholic does not mean giving up the venerable rites of the East. In 1904, at the nine-hundredth anniversary of his death, they put a statue of St Neilos in the court before the church. He stands there looking towards Rome across the hot Roman plain; while his successor rules his monks under the authority of the successor of the Pope he came to Rome to see.[2]

2. The Greek College at Rome.

The second great centre of the Italo-Greeks is the " Pontificium Collegium Græcorum de Vrbe." I doubt if any of the Roman colleges has so interesting or so important a history as this; though it has not always been quite a glorious one. The Greek college was founded in 1577 by Pope Gregory XIII (1572–1585). Gregory founded a number of colleges at Rome for different nations. Among others he thought of the Greeks, at that time groaning under the yoke of the Turk, and lost to the Church through their schism. His idea was that Greek boys should be educated here, that they should have the advantage of what was then one of the chief centres of Western civilization, and at the same time be well grounded in the

---

[1] There were altogether fifteen Commendatorii. The list is given in A. Rocchi, " La Badia di Grottaferrata " (Rome, 1904), p. 37, n. 1; the real Archimandrites, *ibid.*, pp. 31-32.

[2] The chief work about Grottaferrata is A. Rocchi, " De Cœnobio Cryptoferratensi eiusque bibliotheca et codicibus præsertim græcis commentarii," Tusculi (Frascati), 1893. More popular are A. Rocchi, " La Badia di Grottaferrata " (2nd edition, Rome, 1904); F. Pometti, " Nel Centenario della fondazione della Badia di Grotta ferrata " (Bergamo, 1903); A. Pellegrini, Ἡ ἑλληνικὴ μονὴ τῆς Κρυπτοθέρης (Syra, 1904); C. Mencacci, " Cenni storici della Badia di S Maria di Grottaferrata " (Rome, 1875).

Catholic faith; that they should eventually go back to the Levant as missionaries to their countrymen. The Bull of erection is dated January 13, 1577.[1] The college was built by the architect James della Porta. It is a handsome building, of the usual type of sixteenth-century Roman work, in the Via Babuino. By the side of the college is the Church of St Athanasius, the "Greek" church in Rome, where the Byzantine rite is celebrated, served by the students of the college. The church was finished in 1581. Certain changes in the buildings have been made at later dates.[2] Gregory XIII endowed the college generously; he appointed a commission of five Cardinals as its protectors; among these were Sirleto and Santoro. Santoro became the special protector and head of the establishment. He appointed the rectors and looked after its interests for twenty-five years.

One of the chief difficulties of the college has been the constant change of rectors, and even of the manner of its direction. The first rector was a Latin regular of the Crociati order, Nicholas Stridonio; then came secular priests, among them a Scotchman, even laymen. Cardinal Santoro drew up the rule in 1583, and ordered that it should be read aloud in the refectory once a month. In 1591 the direction was given to the Jesuits. Under them it flourished, and the number of students grew steadily. But in 1602, when Santoro died, Cardinal Giustiniani was made Protector. He was a Greek of Chios. He made all kinds of changes in the arrangements of the college, so that the Jesuits quarrelled with him and retired in 1604. There was again a period of continual changes in the direction; the Dominicans held the office for a time, then secular priests and a layman. In 1622 the Jesuits came back. Soon after this Ruthenian students were admitted as well as Greeks, so that, till the reform of Leo XIII, it was the "Collegium Græco-Ruthenum." Then things went badly again. There were constant disorders; the Greeks had the reputation of being the most difficult students to manage in all Rome; by 1693 there were only eighteen students in residence, and there was a question of closing the college. Later Latins from the Greek islands were admitted; so that the college began to change its nature. It was becoming a school for Latin missionaries in the Levant. Italo-Greeks and Albanians were also admitted; the number of Greeks from the

---

[1] Bull. Rom., *ed. cit.*, tom. iv, part iii, p. 328.
[2] For these see P. de Meester, O.S.B., "Le Collège pontifical grec de Rome" (Rome, 1910), pp. 9-14.

East in 1763 was only seven. Under Clement XIV (1769–1774) the Jesuits again retired and secular priests came back. The Revolution put an end to the college altogether for a time. Gregory XVI (1831–1846) reopened it in 1845, admitting fifteen students, eight Ruthenians, four Melkites, and three Italo-Albanians. In 1849 Pius IX (1846–1878) founded four burses for Rumanians. In 1886 Leo XIII made Resurrectionists rectors; three years later he gave the college back to the Jesuits.

Then came the last great change. In 1897 Leo XIII first founded a special Ruthenian College, which was endowed by the Emperor of Austria. The Ruthenians of the Greek College went to this. Then the Greek College, now only for Greeks of the Byzantine rite, was entrusted to the Benedictines; they are to accommodate forty students. The students attend lectures at Propaganda; but they have their own courses of Greek, Canon Law, liturgy, and such subjects as interest them particularly.

The Greek College has produced a surprising number of great men. Ever since it was founded many famous people in Greece and all over the Levant owed their education to it. These are by no means all priests. For instance, a number of physicians were educated there, who afterwards became famous in their own country. The college also sent professors of Greek language and letters to Italian universities: Padua, Venice, Pisa, Bologna, Naples. It educated many monks for Grottaferrata and other monasteries. It has fulfilled the object of its foundation by sending countless Catholic missionaries to the East, to Greece, the Greek islands, the Slav countries, and so on.

Among so many famous students we may notice especially Allatius and Arcudius. *Leo Allatius* (Allacci) is certainly the most distinguished of all, perhaps the most learned Greek since Photius. He was born at Chios in 1586, when it was a Venetian possession. He was always a Catholic. Quite young, he came first to Naples; then, in 1599, he entered the Greek College at Rome. He studied medicine at first, so that among his many accomplishments he was also a skilled physician. But he soon gave up the profession of medicine in order to devote himself to letters. He became *scriptor* at the Vatican library; from now till his death in 1669 he gradually acquired erudition in all branches of Greek studies, and wrote a vast number of learned dissertations which obtained for him more than a European reputation. There seems no branch of classical scholarship in which Allatius did not distinguish himself. He edits classical authors, writes on Homer's birth-place, on Etruscan antiquities, on every kind of obscure point of Byzantine scholarship, on Byzantine architecture, lives of Popes and famous men; he was a poet, philologist, theologian, ritualist, philosopher, and physician. His works include Biblical criticism, dogmatic and archæological treatises. In short, there are very few questions of Oriental study on which Allatius has not written a work which may still be consulted with profit. Especially on all sides of Byzantine liturgy and theology are his writings invaluable. Altogether fifty-five complete books by him are published; and there are quanti-ties of others, letters and treatises, in manuscript still. Out of so many valuable works I name only his *magnum opus*: *De Ecclesiæ occidentalis atque orientalis perpetua consensione libri tres.*[1] He left his valuable library and all his property to the Greek College. The Greeks of the East have never ceased to profit by his immense erudition. They are justly proud of Allatius as one of their greatest scholars. One thing, however, they can never forgive him, that he was a Catholic.[2]

Peter Arcudius[3] (1562–1633), less illustrious than Allatius, was also a famous scholar. He, too, wrote many works of standing importance. Arcudius took his degree in theology at the Greek College before a brilliant audience, which in-cluded such men as Santoro, Bellarmin, Baronius. He was ordained priest, was for a time missionary in Ruthenia, then came back to Rome in 1609, was paralyzed, and so remained all the rest of his life at the college, being carried every morning to the library, and then back again to his room in the evening. Arcudius is not a universal genius, like Allatius; but he is a theologian of great learning. Like that of Allatius, his theological work is nearly all in defence of points of the Catholic creed (the *Filioque*, Purgatory, and so on; especially, of course, the Roman Primacy) against his schismatical country-

---

[1] Köln, 4, 1648. The professed object of this work is to prove that both Churches always held the same faith. Incidentally it contains a mass of information about Greek theologians, their theories, movements in the Orthodox Church, and so on. He always gives long quotations.

[2] A Life of Allatius, with a complete list of his published works, will be found in Cabrol and Leclercq's " Dictionnaire d'Archéologie chrétienne et de Liturgie," tom. i (1), Paris, 1907, cols. 1220-1226 (by L. Petit, Aug. Ass., now Latin Archbishop of Athens). See also Rodotà, " Del Rito greco," iii, 169-171; de Meester, " Le Collège pont. grec.," 54-56.   [3] Ἀρκούδιος.

men. Arcudius, too, among many works has left one classic, his treatise on the Sacraments.[1]

Among the students of whom the Greek College is justly proud we may notice also *Joseph Velamin Rutski*, a Ruthenian, Metropolitan of Little Russia, and a mighty champion of the faith in his time (1637);[2] *Josaphat Azales*,[3] in the time of Paul V (1605–1621), who went to Athos and persuaded the monks there to send a letter of submission to the Pope; further, *Demetrios Phalereus Kyriakos*,[4] professor at the Sapienza at Rome and one of the famous Hellenists of the seventeenth century; *Neophytos Rhodinos*(† 1655),[5] scholar and missionary in Poland, Macedonia, and Greece; *John Tzigalas* († 1687),[6] professor at Padua, and many others. Rodotà in his book draws up a list of the distinguished students of the college: missionaries, monks, bishops, theologians, philologists, Hellenists, philosophers, physicians.[7] To these I must add his own name. *Peter Pompilius Rodotà* was an Italo-Greek of Calabria, nephew of Felix Samuel Rodotà, the first ordaining Byzantine bishop in Calabria (p. 123). He was a student of the college, then became professor of Greek and *scriptor* at the Vatican library. By order of Benedict XIV he wrote his monumental history of his rite in Italy.[8] It was published in three volumes at Rome in 1758–1763. The first volume is about the older Greek element in Italy, the second about the Basilian monks, the third about the Albanians, the Greek College, and other contemporary Greek colonies. This work remains the chief one on the subject. With incomparable patience Rodotà has gathered up all there was to say about the Italo-Greeks down to his time. Other books are needed to continue the story to later times; but it will be long before any other can take the place of this, as the quarry from which all kinds of information is to be gathered. A reference to my notes will show how much

[1] " Libri VII de Concordia Ecclesiæ occid. et orient. in septem sacramentorum administratione," Paris, fol. 1626. For his Life see Rodotà, *op. cit.*, iii, 164-165; De Meester, *op. cit.*, 52-54.

[2] Rodotà, iii, 192-198; De Meester, 43-44.

[3] Rodotà, iii, 183-184; De Meester, 45-46.

[4] De Meester, 51.

[5] Rodotà, iii, 184-188; De Meester, 59-60.

[6] Τζιγάλας or Κιγάλας, *Cigala* in Italian; E. Legrand, " Bibliothèque hellènique du XVIIᵉ siècle " (Paris, 1885), iii, 315-318.

[7] " Del Rito greco," iii, cap. vii, §§ iv-v, pp. 161-216.

[8] " Dell' origine, progresso, e stato presente del rito greco in Italia osservato dai Greci, Monaci basiliani, e Albanesi; Libri tre scritti da Pietro Pompilio Rodotà professore di lingua greca nella biblioteca vaticana."

I owe to Rodotà. Indeed, without his work all this account of the Italo-Greeks would shrink to a very small compass.

Against so many great names we must reckon a few defections. There have been students of the Greek College who, when they returned to the East, forgot the lessons they had learned there and joined the schismatical majority. The chief of these are Pantaleon Ligarides and Hilarion Tzigalas. *Ligarides* entered the college in 1623. He took his degree in theology brilliantly in 1636, and was ordained priest at Rome. Propaganda then sent him as a missionary to Zakynthos; thence he passed to Constantinople and eventually to Rumania. Here he began to play a double game. To the Orthodox he represented himself as one of them; while all his life he went on writing to Propaganda for money. He met Paisios, Orthodox Patriarch of Jerusalem (*c.* 1646–1660), who made him an Orthodox monk, with the name Paisios. So he became Orthodox Metropolitan of Gaza in 1652. But he quarrelled with the Patriarch of Jerusalem, and was by him degraded. Then he went to Russia and helped the famous Patriarch of Moscow, Nikon (1652–1665), in his revision of the Russian service books. But soon he quarrelled with him too. Propaganda had long begun to suspect him, and had ordered him to come back to Rome. But he did not obey this order either; and so he died (1678) rejected by all. Ligarides is an unhappy example of what often happened; trying to please both sides, to pretend to each that he was with them, lying to both, he ended by being denounced by both.[1]

Tzigalas is also an ambiguous person. Less culpable than Ligarides, he committed one great fault which placed him permanently in a false position. His original name was Jerome; after he had left the college he became a monk in the East and then took the name Hilarion. For a time he was a missionary in Greece under Propaganda and a firm defender of the Catholic faith. Then he became professor at Padua. Eventually he went back to the Levant, and again for a time preached Catholic principles. But it appears that he was hurt at not receiving promotion or as much recognition from Rome as he expected. So he came to Constantinople. Here there was no lack of appreciation of his talents. So he went over to the Orthodox, and allowed the Orthodox Patriarch of Jerusalem to ordain him to the Archiepiscopal See of Cyprus. He is thus counted one of the Orthodox Archbishops of Cyprus (1674–1678). But he remained a Catholic at heart, in spite of his

---

[1] Rodotà, *op. cit.*, iii, 208-209; De Meester, 65-66.

false position. As Archbishop he was considered a bad latinizer by the Orthodox. At the end of his life he seems to have come back to the Church. At any rate, he was accused of betraying the Orthodox Church and was deposed in 1678. He died at Constantinople in 1682. From the great dislike to him shown by the Orthodox we may hope that he died a Catholic, repenting of his schism.[1] Rodotà calls both Ligarides and Tzigalas " bitter fruits of our college," but thinks that both, in spite of their defection, kept some good and some Catholic principles to the end.[2]

The Greek College counted among its difficulties the efforts of the Jesuit rectors to persuade students to enter their Society. This has always been the difficulty of the Roman Colleges ruled by Fathers of the Society. It is a real grievance, since the money spent on the education of these boys was certainly not intended to provide a nursery for future Jesuits. So at the Greek College, as at all those in Rome, severe oaths were required of the students, that they would enter no religious order, except that of the Basilians.[3] In spite of these oaths the Jesuits continually managed to get dispensations for the more promising students; so that a large number of the students enter the Society. In view of the constant complaints of Propaganda on this head, one rather wonders why they were not more firm in refusing to grant the dispensations.

It is strange that at the beginning the students of the Greek College had to conform to the Roman rite. It would seem that everyone would have realized from the beginning the importance of training these boys in their own rite. However, it was not so; indeed, till almost the other day, their position was not so much that of Byzantines with Roman infiltrations, as rather that of Romans with occasional observance of the Byzantine rite. The rectors were always Latins (this was an obvious abuse; it would have been easy to find priests of sound Catholic principles and of the Byzantine rite from the South of Italy); they kept their own rite, said Mass and all their offices in Latin; the students had to hear this Mass and to make their Communion in the form of azyme bread only. At first the Roman rite alone was observed in the college chapel; though

---

[1] Rodotà, *op. cit.*, iii, 209-210; De Meester, 67; J. Hackett, " A History of the Orth. Church of Cyprus " (Methuen, 1901), pp. 214-215; quotation from his contemporary, Paul Ricaut, about him, p. 681.

[2] *Op. cit.*, iii, 210.

[3] So Urban VIII (1623-1644), Alexander VII (1655-1667), etc. Rodotà, iii, 156; De Meester, 31.

in the Church of St Athanasius there were occasional Byzantine functions. The only precaution against this latinization was that the students had to take an oath to keep the Byzantine rite as soon as they returned to their own country.[1] In 1592 the Jesuit rector made a great pretence of introducing the Byzantine rite " to be observed exactly in all things possible by all the Greek students."[2] Yet they still had to attend his Latin Mass every morning, and were bound to receive Holy Communion from him at least once a month " in azyme, according to the Latin manner."[3] This is, of course, the cardinal matter of all. It is absurd to say that a man observes the Byzantine rite when he receives Communion in one species and in azyme.

There were always many Latins at the college, Jesuits and others who, naturally, kept their own rite;[4] this, too, helped to prevent a whole-hearted use of that of Constantinople. Again, I wonder why they did not employ Italo-Greeks as servants. Then, gradually, there was some feeling about the disadvantage of bringing up these boys in ignorance of the rite they were afterwards to practise all their lives. Urban VIII (1623–1644) made a rule that three times a year, at Christmas, Easter, and Pentecost, they were to make their Communion in their own rite.[5] This really only made things worse liturgically; in opposition to the normal principles of the Holy See (p. 34) it introduced promiscuity of rite. Meanwhile, although they were not allowed to use their rite, these wretched boys had to keep all its fasts, and the Roman ones too. They had not only the enormously sterner Byzantine fasting, with its four Lents and innumerable days of fasting and abstinence;[6] but when the Romans had a fast, not kept in the East, they had to keep this as well. Thus they had to fast on Saturday; though it had long been a great principle in the East not to do so.[7] So the students were brought up in the strangest mixture of rites, with the inconveniences of both and the advantages of neither. Small wonder that liturgical study made little progress among them. Small wonder either that their rivals in the East were never tired of mocking them as hybrids, semi-latinized Greeks.

---

[1] De Meester, 30-31; Rodotà, iii, 156.

[2] Diary of the college published by C. Karalevsky, " Documenti inediti per servire alla storia delle chiese italo-greche " (Rome, 1911), fasc. i, p. 27.

[3] *Ibid.*, p. 30.   [4] *Ibid.*, p. 28.

[5] De Meester, 31-32.

[6] College diary, *op. cit.*, p. 27.

[7] *Ibid.*, p. 29; De Meester, 32-33.

During the time of the Jesuit Superiors the students were ordained at the Lateran—that is, according to the Roman rite,[1] again a bad case of promiscuity of rite. This has now been abolished by the institution of a Byzantine ordaining bishop for them (see p. 177).

With the removal of the Jesuits by Leo XIII in 1897 a better tradition has been established. According to the Pope's express order everything in the college is now done according to the Byzantine rite. It is true that the Benedictine Superiors are also Latin; but the Pope gave them the special faculty of using the Byzantine rite during their domicile there.[2] Now all services, offices, prayers at the Greek College are exclusively Greek and Byzantine.[3] They are carried out with great care and exactness; the Benedictines of the college make a great point of exact knowledge of the rite, and the students are taught it carefully. In the great churches of Rome these students have plenty of opportunity of seeing the Roman rite; their lectures at the Propaganda College are in Latin; they talk Latin (with an Italian pronunciation) at least as well as any other Roman students; but they themselves are purely Byzantine. No one can now accuse them of being hybrids of a mixed rite.

The old costume of the Greek College was a purple cassock with a red belt and purple *Soprana*. This costume, borrowed from them, is still worn by the students of the Greek-Albanian College at Palermo (p. 164). But at Rome they have changed it. It is now a very pretty grey-blue with red belt, perhaps the prettiest costume in Rome. Under the Jesuits they wore Italian birettas and such things in the house, and the usual Italian hat out of doors. The Benedictines have given them a proper black *Rason* and the *Kalymaukion* of their rite. Under the Rason they still wear their blue cassocks.

3. The Albanian Colonies in Calabria and Sicily.

All that is now left of the Byzantine rite in Southern Italy is represented by a few villages of Albanians. We have seen that the immigration of Albanians in the fifteenth century meant a great revival of this rite (p. 120). But since then the

---

[1] College diary, *op. cit.*, p. 35.

[2] De Meester, 37.

[3] In 1908 the Rector, Dom Athanasius Gaisser, obtained from the Holy Office in 1908 leave to transfer the Roman abstinence on Saturday to Wednesday; so that the students should not incur the old Byzantine reproach of fasting on Saturday (De Meester, *op. cit.*, 34).

Albanians, as far as they represent Italo-Greek rites, have greatly diminished in numbers. Many of their descendants have become Italians of the Roman rite; others have adopted the Roman rite, though they still keep their own language. Lastly, in late years, driven by the economic difficulties of Southern Italy, large numbers of them have emigrated to America. There now remain twenty places in Calabria and five in Sicily where the Byzantine rite survives. In Calabria all are included in the four dioceses Anglona and Tursi (united), Cassano al Ionio, San Marco and Bisignano (united), Rossano, in the provinces of Basilicata and Calabria Citeriore. They fall into three groups. In the diocese of Anglona and Tursi are five villages. *Castoreggio*[1] has nearly 2,000 Albanians with a church, S Maria ad Nives, and a priest of the Byzantine rite. *Farneta*[2] has about 800, *San Paolo*[3] 1,800, *San Costantino*[4] about the same number. South of these we come to the two more important groups on either side of the valley of the Crati. The Crati[5] is a river which flows into the Gulf of Taranto just south of the old Greek city Sybaris. The railway follows its course from Bisignano to Sibari. The river forms a fertile and most beautiful valley. North and south of this are lines of hills. To the north is Monte Pollino, to the south Monte Sila. It is on the slopes of these mountains that the Albanian villages are found.

There is first the line along the northern slopes. *Lungro* is the chief of these. The Albanians settled here in 1500. In 1576 they had twelve priests and six deacons. For their principal church they took an old Basilian monastery church; this is S Nicholas, still the parish church and " matrice " of the place. There are, I think, two others, all Byzantine in rite. The Roman priest who wishes to celebrate at Lungro may do so; but he must use Byzantine vestments, because they have no others. The parish priest, who is a Protopapa,[6] is fond of telling visitors that, when he was a boy, there were ten

---

[1] Rodotà, " del Rito greco," iii, 62; Charon, " Le quinzième Centenaire de S Jean Chrysostome " (Rome, 1909), p. 262, n. 2.

[2] Rodotà, *op. cit., ibid.*; Charon, *op. cit. ibid.*

[3] Charon, *ibid.*

[4] Rodotà, iii, 61; Charon, *ibid.*   [5] The Greek Κράθις.

[6] Incidentally I may mention at once that nearly all the Albanian parish priests in Italy are Protopapi, wear rings, and have various privileges of which each is very proud, which seem to mark each as a distinguished prelate, till one finds that all the others have the same. Throughout Italy the multiplication of ecclesiastical titles has destroyed any meaning they once had, nowhere more than among the Albanians.

priests in the town. Now there are only two. From Lungro
especially a great number of Albanians have gone to America.
However, it is still the chief Albanian colony of these parts.
It has about 6,000 inhabitants; all speak Albanian and keep their
rite. The church is the handsomest of its rite in Calabria.
It has three cupolas, a nave and transepts, three altars,[1] and
no Ikonastasion.[2] About 3½ kilometres south-west of Lungro
is *Acquaformosa*[3] with 2,000 Albanians. There are no Latins.
The Albanians came here in 1502, and began to reclaim what
was then a quite desolate place. They have a priest and a
parish church, St John the Baptist. Five kilos. south-east
of Lungro is *Firmo*,[4] also all Albanian, with about 2,000 souls,
a priest, and the church, B.M.V. Assumpta. Going north of
Lungro we come first to *San Basile*[5] with nearly 2,000
Albanians; then to *Frascineto*,[6] over 2,000 Albanians. Five
kilos. to the east is *Civita*,[7] 2,500 souls. There are also in this
region two small villages, *Plataci* and *Porcile*,[8] of no great
importance. All these, I believe, are entirely Albanian and
Byzantine. At Cassano al Ionio, the diocesan city, there is
no Albanian colony; but Mgr. Pietro Camodeca de' Nobili
Coronei, the Vicar General for the Byzantine rite,[9] resides here
near the bishop.

Crossing the valley of the Crati we come to the third group,
along the slopes to the south. Here, too, is a line of Albanian
villages stretching from west to east between the two diocesan
cities, Bisignano and Rossano. First, west of Bisignano, there
is a place which has played a great part in the past, *San
Benedetto Ullano*.[10] Here once stood the seminary for the
Calabrian Albanians. In the early eighteenth century it was
a disused Benedictine monastery. By the advice of Samuel
Rodotà, Clement XII (1730–1740) turned this into an Italo-

---

[1] This is one of the un-Byzantine features common here. A
Byzantine church should have only one altar.
[2] For Lungro see Rodotà, " del Rito greco," iii, 79-88; V. Vannutelli, O.P., " Le Colonie italo-greche " (Rome, 1890), 147-152.
[3] Rodotà, iii, 88-89; R. Netzhammer, O.S.B., " Unter den
Albanesen Kalabriens," in the *Studien u. Mitteilungen aus dem Ben.-
u. Cist.-orden*, 1906, p. 100.
[4] Rodotà, iii, 89-91.   [5] *Ibid.*, 91.
[6] *Ibid.*   [7] *Ibid.*, 92.   [8] *Ibid.*
[9] His portrait may be seen in Charon, " Le quinzième Centenaire,"
p. 260.
[10] Also called " San Benedetto d'Ullano," Latin " S Benedicti
Vllano " or " in Vllano." There was an old village, Vllanum,
destroyed by the Saracens in the ninth century (Rodotà, iii, 70).
The form in the text seems the usual one now.

Albanian seminary in 1732.   It was to be called the " Collegio
Corsini."[1]   It was also to be the residence of the ordaining
Byzantine bishop for Calabria.   Samuel Rodotà himself was
the first bishop of this line (p. 123) and the first rector of the
seminary.   In 1791 the college and bishop's residence were
transferred to the monastery of St Adrian at San Demetrio
Corone.   Now there are 2,100 Albanians at San Benedetto
Ullano, who use the old church.[2]   Five kilos. north-east of
Bisignano we come to the village *Santa Sofia d'Epiro*.[3]   The
principal church of this place, built by the Albanians in the
sixteenth century, had the title " Hagia Sophia," and the
Albanians themselves are constantly called " Epiroti."
Hence the name.   It has about 1,800 Albanians.

Four kilos. again to the north-east is *San Demetrio Corone*,
the chief Albanian colony of this group.   Just outside the town
is the college of St Adrian.   It was once a Basilian monastery.
In 1791 the Italo-Albanian seminary for Calabria was moved
here from San Benedetto Ullano.   At that time the monastic
community was almost extinct.   So the Pope, Pius VI (1775–
1799), thought the buildings would be more useful in this way.
Then for about a century the seminary at Sant' Adriano did
useful work in educating Calabrian Albanian boys for the
priesthood.   The Byzantine ordaining bishop, who was also
rector of the college, lived here.   But gradually the prosperity
of the institution dwindled.   The Albanians were turning Latin
or emigrating.   There were fewer students, the revenue of the
college diminished.   After the revolution in Naples (1860)
the Italian Government appointed a commissioner to look after
the affairs of the college.   He seems to have been an anti-
clerical person, so he confiscated most of what was left of the
property.   A series of lawsuits and quarrels followed.   At
last, in 1900, the seminary was closed.   Then the Government
confiscated the whole place, repaired the buildings, and in 1903
reopened it as a college for the Albanians, but a purely lay
one.   There are now no clerical students.   It contains about
150 boys, all laymen destined for lay professions.   Through
this college the Italian Government does much work to
italianize the Albanians.[4]   The boys go now and then to assist

---

[1] Clement XII was Lawrence Corsini.
[2] Rodotà, iii, 68-78; Moroni, " Dizionario di erudizione storico-
ecclesiastica," vol. xxxii (Venice, 1845), 152-153; Vannutelli, *op. cit.*,
153-154.   [3] Rodotà, iii, 68; Vannutelli, 145.
[4] On the whole the Italian Government is very kind to its Albanians.   It has great hopes of getting Dalmatia and Epirus as an
Italian colony, and it looks to the Albanians of Italy to influence their

at the Byzantine liturgy in the church; and I suppose no particular hindrance would be made if they wanted to receive a sacrament in it. But it is not a pious institution. Even before the secularization the college was a great centre of liberal ideas. The Albanians in general were enthusiastic for Garibaldi and the revolution. It is said that, even when it was a seminary, there were more pictures of Garibaldi on the walls of the students' rooms than pictures of saints.[1] In theory this should still be the residence of the Byzantine ordaining bishop for Calabria. His throne may still be seen in the church. But because of difficulties with the governing body of the college, he now lives at Naples (p. 178). However, the town of San Demetrio Corone is still an important Albanian centre. It was originally one of the settlements of the Albanian refugees from Korone in the Peloponnesus, and the church was dedicated to St Demetrius. The village is still entirely Albanian; there are nearly 4,000 of them here.[2] *Macchia*[3] is 2 kilos. north-east of San Demetrio. It has 700 Albanians. *San Cosimo*,[4] 3½ kilos. east of Macchia, has about 1,000, *Vaccarizzo Albanese*,[5] a kilo. and a half north-east again, has 2,000. *San Giorgio Albanese*,[6] 1½ kilos. south-east, has 1,770. These are all the Albanian villages of this group. Five kilos. east of San Giorgio we come to the town of Corigliano Calabro, and then, 10 kilos. south-east, to Rossano. In neither of these are any Albanians left. Of this group San Benedetto and S Sofia are in the diocese of San Marco and Bisignano; the others in Rossano.

Except perhaps Lungro, all the Albanian villages of Calabria give the impression of great poverty. All Calabria

---

countrymen across the Adriatic. So it protects their missions to Albania. There is now a chair of Albanian at the University of Naples. On the other hand, the clergy complain that the Government is trying to italianize the people and make them anti-clerical. And the Albanians, who are inordinately proud of their own race, dislike and affect to despise their Italian neighbours. The first thing they tell you in every Albanian village is, " We are not Italians; we are Albanians."

[1] Vannutelli, *op. cit.*, 129; Netzhammer, *loc. cit.*, p. 92. When they do go to church, they scribble things in pencil on the walls during the Liturgy.

[2] For S Demetrio Corone see Rodotà, *op. cit.*, iii, 110; Vannutelli, pp. 143-145; Netzhammer, pp. 90-92.

[3] Rodotà, iii, 101; Vannutelli, 123-125.

[4] Rodotà, iii, 101; Vannutelli, 122-123.

[5] Rodotà, iii, 101-102; Vannutelli, 117-121.

[6] Rodotà, iii, 102.

is a poor land; want of water, natural barrenness of the soil, and the economic difficulties of South Italy combine to make it so. But even in a poor district these Albanian villages stand out as poorer than any. They are also extremely dirty. Their poverty is reflected in their churches. Except at Lungro, the Byzantine churches seem almost abjectly poor and dirty; some are almost in ruins. I can agree to what Father Vannutelli says about them: " Often they plead as an excuse their poverty and misery. But this is not a sufficient reason; because, if they had a little more zeal, there would be more order and cleanliness. In villages one does not expect that the churches be rich or well provided; but at least let there be that decency which can be found with poverty."[1]

Nor is there enough care for their rite among the Calabrian Albanians. They are proud of being Albanians, and they despise their Italian neighbours. They are proud of their Byzantine rite as marking their nationality. They are always ready to explain that they are not just ordinary Latins, like the rest of us. But they do not take enough pains to present this venerable rite worthily. I do not mean that their uses are not pure Byzantine. That is true; we shall come back to the fact (p. 179); but as far as that goes, I think there is a good deal to be said for the special peculiarities of the so-called Italo-Greek rites. My point now is rather that, allowing for their local customs and special traditions, they do not, even so, celebrate their services with sufficient reverence. Even for Southern Italy their churches are too dirty and their ceremonies too carelessly done. However, things are now gradually getting better. Influence of the Greek College at Rome and of the admirable college at Palermo, the growing interest in liturgical study on all sides, the special interest so many students have in this remnant of so great a tradition, all these affect the Albanian clergy in Calabria, so that many of them are now anxious to do things better.

Across the water, in *Sicily*, there is also a group of Albanian colonies. The impression made by these is more favourable in every way. In Sicily we have first Palermo itself, then five villages to the south of the city. The Albanians have a church at *Palermo* since 1547. Their colony here is not very great nor important in itself; but at Palermo is the seminary where the clergy are educated, and the seat of the ordaining Byzantine bishop for Sicily. The seminary was founded by Father George Guzzetta of the Oratory, who in various ways

[1] *Op. cit.*, p. 144.

did so much for the Sicilian Albanians (p. 124). It was opened in 1715. Since 1784 the rector is the ordaining bishop. The college not only supplies the clergy for its rite in Sicily, it is also a centre from which Catholic missionaries set out for Albania. It publishes a little periodical in Albanian *Fiála e t'in' Zoti*, which appears to mean " The Word of the Lord."[1] The students come from the Albanian villages, Piana, Mezzoiuso, and the others. They wear what was the old dress of the Greek College at Rome, a purple cassock with red belt and trimmings and a purple *soprana*. They seem well-kept, intelligent, hard-working and happy. To the stranger they talk quite nice Italian; but they are careful to explain that this is not their own language.

Next to the college is the parish church for all Byzantine Panormitans, dedicated to St Nicholas. It is a little difficult to find the church and college. You must go into the back streets, behind the great Dominican church, till at last you find the tiny " Via dei Greci." The church is not strikingly small or mean; it would make a fair average village church. It is clean and well kept. All the same, when one sees the great number of enormous Latin churches in every street of Palermo, it seems a pity that one of them could not be set aside for a rite that has so many historical associations with Sicily. The church of St Nicholas is served by a parish priest, a curate, and two " coadjutors "; the students of the college attend its services and sing on Sundays. There is a colony of about 2,000 Albanians at Palermo, who frequent this church. The bishops of Palermo and Monreale share the administration of the college; each has burses in it for Albanian students of his diocese.[2]

Fifteen kilos. almost due south of Palermo is *Piana dei Greci*,[3] the chief colony of Sicily. The Albanians came here first in 1488. It has always been one of the most important Albanian settlements in the West, and is still the largest. For a long time the Byzantine ordaining bishop for Sicily resided here. It was at Piana that George Guzzetta founded his Congregation of the Oratory for the Byzantine rite. Here also he founded a Congregation of religious women, the " Sisters

---

[1] Weekly; in Italy fr. 2.50, abroad fr. 3.00. See " Roma e l'Oriente," iv (1912), pp. 249-255.
[2] For Palermo and the college see Rodotà, *op. cit.*, iii, 120-122; Moroni, " Diz. di Erud.," xxxii, 153; I. de Iohanne, " de diu. Sicul. officiis," p. 83; Vannutelli, *op. cit.*, 43-48; " Roma e l'Oriente," iii, 270. [3] It was formerly called Piana degli Albanesi.

of the Holy Family," who had schools "of Mary" for the education of Albanian girls. The Byzantine Oratorians have disappeared (see p. 124); but the Sisters remain. They have at Piana a " College of Mary," where girls are educated in their own rite and language. The whole of Piana talks Albanian; but about a third of the people have passed to the Roman rite. Out of 10,000 inhabitants 7,000 are Byzantine. They have two parishes, altogether five churches, and two country chapels of the Byzantine rite. The chief church, the " matrice " of the place, is St Demetrius of Thessalonica. The Protopapa of this church has jurisdiction over all the Byzantine clergy, except the one of the " Annunziata," who is exempt. There are now ten Byzantine priests at Piana. There is also one Latin parish church; but in all they preach and teach catechism in Albanian. The Byzantine rite is celebrated with great care and even pomp, though naturally with the special features of the Italo-Greeks. They have extra-liturgical devotions and hymns in Albanian. The music they sing is very curious; here best of all you may hear the traditional Italo-Greek chants and popular Albanian hymn-tunes. In short, if the traveller wishes to get an impression of the Italo-Greeks he should undoubtedly go to Piana.[1]

Six kilos. south-east of Piana is *Santa Cristina Gela.*[2] This colony was founded from Piana in 1691. Its present position is ambiguous. All the inhabitants speak only Albanian and are of the Byzantine rite. But since about fifty years ago the parish priest is a Latin; so they have to receive sacraments and attend services in that rite. There is now a movement to restore the Byzantine rite here.

Then, 17 kilos. south-east again, we come to the village with the strange name *Mezzoiuso.*[3] The people here are all Albanians by descent; but (as far as I know) not one of them speaks that language; all are now italianized. The greater part have also passed to the Roman rite. Of about 7,000 in-

---

[1] For Piana see Rodotà, iii, 117-120; Vannutelli, 91-98; " Roma e l'Oriente," iii, 265; Moroni, " Diz. di Erud.," *loc. cit.*

[2] " Roma e l'Or.," iii, 267; Vannutelli (p. 98) is mistaken in saying that at S Cristina all are now Latins.

[3] It has had various strange forms of its name in the past, Muniussum, Miziliusum, Minziliusum, etc. Now it is Mezzoiuso, or Mezzoiusso, in Latin Medium iussum, or Oppidum Dimidii Iussi. The usual explanation is " medium ius," meaning that rights or property was divided, or that it stood half-way between two boundaries I am rather inclined to see in it an Arabic word, possibly a participle of the tenth form.

habitants only 2,500 are still Byzantine. But they have five Byzantine churches, served by six priests.[1] Twenty-nine kilos. south-west is *Contessa Entelina*, where the Albanians came in 1450. All here speak Albanian. The population is about 3,000, of whom half are still Byzantine. Contessa has three Byzantine churches, and six priests of the rite.[2]

Lastly, 17 kilos. south-east, is *Palazzo Adriano*,[3] where the Albanians came in 1482. It was originally all Byzantine; the Byzantine parish church was the undisputed " Matrice " of the place. Then some of the inhabitants turned Latin; a church of the Roman rite was built, and there began one of those curious long and angry disputes as to which church was the " Matrice." It does not seem of much importance, since in every diocese the only head really is the Ordinary; but in these Albanian colonies there have been fierce disputes as to which church, Latin or Byzantine, should bear this rather senseless title. Now at Palazzo Adriano, as for the matter of that at Mezzoiuso, too, there are two " Matrici." Both churches claim the title, and they still quarrel over it. The Latin parish priest calls himself the " Arciprete," his Byzantine colleague is the " Protopapa "; and each loudly declares that he is the real archpriest of the place. The Bishop of Monreale might do worse than take away the title from both, and stop their quarrelling that way.

[1] Mezzoiuso used to pride itself on its pure Byzantine rite, as opposed to the " mixed " Italo-Greeks. I do not know how far this was justified. Andrew Reres founded a monastery here, and endowed it (1609) on condition that it remained always Byzantine. Then it came into the Basilian Congregation (p. 132); his heirs disputed its right to keep the property, on the plea that it had turned " Italo-Greek." There was a lawsuit which lasted four years, from 1694 to 1698. Finally the monks of Mezzoiuso were compelled to keep the strict rule, as in the East. The story is told at length by Rodotà, " del Rito greco," ii, pp. 204-214. For Mezzoiuso see Rodotà, iii, 122-126; Vannutelli, *op. cit.*, 56-71; Moroni, " Diz. di Erud.," xxxii, 152-153; " Roma e l'Oriente," iii, 267; especially Onofrio Buccola, " La Colonia greco-albanese di Mezzoiuso," Palermo, 1909, and " Nuove Ricerche sulla fondazione della Col. gr.-alb. di Mezzoiuso " (*ibid.*, 1912). In the seventeenth century the monks of Mezzoiuso were zealous missionaries in Albania (" Roma e l'Or.," v, 97-112; 159-166; vi, 209-231).

[2] Spiridon lo Jacono, " Memoria sull' origine e fondazione della comune di Contessa," Palermo, 1851; Rodotà, *op. cit.*, iii, 114-115; Vannutelli, pp. 83-91; " Roma e l'Oriente," iii, 269-270.

[3] This is not the site of a palace of the Emperor Adrian, but of a castle built by a rich Albanian who had the same euphonious and respectable name. Crispi, " Memoria sulla origine e fondazione di Palazzo Adriano," Palermo, 1827; Rodotà, iii, 106-114; Vannutelli, 71-83; " Roma e l'Or.," iii, 268-269.

At Palazzo Adriano Albanian is still spoken; but it is dying out. The younger generation know only Italian. Of about 5,000 people nearly 4,000 are Byzantine. They have three churches and six priests of their rite. The dioceses to which these places belong interlace curiously. Piana is in Monreale, S Cristina in Palermo, all the others in Monreale. Palazzo Adriano was in Girgenti till 1846; then, by a new arrangement of boundaries, it passed to Monreale. These six places are the only Albanian settlements in Sicily.

At *Messina*, once so great a centre of the Byzantine rite, there are now hardly more than memories. The great monastery of St Saviour has gone (p. 125); the cathedral keeps only its title " Santa Maria del Grafeo " (p. 110) as evidence that once it was Greek. But there is one Byzantine Uniate priest here with a small chapel. As far as I know, he ministers to the few Uniates who may happen to stay in the city. In *Malta*, at Valletta, there is one Uniate Byzantine priest, with a small church. Both Messina and Valletta have large and prosperous Orthodox churches for the Greeks there; so have Naples (p. 144) and many cities in Italy. At Malta notably the two priests, Uniate and Orthodox, seem to be on the best possible terms; which is pleasant to note. In spite of the schism, they seem to realize that they have much in common. The Uniate looks upon his Orthodox rival as a good man, unimpeachable in rite, though unhappily *materialiter* in schism; the Orthodox thinks the Uniate a Greek and a colleague, though he does bend his neck to the horns of Roman pride. They visit each other and talk pleasantly. Each, of course, tries to capture the flock of the other; but I think each has the good sense to see that this is inevitable under the circumstances, and so bears no malice.

Altogether there are 50,000 to 60,000 Albanians in the south, about 37,000 in Calabria, and 20,000 in Sicily.[1]

---

[1] This is Charon's estimate (" Le XVe Centenaire," p. 262). I find no attempt at a total estimate in Rodotà. Moroni (" Diz. di Erudizione," xxxii, 149) says that about 100,000 came in the sixteenth century, that emigration and latinization has (1845) reduced that number to half. S. Vailhé (" Dict. de Théologie cath." iii, 1368) estimates the number as about 50,000; Netzhammer (" Unter den Albanesen Kalabriens," *loc. cit.* p. 100) says there are 35,000 in Calabria. " Roma e l'Oriente," vii, 278, says 80,000 altogether. O. Werner (" Orbis terrarum catholicus," Freiburg, 1890, p. 36), 41,556 (in 1858), C. Streit (" Atlas hierarchicus," Paderborn, 1913, p. 122), 49,000.

4. The Greeks of Corsica and Leghorn.

Apart from the Albanians in Southern Italy are these two colonies. Both have a curious history.

When the Turks conquered Greece they found stubborn resistance, especially in the Peloponnesus. Here, along the eastern side of the Gulf of Messenia, is the land *Maine*,[1] and in the middle of the long strip of land stands the village Boitylos, formerly Oitylos.[2] The people of Boitylos made a long and stubborn resistance to their enemies. At last they saw that the struggle was hopeless. Rather than stay under Turkish rule, they decided to wander from their homes to the West, where they could find a Christian and civilized government. They sent to Genua and made an arrangement that they should come and receive the barren district of Paomia in Corsica (at that time Genoese territory).

They came in several groups. The first started in September, 1675, having escaped the vigilance of the Turks, on a French ship.[3] They were led by the Stephanopulos family and their bishop, Parthenios Kalkandes. The Metropolitan of Maine wanted to come too. But the captain of the ship, seeing his great age, and fearing lest he die on the way, refused to take him. The Mainotai in Corsica still tell the story how the old man stood on the shore weeping as the ship sailed away, and cursing them for refusing to have pity on him. Part of the story is that he then prophesied that they should never stay a century in one place.

They got to Genua and asked to be allowed to stay in the city a few days, to rest after their journey before going on to Corsica. Meanwhile they accepted certain capitulations of the Genoese Government.[4] As in the case of all these immigrants

---

[1] Μαινή.

[2] Οἴτυλος—Βοίτυλος, pronounced Vítilos, then (as they often cut off the last letter) Vítilo. Tozer (*Journ. Hell. St.*, iii, 354) calls it Vitylo—rather a compromise. If you are going to transliterate β phonetically into *v*, you may as well do the whole thing and make *v* into *i*. The reasonable principle seems to be to transliterate the *written* word, letter for letter, and to let the reader take his chance of pronouncing it right. We do not spell French or German names in a way that would be phonetic to an Englishman.

[3] The *Sauveur*, Captain Daniel. The text of the contract between the Captain and the leaders of the emigrants is given in P. Stéphanopoli (*op. cit.* below, p. 173, n. 2), pp. 23-25. It is dated September 20, 1675. Here also (pp. 26-29) is a list of them. According to Parthenios Kalkandes they were 570, all told (*ibid.*, p. 34).

[4] There were altogether three capitulations, dated 1663, 1671, 1676 (text in Stéphanopoli, pp. 52-54).

into Italy, the capitulations contained clauses about religion. They were to keep their rite unchanged; but they were to be Uniates. They must accept a profession of faith and of union with the Holy See, on the same terms as the Albanians in Italy. When their bishop, priests, and monks were dead, the successors were to be ordained by the Pope or his delegate. They were to be subject to the Latin bishop in whose diocese they should be. It would seem as if the Republic meant that Parthenios was to have successors, ordaining bishops for these Greeks. As a matter of fact, he had none. They had many priests, deacons, and monks with them. In March, 1676, they sailed off on a ship of the Republic to Paomia in Corsica. The Government treated them exceedingly well; it gave them grain to sow, cattle, and all things necessary for colonists. Meanwhile other ships brought their relations from Boitylos, till gradually there was a large number of them. I find the names of seven churches and a monastery that they built at Paomia. There seems to have been no difficulty about their ecclesiastical position. No doubt they accepted it without either dislike or enthusiasm. The bishop at least must have understood from the first that it would be impossible to secure the favour and protection of the Genoese Government unless they were Catholics. Probably the simple peasants hardly noticed the difference, as long as their rites were untouched. Modern Orthodox writers are extremely indignant at the force used to bring them under Roman domination.[1] It was inevitable, according to the ideas of the time. So, quietly, the Mainotai in Corsica all began to believe that the Holy Ghost proceeds from God the Father and from the Son, and they blessed God who had brought them to this peaceful asylum.

However, in time they got into difficulties with their neighbours. Corsicans are not naturally peace-loving people: nor are they fond of strangers. So in the eighteenth century feuds begin between them and the Greeks. The Greeks asked and obtained protection from the Government; but at last things got so bad that they complained that they could not go out for a walk without being stuck by a knife. Of course, if you lived in Corsica in the eighteenth century, you must expect that sort of thing; but the Mainotai do not seem to have understood the Corsican character, and they did not like it. Then, in 1728, the whole island rebelled against the Genoese. The Mainotai, remembering the kindness of the Government, refused to join in the rebellion; so things got worse. Paomia

---

[1] *E.g.*, Vlasto in his article (p. 173, n. 2), p. 223.

was attacked by the rebels, and many of its Greeks were killed. After a regular siege they fought their way out and sailed off by sea to Ajaccio in 1731. This was the first fulfilment of the Metropolitan's prophecy that they should never stay a century in one place. Only 900 came to Ajaccio. Here they formed themselves into a guard in the service of the Government. Here also they gave up their national Greek dress, and the process of losing their language began.

In 1768 Corsica was ceded to France. The Count de Marbœuf was made governor. He was, all his life, a good friend to the strangers; and he suggested that they should settle at the village of Cargese.[1] Only a few remained at Ajaccio, where they became Latins and practically Corsicans. The rest, keeping their rite and their language (though this was already dying out) settled at Cargese. Here the quarrels with their neighbours began again. During the French Revolution the Corsicans seized the opportunity to burn down Cargese and kill a lot more of the Mainotai. Under the Directory they were able to return and build their village up again. In 1814 and again in 1830 they had trouble with the neighbours; but these were the last quarrels. Hard-working, temperate, and economical, the Greeks make excellent citizens; so that at last they conquered the respect of everyone. Here at Cargese they still are.

In the early nineteenth century some Latin Corsicans came to settle at the same place; so for their use a Roman church was built, besides the Byzantine one. Unfortunately a number of Greeks turned Latin and now frequent this church.[2] It seems, too, that the bishops of Ajaccio were only too ready to welcome such change of rite, in spite of the formal decrees of the Holy See.

But the Greeks were forgetting their language. In 1865 the French Government had the happy idea of appointing a professor of Greek for them. Then the Bishop of Ajaccio did what seems to be an unjust thing. He deposed the old Byzantine parish priest and appointed a successor. The people resented this very much, rebelled against the bishop's orders, and sent to the *Orthodox* of Marseilles for a priest. This argues how little, even after their long residence in Corsica, they appreciated the situation. The Orthodox of Marseilles could do nothing for them; but the Holy Synod of Athens seized the

[1] Also called Carghese.
[2] One of them, Elias Papadacci, was ordained in the Roman rite, became Latin parish priest in 1817, and persuaded many to change their rite (Stéphanopoli, *op. cit.*, p. 133).

opportunity, and sent them an Archimandrite named Bersi. However, he only stayed three days; so he could not have done much harm.   The Greeks of Hellas have several times made attempts to bring their countrymen of Corsica back to Orthodoxy, generally under the pretext of preserving their nationality and teaching them Greek.   In 1885 they sent a teacher, Mr. N. B. Phardys (Orthodox, of course) to open a Greek school at Cargese;[1] but the school was a failure and was closed after a year.   Greek (without theological bias) is taught regularly at the Cargese school by a native of the colony, Mr. Ragazzacci-Stephanopuli.

Between 1874 and 1876 a number of the Greeks of Cargese emigrated to Africa, thus again, though only partially, fulfilling the prophecy.   They settled in Algeria, at a place called Sidi-Meruan, in the province of Constantine.   There are now about 300 of them here; they keep their rite, have a church and a priest.   But the use of the Greek language is dying out here too.

At Cargese there are about 1,000 inhabitants, of whom rather more than half are Byzantine.   Each group (Roman and Byzantine) has its church and its parish priest.   The Byzantine priest is the Archimandrite Cæsar Cotti.   In his church is a fine Ikonostasion, given by Cardinal Simeoni, four holy eikons brought from Boitylos in the old days, and the flag under which they sailed when they came to Corsica, argent, a cross throughout gules, made in silk.   Fr. Cotti preaches occasionally in Greek; but he admits that the use of that language is dying out.[2]   French is taking its place, as it is taking the place of the Corsican dialect.   In general the Greeks of Cargese conform to the uses of the Italo-Greeks. They use the Byzantine service-books published by Propaganda, the bishop confirms (the Bishop of Ajaccio, according to the Roman rite, I regret to say); they have Benediction of the blessed Sacrament (as do many Uniates now; see p. 181), and they sing popular hymns in modern Greek.   The patronal feast of their church is St Spiridon, December 12; but they still keep another patronal feast, August 15, the falling asleep of the All-holy Theotokos, which was that of the

---

[1] Vlasto gives an enthusiastic account of this school (loc. cit., pp. 223-226).

[2] However, Vlasto prints some interesting Greek dialect songs they still sing (loc. cit., pp. 219-221); but, just like a modern Greek, he says he takes no interest in the δημοτική, and does not understand it properly.

original church at Boitylos. The people cultivate the land. They produce wine and cereals, and are well-off and prosperous.

But here is a wonderful story. In 1872 Mr. H. F. Tozer was at Cargese. He made some studies of their Greek dialect and noted some of their popular songs. Then, in 1882, he was in the Peloponnesus and went to Boitylos. He found that the people there perfectly remembered the fact that once, long ago, some of their forbears had sailed away to the West. He recited one of these songs from Cargese[1] to them, and they said: " That is just what our boys still sing in the streets." He found, too, that both had the same peculiarities of dialect.[2]

The other Italo-Greek community in the north is that of *Leghorn*. This, too, has a curious history. It began at the end of the sixteenth century. Cosimo I, Grand Duke of Tuscany (1537–1574), seeing the advantages of having the industrious, law-abiding Greek refugees in his state, invited a number of them to come and settle at Leghorn. This was in 1572. They came, not directly from the Levant, but from other Italian cities where they had already settled. The first group was from Ancona. Cosimo granted them extensive privileges, and obtained from the Pope (Pius V, 1566–1572) leave to hand over the old Augustinian church of St James " in Acquaviva." The Greeks rendered good service to the Tuscan state. As successful merchants they increased the general prosperity; as skilful sailors they manned the Tuscan galleys. They were always loyal to the Government; some of them occupied important posts in the army. Soon they had a special quarter of the town, the " Borgo dei Greci," around their church. Then they became too many for the church of St James; so they built the one they still use, S Maria dell' Annunziata. This was finished in 1605 and consecrated by

---

[1] " Κρέμασε ταὶς πλεξίδες σου ὄξου στὸ παναθύρι
νὰ κάμω σκάλα ν'ἀνεβῶ νὰ σὲ φιλῶ στὰ χείλη."

(" Hang down your braids outside the window, for a ladder for me to climb, that I may kiss your lips.")

[2] *E.g.*, K = tch. 'Εκεῖ, pron. Etche, etc. H. F. Tozer, "Vitylo and Cargese," in the *Journal of Hellenic Studies*, iii (1882), pp. 354-360. For the story of the colony at Cargese see P. Stéphanopoli, " Histoire des Grecs en Corse," Paris, 1900; E. A. Vlasto, " Relation d'un Voyage en Corse," in the " Annuaire pour l'encouragement des études grecques en France," xxi, Paris, 1887, pp. 207-226; Th. Xanthopoulos, " La Colonie grecque-cath. de Cargèse," *Échos d'Orient*, v, 1901, pp. 33-39; N. B. Phardys, Ὕλη καὶ σκαρίφημα ἱστορίας τῆς ἐν Κορσικῇ ἑλληνικῆς ἀποικίας, Athens, 1888.

their priest Athanasius, formerly Orthodox Archbishop of Cyprus.[1] Among the priests of this colony there are many who had been Orthodox bishops, who for some reason quarrelled with their people in the East, came to Italy, were converted, and then accepted this post at Leghorn. The colony never had a bishop, on principle; but the fact that its chaplain was in bishop's orders incidentally gave them for continual periods the advantage of having an ordaining bishop, like the Albanians in the south.

From the time of the quarrel between Melkites and Orthodox in Syria—that is, from the first quarter of the eighteenth century (see pp. 194 *seq.*)—many Syrian Melkites, speaking Arabic, came to join the colony at Leghorn. So comes a period of disputes, partly between the Greeks and the Melkites, partly between the Uniates and Orthodox. For many Orthodox merchants and refugees had also settled in the town. The Orthodox, having no church of their own, had attended the holy liturgy at the Uniate church. About the year 1757 they made an effort to turn it into an Orthodox one. But the Melkites and the Uniate Greeks joined forces to prevent this. Eventually, in 1757, the Grand Duke allowed the Orthodox to build a church for themselves, on condition that outside, where the door faced the street, there should be no symbol; inside they could put what they liked. It was to be quite distinct from the Uniate church; a list was to be kept of the members of both groups. No one was to be prevented turning Uniate if he wished to do so.[2] For Italy at that time these terms are not harsh. Then the Melkites began to make difficulties. They wanted a Melkite priest at the Annunziata church, and to have the services in Arabic. As they could not get this, most of them turned Latin. In 1763 Pope Clement XIII (1758–1769) tried to stop this; he issued a decree that all Catholics of the Byzantine rite, including the Melkites, should remain in, or return to, that rite. But the disputes went on. In 1816 the Melkites again petitioned Pius VII (1800–1823) that they might become Latins. This time at first they got the leave they wanted. It is odd, but characteristic of the Levantine Christian, that these people should prefer to become Latins rather than hear the prayers of their own rite said in another language.

[1] For Athanasius' history and deposition at Cyprus see J. Hacket, " A History of the Orth. Church of Cyprus " (Methuen, 1901), pp. 200-202.

[2] The document is in Rodotà, " del Rito greco," iii, 230.

Ten years later, in 1826, the Melkites got all they wanted. The Greeks seem to have given way suddenly. The Melkites sent to their Patriarch of Antioch, Ignatius V (see p. 204), and he sent them a Melkite priest, a Salvatorian Basilian monk, Michael Bāhūs. The famous Maximos Mazlūm (p. 210) was then at Rome. From this time the Melkite hierarchy assume the chief part in the direction of the church at Leghorn. As soon as they had succeeded in their object, the Melkites who had become Latins turned again and came back to their own rite. From this time there is always at least a Melkite curate at the church, named by the Melkite Patriarch. Mazlūm in 1840 came and baptized their bell; the direction of the clergy seems to pass entirely to the Melkites. In 1807 John Doxaras, the chaplain, a Greek, obtained from Rome the privilege of wearing the Byzantine mitre and of being a titular Archimandrite. The chaplains also wear the Epigonation and generally call themselves Chorepiskopoi. All these privileges are now so common in the Melkite church that they mean nothing more than when a priest is a Monsignore with us.

Since 1887 the chaplain is Joseph Shalhūb, a Melkite Salvatorian. But he is the only Melkite in the place. All the others have either turned Latin or have gone away. So we have the odd situation that a Congregation consisting exclusively of Italo-Greeks is served by an Arab Melkite priest. Till 1892 there was a committee of Greeks to arrange the temporal affairs of the church. Then the number of Greeks was so reduced that Italian Latins were admitted to this committee. In 1904 the committee was dissolved by the Government; they have now appointed a commission to consider the formation of a new one. There are about eighty people who attend this church, all Italo-Greeks, by descent Albanians. The services are in Greek, which Fr. Shalhūb knows well; the books and registers are also kept in Greek. But the people speak Italian, and the priest is an Arab. The church, according to rule in Italy, depends on the Bishop of Leghorn; the priest is presented by the Melkite Patriarch of Antioch, appointed by the Ordinary.[1]

[1] See Giuseppe Scialhub (= Yūsuf Šalhūb), " La chiesa greco-unita di Livorno, memorie storiche edite nel terzo centenario civile di Livorno e dell' inaugurazione della chiesa greco-unita," Leghorn, 1906, where a list of the rectors will be found; Rodotà, " del Rito greco," iii, 229-230; C. Charon, " L'Église grecque cath. de Livourne " in the *Echos d'Orient*, xi (1908), pp. 227-237.

5. Italo-Greek Canon Law and Rites.

Since the Italo-Greeks are the nearest Uniates to Rome, it is natural that the Holy See should have given to them, if not most, at any rate the first attention. So it happens that many rules, made in the first case for them, have since been applied, sometimes with modifications, to the other Uniates. It follows that much of the Italo-Greek Canon Law has become general Canon Law for all Uniate churches. In other ways they stand apart from all the others. For instance, they are considerably the most influenced by Latin principles. During the centuries in which they have lived in Italy, surrounded by Latins, they have adopted many Roman customs; in some cases the Popes imposed such customs on them, no doubt thinking these to be essentially Catholic. Later bodies of Uniates have escaped this influence. On joining the Church they brought with them their independent customs. Since they joined at a later period, when the study of rites and canons was more advanced, it was then recognized that these customs and ritual observances were in themselves perfectly legitimate. Here I note one or two of the main features of Italo-Greek law.

Although we put the Italo-Greeks first among the Uniate Churches, although in the past they have played so important a part in Church history, it is a curious point to note that they are not really a Church at all. For to be a Church—that is, a local Church in the one great Catholic Church, people must at least have bishops with ordinary jurisdiction. Lower than one diocese the concept of a Church cannot go. But the Italo-Greeks have no Ordinaries. We have seen that the last lines of Byzantine bishops in Italy died out—that is, became Roman—before the Albanians arrived (p. 102). The Albanians, scattered about Calabria and Sicily, have never had dioceses of their own. They have been counted, quite correctly, simply as so many Catholics more in each Latin diocese already existing. Indeed, unless they had been all herded together in one district, and all the Latins turned out of it, it would have been impossible to make them into a diocese on the normal lines. It is true that in later times cross-jurisdiction over the same territory has become common; so that now, in the Levant, there are many cases of bishops ruling their subjects, not by geographical area, but according to the rite these subjects use, wherever (within limits) they may dwell. But in the fifteenth century, when the Albanians arrived in Italy, there was thought to be a great principle against this.

It was then accepted that there could not be two bishops in one place, according to the axiom of the Fourth Lateran Council.[1] In short, the only possibility recognized was the geographical diocese; where one bishop ruled in a town there could be no other ordinary episcopal jurisdiction but his. So, at first, as we have seen (p. 122), the Holy See provided for the Albanians by requiring each Latin bishop, in whose diocese they settled, to have a special Vicar General of the Byzantine rite for them. That is still the law; and so far it works well. Mgr. Peter Camodeca de' Nobili Coronei is Vicar General of the Bishop of Cassano al' Ionio for the Albanians (p. 161).

Yet it was impossible that their condition should be satisfactory as long as they had no one in episcopal orders of their rite. They needed someone to ordain their clergy, to bless their chrism, and (since in this point they are latinized) to confirm them. For over two centuries the Italo-Greeks had to get on without such a bishop. During that time all kinds of curious compromises were made. Sometimes a wandering Uniate bishop from the Levant was called in to ordain (sometimes, by mistake, he was not even a Uniate); generally the Latin ordinaries, in spite of the Canons, themselves ordained and confirmed their Byzantine subjects, according to the Roman rite. This is directly opposed to one of the principles of the Holy See—namely, that every man should receive sacraments in his own rite. But there was already a precedent at Rome itself. Here, too, the same difficulty had occurred. Who was to ordain the students of the Greek College ? Already, in 1595, Clement VIII (1592–1605) had provided for this by appointing a Byzantine bishop *in partibus infidelium* to ordain the students, and (so he intended) all Italo-Greeks. This bishop was to have no jurisdiction. But the line does not seem to have lasted. There is considerable obscurity about these Byzantine bishops in Rome, till they were revived in 1629. In 1624 Urban VIII (1623–1644) drew up a new Constitution for the Greek College, in which, among other things, he ordered that there should always be a Byzantine ordaining bishop in it.[2] In 1629 Gabriel, titular Metropolitan of Mitylene, was appointed to this place. From his time the line continues regularly. The bishop lives at the Greek College, has nothing to do with its management, but ordains

---

[1] See p. 123, n. 2.

[2] Const., *Uniuersalis Eccl.*, November 23, 1624. Bull. Rom., tom. v, part v, p. 277, No. lxxxviii. " Curet Protector . . . ut Græcus aliquis . . ." (p. 280).

the students when he is required to do so.   The present bishop is Joseph Schirò, titular of Neocæsarea.[1]

But this one bishop at Rome was not enough for the Italo-Greeks of the south.   In 1717 an Albanian priest, former student of the Greek College, Stephen Rodotà, came to Rome and explained to Pope Clement XI (1700-1721) the needs of his people.   The Pope then, after some provisional measures, founded the college at San Benedetto Ullano (p. 161), and in it ordered that there should be an ordaining bishop for the Albanians of Calabria, on the same footing as the one at Rome. Felix Samuel Rodotà was the first rector of the college and the first Calabrian Byzantine ordaining bishop (1732).   This line also continues regularly to the present time.   At first the bishop resided at the college at San Benedetto; then he migrated with it to San Demetrio Corone (p. 162).   Of late years, owing to difficulties with the administration of the college (now secularized), he has a house at Naples.   The last bishop was John Barcia, titular of Croia in Albania.[2]   Then in 1784 the Albanians of Sicily asked and obtained of Pius VI (1775-1799) the same privilege.   The first bishop of their line was George Stassi (1784-1801), the present one is Paul Schirò, titular of Benda in Albania, ordained in 1904.[3]   He resides at the Greek-Albanian College at Palermo.   These three bishops are to be considered as auxiliaries of the Latin Ordinaries.   They have no ordinary jurisdiction; but they have a considerable measure of delegate jurisdiction for the churches, clergy, and faithful of their rite.   In theory, perhaps, each Ordinary in whose diocese Albanians live should have such an auxiliary; but there are not enough Albanians to make this worth while. So the Byzantine auxiliary in Calabria gets his faculties from the Archbishop of Rossano and the Bishops of Cassano and San Marco; the Sicilian auxiliary from the Archbishops of Palermo and Monreale.

Dating, perhaps, partly even from the time of the Norman conquest, the Italo-Greeks had evolved certain peculiarities of rite which lead some people to speak of a special " Italo-Greek " rite.[4]   It hardly amounts to that.   But there was (to some extent there still is) considerable latinization among

[1] Rodotà, iii, 218-220 gives an account of these bishops down to his time.   The complete list is in Charon, " Le XVe Centenaire," p. 48.
[2] See the complete list in Charon, op. cit., p. 261.   Mgr. Barcia died in 1914; his successor has not been appointed.
[3] Ibid.
[4] Rodotà, for instance, uses this expression always.

them. In connection with this there is a point to notice. Of
late years, with the spread of liturgical study, there is a movement among the Byzantines of Italy in favour of purity of
rite. This means conforming to the pure Greek Typika.
Grottaferrata, now full of enthusiasts for the Byzantine rite,
sets the standard of this movement; from Grottaferrata it
is spreading to the Albanian colonies of Calabria and Sicily;
so that now it is looked upon almost as a disgrace to practise
any Latin infiltration at all. The student might think that
the pure rite he will see at Grottaferrata itself, and in a lesser
degree at Piana and other places, is the old tradition; that the
Latin influence that he will notice in some of the churches is a
later corruption. Really the opposite is true. This pure use is
the latest development of all; those despised latinizations have
many centuries of use behind them. And so, if one cares for
local customs in rite too, one may perhaps ask whether this zeal
for theoretic purity is entirely an advantage. It is rather like
the zeal for doing everything exactly as is done at Rome among
Latins of different countries. I should rather be inclined to
say that local variety in a rite also has its interest, that it is most
natural that during the long centuries of Roman neighbourhood
the Italo-Greeks have gradually acquired some latinization,
that liturgically this is harmless and historically it is interesting, that it is, on the whole, rather a pity to destroy so old a
tradition. If specific identity is so important, why not recognize a special Italo-Greek use, and maintain that according
to its own tradition ?

In general the Italo-Greeks use the Byzantine rite in Greek.
The great authority for them is the Typikon of Grottaferrata[1]
used as the basis of the books printed at Propaganda. They
use these books, of which the first was the *Liturgikon*,[2] printed
at Rome in 1738 by order of Benedict XIV and Clement XII.
The first Roman edition of the complete *Euchologion* was
issued in 1754. Benedict XIV accompanied it with the Bull
Ex quo primum.[3] There is, then, nothing much to say about
the rite of the Italo-Greeks in general. It is simply the

---

[1] Compiled by St Bartholomew, the fourth Archimandrite
(† *c.* 1050), revised by Blasius II, twenty-fifth Archimandrite,
in 1300.

[2] The book containing the celebrant's part of the liturgies, really
an extract from the " Euchologion." In 1683 Card. Nerli, Protector
of the O. S. Bas., edited a book of the liturgy for them, on the lines
of the Roman missal.

[3] " Bullarium Ben. XIV " (ed. Prati), iii, pars ii, pp. 299-329
(March 1, 1756).

Byzantine rite, with the inevitable notes of Catholic use.[1]   The peculiarities of the Italo-Greeks are, in outline, these.   Rodotà calls them peculiarities of the Basilian monks in Italy.[2]   But that, I think, is only because at his time the Byzantine rite in Italy was maintained chiefly by the monks.   The other churches seem to have had the same points.   What they come to is that there are Roman infiltrations, some of great, some of hardly any, importance.   The chief point of all was the use of azyme bread for the holy Eucharist; next to this, in importance, are feasts taken from the Roman Calendar and the use of Latin vestments.

We have noted that some at least of these Italo-Greek peculiarities go far back into the Middle Ages.   After the Norman conquest it was almost inevitable that there should be Latin influence among the Greeks in Italy.   There is, for instance, a curious combination of the Byzantine Proanaphora with a translation into Greek of the Roman Canon, called the Liturgy of St Peter, dating from the ninth or tenth century.[3] It is commonly said that the chief Romanizing points, azyme bread and Roman vestments, were introduced by Cardinal Bessarion at Grottaferrata, and then spread among all the Italo-Greeks.   This, however, is a mistake.[4]   Rodotà says roundly: " The Basilians of our time celebrate the holy

[1] The Pope's name in the intercessions, etc.

[2] Rodotà, " del Rito greco," ii, cap. xii, pp. 224-233.

[3] Printed in C. A. Swainson, " The Greek Liturgies " (Cambridge, 1884), pp. 191-203; see F. E. Brightman, " Eastern Liturgies " (Oxford, 1896), p. xci.

[4] The use of azyme bread seems to have begun, almost insensibly, from the frequent inter-communion between Italo-Greeks and their Roman neighbours.   The XIVth Roman Ordo (by Card. James Gaetano, fourteenth century) describes the communion of an Abbot from the Pope's hand, when he is blessed by the Pope.   It is, of course, Roman, in one kind and with azyme (§ 57, P.L., lxxviii, 1173, B); no exception is made, though at that time Archimandrites of Grottaferrata were frequently blessed by the Pope himself.   At least, then, they must have made their Communion in the Roman form.   Eugene IV (1431-1447), by Bessarion's advice, allowed the Italo-Greeks to consecrate bread, leavened, but made in small, thin, round cakes, looking like the Roman azyme altar-breads.   At first many opposed this.   Then, when the custom had obtained, the further change to azyme must have followed easily.   Side by side with this change went that into Communion under one kind alone.   Rodotà (ii, 229) quotes a letter to the Inquisition by a Byzantine Protopapa in the province of Otranto (1603), which shows that it had then been made there.   A detailed discussion of the whole question, with many curious details, will be found in Rodotà, " del Rito greco," ii, pp. 226-231; see also " Roma e l'Oriente," vii (1914), p. 341.

Mysteries in the Greek language with Latin ceremonies."[1] That is a great exaggeration. The prayers and the chief ceremonies were always Byzantine. As Latin elements we have first the use of azyme bread. This is certainly a very grave matter, by far the gravest of all. Nothing could be more opposed to Byzantine use. Another important latinization is the adoption of feasts from the Roman Calendar. Ever since Pope Gregory XIII (1572-1585) reformed it in 1582 the Italo-Greeks have followed this Gregorian Calendar. Indeed, at first they were the only Uniates on whom it was imposed by authority; the others have adopted it later, some only the other day (see p. 221). However, this is but a small point. There is nothing essential to any rite in such a matter as the Julian or Gregorian calculation of the year; it is obviously most desirable that all Catholics should, for nstance, keep Easter on the same day. The whole Byzantine cycle of feasts and fasts could remain unchanged, though calculated in the Gregorian manner.

Much more vital is that the Italo-Greeks keep a number of Roman feasts. The chief of these are St Joseph on March 19, All Saints on November 1, All Souls on November 2,[2] Corpus Christi; they also have our Lady of the Rosary (τοῦ ʽΡοδαρίου ἤτοι τοῦ ʽΡοσαρίου) on the first Sunday of October, St Michael *in Monte Gargano* on May 8,[3] the Sacred Heart (Friday after the octave of Corpus Christi) and some Western Saints, whose names look odd in Greek letters.[4] Less important was the use of Roman vestments. Further, they say the *Filioque* (καὶ ἐκ τοῦ ʽΤιοῦ) in the Nicene Creed;[5] the priest at baptism does not confirm the child; but it is confirmed later by a bishop. There is no Ikonostasion in most of their churches[6]; they have side-altars, solid statues, Benediction of the Blessed Sacrament, and other popular devotions

---

[1] " del Rito greco," ii, p. 225.

[2] But they also keep these days according to the Byzantine Calendar, St Joseph (with our Lady) on December 26, All Saints the first Sunday after Pentecost (our Trinity feast), All Souls the Saturday before Sexagesima.

[3] This is natural, since M. Gargano is in what was once their country.

[4] *E.g.*, December 3, ʽΗ μνήμη τοῦ ἁγίου ἰσαποστόλου φραγγίσκου Ζαβερίου τοῦ ὁμολογητοῦ. For the Italo-Greek Calendar see Nilles, " Kalendarium manuale," ii, 547-551.

[5] It is not said at the Greek church at Rome.

[6] There are Ikonostasia now only at Grottaferrata, Cargese, Leghorn, Palermo. Mgr. John Barcia (p. 178) left money in his will for one at Palazzo Adriano. This is being made.

borrowed from us. The monks used to shave the beard, did not always abstain from flesh-meat, cut their hair short, and wore a Latin form of habit.[1] Most of the priests have short hair and Latin cassocks. In some churches a few Latin prayers were interpolated in the liturgy.[2] The use of a " low " liturgy (like low Mass) can hardly be called latinization, since it is a development in most Eastern rites.[3] That is about all.

I have already noted that there is now a great movement against these latinizations. It began under Leo XIII, as part of his tendency in favour of Eastern rites, with the hope of bringing the schismatics back to reunion. So on April 12, 1881, the Congregation for Eastern Rites published a decree, of which the first article was that " In the monastery of Grottaferrata, all variations of any kind and customs to the contrary being abolished, the Greek rite be observed restored integrally in the divine offices and other sacred functions." So Grottaferrata set about the reform; on the Koimesis of our Lady of that year (August 15) the holy liturgy was celebrated with leavened bread, the proper Byzantine vestments, without elevation after the Consecration, in short, with all desirable correctness.[4] We have seen that they have now made an Ikonostasion in their church.[5] The monks all wear the beard and long hair; their *Rasa* are quite correct—in short, everything now is scrupulously Byzantine. The movement has spread throughout the Italo-Greek churches. It is now a reproach,

---

[1] At the Council of Florence (1439) the silly Italians made fun of the dress of the Eastern monks (see the letter of Lapo Castelliunculo, quoted in Rodotà, ii, 232-233, note 6).

[2] Thus at Grottaferrata before the reform of 1881 they read the epistle and gospel in Latin after they had done so in Greek. Before the Apostolos (epistle) the celebrant said *Dominus uobiscum* and the Roman collect of the day, in Latin. An elevation after the words of institution was common in most Italo-Greek churches. I believe that all this is now abolished.

[3] In 1755 Benedict XIV allowed a shortened form of the liturgy and divine office for the O.S.Bas. for private use only. He expressly excepted the monks of Mezzoiuso, who were always supposed to be rigidly Eastern (see p. 167, n. 1). The Bull is *Quem religionis* (" Bullarium Ben. XIV," ed. Prati, 1847, iii, pars ii, pp. 273-275). The diocesan clergy tried in vain to share this privilege. Rodotà (ii, 226, note) makes mock of the situation—that the monks had a special privilege to say fewer prayers than the secular clergy. Now all Uniates have shortened private liturgies, and say only part of their office when it is not said in choir.

[4] A. Rocchi, " La Badia di Grottaferrata " (Rome, 1904), pp. 74-75.   [5] Above, p. 149.

which they resent greatly, to say that they are not pure Byzantine. I do not think that any church now uses azyme bread or Roman vestments. The *Kalymaukion* has come back to the Greek College at Rome, and, at least for State occasions, among the Albanian clergy. Their dress out of doors is still rather Roman or Italian; but they wear beards. Where there are no Ikonostasia they declare that they are going to have them, as soon as they can afford it.[1] In short, the movement has set so firmly in the other direction that there is very little that is peculiarly Italo-Greek and not pure Byzantine among them now.[2]

Summary.

In this chapter we have considered what remains of the Byzantine rite in Italy. Except for the colony in Corsica it is represented now only by the Albanian refugees of the fifteenth and sixteenth centuries (though there were Greeks among them too). The most important Byzantine institution in the country is the venerable monastery of Grottaferrata, founded by St Neilos the Younger at the beginning of the eleventh century. Grottaferrata has always kept its rule and its rite, though both at one time suffered from Roman infiltrations. Now it is again purest of the pure Byzantine. The other great centre is the Greek College at Rome, founded by Gregory XIII in the sixteenth century. Then there are the Albanian villages in Calabria and Sicily, containing altogether about 50,000 Italo-Greeks. At Cargese in Corsica is a colony of Greeks, numbering about 600; these have a further colony in Algeria. At Leghorn is a parish containing about eighty Italo-Greeks, with a Melkite priest. None of these people have diocesan bishops of their own. They are subject to the

---

[1] So they say at Piana de' Greci. An example of their feelings may be seen in " Roma e l'Oriente " vii (1914), 224-231, where the clergy of Piana are accused of doing certain unbyzantine things in Holy Week; and their angry denial, pp. 353-364. See also iii (1911-1912), 344, " Risveglio fra il clero greco (di Sicilia)."

[2] The Italo-Greeks have their own church music, derived ultimately from Constantinople. It is enharmonic, obeys the rules of the Byzantine modes, and forms a very interesting parallel to the development in the Levant. There is a dissertation on it, with examples and parallel Eastern forms, by Dom Hugh Gaisser, O.S.B., " I canti ecclesiastici italo-greci " (estratto dalla *Rassegna gregoriana*, sett.-ott., 1905), Rome, Desclée, Lefebvre, 1905. They also sing curious Albanian popular hymns, of which a specimen may be seen in " Roma e l'Oriente," iii (1911-1912), 271.

Latin Ordinaries; but they have three ordaining bishops, auxiliaries of the Ordinaries, at Rome, in Calabria, and Sicily. In the past, since the early Middle Ages, their rites were considerably latinized.   They used azyme bread for the holy Eucharist, Roman vestments, and many Roman feasts in their Calendar.   Nor were their churches arranged according to Byzantine principles.   Now there is a great movement in favour of a return to pure Byzantine use.   I might have added before that they are all excellent Catholics.   They think it better to be Byzantine than Roman; but they think it atrocious to be a schismatic.   It would be a great pity if what is left of so ancient a tradition as the Byzantine rite in Italy were ever to disappear.   The Roman rite, extended over vast continents in unquestioned predominance, cannot fear the rivalry of this little remnant; no Latin could possibly be jealous of any other rite.   May the Byzantine rite remain ever in this ancient home, and may it flourish always as the memory of so great a past.

CHAPTER III

THE MELKITES

THE next group of Byzantine Uniates is that of the Melkites. These are the Catholics of this rite in Syria, Palestine, and Egypt, who all now speak Arabic. They are the most closely organized of the Byzantine Uniates; they alone in this rite have a Patriarch of their own. Perhaps the most striking fact about them is that it is their Patriarch who, by direct descent and undoubted historical continuity, represents the original line of Antioch. It is the same case as that of the Chaldees and Malabar Christians. The Uniates are the old line, which after several vicissitudes has at last come back definitely to union with the Holy See. The Orthodox of Syria, who pretend to be the old Church, are a schism away from that Church, formed in the eighteenth century, when she returned to her original Catholic obedience.

1. Before Cyril VI (1724)

The word " Melkite " is now commonly used for Uniates of the Byzantine rite in Syria and Egypt.[1]   Originally it meant

[1] For all the following account of the Melkite Church I am indebted, most of all, to the admirable work of Father Cyril Charon. Charon is a Frenchman by birth and a Catholic priest of the Byzantine rite. He spent many years as a member of the Melkite Patriarchal clergy in Syria, where I knew him. In 1907 he came back to Europe, changed his name to Karalevsky, and took up work among the Catholic Slavs of his rite. He commands an astonishing number of languages, to which he adds an intimate knowledge of the Melkite clergy and people, and a sound historical, theological, and liturgical instinct. Nothing could exceed his care to verify his facts from the original documents, the patience of his research, and the accuracy of his transcriptions. Armed with every possible qualification, he began a detailed history of the Melkite Church in the *Echos d'Orient*, iv (1900-1901), p. 268. Charon's articles continue to vol. xi (1908), bringing the story to the end of Maximus III (1855). Now he is engaged in remodelling and continuing his history in a complete work in three large volumes, " Histoire des Patriarcats melkites " (Paris, Picard, 1911 *seq.*). Of these all published so far are vol. iii,

those who accepted the Emperor's religion—that is, the faith of Chalcedon—as opposed to the Monophysites.[1] Then, after the schism of the ninth and eleventh centuries, it meant both Catholics and Orthodox in these parts, though for many centuries there were but few Catholics. As far as opposition to Monophysism went, these two agreed. It is a curious development that the name is now commonly used for the Catholics only. This is the result of the proceeding of the Uniate Patriarch Cyril VI (see p. 201) at the beginning of the eighteenth century. At that time the two names " Orthodox " and " Melkite " meant the same thing in Syria. Cyril tried (in vain) to get the Turkish Government to recognize the Uniates as a separate body from the Orthodox. It is one of the early attempts to procure civil emancipation for the Uniates, which was at last obtained by Maximos III (p. 218). So, in order to describe his people and to distinguish them from the others, he left the more common name to his rivals and annexed " Melkite " for his flock. He did not succeed in his attempt to procure emancipation for the Uniates; but his artificial distinction of name has remained ever since. To this day the people of Syria and Egypt mean one thing by " Orthodox," another—namely, Uniate of the Byzantine rite—by " Melkite."[2]

---

containing exhaustive information about the present state of the Church, its liturgy, Canon Law, organization, hierarchy, statistics (the account of liturgical books especially is a model how such things should be done), and the first part of vol. ii (history from 1833-1855). When this work is complete the Melkites will have a history of their Church which any other in Christendom may envy. May members of the other Uniate Churches be inspired by this model to write a history of their Patriarchates in the same way. Paul Bacel and Constantine Bacha (Bāsā), Melkite monks, have also contributed valuable articles to the *Echos d'Orient ;* there are other sources, which will be mentioned in the notes below.

[1] " Lesser Eastern Churches," pp. 184-185.

[2] It does, however, still happen occasionally that " Melkite " is used for both Catholics and Orthodox. Since 1914 the *Echos d'Orient*, in its " Chronique religieuse " has begun to write two headings, " Melkites catholiques " and " Melkites orthodoxes." There is here the idea of harking back to the original meaning of the name. But it is a mistake. There would be no end to the confusion if we began to claim technical terms in what we believe to be their proper meaning, for, in this sense, we certainly claim that we are the orthodox Christians, and we are evangelical and unitarian. The only sensible course is to use all such names as commonly received technical terms by which no one is understood to concede what their origin or etymology implies. Note that the spelling " Melchite " is wrong. The third radical is *Kaph;* CH represents *Ḥeth*.

It is merely a fictitious distinction, as far as any meaning of the name in their natural sense goes. Indeed, " Melkite " seems specially inappropriate for Catholics; it has an Erastian sound, and, of course, we think we are really the Orthodox Christians. Yet, on the general principle of common sense, I keep this term, and by a " Melkite " mean always and only a Catholic of the Byzantine rite in Egypt or Syria.

There is a question, really superfluous, of which we must notice something before we go on to the history of the Melkites—namely, the much vexed one of their ethnological origin. Really there is no question here at all. They are of the same race, of the same mixed blood as all the other inhabitants of these lands, whether Christian or Moslem. The religious body to which a man belongs does not affect his blood; though the Melkites themselves think it does. They protest eagerly that they are Greeks, in the ethnological sense, descended from Greeks of Hellas. At first it seems to the Western reader absurd that anyone should hold this theory, with its obvious confusion between religion and race. No one in England discusses of what blood Methodists may be. But it is the commonest confusion in the East. Its origin is the way the Turks always class people by fictitious races according to their religions. Each religious body is a " nation " (*millet*) to the Turk. He has some confused idea that the differences of religion in his empire come from the fact that each group is descended from a race which once held that particular religion. Since so much civil law, and the state of each subject in temporal matters, depend on the religious body to which he belongs, it is not so surprising that, at last, the Christians themselves have begun to look upon themselves as different nations, in the ordinary sense. This is encouraged by the fact that it has always been extremely difficult for a man in the Turkish Empire to change his religion. We are so used to seeing people change from one religion to another that it would be impossible for us to confuse religion with race. But out there this hardly ever happens. Each man is, in religion, what his fathers were before him; he marries a woman of the same Church; so something like a distinction of blood often does, at last, occur between the Churches. They think that it is so essentially. They talk of their " nation," meaning their Church, and they do not realize that this is a purely artificial use of the word introduced by the Moslems, because these had no other way of classifying their Christian subjects.

As a matter of fact, the situation is simple enough; it applies

to all the inhabitants of Syria, whatever their religion may be.
In origin they are the old Semitic population of the land,
Aramæans, called in later language Syrians. From the time
of Alexander the Great there was considerable Greek influence
throughout Syria, mostly in the towns. Greek became the
common language of all the Eastern Mediterranean basin,
spoken by the more educated townsmen; while peasants went
on speaking Syriac and Coptic. Certainly there was considerable infiltration of Greek blood. Alexander and the
Seleucid kings brought many Greeks from Hellas to Syria.
But this strain of Greek blood has long been lost in the general
mass. It has not formed one " nation " among the others.
As far as blood is concerned, a Moslem of Syria is just as likely
to have Greek blood as a Melkite. Then, with the Moslem
conquest of the seventh century, came a new influence. Arabic
became the language of the Government, then of the whole
people. The Greek influence died out; even Syriac was forgotten; so now they all talk only Arabic. No doubt, from the
time of the Moslem conquest there have been infiltrations of
Arabic blood too; but this is lost in the general mass, as
the Greek blood was before. The language people speak is
never a safe nor a final test of their blood. The population
of Syria, then, is mixed, as is that of nearly all countries.
Fundamentally it is Syrian; it has Greek and Arabic elements.
The case is exactly parallel in Egypt. Here we have a population, originally Egyptian, with Greek and Arabic strains lost
in the general mass. Probably no single person in either land
knows how much of each element he has in his veins. The
mixture is the same for all. It has nothing whatever to do with
the various religious distinctions, which owe their origin to
entirely different causes.[1]

Now we turn to a more serious question, the ecclesiastical
origin of the Melkite Church. We have not here the case of

[1] The discussion about the ethnological origin of the Melkites is
still lively over there. See C. Charon, " L'origine ethnographique
des Melkites," *Echos d'Orient*, xi (1908), pp. 35-40; 82-91. H.
Lammens, S.J., wrote against the supposed Greek origin in the Arabic
review *alMašriḳ*, vol. iii (1900), pp. 267-273. Evangelos 'Id wrote,
angrily defending it, " Étude sur les origines des Grecs melkites,
réponse au R. P. H. Lammens, S.J.," Rome, 1901. Next year he
published an Arabic version of this at Beirut. Constantine Bāšā,
O.S.Bas. (Salv.) also wrote to defend their Greek descent, " Baḥthu-
ntiḳādiyy fi aṣli-rrūmi-lmalakiyin, waluġatihim " (" Critical Research
Concerning the Origin of the Melkites and their Language "), Cairo,
1900. S. Vailhé sums up this discussion in the article, " Melkites et
Maronites." *Echos d'Orient*, vi (1903), pp. 143-147.

a Church springing up suddenly at some definite moment by
the conversion of a large number of people. The situation is
more complicated, so that it needs attention. To begin with,
the matter of the schism of the East is not so simple as many
people think. Indeed, it is very difficult to say exactly when
the Orthodox, outside Constantinople, became schismatics.

It will be remembered that both the quarrels with the Holy
See, that of Photius in the ninth and of Cerularius in the
eleventh century, were, in themselves, purely local quarrels of
Patriarchs of Constantinople. Nor has the Holy See ever
excommunicated the Eastern or " Orthodox " Church as
such.[1] It is only because, eventually, the other Eastern
Patriarchs and bishops took the side of Constantinople, remained in communion with the Œcumenical Patriarch, that
they, too, share his state of schism. But when did they do so ?
In the first schism, of Photius, apparently they never did.
I doubt very much if we can speak of a general schism of the
East, or of an " Orthodox " Church, meaning a separate
religious body, at that time at all. At the eighth General
Council (Constantinople iv, 869), when Photius was tried and
condemned, the Imperial Commissioner asked the Legates of
the other Eastern Patriarchs why they had not condemned him
long ago. They answered that the right of Ignatius was so
evident that it did not need their support, and that, in any case,
the Pope had done all that was wanted.[2] From this it appears
that they had never intended to share Photius's schism. It
would seem, then, that the other Eastern Patriarchs had
remained in communion with the Holy See throughout that
quarrel. So I do not think we can speak of a general schism
in the East, at least till the time of Cerularius.

Nor did such a state of things occur at once under Cerularius.
His quarrel, too, was a purely local one at Constantinople, perhaps even more so than that of Photius. In one case, especially,
we know that one of his brother Patriarchs protested vehemently
against his course, and declared that he would not break communion with the Pope. This Patriarch, Peter III of Antioch,
was certainly not a schismatic.[3] Nor can we say exactly when his
successors fell into schism. The final test would be when they
removed the name of the Pope from their diptychs. But we
do not know when this happened. Probably for a long time
none of them realized that a permanent state of schism between
East and West had broken out. Hitherto they had been in

[1] " Orth. East. Church," p. 185.
[2] *Ibid.*, pp. 157-158.   [3] *Ibid.*, pp. 188-192.

communion with both the Pope of Rome and the Patriarch of Constantinople. They knew, of course, that these two were now quarrelling, but, presumably, they thought that this quarrel was no business of theirs. They, no doubt, hoped that it would be made up in time; meanwhile they intended to keep out of it and to remain in communion with both. It is true that eventually the nearness of Constantinople, the unhappy and degrading dependence that these other Patriarchs had learned to accept under the Emperor's Patriarch dragged them, too, with him into schism; but it would be most difficult to define exactly when this happened. In their case it was always the participation in the guilt of another rather than any spontaneous movement of their own. And, as they went into schism only dragged by Constantinople, so ever since there have been times and periods when, it would seem, they renewed relations with Rome and were not in schism at all. For one thing, we must remember that, even as far as Constantinople itself, the home of the schism, was concerned, the excommunication of Cerularius was not the last step. Since then there have been the reunions of Lyons in 1274 and of Florence in 1439. These applied to the other Patriarchates too. If they were in schism after Cerularius they came back to union in 1274; if again they glided into schism after that, they came back in 1439.

But the curious thing is that besides these two famous cases there have been many relations between the other Eastern Patriarchs and Rome. They never seem to have forgotten that, in theory, they should be in communion with the chief Patriarch of all, in the West. Communications were difficult; yet, even so, there are a number of cases in which a Patriarch of Antioch, or of Alexandria or Jerusalem, succeeded in renewing relations with the Pope, and so must be counted as a Catholic. Often, no doubt, when they could not do so, being then under the heel of the Turk, they believed all the Catholic faith, and intended to be in communion with the Pope. So we must look upon the present distinction between the Orthodox and the Melkites in Syria and Egypt as the result of a gradual, a very gradual, parting of the ways. The Melkites represent the tendency, never quite extinct, towards union with Rome, now crystallized in one Church; the Orthodox represent the other tendency towards Constantinople crystallized in another.

The late Melkite Patriarch, Peter IV (Giraigīrī, p. 222), said that between Nicholas I of Antioch (847–869) and Cyril VI (Tānās), under whom the final reunion took place

(p. 197), there were no less than twenty-five Patriarchs of Antioch of whose catholicity we can be absolutely certain.[1] This number is perhaps an exaggeration; but there are a surprising number of perfectly authentic cases of Patriarchs of Antioch in union with Rome in that interval. First among them again I name Peter III.[2] His correspondence with Pope Leo IX (1048–1054) leaves no doubt at all that just then, when Cerularius was causing his schism, Peter was entirely Catholic.[3] His successor, Theodosius III, however, seems to have been a schismatic. In 1057 he came to Constantinople and made common cause with that Patriarch. It was he who proclaimed Isaac Komnenos (1057–1059) Emperor. But now we see how the defection of one Patriarch was not considered as contaminating the whole line of his successors. When John IV was Patriarch of Antioch (*c.* 1090–*c.* 1103) the Crusaders took the city (1098). They would not set up a Latin Patriarch, because it is against the canons that there should be two bishops in one see. Clearly they treat him as a Catholic. Very likely at first he was. But later the Crusaders behaved badly to him; he quarrelled with them and fled to Constantinople (he was himself a Greek). Here he must have joined the Byzantine schism, and the Crusaders, considering the see vacant by his flight, appointed a Latin successor, Bernard of Valence. When John IV died at Constantinople, the Greeks of that city gave him a Greek successor (Theodosius IV). It was the beginning of that series of absentee Patriarchs, Greeks living at Constantinople, which was not only a deplorable calamity for the Christians of their lands, but also did much to fix the state of schism.

The Greeks of Constantinople were naturally the great promoters of the schism. Theodore IV of Antioch (1186–1203), the famous Theodore Balsamon, was undoubtedly a schismatic. He is still the chief Orthodox Canonist. This Theodore, a Byzantine Greek, is responsible for the last degradation of the other Patriarchal Sees by the Œcumenical Patriarch, inasmuch as it was by his advice that their own far more venerable rites were taken from them and they were forced to adopt the modern one of Constantinople.[4] Theodosius V signed the union of Lyons in 1274. He was himself of Frank blood, of the family of Villehardouin, Princes of Achaia. When

---

[1] *Echos d'Orient*, iv (1900-1901), p. 268.

[2] His reign began in 1053. The date of his death is not known; before 1057.

[3] " Orth. East. Church," pp. 188-192.

[4] The works of Balsamon are in P.G., cxxxviii.

the union was rejected by the Emperor (Andronikos II, 1282–1328), Theodosius was consistent to his principles, and resigned his see rather than go into schism. Dorotheos I (1464) accepted the union of Florence (1439). This union was broken at Constantinople when the Turks took the city in 1453. It was their machinations that broke it. They did not want the Christians under them to be friendly with the West, so they set up Gennadios II (of Constantinople, 1454–1456), a fanatical hater of the Latins, just because he would undo the work of Florence. He did so, as far as his own city is concerned. It is often said that the Florentine union was abandoned by the whole East as soon as the delegates got home. This is not true. It is true that in 1443 the Patriarchs retracted their adherence to Florence,[1] yet later they came back on several occasions. The successor of Dorotheos, Michael III of Antioch, as soon as he succeeded, summoned a synod and formally renewed his profession of union with Rome.[2] He sent an archdeacon, Moses, to Rome to tell the Pope of this. The Pope (Pius II, 1458–1464) received Moses in full audience in 1460 and sent him back with letters, confirming Michael's union with himself.[3]

Michael's successor, Theodore V († 1465), was also a Catholic. He maintained union with the Pope and died in his communion.[4] It seems that the union of the Patriarchate of Antioch lasted at least a century. Joachim V (living in 1560) was also a Uniate. " He kept the definitions of Florence, published an encyclical in which he forbade any injurious language about the Pope, and proved his primacy over the whole Church, appealing to the Holy Canons of Councils."[5] From the time of Athanasius III († 1619) there is a very strong movement for union in the Antiochene Patriarchate. Athanasius himself was a Catholic. He held a synod at Damascus, in which he accepted the definition of Florence.[6] Euthymios II (1643) received the Council of

---

[1] *Cf.* Lequien, *op. cit.*, ii, 769; Allatius, " de Eccl. Or. et Occ. perp. Consensione," lib. iii, chap. iv, n. 1.

[2] Cyril Rizk, Melkite priest (now Patriarchal Vicar at Cairo), quoting the unpublished *Taktikon* of Antioch, in the *Revue des Églises d'Orient*, ii, pp. 411–412. See Charon, " L'Église grecque melchite catholique," *Échos d'Orient*, iv (1900–1901), pp. 273–274.

[3] Raynauld, *Annales eccl.* ad ann. 1460, No. lv (Lucca, 1753, tom. x, pp. 239–240). Lequien, " Oriens christ.," ii, 769–770.

[4] C. Rizk, quoting a contemporary Arabic manuscript by David, son of Moses Ganaf of Kūra, *Rev. des Égl. d'Or.*, ii, 485; *Éch. d'Or.*, *loc. cit.*, p. 274.

[5] Rizk, *loc. cit.*   [6] *Ibid.*, ii, 412; Charon, *loc. cit.*, p. 275.

Florence and gave the Jesuits, then first establishing their missions in the Levant, the charge of educating the boys of his Patriarchate. They were to teach these boys to " despise the sayings of the enemies of the Roman religion."[1] The Greeks of Constantinople persecuted him for this; so that he was called upon to pay a large fine to the Turks. He could not find the money and resigned. His successor, Eutychios (1643), also adhered to the Council of Florence.[2] Then came Makarios III (Za'īm, 1643). Lequien counts Makarios as a Catholic, and says that he made a formal profession of the Catholic faith in 1646.[3] However, in 1668 he was present at the Synod of Constantinople which approved the Confession of Peter Mogilas[4]; so he can hardly be counted as having remained one.

But all this time there was a very considerable Catholic movement throughout the Patriarchate. The Jesuits converted Euthymios, Metropolitan of Tyre, who " proclaimed loudly that the Church of the Franks and Maronites is most holy and the true Church. . . . He allowed all those whom the missionaries brought to preach in his church."[5] Meanwhile at Damascus there were 7,000 recognized Uniates, with the most handsome church in all Syria.[6] It is noticeable that at this time there was still no external parting of the ways. The union of Florence had never been irretrievably broken; the local bishops were, apparently, recognized by the Jesuit missionaries as the Ordinaries; there was no opposition hierarchy. The point of view of the missionaries seems to be that all these people were, at least officially, Catholic, until any of them formally went over to schism. The missionaries' work was rather to purify these Catholics from schismatical tendencies.

After Makarios III came Cyril V († 1720). He appears to have come to a clearly Catholic position through a conference he held with the Maronite Patriarch Stephen II (1671–1704). One of the Jesuits writes at that time to his

---

[1] So the report of Fr. Queyrot, S.J., at Aleppo. Charon, *Echos d'Orient*, iv, p. 326. Rizk, *Rev. des Églises d'Orient*, ii, 412.

[2] Rizk, *loc. cit.*, ii, 412.

[3] " Oriens Christianus," ii, 774.   [4] *Ibid.*

[5] *Echos d'Orient*, iv, 327, quoting Jos. Besson, S.J., " La Syrie Sainte " (Paris, 1660). This Euthymios (Aftīmūs ibnu-ṣṢaifi) is a very important person who forms the starting-point for the whole Melkite Church. He was uncle of the Patriarch Cyril VI, who brought about reunion, and founder of the first Uniate Congregation of monks (p. 205). It seems that nearly the whole movement in favour of reunion begins with him. We shall often have occasion to mention him (pp. 197, 201, etc.).

[6] *Echos d'Orient*, iv, 326 (again from Besson, *op. cit.*).

Superior about this Patriarch: " Far from opposing the conversion of the Greek schismatics, his flock, he favoured, as much as he could, their return to the Roman Church. He admitted that he was displeased with the Greeks of Constantinople for having separated themselves from her."[1]   Still, for a time, he had not the courage to proclaim union with Rome. The Patriarch of Alexandria had done so (p. 196): Cyril would have liked, had he dared, to follow this example.[2]   Yet he was so well known as a favourer of the Latins, that the Turks, always afraid of relations with the West, put him in prison in 1707.   As soon as he came out he received a most cordial letter from Pope Clement XI (1700–1721), encouraging him to proclaim his Catholic sentiments aloud.   He received this letter with all respect, summoned a synod, and proclaimed the decrees of Florence.   With him several other bishops made their submission to Rome, notably the Metropolitan of Beirut and Euthymios of Tyre.[3]   Cyril V wrote a book in favour of reunion.   He died in 1720, and was succeeded by his old rival Athanasius IV (Dabbās, 1720–1724).   Athanasius, too, had already taken steps in favour of reunion.   The movement seems at this time to have gained nearly the whole Patriarchate.   But his opposition to Cyril drove him into the other camp.[4]   For a time, at least, he persecuted the Catholic party, and imprisoned its leaders, including Euthymios of Tyre.   It is disputed whether he died a Catholic or not.   His successor, Cyril VI, finally and definitely brought this line back to union with the Pope; then the schismatical party set up a rival one.

In Egypt we see the same state of things.   The Alexandrine Patriarchate was never excommunicated by the Pope.   At first the quarrel of Cerularius was no affair of the Egyptians. Then, certainly, the Orthodox of Egypt slipped into schism, through the fact that they maintained communion with Constantinople.   But here, too, it seems to have been a gradual and almost unconscious process.   Then in Egypt, as in Syria, there are an astonishing number of cases of Patriarchs in union with Rome since the eleventh century.   In Egypt, too, Catholics

---

[1] P. Nacchi, S.J., " Lettres édifiantes et curieuses; Mémoires du Levant " (in Bousquet, " Les actes des Apôtres modernes," Paris, 1852, tom. i, 182-183).

[2] Bousquet, i, 183.

[3] Antoine Nacchi, S.J., to M. A. Tamburini, General, S.J. (Bousquet, op. cit., i, 183-184).

[4] Athanasius IV was present at a synod at Constantinople against the Catholic movement, in 1722.

seem to take the line that the whole Patriarchate is not con-
taminated finally; so that each individual Patriarch, or even his
subjects, were judged on their own merits. If one Patriarch
was a schismatic, that did not exclude the possibility that his
successor might be a Catholic.

The first case of, at least, friendliness towards the Latins
is perhaps only a small one; but it is significant. The Emperor
Manuel I (Komnenos, 1143–1180) was notorious for his Latin
sympathies. Because of these he made himself very unpopular
at Constantinople. He was accused, not without reason, of
trying to impose Frank customs and the Frank religion on his
subjects. For a time he was allied with the Norman kings of
Sicily; he married twice, both his wives (Bertha of Sulzbach
and Mary, daughter of Raymund, Prince of Antioch) were
Latins, and he gave his children in marriage to Frank princes.
He wrote to Pope Alexander III (1159–1181) asking that
Greeks and Latins might again be united as one flock under one
shepherd, the Pope. In short, Manuel I must almost, if not
quite, be counted a Catholic.[1] His second marriage with
Mary, in 1166, was most unpopular among the Greeks. I
suppose we should count it as a Catholic marriage; or, if it
was mixed, it was only very slightly mixed. I do not know
what rite was used, no doubt that of Constantinople; but the
significant thing is that, not the then formally schismatical
Patriarch of Constantinople, but Sophronios II of Alexandria
(*c.* 1166–*c.* 1180) came to bless this marriage.[2]

Then, in the thirteenth century, we find Athanasius III of
Alexandria (1268–1271), of whom Lequien says that he would
never pronounce either for or against the schism.[3] That certainly
does not make him a Catholic; but it shows again how much less
bitter was the feeling against the Latins in these other Patriarchates than at Constantinople. Niphon (*c.* 1367) is said
definitely to have made his submission to the Holy See. He
received a friendly letter, exhorting him to do so, from Pope
Urban V (1362–1370).[4] Philotheos I (*c.* 1439 and 1450)
signed the union of Florence, retracted it, and then accepted

[1] For Manuel I's latinizing policy see G. F. Hertzberg, " Gesch.
der Byzantiner " (in Onckel's *Allgem. Gesch.*, Berlin, 1883), pp. 291-
305, and K. Dieterich, " Byzantinische Charakterköpfe " (Leipzig,
Teubner, 1909), chap. iv, pp. 35-48.

[2] Kinnamos, " Hist.," v, 4 (P.G., cxxxiii, 561).

[3] *Op. cit.*, ii, 493.

[4] Raynauld ad ann. 1367, No. x (tom. vii, p. 153); Lequien, ii,
498-499. It was the time of proposed reunion under John V,
Palaiologos (1341-1376).

it again.[1]   Philotheos II (*c.* 1523) sent his submission to Pope
Adrian VI (1522–1523).[2]   In 1711 a Jesuit missionary in
Egypt, Father William du Bernat, writes of the Patriarch of
Alexandria (not named): " He kept up relations with Rome,
and in conversation he wanted to appear orthodox.   He told
me that Prelates from Italy pressed him to declare himself
publicly and to reunite his Church with the Roman Church;
but, he says, they do not know what it is to be under Turkish
dominion.   If only they will set us free, reunion will be
accomplished at once."[3]   We must not think this too important.   It may be only civil things said to a Latin missionary;
Eastern people are often great flatterers.   Very likely the same
man would have said to a Greek of Constantinople how thankful
he was to be free of the tyranny of Rome.   However, it is
certain that at that time there was a great movement towards
reunion in Egypt, as in Syria.   The French missionaries had
done much work; already there was a large number of people
who professed the Catholic faith, recognized all the rights of
the Holy See, and declared their intention to be in union with
the Pope; though they were not yet constituted as a separate
body.   In Egypt, too, we hear of Uniate churches, priests, and
congregations.

Then we come to a Patriarch of whose catholicity there is
no doubt at all.   This is Samuel Kabasilas, Patriarch of
Alexandria (*c.* 1721).   During his reign he heard that Lawrence
de Saint Laurent, O.F.M., then Guardian of the holy Sepulchre,
was in Egypt.   So he sent for him, had conversations with
him, in which he " found consolation and light."   So he was
converted to the Catholic Church.   He made his profession
of faith before Franciscan missionaries, gave every assurance as
to the disputed points of faith, and then sent a Franciscan to
Rome with a letter for the Pope in 1713.   The Pope (Clement
XI, 1700–1721) received this ambassador in solemn public
audience, accepted the Patriarch's profession, and sent him a
pallium.   He also wrote to Louis XIV of France and the Doge
of Venice, asking them to use their influence with the Turkish
Government that Samuel should not be annoyed.[4]   There is,
then, no doubt that this Samuel was a Catholic.   After him we

---

[1] Lequien, ii, 500.   Allatius, " de Consens," lib. iii, chap. iv, n. 1.
[2] Raynauld ad ann. 1523, No. cvii (who calls him Theophilus;
tom. xii, p. 444); Lequien, ii, 501.
[3] *Echos d'Orient*, iv, 331, quoting the " Lettres édifiantes; Mémoires du Levant."
[4] M. Picot, " Mémoires pour servir à l'Histoire ecclés. pendant
le XVIIIme Siècle," 3rd edition, Paris, 1853, tom. i, pp. 326-327.

hear no more about the union in Egypt; it must have fallen through. At any rate, the line of Patriarchs of Alexandria became schismatical again, and the Catholics in Egypt remained without a Patriarch till their Patriarchate was joined to that of Antioch (p. 203).

For the third Patriarchal see, Jerusalem, there is only one little incident to note here. A Metropolitan of Palestine assured Father John Gauthier, S.J., that both Sophronios V of Jerusalem (1579–1608) and his successor, Theophanes IV (1608–1646), were in union with Rome.[1]

2. Union under Cyril VI of Antioch (1724-1759).

Turning back to the Antiochene Patriarchate, we come to the final reunion which constituted the present Melkite Church. This was the work of the Patriarch Cyril VI.

Athanasius IV died in 1724. There was at that moment a very strong movement in favour of reunion with Rome throughout the Patriarchate. Latin missionaries (chiefly French Jesuits) had worked hard for this; they had already converted many, and had convinced others that reunion was at least most desirable. The Metropolitans, Euthymios of Tyre (Aftīmūs Ibnu-ṣṢaifi) and Neophytos Naṣrī of Ṣaidnāiā, were Catholics; at Damascus, Aleppo, Sidon, Tyre, Acre, the majority of Christians of the Byzantine rite were Catholics, at least at heart. Now it seems that Athanasius IV had intended that a certain Silvester, a monk from Cyprus, his friend,[2] should succeed him. Some say that he actually nominated Silvester his successor; this would make no difference, as he had no power of doing so. It seems that rivalry between the communities of Aleppo and Damascus is at the bottom of the quarrel which now follows.[3] Silvester was considered to be the nominee of Aleppo. So hurriedly, to prevent his election, the people of Damascus elected Seraphim Tānās. Seraphim was a Catholic, nephew of Euthymios of Tyre;[4] he was also in favour with Othman Pasha,

---

[1] *Echos d'Orient*, iv, 333, quoting Gauthier.

[2] The origin of this Silvester is disputed; he is said to be a relation of Athanasius IV (Dabbās). *Echos d'Orient*, v, 18.

[3] *Echos d'Orient*, xi, 41 (article by S. Vailhé). Although Silvester represented the schismatical party, the Catholics, and even Latin missionaries of Aleppo, for a time took his side. See the documents and letters in A. Rabbath, S.J., " Documents inédits," i, pp. 566-574.

[4] Seraphim Tānās was born in 1680, at Damascus, of Naṣr Tānās and his wife, Sispina, sister of Euthymios Ibnu-ṣṢaifi of Tyre. Both were Catholics of the Byzantine rite. His uncle, the bishop, educated him, sent him to the Propaganda College at Rome from 1702 to 1710,

Abu-Tauk,[1] the Wali of Damascus. The election was held
on September 25, 1724. No bishop was present;[2] it was made
by priests and lay " notables." Seraphim was then ordained
Patriarch by Basil Fīnān, Metropolitan of Baïas,[3] Neophytos
Naṣrī of Ṣaidnāiā, and a third bishop, Euthymios of Furzul,
himself ordained for this occasion. According to custom,
Seraphim changed his name as Patriarch and became Cyril VI.
There were then fifteen sees in the Patriarchate; of these ten
bishops adhered to Cyril VI.[4]

Meanwhile his rival, Silvester the Cypriote, did not remain
idle. He went off to Jerusalem, and told that Patriarch of the
alarming progress Popery was making in the neighbouring
country. He presented his own claim, as nominee of the last
Patriarch of Antioch, and explained that, if he were appointed,
he would put down this tendency. So Jerusalem took his side
and informed the Synod of Constantinople of what was happening. Constantinople and Jerusalem now declare for Silvester.
He was then ordained at Constantinople. He succeeded also in
alarming the Turks about the defections of so many Syrians
to the Frank religion, and came back to Syria armed with laws
against Catholics. All those who have joined the communion
of the Pope are to return, no intercourse with the missionaries
is tolerated, and they are to be expelled. The Government

---

and ordained him priest at his return. In 1711 he was brought to
Damascus by the Patriarch Cyril V († 1720) and made Khūrī biskūbūs
(chorepiskopos). He went to Rome to assure the Pope (Clement XI)
of Cyril V's catholic sentiments, and in 1716 received a Brief for
Cyril in which the Pope exhorts him to declare himself openly (see
above, p. 194). Then, while Athanasius IV was persecuting the
Catholics, Tānās was put in prison. His election in 1724 is the sign
of definite wish for reunion among the electors (see Bacha in *Echos
d'Or.*, x, 202-203).

[1] Abu-Tauk is the man's *kunyah*.

[2] Charon is mistaken in saying that the bishops elected Ṭānās
(*Ech. d'Or.*, v, 18); they confirmed the election later (see the dis-
cussion by Paul Bacel, *Ech. d'Or.*, ix, 283, C. Bacha, *ibid.*, x, 200-206;
S. Vailhé, xi, 40-41).

[3] Baïas, near Aleppo, not Bānīās (Cæsarea Phil.), which was not
restored as a diocese till 1886 (Charon, " Hist. des Melkites," iii,
p. 295). But C. Bacha insists that all the documents call Basil Fīnān
Metropolitan of Bānīās (*Ech. d'Or.*, x, 206, n. 2).

[4] So the answer of Benedict XIV to the petition in his Consistory
of February 3, 1744, " Cyril is head of a people which now includes
a vast number of Catholics, governed by ten bishops who respect and
honour him as lawful Patriarch " (" Bullarium Ben. XIV," ed. of Prato,
1845, tom. i, p. 643). The ten were the Metropolitans of Aleppo,
Beirut, Sidon, Tyre, Ṣafad, Acre, Ba'albek, Baïas, Furzul, and Ṣaidnāiā.

recognizes Silvester as Patriarch; the Synod of Constantinople[1] imposes a profession of faith on all who recognize Silvester, and all whom the Turks force so to do, explicitly denying the *Filioque*. Cyril flees before his rival to a monastery in the Lebanon.

Much depends on the question of Cyril VI's election. Was it valid? There is no uniform rule for the election of bishops, recognized throughout Christendom, nor even throughout the Catholic Church. All one can say is that an election is valid if it conforms to the Canon Law (either written or by custom) of the time and place. Against Cyril is the fact that no bishop took part in his election. It was conducted by priests and laymen. That certainly seems an argument against it. On the other hand, there is evidence that, since the transference of the Patriarch's seat from Antioch to Damascus, the right of the Damascenes to elect had been recognized and used repeatedly.[2] The Pope's Consistory later said expressly that Cyril had been elected " according to the custom of the Greeks."[3] More important is the fact that the considerable majority of his Metropolitans acknowledged him. This gives him a later ratification, a *sanatio in radice* for whatever may have been irregular in the actual election. At any rate, so many Eastern Prelates have been elected by a popular vote and under all kinds of irregular conditions, yet by the acceptance of their Suffragans have held their position undisputed, that it would be impossible for the Orthodox to lay down a general principle that only one method is valid. Patriarchs of Constantinople have been nominated by the Sultan, yet no one hesitates to count them in that line. The only possible rule, in the East especially, is that the bishop *de facto* becomes bishop *de iure* by tacit consent. Cyril was certainly Patriarch *de facto*, recognized by the great majority, till his rival began to persecute his adherents. Indeed, the Synod of Constantinople itself acknowledged him, since in 1724 it deposed him. In this pronouncement the only argument against his election is the nomination of Silvester by the former Patriarch.[4] Five years later, in 1729, Propaganda, having examined the whole question at leisure, declares as its first resolution that " nothing is

---

[1] Charon says a synod was then being held at Constantinople (*Ech. d'Or.*, v, 19). I think it must have been the permanent σύνοδος ἐνδημοῦσα.

[2] See the witness of a contemporary, Nihmet (*sic*, for Ni'mah) of Aleppo, quoted by Bacel, *Éch. d'Or.*, x, 205.

[3] February 3, 1744. " Bullarium Ben. XIV " (Prato, 1845), i, p. 642.

[4] See the acts of this synod in Mansi, xxxvii, cols. 219-226.

against the valid and free election of Cyril as Patriarch of Antioch."[1]   This was after his enemies (for he had some among the Catholics too[2]) had presented every argument against him. In any case, the appointment of his rival was utterly invalid. Silvester of Cyprus was simply nominated by the Synod of Constantinople.   Now there is nothing that the Orthodox of Syria, Egypt, and all parts outside Constantinople hold more firmly than that the Œcumenical Patriarch has no jurisdiction beyond his own Patriarchate.   The modern Orthodox, who trace the line of their Patriarchs of Antioch through Silvester, cannot object to the proceeding of Cyril's election; because equally irregular elections have been the commonest thing in all their sees.   Their real reason for rejecting him is not that, but the fact that he came into communion with the Pope.   But, if that is an impediment, what becomes of all the Antiochene Patriarchs of the first centuries ?   They have also in their favour the shameful protection that Silvester sought and obtained from the Turkish Government.   It is indeed surprising that Christian bishops should seek such an argument; but it has been the constant recourse of the Orthodox, ever since the Turk first held their lands.   Silvester of Cyprus at Antioch is only one out of countless Orthodox bishops who have rested their claim to rule in the name of Christ on the approval of Mohammed.

Unless we admit such arguments as these, it seems impossible to deny that the present Orthodox line of Patriarchs of Antioch, coming through Silvester, is not historically the old line, but a new schism therefrom beginning with him. The old line of Antioch is in union with Rome since Cyril VI.

Fortified then by the protection of the Turks, by the recognition of Constantinople and Jerusalem, Silvester carried on a fierce persecution of the Uniates, to restore the Orthodoxy —that is, schism from Rome—which had been so endangered in the Patriarchate for the last century.   Meanwhile Cyril VI sought refuge from him in the famous monastery of St Saviour (Dair al Mukhallis) in the Lebanon.[3]   The Turks imprisoned Germanos, Metropolitan of Aleppo, a partizan of Cyril, also Euthymios Saifi of Tyre, and many Uniates at Damascus, Aleppo,[4] Tripoli, Sidon.   The greater part of the clergy then

[1] *Coll. Lacensis* (Freiburg, 1876), tom. iv, col. 442 *seq.*
[2] See pp. 201-202. [3] For this monastery, see pp. 205-206.
[4] Aleppo has always been so great a centre of Melkites that, to this day, among the Greek-speaking Orthodox (for instance, at Constantinople), all Melkites are commonly called Χαλεπίδες.

submit to Silvester; the others go off to Cyril in the Lebanon. There is now a clear parting of the ways, and two Churches, that of the Orthodox under Silvester, that of the Melkites under Cyril; though for a time each still claims the whole body and tries to attract his rival's supporters. Aleppo for a long time remained one of the chief centres of the Melkite party. In 1732 the Metropolitan Germanos resigned; but his successor, Maximos Ḥakīm, also declared for Cyril. After he had opened his campaign Silvester went off and wandered about Wallachia; then he came back to Damascus and began ordaining bishops to replace those who were faithful to Cyril.

Both rivals then asked for and obtained a firman from the Government. Cyril did so, in spite of the laws against him, in 1743; Silvester then got one too. It seems that already the Turk was beginning to recognize the existence of two Churches. The Orthodox succeed in seizing the Church at Aleppo. Nevertheless Cyril has many Catholics, especially among the laity, who were less exposed to persecution. He had 9,000 followers at Damascus.[1]

But all this time Cyril was still unrecognized at Rome. Now that he had taken a definitely Catholic line, naturally he was much concerned to regulate his position on Catholic principles.[2] In 1729 Pope Benedict XIII (1724–1730), who had heard of the events in Syria, sent a Capuchin, Father Dorotheus a SS Trinitate, to receive Cyril's profession of faith according to the formula of Urban VIII. Then another question had to be considered. The famous Euthymios of Tyre had introduced certain changes in the liturgy. Cyril, his nephew, adopted and defended these. But many of his people were vehemently opposed to them; so there was already division among the Melkites. The Pope demanded that he should undertake to change nothing in the services of the Church without the consent of Propaganda. Cyril made the profession of faith and all the engagements required; then there was further delay because of the death of the Pope (1730). It was not till 1744 that Benedict XIV (1740–1758) at last sent the pallium.[3] It was on this occasion that he published his

---

[1] Ech. d'Or., v, 22.

[2] He was always a Catholic at heart. Only the difficult circumstances had prevented him from applying to the Pope for recognition sooner.

[3] In the Consistory of February 3, 1744, Benedict XIV made an allocution praising Cyril's predecessors and explaining that there was a great movement for reunion in Syria (" Bullarium Ben. XIV," ed. cit., i, 643). The Brief accompanying the pallium is Dum nobiscum,

famous Constitution *Demandatam cælitus* for the regulation of the Melkite Church (see pp. 34, 35).

But the Patriarch still had difficulties. He had opponents among his own Melkites; he also had trouble with the other Uniate Churches; notably the mutual dislike of Melkïas and Maronites, so long a disturbance among the Catholics of Syria, already showed itself. The Latin missionaries, too, gave him trouble. He complained that they administered sacraments, baptized in the Roman rite, heard confessions, and collected money from his people without his authority. The Maronite Patriarch also, on the strength of an ancient Roman Constitution authorizing him to receive heretics and schismatics into the Church, began turning Melkites into Maronites. This so annoyed Cyril that he tore up certain pictures of St John Maro, declaring that he had been a Monothelete. The Maronites complained of this at Rome, and Benedict XIV wrote a stern letter, *Inter cætera*, in 1753.[1] At last, worn out with his troubles, Cyril VI made up his mind to resign his see. First he nominated the son of his nephew, Ignatius Gauhār, as his successor, and then abdicated in 1759. The next year he died.[2]

3. History to Maximos III (1759-1833).

Ignatius Gauhār assumed the name Athanasius V. There were then eleven Melkite bishops. Seven of them recognized him;[3] but the other four[4] protested against his nomination and appealed to Rome. As a matter of fact, Cyril had no right at all to nominate his successor, nor had he the right to resign without the Pope's consent; further, Gauhār was only twenty-seven years old, under the canonical age. So, in 1760, Clement XIII (1758-1769) quashed the resignation and nomination. But, as meanwhile Cyril was dead, the see was vacant. The Pope therefore himself appointed Maximos Ḥakīm Metropolitan of Aleppo. In doing so he declared that this was only the result of the special dispute then raging, that he did not intend to interfere with the right of the Metropolitans

---

February 29, 1744 (*ibid.*, i, 348-349). The pallium was conferred by the Latin Bishop of Babylon.

[1] " Bullarium Ben. XIV," *ed. cit.*, tom. iii, p. ii, pp. 135-138.

[2] For the Patriarchate of Cyril VI see Charon in *Echos d'Orient*, v, 18-25; 82-86.

[3] The Metropolitans of Tyre, Homs (Emessa), Acre, Baïas (or Bānïās ?), Furzul, Cana, Ḳara.

[4] Maximos Ḥakīm of Aleppo, Athanasius Dahān of Beirut, and two others.

to elect their Patriarch in general. Maximos II reigned from 1760 to 1761 only. At first Ǵauhār had a party which protested and sent complaints of Maximos to Rome. Then he submitted and was given the see of Sidon. Maximos II represented the party of the Shuwair monks, as opposed to those of St Saviour (see pp. 205–208). He resided at Shuwair, where he died on November 28, 1761. The chief event of his reign is that he introduced the feast of Corpus Christi in his Patriarchate, for which he composed an excellent office, according to Byzantine rules.[1] Before he died he appointed Athanasius Dahān, Metropolitan of Beirut, his coadjutor.[2]

After Maximos's death this Athanasius Dahān was elected his successor, and took the name of Theodosius VI (1761–1788). Ignatius Ǵauhār made another attempt to get himself made Patriarch, and sent a protest to Rome against Theodosius; but he did not succeed, and again had to submit. Theodosius resided at the monastery of St Antony at Ḳarḳafah.[3] In 1773 Clement XIV (1769–1774) submitted the few Melkites of Palestine and Egypt to the Patriarch of Antioch. But no title was yet given for these.

Then, when Theodosius died,[4] at last Ignatius Ǵauhār, who had so long tried to be Patriarch, was elected lawfully. Rome confirmed his election, and he became Athanasius V (1788–1794). He was of the party of St Saviour, and resided there. In 1790 he summoned a synod, which made twenty canons against the monks of Shuwair. These were all quashed at Rome.[5] Cyril VII, Sīāḡ, a monk of St Saviour, succeeded (1794–1796), but died before he received the pallium.[6] Agapios Maṭār (Agapios III, 1796–1812), formerly Metropolitan of Sidon, monk of St Saviour, had trouble with the Latin missionaries, and obtained decrees from Rome against their attempts to turn his Melkites into Latins. In 1806 he held the famous Synod of Ḳarḳafah (p. 209). He summoned another synod in 1811, at 'Ain Trāz,[7] and founded a seminary

[1] A French version of this will be found in John Oquet, " Manuel de Prières à l'usage des fidèles du Rite grec " (Beirut, Alex. Coury, 1902), pp. 618-624.

[2] For Maximos II, see Charon in *Echos d'Orient*, v, 86-89.

[3] Afterwards famous for its synod (p. 209).

[4] Theodosius VI, *Ech. d'Or.*, v, 141-145.

[5] Athanasius V, *Ech. d'Or.*, v, 145-147.

[6] Cyril VII, *ibid.*, 147.

[7] 'Ain Trāz is a village near Rishmaia, about fifteen miles south-east of Beirut. The seminary there was for a long time the only one for Melkite clergy. It became a centre of their Church, and the Patriarch often resided in it.

there for the education of his clergy. As first rector of this seminary he appointed the famous Maximos Maẓlūm, who was to become the greatest Patriarch of this line (pp. 210–221). He also had great trouble with one of his Metropolitans, Ignatius Ṣarrūf of Beirut, who founded a religious Congregation at Mār Simʿān, near Biskinta.[1] The Patriarch would not recognize this Congregation. Ṣarrūf was defended by the Latin missionaries and appealed to Rome. Meanwhile Agapios suspended him from the use of pontificalia. After a long quarrel Propaganda declared for the Patriarch and Ṣarrūf had to submit.[2] When Agapios died Ṣarrūf succeeded him, becoming Ignatius IV (1812). He was murdered ten months later by a Christian before he had time to receive the pallium.[3] Athanasius VI (Maṭār, 1813)[4] and Makarios IV (Ṭauwil, 1813–1815)[5] succeeded in short periods, each dying of the pest soon after his appointment.

Then came Ignatius V (Ḳaṭṭān, 1816–1833). Several important events took place in his reign. There was a great persecution of the Melkites, which lasted from 1817 to 1832. The Orthodox, seeing the growing power of the Melkite Church, persuaded the Turks that these people were turning *Frangi* and becoming a danger to the state. The persecution which followed raged chiefly at Aleppo and Damascus. Many Melkites were murdered, others were exiled, imprisoned, flogged. Only in the Lebanon under the powerful Christian (mostly Maronite) Emirs[6] was there peace. Lately the question of the cause of these martyrs has been discussed at Rome.[7] It was also under Ignatius V that the separation of the Shuwair Congregation of monks into two took place (p 2c8). He ordained the first Catholic Coptic bishop since the old schism; lastly, in his time the Sultan Maḥmūd II (1808–1839) granted the Melkites civil independence from the Orthodox, making the Uniate Patriarch of the Armenians civil head of all Uniates in his empire. Ignatius went blind at the end of his life, and died at the monastery Ẓuḳ Mīkhā'īl[8] on February 9, 1833.[9] His successor was the great Maximos III.

---

[1] Biskinta (Basconta) is a village twenty miles north-east of Beirut.

[2] For Agapios III and the quarrel with Ṣarrūf see Charon, *Echos d'Or.*, v, 203-206; 264-270.   [3] *Ech. d'Or.*, vi, 16-17.

[4] *Ibid.*, vi, 17.   [5] *Ibid.*, vi, 17-18.

[6] The Emirs of the Shabāb family were then most powerful in the Lebanon. Many of these were Maronites.

[7] *Echos d'Orient*, vi, 113-118.

[8] By the sea between Beirut and Gibail.

[9] For Ignatius V, see *Echos d'Orient*, vi, 18-24.

4. The Monks of St Saviour and the Monks of Shuwair.

Two Congregations of Melkite monks have played so important a part in the history of their Church that we must add some notice about them here.   It is well known that in Eastern Churches, at least originally, there was no such thing as a distinction of religious orders.   An Eastern monk is simply a monk; no further description is needed.   All, or nearly all,[1] follow the rule of St Basil; each monastery, possibly with its dependent houses, is a community independent of all others, though subject to the jurisdiction of the Ordinary.[2]   However, this old principle has been considerably modified in the case of the Uniate Churches.   Under Western influence most of these now have what comes to much the same thing as our distinction of religious orders.   That is to say, Congregations are formed under one general head.   Such a congregation adopts the rule of St Basil to its own special needs and circumstances, so as to make practically a rule of its own.   Generally, all are Basilian, but with differences.   Perhaps the best parallel in the West would be the various divisions of the Franciscan order.   And then, of late years, there have been totally new Congregations, founded entirely on Western lines, like our Jesuits, Redemptorists, Passionists, and so on.

Two such Congregations of monks, eventually three, play a great part in Melkite history, forming rival centres, around which parties are grouped.   These are the Congregations of the Salvatorians and the Shuwairites.   The *Salvatorians*[3] were founded by the famous Euthymios Ibnu-ṣṢaifi, Metropolitan of Tyre and uncle of the Patriarch Cyril VI.   In 1687, under Cyril V, Euthymios founded the monastery of St Saviour (Dair alMukhallis), near the village Ġūn in the Kharrūb district of the Southern Lebanon.[4]   He sent there a certain Father Naʿamatullah as Superior, with several monks.   In 1708 they began building their monastery.   Needless to say, in view of their founder's known zeal, this monastery became a great centre of reunion.   It was, of course, faithful to Cyril VI in his quarrel with Silvester of Cyprus; as soon as the Uniate Melkite Church was organized the monks of Dair alMukhallis

---

[1] There are some monasteries that follow a rule ascribed to St Antony, the first hermit.

[2] Stauropegia monasteries are subject immediately to the Patriarch.

[3] Their early history is told by C. Charon, *Echos d'Orient*, v, 24. They occur again throughout all accounts of the Melkite Church.

[4] Between Ṣaidā (Sidon) and Beirut.

were part of it. In 1743 they asked for, and obtained, confirmation of Pope Benedict XIV for their Constitutions—that is, the rule of St Basil adapted to their circumstances. In 1745 the rule was printed in Arabic at Rome for them. They formed a chapter which, in 1751, elected Augustine Za'arur Superior General. In the same year Benedict XIV sent them a Brief, *Etsi persuasum*,[1] telling them to observe their rite exactly, and to send all acts of their chapters to Rome to be confirmed. Gradually a number of other houses were built for the Salvatorian monks, so that they became a large Congregation. Many of them have always served in parishes. Indeed, it seems that this was their founder's idea. They are less strictly organized as a monastic order than their rivals of Shuwair. Cyril VI resided at their mother-house, Dair alMukhallis. His successor, Maximos II, represented the other party, of Shuwair. Athanasius V was again a Salvatorian and lived there. So there has been an alternation of influence between the two Congregations.

The story of Shuwair[2] begins a little later. Gerasimos and Sulaimān, formerly students of the Jesuit missionaries, entered the monastery of Balāmand[3] near Tripoli. They converted many monks to union with Rome; but the others finally expelled them and their party. So they went to Cyril V and received his approbation. Encouraged by him, they then founded a monastery of St John the Baptist (Mār Ḥanna) near the village of Shuwair, in the district Kesruān, between Beirut and Ba'albek. Others came to join them. But Gerasimos and Sulaimān disagreed; so that Sulaimān went back to Balāmand.[4] Gerasimos remained Superior of Mār Ḥanna at Shuwair. In 1718 these monks built their church; soon

---

[1] " Bullarium Ben. XIV " (ed. Prati, 1846), tom. iii, pars i, pp. 274-275.

[2] The history of the Shuwairites is told at full length by one of their monks, Paul Bacel, in the *Echos d'Orient*, vi-xvii, in a series of twenty-two articles, bringing it down to 1794. Here will be found a translation of their Constitutions, lives of their great men, and full details of their story. Like most French writers, he spells *Ghouér* and *Chouérite*. I apply my usual principle of transliteration. " Shuwairite " is an ugly hybrid compound; but I fear " Shuwairiyin " would look too odd in English.

[3] Balāmand is an old Cistercian monastery, built and then abandoned by the crusaders. The name is said to be " Bel mont." Another explanation is ἡ παλαιὰ μάνδρα.

[4] This was not apostasy. Sulaimān became Archimandrite of Balāmand and spent his life trying to make his monks Uniates. He died in 1712.

after a considerable sum of money was left to them. Gerasimos became Metropolitan of Aleppo. Other monasteries joined them. In 1727 Nicholas Ṣā'īgh was elected Superior; they then determined that there should be a new election every third year. Ṣā'īgh († 1756) was a poet of some reputation.[1] They wanted to be joined to the Italian Basilian Congregation; but Propaganda did not encourage this idea. However, in 1734 Pope Clement XIII (1758–1769) gave them the church of St Mary in Dominica at Rome, commonly called " Santa Maria della Navicella."[2] This still belongs to the Congregation; they use it as their agency at Rome. Ṣā'īgh composed their Constitutions, which were approved by Benedict XIV in 1756. The Shuwairites are rather more strictly organized than the Salvatorians. But they, too, serve the parish churches. They have had a number of famous men, including bishops and Patriarchs.

Neophytos Naṣrī, Metropolitan of Ṣaidnaia, is one of the chief Catholic bishops of the first period, under Cyril VI. He was one of Cyril's ordainers (p. 198). He died at Rome in 1731, leaving the reputation of a saint. There has been a great dispute as to whether he was a Shuwairite monk. On the whole, the evidence seems that he was.[3] 'Abdullah Zakher (1680–1748), who entered Shuwair in 1722, was famous for his learning. At four years old he could read Arabic easily. As a Shuwairite monk he founded a printing press which produced many liturgical and other useful books; this was one of the first presses for printing Arabic.[4] The Congregation also had nuns, whose rule was approved at Rome in 1763. In 1735 Cyril VI made an attempt to unite the Congregations of St Saviour and Shuwair; but it came to nothing. He was himself a partizan of St Saviour, being nephew of its founder; the Shuwairites represent his plan as an attempt to merge

---

[1] His Life (with portrait) is in *Ech. d'Or.*, xi, 71–76; 154–161. His Dīwān (collection of poems: " Dīwān alkūrī ") is published by the Imprimerie Catholique of Beirut, 1883.

[2] Alexis Kateb, " Église diaconale cardinalice de N.-D. de la Barque," Rome. *Ech. d'Or.*, ix, 155–159.

[3] In the *Echos d'Or.*, vii, 213-214, Haissa Boustani says he was a monk of Shuwair; viii, 87-88, C. Bacha (Salvatorian) denies that he was a monk at all (a Byzantine bishop in the eighteenth century not a monk ?); viii, 361-363, P. Bacel (Shuwairite) agrees with Boustani and is angry with Bacha; ix, 160-161, Bacha returns to the charge and S. Vailhé sums up against him.

[4] Life of Zakher, with his portrait and list of works he wrote or printed, *Ech. d'Or.*, xi, 218-226; 281-287; 363-372 (by P. Bacel).

Shuwair into Dair alMukhallis. At any rate, they resisted it successfully.[1]

Instead of union between the two existing Congregations, a dispute a hundred years later produced three, by dividing the monks of Shuwair. For some time there seems to have been mutual jealousy and unfriendly feeling between the Shuwairites at Aleppo and their brethren in the Lebanon. The monastery at Aleppo was at some distance from the others, and developed independently of them. It is said that the Aleppo monks affected to be superior to those of the Lebanon, despising them as rude mountaineers. In 1826 there was a schism (monastically, of course, not ecclesiastically) between Aleppo and the mountain monks. But the Emir Bashīr Shahāb reconciled them. However, the feeling persisted; in 1829 it broke out again. This time the quarrel was too serious to be healed by reunion. So the Patriarch Ignatius V (1816–1833) and Propaganda agreed that they should be separated. Each then formed a separate Congregation with its own Superior General. At first they were the " Country Shuwairites "[2] and the " Aleppo Shuwairites."[3] Now it seems that the country branch has kept the old name; so they are Shuwairite Basilians, the others Alepin Basilians. This makes, with St Saviour, three Congregations.

5. Germanos Ādam and the Synod of Karkafah.

With the constant opposition of the Orthodox at their side, one would have thought that the Papacy was so much the cause of the Melkites that they would have been always Ultramontane to excess. It is, then, rather startling to find that in the early nineteenth century there was a considerable movement among them of what is called variously Gallicanism, Febronianism, even Jansenism. This was the work chiefly of a Melkite theologian of unimpeachable piety and considerable learning.

Germanos Ādam was born at Aleppo[4] and studied at Propaganda, which shows that not even the things they teach at Rome are a quite safe guarantee. From the beginning he had a great reputation for his knowledge. He spoke Arabic, Greek, Latin, Italian, and French fluently. In 1774 Ādam

---

[1] Echos d'Orient, x, 102-107; 167-173, " Essai de Réunion des Chouérites avec les Salvatoriens, 1734-1737 " (by P. Bacel).

[2] Ash-Shuwairiyīn al-baladiyīn.

[3] Ash-Shuwairiyīn al-halibiyīn.

[4] The year of his birth is not known. For all this paragraph see C. Charon in the Echos d'Orient, v, 332-343.

became Metropolitan of Acre; in 1777 he was translated to Aleppo, the second see of the Patriarchate.[1] As Metropolitan of Aleppo he had many quarrels with the Latin missionaries. Cyril Charon says, with truth, that not all the wrongs in these quarrels were on his side.[2] Thus the *Custos Terræ sanctæ* wanted to reconfirm children confirmed at their baptism according to their own rite. Germanos supported his Patriarch in the affair of Ignatius Sarrūf of Beirut (see p. 204); but on other occasions he seems to have quarrelled with him too.

Now comes the great matter of his Gallicanism. He had made friends with Scipio Ricci, Bishop of Pistoia, while he was in Italy. No doubt it was from him that he acquired these ideas. In 1799 he wrote against the missionaries in the affair of Sarrūf. Here already appears the poison. He thinks that the Primacy of the Pope is only of honour, that a General Council is above the Pope. In the controversy that followed he appealed to the Declaration of the Gallican clergy of 1682. Then he took up and defended the ideas of Febronius. Already in 1802 the news of his ideas had reached Rome. Pius VII (1800–1823) then ordered his works to be sent to be examined.

On July 23, 1806, the Patriarch Agapios III opened the Synod of Ḳarḳafah, in the monastery of St Antony at that place. Nine bishops attended, as also the Superiors General of St Saviour and of Shuwair; the Egyptian Melkites were represented by a Salvatorian monk, those of Damascus by another, those of Aleppo by Michael Maẓlūm, the future Patriarch. Lewis Gandolfi, the Papal Visitor, was also present, and signed the acts. The only explanation of this seems to be that he did not know enough Arabic to understand what they were. The Maronite Patriarch Joseph Tiān also approved of them. There is no doubt that Germanos Ādam was the soul of the synod, and that he drew up the acts. They contain all his views, that a General Council is above the Pope, that not the Pope, but only the whole Church, is infallible; the Primacy is reduced to hardly more than an honorary precedence.

Ādam defended other theories displeasing to the authorities at Rome in his many works, notably that the Consecration of the holy Eucharist is effected not only by the words of Institution, but also by the Invocation of the Holy Ghost. But not

---

[1] In practice Aleppo seems always to have been the second see and chief Melkite centre. But Tyre has historic and canonical claims to be the πρωτόθρονος. Hence frequent disputes (see pp. 212-229. [2] *Ech. d'Or.*, v, p. 333.

all he wrote is of this kind. He was a good theologian, and published many works of acknowledged merit. Chief among these is the Smaller Catechism he wanted to see adopted in the Patriarchate in place of a translation of Cardinal Bellarmine's Catechism, hitherto used. Although this was condemned by name specially, nevertheless, after correction, it has been reprinted and is still used in the Jesuit schools in Syria.

Ādam died in 1809, submitting all he had written to the judgment of the Holy See. In 1816 Pius VII condemned all his writings, especially the Catechism. It was not till 1835 that Gregory XVI (1831–1846) condemned the acts of the Synod of Ḳarḳafah. The Melkite Patriarch, Maximos III, adhered to this condemnation; gradually the whole movement disappeared. No one need fear Gallicanism among the Melkites to-day. The Jesuits have schools and missions all over the Patriarchate.

6. Maximos III (1833-1855).

By far the greatest man of the Melkite Church is the Patriarch Maximos III.[1]   Michael Maẓlūm was born at Aleppo of Melkite parents in 1779. He studied at his native city under a priest, Michael Naḥāwī, who is said to have been imbued with the ideas of Germanos Ādam. No doubt it was from him that Maẓlūm acquired those Gallican ideas that he never quite abandoned. He went to no seminary. Among the Melkites then it was still common (as in the schismatical Eastern Churches) that a priest should take young men to his house and teach them what theology, liturgy, and so on he could. Maẓlūm was ordained priest by Germanos Ādam of Aleppo and, at least for a time, became one of his foremost defenders.[2]   He was secretary of the Synod of Ḳarḳafah; there is no doubt that he then shared all its opinions. In 1810

[1] The figure of Maximos III looms large in every history of the Melkites. Paul Bāshā has published a contemporary account, " Historic notice of what happened to the nation of the Rūm Kāthūlīk (=Melkites) in the year 1837 and afterwards " (in Arabic, " Nabḍat tārikhīyat fīmā ġarā litā'ifat arrūmi-lkāthūlīk munḍ sanat 1837 fīmā ba'dhā." Beirut, 1907). Although it is anonymous, he says the author is Maximos himself. Charon's " Histoire des Patriarcats Melkites," vol. ii, part i, now published (see p. 185, n. 1), begins with Maximos's life, and gives an exhaustive account of his life, reign, and times. Many more details will be found here (pp. 1-400).

[2] Afterwards he denied that he had ever been a partizan of Ādam. There is something of the nature of a mental restriction about this (Charon, " Hist. des Melk.," ii, p. 9).

he was ordained Metropolitan of Aleppo by the Patriarch Agapios III, and took the name Maximos. In 1811 he became the first rector of the new seminary at 'Ain Trāz. But in the same year Propaganda refused to recognize his appointment to the see of Aleppo. The Patriarch and nearly the whole Melkite hierarchy refused to submit to this measure. In 1813 he went to Rome to regulate his affair. At last he submitted to his deposition from Aleppo and was made titular bishop, first of Abydos, then of Myra. Basil 'Arakṭingī, Superior General of Shuwair, became Metropolitan of Aleppo. Then the seminary at 'Ain Traz, suspect of the ideas of Ādam, was closed.[1]

In 1818 Maẓlūm went to Trieste, where he had an audience of the Emperor Francis I, who made him protector of all Melkites, as far as Austria was concerned. Then Maẓlūm founded the still existing Melkite Church at Marseilles.[2] He was still supposed to be not sufficiently submissive to Papal authority, and all this time was under a cloud. He went back to Rome and stayed there till 1831. In that year Gregory XVI (1831–1846) became Pope. He was much more friendly to Maẓlūm, and the old quarrel of Melkite Gallicanism was becoming forgotten. Maẓlūm was sent back to Syria with two Jesuits, who apparently had the duty of looking after him. Before going he had to sign a promise of fidelity to the Holy See. As soon as they landed in Syria he dodged his Jesuits, and went off to the Patriarch Ignatius V, at Zūk Mīkhā'īll. He now wanted to be made Patriarchal Vicar; but he did not succeed. Ignatius V died in 1833. There were then eight bishops to elect a successor. The Papal Delegate warned them that they must not elect Maẓlūm. But they did elect him all the same. When the news came to Rome the authorities there seem to have hesitated. First they demanded of the Patriarch-elect a denunciation of the Synod of Karkafah and of the ideas of Germanos Ādam. In 1835 the Pope published the Bull, *Melchitarum catholicorum synodus*, condemning Karkafah. Maximos accepted this with entire submission. But he had still not received his pallium when he summoned and held the Synod of 'Ain Traz in 1835. At last, in the same year, Gregory XVI confirmed his election.

The Synod of 'Ain Trāz is of great importance to the

---

[1] It was reopened soon after by the Jesuits.

[2] Polycarp Kayata (tit. Archimandrite and present rector of the church), " Monographie de l'église grecque catholique de Marseille et vie de S Nicholas de Myre," Marseilles, 1901. A view of the inside of the church will be found in Charon, *op. cit.*, ii, p. 35.

Melkites. It is the only one that has been approved at Rome, that has real force of law. It was opened on December 1, 1835. At the opening only two bishops,[1] besides the Patriarch, were present. Aleppo sent a procurator, Ba'albek did not appear;[2] the Metropolitans of Tyre, Acre, and Zaḥleh were dead. Maximos ordained a bishop for Tyre at the opening of the synod. Twenty-five canons were drawn up, concerning the administration of sacraments, the rite, offerings to churches, holidays of obligation, life and manners of clerks, regulars, the seminary of 'Ain Trāz, canonical visitations, care of the poor, fast and abstinence, vows and pilgrimages, usury.[3] All bishops present signed, and Maximos added the signature of the Metropolitan of Ba'albek, though he was not there.

There was a quarrel about the precedence of Aleppo and Tyre, each of these sees claiming to be the Protothrone— that is, first See of the Patriarchate.[4] The question of the Gregorian Calendar was discussed, but put aside for the present.

When the acts of the synod were sent to Rome, at first Propaganda was much annoyed because Maximos had held it before he had received the pallium. This is a violation of Canon Law. He had performed other Patriarchal acts before he had the pallium. It seems clear that he was acting on his Febronian theory that synods may be held without the intervention of the Pope. However, he had received the pallium meanwhile, so, after a good deal of discussion, at last the acts of 'Ain Trāz were formally approved by Propaganda in 1841.

Meanwhile Maximos obtained leave of the Government and came to Damascus. It was the first time a Melkite Patriarch had done so since Cyril VI fled to the Lebanon (p. 200). Then he made a journey in the Haurān[5] and ordained a bishop for that district. There were very few Melkites in it; afterwards his enemies said that he did this only to increase the number of his adherents by ordaining useless bishops. There are other cases in which the same was said of him. He

---

[1] Agapios Rī'āshī of Beirut and Basil Kaḥīl of Sidon.

[2] Athanasius 'Ubaid of Ba'albek was then quarrelling with his Patriarch.

[3] The acts of 'Ain Trāz are in the " Collectio Lacensis," ii, cols. 579-592.

[4] For this dispute see Charon, *op. cit.*, ii, pp. 115 and 243.

[5] The Haurān is the wild desert land south of Damascus (Basan in the Old Test.). Its chief town is Boṣrā. It is inhabited by Moslem Badawiin and Druses. There are few Orthodox Christians there, and still fewer Melkites.

ordained a bishop for Ḥomṣ, Ḥāma, and Yabrūd, thereby taking those places from the diocese of Beirut. Athanasius 'Ubaid of Beirut complained to Rome of this, and Propaganda took his side. This did not prevent Maximos from carrying out his plan. He ordained a bishop for Diyārbakr; but this time the result was most tragic. The bishop was Peter Sammān, who took the name Makarios. In 1843 the see of Aleppo was vacant, and Makarios of Diyārbakr applied for it. The Patriarch, however, did not give it to him; so he turned sulky and, after a period of playing a double part, finally he went off to the Orthodox at Constantinople. The apostasy of this wretched man acquired some fame because of the extraordinary things the Orthodox did to him. He was to be Orthodox Metropolitan of Diyārbakr. He had received all sacraments, including his bishop's orders, according to the Byzantine rite, exactly the same as that of the Orthodox. Nevertheless they not only reordained him, but began proceedings by rebaptizing the man. It is a famous case illustrating their belief that no sacraments are really valid except those administered in the Orthodox Church.[1]

Another bishop of unhappy memory in the time of Maximos III was the once notorious Athanasius Totūnǧī of Tripoli. His ordination was a further mistake of Maximos, always too ready to multiply bishops. He was Superior of the seminary of 'Ain Trāz. Maximos had turned out the Jesuits who had been in charge of that seminary after the troubles of Germanos Ādam (p. 211), and had put this Totūnǧī there as rector. There was not the slightest need to make him a bishop. Seminaries get on quite well with a priest as rector. Still less was there any need to make a bishop for Tripoli. Charon says there were then at most ten Melkites there.[2] The Patriarch's idea was that he should administer the diocese while residing at 'Ain Trāz and conducting the seminary. Then very serious rumours about Totūnǧī's moral conduct got abroad. Maximos examined them; Totūnǧī pleaded guilty and gave the Patriarch a written confession. Maximos then told him to go to Ḥomṣ, to be quiet, and out of the way till the scandal had blown over. However, Totūnǧī fled to the refuge of all discontented Melkites,

---

[1] For the story of Makarios Sammān see Charon, *op. cit.*, ii, pp. 117-122. His admission to the Orthodox Church has become a kind of test case and precedent. From this point of view it is discussed by L. Petit, " L'entrée des catholiques dans l'Eglise orthodoxe," *Ech. d'Or.*, ii, 129-138.

[2] *Op. cit.*, ii, 141. All Totūnǧī's story is told, ii, 140-146.

Rome. Here he accused his Patriarch of tyrannical conduct towards himself, and told many lies. At Rome they were quite kind to him, they even gave him a pension; but they told him to go back to Syria. He got as far as Malta, then dodged and came to Marseilles and Paris. Maximos ordered him home; but now, in open disobedience to his Patriarch and the Roman authorities, he came to England, pretending that he had been sent to collect alms for his poor flock. Wiseman, then Vicar Apostolic of the London district, gave him a *celebret* and leave to collect alms. People were less suspicious then of these begging Orientals than we have become since. For a time he celebrated in the Catholic church at Chelsea. But meanwhile he was talking to the Anglicans, and telling them a very different story. This came out, and Wiseman withdrew his faculties. Totūngī went off to Lord Palmerston and the Archbishop of Canterbury. The Anglicans, of course, were delighted. They seem not to have had the vaguest idea who he was. Anglicans never do understand who these people are who come and beg from them. All they thought was that he was a " bishop of the Syrian Church " (whatever that might mean) who was persecuted by the Pope of Rome. Needless to say, every Anglican heart went out to the Apostolic person so ill-used (hardly an Anglican alive understood the difference between a Melkite and the Orthodox; very few knew that between Orthodox and Jacobites). So the Archbishop of Canterbury gave him a sum of money, just to show, says he, " the sympathy between the Catholic Church of England and the Church of Syria." Totūngī got up a meeting at Leamington under the auspices of Anglican bishops. There was a great crowd and much enthusiasm. A parson, Mr. Craig, explained to the meeting that the illustrious person before them wanted to become a British citizen in order to enjoy the protection of our Empire. " The presence of this eminent Prelate in our country will help to convince the members of our Church that our brethren in the East have preserved the doctrines of the Church of England.[1] . . . The creed of the Bishop of Tripolis is in perfect accord with that of the Catholic Church of Jesus Christ.[2] Deprived of help from France and Austria,

[1] Observe the gorgeous muddle of all this. " Our brethren in the East "; as if they were all one body in union with Totūngī, and committed to his views. " Preserving the doctrines of the Church of England," as a standard for Syria, is very funny.

[2] Mr. Craig did not know, of course, that the eminent Prelate was Bishop of Tripolis only on the strength of appointment by a Popish Patriarch. There was an Orthodox Metropolitan, his rival,

he turns to the Church which, like his, acknowledges two sacraments as necessary to salvation."[1]   Then Totūnǵī, having learned the right sort of patter for his audience, assured them that his object was to educate his people " on true scriptural principles."   He implored them to provide his flock with copies of the unmutilated Word of God; and hoped that the money for this purpose would be entrusted to himself.   He also received Communion in an Anglican Church from Mr. Craig. Great was the joy of the Anglicans at this reunion of Christendom.   But then the fellow got arrested, was sent about his business, and finally, having exhausted the credulity of everyone over here, did go back to Syria.   There he wanted to follow the example of Makarios Sammān and turn Orthodox. But they would not promise him a diocese; so he made an attempt to start a private little schism of his own at Aleppo. This came to nothing; finally the poor fellow came back to the Church, repented, did penance, and died a Catholic at Aleppo in 1874.   His queer story is typical, and should be a warning to High Church enthusiasts.   It is not always safe to believe Orientals who come here and say they are persecuted by the Pope because they want the pure Bible and two sacraments. It would also be wise to acquire some little knowledge of Eastern Christendom, so as not to talk nonsense about " the Church of Syria."

We have seen that, already under Theodosius VI, Propaganda had made the few Melkites of Egypt and Palestine subject to the Melkite Patriarch of Antioch (p. 203).   Since then their number had increased.   In 1836 Maximos III made a journey to both these lands, built churches, and left Patriarchal vicars at Cairo and Jerusalem.   He showed great zeal in maintaining the Byzantine rite among his people there.   There were many children of Byzantine parents who, for want of clergy of their own rite, had adopted that of Rome.   Maximos insisted on their coming back to the custom of their fathers.   Not all of them were willing to do so, after having accustomed themselves to Roman ways.   Again there was a dispute; Propaganda in

---

all the time; the Anglicans ought to have put their money on that man—if they had known anything about it.   How far had Mr. Craig examined Totūnǵī's creed before committing himself to this assertion ? As a matter of fact, his creed was exactly that of the Pope of Rome, though his morals were not.   So Craig, like Caiaphas, was right for once.

[1] These "two sacraments " are the gem of the whole story. Poor Mr. Craig; and what monumental lies Totūnǵī must have told !

1843 made one of the important decisions which still affect this difficult question. We shall come back to the laws[1]; here it will be enough to say that, as always, this decision was scrupulously respectful of the rights of the Uniate Church. Now comes a great and famous quarrel, which to the Western reader may seem slightly ridiculous, though it caused much heartburning at the time. It is the question of the hats of the Melkite clergy.

In 1837 the Orthodox Patriarch of Constantinople, Gregory VI,[2] alarmed at the progress of the Melkite Church, obtained a firman from the Sultan which forbade the Melkites to make any converts from the Orthodox and commanded their clergy to change their dress, so that no one should mistake them for Orthodox. Naturally, since the division under Cyril VI, the clergy of both sides kept the same dress as before. It was a black cassock without buttons (ἀντερίον, Arabic ḳumbāz), with a cloth belt, a cloak with wide sleeves (ῥάσον, ǵubbah), and the kalymauchion (καλυμαύχιον, ḳallūsah).[3] This is the cylindrical hat without a brim worn by all the Byzantine clergy.[4] Now the Orthodox wanted to make the Melkites change their dress. This was a humiliation for them. It would make them look like some new strange sect. Why should they not go on wearing the same dress, respected by their people, as had been worn for centuries by their predecessors ? Indeed, since the Melkites represent the old Patriarchate of Antioch, they could urge with reason that, if there is to be any change, it should be made by the followers of the new schismatical line of Silvester the Cypriote. First the Orthodox insisted that, as the Melkites were practically Europeans, they should be made to dress like French priests, wearing the French hat. The malice of this is obvious. It would have stamped them as foreigners at the first glance, would have confused them with the Latin clergy, and would

---

[1] The chapter on the Canon Law of the Uniates was never written. For the decision referred to, see Charon, " Hist. Melk.," ii, p. 148. [*Editor's Note.*]

[2] Gregory VI of Constantinople, 1835-1840 (deposed); after eleven other Patriarchates in between, restored 1867-1871. Then he was deposed again.

[3] Kalymauchion, kalymmaukion, also kamalaukion (and other spellings); supposed to be from κάμηλος, hat, and αὐχήν, neck. Arabic ḳalansuwah, then ḳallūsah (the usual word now).

[4] It is worn both out of doors and in choir; so it corresponds to both hat and biretta. Dignitaries wear a black veil over it, ἐπανωκαλυμαύχιον. You can distinguish all the Eastern clergy by the shape of their hats.

have lost to them the sympathy of natives. It is a common trick to injure a rival religion by representing it as foreign, and so hostile to all patriotic citizens. Then it was proposed that they should wear a square kalymauchion. The Melkites persisted in claiming that they would go on dressing exactly as their fathers had dressed, in the traditional costume of their rite.[1] The quarrel lasted with great bitterness for ten years. At last a compromise was made by the Government. The Melkite clergy were to wear a kalymauchion, not round, but six-sided;[2] their cassock was to be, not black, but blue or violet. This was made law by the Turk in 1847. But it was not long observed. The blue or violet got darker and darker, the six angles of the hat became more and more blunted, till there is now nothing to distinguish the Melkites from the Orthodox in dress.

A greater work, the greatest work of Maximos's life, was the civil emancipation of his people. It is known that, at any rate till the revolution of 1908, the Turkish Government grouped its Christian victims according to their religions. Each religion was a " nation," dependent on its religious head in civil matters too; these heads were responsible to the Porte for the behaviour of their people. When the division between Melkites and Orthodox came, at first that made no difference to the Turk. He still looked on them as one nation. Since the Government eventually took the side of the Orthodox Patriarchs, Silvester and his successors, these still had civil jurisdiction over the Melkites. Such a state of things was intolerable to them. Naturally, the Orthodox used their authority to vex, annoy, and persecute the followers of the Melkite Patriarchs in every possible way. It was not till 1830 that the Sultan freed all Uniates from dependence on their rivals. At first he put all under the civil authority of the Armenian Patriarch, as representing the largest and best known

[1] Naturally, they exaggerated its importance. In a protest of 1841 the Melkites declare that their kalymauchion has been worn by all their clergy since the birth of Christ ! (Charon, *op. cit.*, ii, p. 193). The high cylindrical cap seems to be of Persian origin. It is, no doubt, originally the same thing as the red tarbūsh worn by everyone, Moslem or Christian, in the Levant. Modern Persians wear a cap of the same shape, but of black wool. The brim at the top of the kalymauchion is not earlier than the nineteenth century. Students and clerks in minor orders still wear it without this brim.

[2] It is said that the Grand Wazīr suggested this form, taking it from the little six-sided tables on which Turks put their coffee cups and pipes. In Charon, *op. cit.*, ii, p. 149, may be seen the portrait of a Melkite bishop wearing the six-sided kalymauchion.

community of Uniates (p. 204).   Maximos III, after enormous
labours, at last obtained the repeal of this law, and the complete
civil autonomy of the Melkites under their own Patriarch.
First he obtained his own appointment as agent (murakhkhaṣ)
of the Armenian Patriarch for the Melkites.   But there was
then a general movement in favour of separation among all the
other Uniates.   The Syrian and Chaldæan Uniates demanded
the same thing as the Melkites, though they did not obtain
quite so much.   In 1846, after long negotiations, Maximos
persuaded the Government to recognize the Melkites as a quite
separate nation under himself and his successors.   From that
time the Melkite Patriarch has a *berat* from the Porte giving
him this authority.[1]

But the civil arrangements of the Turkish Government are
not quite the same thing as ecclesiastical jurisdiction, given
only by the central authority of the Church at Rome.   Maximos
seems to have thought that it is.   So, on the strength of his
berat from the Turk, he began to assume ecclesiastical jurisdiction also over all Uniates of the Byzantine rite in the Turkish
Empire.   He even tried this over the few Byzantine Uniates
of Constantinople.   He built a church there and quarrelled
with the Latin vicar, who would not allow people to attend it.[2]
Ecclesiastically he was only Patriarch of Antioch.   However,
already in 1773 the Pope had entrusted the Melkites of the
other two Patriarchates, Alexandria and Jerusalem, to the
Patriarch of Antioch; though so far no title had been granted
for these (p. 203).   Maximos now asked at Rome that he might
be recognized as " Patriarch of the Greek Melkite Catholic
Church."   So strange and new a title, with its vague claim,
was not approved.   But Pope Gregory XVI, in 1838, granted
him, as a personal favour which was not to continue to his
successors, the titles of Alexandria and Jerusalem.   Since he

[1] The story of the emancipation of the Melkites is told at length,
with the full text of the documents in Charon, *op. cit.*, ii, chap. iv,
pp. 153-216.   The text of Maximos's *berat* of January 7, 1848 (Mu-
ḥarram, A.H. 1264) will be found at pp. 202-207.   The rights and
privileges conferred are drawn up in twenty-three paragraphs.   Notice
the second.   No one is to prevent him from " reading the Gospel
(Kirā'at alInǧil)".   This is the regular Moslem euphemism for celebrating the holy liturgy.   My Moslem *mukāri* used to take me to
Franciscan convents in Syria that I might " read the Gospel " next
morning.

[2] This question was settled eventually.   The priest serving the
church is nominated by the Melkite Patriarch, but has his faculties
from the Latin Vicar Patriarchal (Charon, " Hist. des Melk.," ii,
p. 212).

was already Patriarch of Antioch, and known under that title, since the other two were, so to say, only accidental additions, not necessarily to continue after his death, Maximos used the form " Patriarch of Antioch, Alexandria, Jerusalem, and of all the East," with Antioch first. We shall see how this title has maintained itself, illegally, among his successors (p. 224). Maximos built a Patriarchal church at Jerusalem, and he had one already at Cairo. For Egypt and Palestine he appointed Patriarchal vicars, which practice has continued ever since.

In 1849 Maximos summoned a synod at Jerusalem, which was to complete the work of that of 'Ain Trāz in 1835. But at once strong opposition showed itself. Three bishops, those of Tyre, Beirut, and Ba'albek, wrote to Rome to protest. They did not see the good of a new synod, they resented Maximos's lordly ways over his Metropolitans, they did not want to go to Jerusalem at all. However, he held his synod, with great external pomp. One of the first questions that came up was what to do with Athanasius Totūnǵī, who had now repented. The folly of Maximos's mania for ordaining bishops was shown most clearly in this case. Had Totūnǵī been a priest, no doubt a post could have been found for him easily; but a bishop must, according to Melkite ideas then, have some sort of diocese. He was not a monk, so they could not send him back to his monastery. The wretched man who had already given so much trouble now gave more by causing the great quarrel between the Patriarch and Ag'apios Ri'āshī, Metropolitan of Beirut. In order to provide Totūnǵī with a see, Maximos said he would cut off Ǵebail from the diocese of Beirut, and make him bishop of that new see. Ri'āshī was furious, and appealed to Rome. Maximos at his synod then told the Metropolitans to suspend Ri'āshī from the use of pontificalia. They said they could not do so till the bishop's case had been heard. Ri'āshī succeeded this time, and Totūnǵī was not made bishop of Ǵebail; but the quarrel between Ri'āshī and the Patriarch continued, and caused the chief trouble of the end of Maximos's reign. The Salvatorian monks also were opposed to the synod, and sent protests to Rome. It made forty canons. There are many things in its acts which would offend Propaganda. First Maximos declares that he holds this synod in the fullness of his Patriarchal power, again ignoring the need of Roman approval. When the acts were sent to Rome, the authorities there also blamed the magnificence with which the Patriarch loved to surround himself, the pomp of his titles repeated over and over again, the exaggerated claim to authority over his suffragans, even a studious imitation of Papal titles and style. No bishop is to settle anything without the Patriarch's leave; whereas he acts with too great independence of his superior, the Pope. There are supposed to be Jansenist infiltrations in expressions about grace and sacraments; there were decrees annoying to the Salvatorians. For all these reasons the synod was said to be tainted with the errors of Ḳarḳafah; it was never approved at Rome. In this synod the old quarrel of precedence between Tyre and Aleppo came up again.[1]

Meanwhile Ri'āshī of Beirut was still in opposition against his Patriarch, and the Shuwair monks of his diocese were in opposition against him. They wanted independence of the Metropolitan and immediate dependence on the Patriarch. After a long quarrel which embittered Maximos's last years, Rome decided for Ri'āshī. Maximos was summoned to Rome, and refused to go. It is even said that very grave remonstrances were about to be sent to him by Propaganda when he sickened and died. Certainly at his death the Patriarchate was in a great state of disorder. Maximos fell sick at Cairo in the spring of 1855. He would not use any relaxation of the severe fast of Lent according to his rite, saying that the Patriarch, above all, should give a good example of fidelity to the laws of his Church. He received the last sacraments, died a holy death on August 11, 1855,[2] and is buried at Cairo.

Maximos III had many enemies during his long career. He was accused of pride and too great pomp. Certainly he loved to surround himself with attendants; he loved grand titles and splendid ceremonies. His weakness was ordaining useless bishops and then quarrelling with them. Yet he was by far the greatest Patriarch, perhaps the greatest bishop, the Melkite Church has had. He was a man of great erudition, author of a score of valuable works on grammar, history, liturgy, and theology.[3] He inherited the Gallican ideas of Germanos Ādam, which he never quite laid aside. For all that, he was a man of unquestioned piety, zeal, and energy for the good of his Melkites. In spite of his Gallicanisms and assumptions of independence, he was never anything approaching a heretic or schismatic. Now all his faults are long forgotten by his people.

---

[1] For the Synod of Jerusalem in 1849 see Charon, *op. cit.*, ii, chap. v, pp. 217-251.

[2] His will is in Charon, *op. cit.*, ii, 261-267. In it he protests his Catholic sentiments and fidelity to the Holy See. The story of his last hours is most edifying and touching (*ibid.*, 259-260).

[3] The list of his works is given in Charon, *op. cit.*, ii, 267-276.

They remember him only as the great Patriarch who did so much for them, who, above all, obtained for them their civil independence.

7. History after Maximos III (1855-1915).

After the death of Maximos III thirteen bishops elected Clement Baḥūth,[1] a Salvatorian monk and Metropolitan of Acre, to be his successor (1855–1864). The great event of his reign was the adoption of the Gregorian Calendar, which led to dreadful trouble and a schism of part of his flock. So far the Melkites had used the old Julian Calendar, like the Orthodox. But it was felt, at least at Rome, that in so vital a matter as this the whole Catholic Church should agree. The question does not affect the special feasts and fasts of each rite. In spite of those, there are the great cardinal feasts of the year: Easter, Epiphany, Pentecost, and others, such as Christmas, kept by all. It was certainly a strange anomaly that Catholics should keep these on different days.[2] Moreover, everyone knows that the Julian Calendar is hopelessly wrong. Already at the synod of 'Ain Trāz in 1835 the question had been discussed; but the feeling against a change was so strong that it was shelved. Now the Patriarch Clement thought it could be no longer put off. The Maronites had already adopted the Gregorian Calendar in their synod of 1736.[3] Clement ordered its use throughout the Melkite Church in 1857. At once there was an enormous uproar. Eastern people are very tenacious of their old customs, especially in such external matters. Many Melkites protested that the Patriarch was tampering with their faith, that he was a Franġi trying to latinize them. Books and violent pamphlets were written on either side. A considerable number of Melkites at last flatly refused to obey the order, and were excommunicated by Clement. Their leader was a secularized monk, Ġibarra. Protected by the Russians, he opened chapels for the sect that gathered round him. He called this the " Eastern Church " (alkanīsat ashsharḳīyah). The schism lasted for about three years. Then, during the

---

[1] His name had been Michael, till he took that of Clement when ordained bishop for Acre in 1836, just after the synod of 'Ain Trāz. He is the only Patriarch of Antioch of this name.

[2] Step by step, and often at the cost of much disturbance, all the Uniate Churches have now adopted the Gregorian Calendar.

[3] Synod of Mount Lebanon (" Coll. Lac.," ii, 77) confirmed (September 1, 1741) by Benedict XIV in the Brief *Singularis* (Charon, iii, p. 368).

troubles of Syria in 1860, many of these Sharḳiyīn came back to the Church. By 1865 nearly all were converted. They kept the feast of Candlemas in union with the Melkites, on the Gregorian date, and the chief trouble was over. Only Ġibarra himself with very few followers kept a schismatical chapel at Beirut. I believe that the whole schism is now ended. But meanwhile Clement, worn out with this trouble, resigned his see in October, 1864, and went back to his monastery, St Saviour.[1]

He was succeeded by Gregory Yūsuf[2] (1864–1897). Gregory had been a student of the Jesuit college at Ġazīr, then of the Greek College at Rome. He was a Salvatorian monk, and Bishop of Acre. He was elected by the bishops of the Patriarchate at Shuwair, and confirmed by Pius IX in 1864. He founded the Patriarchal school at Beirut; in his time the French "White Fathers" opened their admirable College of St Anne at Jerusalem for the education of the Melkite clergy.[3] At the Vatican Council Gregory was an Inopportunist. He died on July 13, 1897. Then came Peter IV, whose family name was Ġiraiġīrī (1897–1902). He was born at Zahleh in 1841, and had studied for four years at the seminary of Blois, to learn French. He was ordained priest in 1862; in 1886 he was made Bishop of Bānīās (Paneas), which is Cæsarea Philippi. He was the first bishop of this see since before the time of Cyril VI.

When the bishops met at the monastery of St Saviour to elect a Patriarch, the Turkish Government declared that it would not allow the presence of any foreigner at the election. But it was the rule that the Apostolic Delegate should be present. The French Ambassador protested, and the Government gave way. Peter IV intended to summon a Melkite synod, and went to Rome to make arrangements for this in 1899. The synod was never held; they still wait for it, and many demand it. At one time Orthodox papers spread the rumour that Peter had tendencies away from Rome and towards their Church. This was, of course, indignantly denied. When Peter died the bishops elected Cyril Ġiḥā, Metropolitan of Aleppo, who became Cyril VIII (1902–1919).

---

[1] Clement Bahūth died, leaving the reputation of a saint.
[2] He is often called "Gregory Joseph." But I believe that Yūsuf, or Ibnu-Yūsuf was his family name. There was a Gregory of Antioch in 579-584; so Yūsuf would be Gregory II. However, I have never seen him so called. I have seen "Grégoire-Joseph I."
[3] This was the beginning of systematic formation of secular clergy for the Patriarchate. Formerly nearly all parishes were served by monks. For the College of St Anne, see p. 229.

8. The Melkite Church at the Present Time.

The Melkites, then, are the Arab-speaking Catholics of the Byzantine rite in Syria, Palestine, and Egypt. The Head of their Church, under the Pope, is their *Patriarch*. As soon as the Patriarch dies, the Holy See appoints a Vicar Apostolic Patriarchal, who corresponds to the Vicar Capitular in the West. He may be any bishop of the Patriarchate. He then summons a synod to elect the new Patriarch. Propaganda always desires that the Latin delegate be present and preside at this synod; but he has no vote. As a matter of fact, synods to elect a Patriarch have often been held without the presence of the delegate. The matter seems still uncertain. All the bishops of the Patriarchate, whether Ordinaries or titular, have a vote, no one else. Till now an absolute majority has been sufficient.[1] As soon as the Patriarch is elected, and has accepted his election, he is proclaimed and enthroned. The president hands him the Patriarchal Dikanikion, all the bishops come up and kiss his hand; then they sing a Polychronion in his honour. It is curious that this ceremony takes place before he is confirmed at Rome. Then the synod and the Patriarch-elect write to the Pope. He sends a profession of faith and begs for the pallium. In theory he should come to Rome for his pallium; but he never does. There have been many cases of Melkite Patriarchs using jurisdiction before they had the pallium, and much dispute about this.[2] If the Pope approves of the election, he sends the pallium, which is given to the Patriarch by the Latin Delegate. On this occasion the Patriarch makes a new profession of faith. He is then confirmed by the Turkish Government and receives his Berat.[3]

The Patriarch's title is the result of the development of his position. Originally he was Patriarch of Antioch only, succeeding Cyril VI in that line. Then, when there were a few Melkites in Palestine and Egypt, but not enough to justify the erection of separate Patriarchates, these were entrusted to the care of the Patriarch of Antioch, at first without any title for them.[4] Then the Pope allowed Maximos III to call himself also Patriarch of Alexandria and Jerusalem; but this was a personal favour, not to continue to his successors.[5] When

---

[1] The new Synod of 'Ain-Trāz (1909) desires a majority of two-thirds (Charon, " Hist. Melk.," iii, 402).   [2] *E.g.*, see p. 212.

[3] All the laws for the election and confirmation of the Patriarch are given by Charon, *op. cit.*, iii, pp. 394-408.

[4] See p. 203.   [5] P. 218.

Maximos died, his successor, Clement, without any justification, used these other titles. For this he was reproved by Propaganda, and at once expressed his regret. Then Pius IX renewed the titles for him, again as a personal favour. They have never been renewed since. Gregory Yūsuf assumed them with no right. Circumstances were at that time so difficult in Syria that Rome left this matter alone. But the *Gerarchia Cattolica* described him scrupulously as " Patriarca antiocheno dei Melchiti " only. All Roman documents still recognize the Melkite Patriarch as of Antioch only.[1] He has no right to any further title. Nevertheless, since Maximos III, each Patriarch adds those of Alexandria and Jerusalem.[2] Maximos made a further change in the title, which remains as used by them. If the three sees are to be united in one person, Alexandria should come first. That see has precedence over Antioch and is second in Christendom. But, since Antioch was the older title for this Patriarch, the only one to which he had right by succession, Maximos and his successors put it first. The old style of Antioch was " Antioch and all the East," meaning the Roman Prefecture of the East. But the Melkite Patriarchs put these words at the end of all, and call themselves " Patriarchs of Antioch, Alexandria, Jerusalem, and all the East." This seems to give a new meaning to the " East." They are not, of course, really Patriarchs of anything like all the East in the usual meaning. The Melkite has jurisdiction over Melkites in Syria, Palestine, and Egypt only. He has never received nor assumed the title of Constantinople; though I have heard it whispered in Syria that Cyril VIII, having already so many titles, had vague dreams of being Œcumenical Patriarch. People in the East love titles. The full style of this Patriarch, used in his solemn $\phi\acute{\eta}\mu\eta$[3], is: " The most blessed, most holy, most venerable, our chief and lord, Patriarch of the great cities of Antioch, Alexandria, and Jerusalem, of Cilicia, Syria, and Iberia, of Arabia, Mesopotamia, and the Pentapolis, of Ethiopia, all Egypt, and all the East, Father of Fathers, Shepherd of Shepherds, Pontiff of Pontiffs,

---

[1] See, for instance, the *Annuario pontificio* for 1915, p. 62, " Antiochen. Græcorum Melchitarum."

[2] I have before me a portrait of Lord Cyril VIII, signed by himself, " Kīrilus ath-thāmin, Baṭrak Anṭākiyeh wAliskandariyeh wUrashalīm wasā'iri-lmashriḳ." Some day, when there are more Melkites in Egypt and Palestine, there will be separate Patriarchs of Alexandria and Jerusalem.

[3] The φήμη is the solemn proclamation of a bishop, in all his glory. It occurs in Polychronia, and (abbreviated) in Diptychs.

and thirteenth Apostle."[1] However, since he is the only Melkite Patriarch, the usual and convenient rule is to call him so simply. According to Eastern custom he is " His Beatitude."[2] At Rome they do not seem to recognize this. To them he is " Eccellenza reverendissima."[3]

Antioch has long been abandoned as the Patriarchal residence. When the Ottoman Turks conquered Syria in 1516 Damascus became the political centre of the province. The Patriarch of Antioch then went to live there. Antioch is now a poor town of about 35,000 inhabitants, mostly Noṣairi. It has a few Orthodox Christians, a handful of Latins, Maronites, and Uniate Armenians, I believe no Melkites at all. The Orthodox Patriarchs then resided at Damascus; for a time there was still a Metropolitan of Damascus as well. Then, since the Patriarch was there himself, he assumed the administration of that see. This is still the case with both Orthodox and Melkites. When the division between Cyril and Silvester came, Cyril had to flee Damascus. From 1724 to 1834 the Melkite Patriarchs resided at the monastery of St Saviour, or at 'Ain Trāz, or Zūḳ-Mīkā'il (p. 204). Meanwhile they appointed Vicars Patriarchal for Damascus. In 1834 Maximos III returned to Damascus (p. 212), but now, having also the administration of Egypt, he spent a great part of his time in his house at Cairo. Peter IV did not like Damascus; so he built himself a large house next to the Patriarchal College at Beirut. But he did not live to inhabit it. Since then this house is let. The present custom is for the Patriarch to divide his time between Cairo and Damascus, at both of which he has houses. It depends on his own preference where he spends most of his time. He is rarely at Jerusalem, where his flock is very small. He has a country house at 'Ain-Trāz.[4]

The Patriarch has *Vicars Patriarchal* representing him. These are generally, but neither necessarily nor always, bishops. At present there are such vicars at Cairo (for Egypt), at Jerusa-

---

[1] A missionary in Syria was much puzzled by this " thirteenth apostle." The idea is simple enough. We all know the twelve apostles. The Patriarch is so great that he is practically a thirteenth, practically equal to the others.

[2] Ġibtah, Μακαριώτης.

[3] For the φῆμαι and titles of Patriarchs and bishops see Charon, *op. cit.*, iii, 409-423. Cyril VIII made up a coat-of-arms for himself. It may be seen *ibid.*, p. 422. It is shocking bad heraldry.

[4] Charon (iii, pp. 452-488) gives a complete list of the Patriarch's ecclesiastical rights and duties, according to the Synod of Jerusalem in 1849, also (pp. 507-519) of his civil rights and duties.

lem (for Palestine), at Damascus, at Constantinople (to repre
sent the Patriarch's interests with the Government), at some
outlying cities in the East, where are a few Melkites; at
Rome, Paris, and other places in the West, including
America.[1]

The number of Melkite *sees* has varied considerably.
At present there are twelve Ordinaries, besides the Patri-
arch himself. Antioch is a mere title; the Patriarch is
Ordinary of Damascus. Then there are Bishops of Tyre,
Aleppo, Boṣra-and-Haurān (united), Homs, Beirut,[2] Acre,
Sidon, Paneas, Tripoli, Ba'albek, Yabrūd, Furzul-and-
Zaḥleh (united). There are no suffragan sees in Palestine
or Egypt.[3]

So far I have generally called all these bishops Metro-
politans. This is the usual term among all Christians in the
East. It is a development of Byzantine law to give to every
Ordinary this title; obviously meaning no more than bishop.[4]
From the Greek μητροπολίτης the Arabs formed the word
Mutrān.[5] This is now used in Arabic as meaning no more than
bishop. Every bishop, even a titular one, is called *Mutrān*.
The Latin translation of the acts of the third synod of 'Ain-
Trāz uses " Metropolitanus " for Mutrān, and gives the title
to every bishop.[6] As a matter of fact, I believe that there are
now no real provinces nor Metropolitan jurisdiction among the
Melkites at all. All their bishops are immediately subject
to the Patriarch. He ordains them all, blesses the chrism for
all, and rules all on the same level. But Cyril Charon desires
a reform in this matter. He points out that, originally, there
were real provinces and Archbishops, as in the West. He
insists on this as the legal position still. His scheme, based
on antiquity, is this: Tyre is the first see under the Patriarch.
Under Tyre as Metropolis he groups Acre, Sidon, Paneas,
Tripoli. Aleppo is the second see, a Metropolis without
suffragans. Damascus is the third Metropolis having as
suffragan sees Ba'albek, Yabrūd, Furzul-and-Zaḥleh. Then

---

[1] See the list in Charon, *op. cit.*, iii, 280-284; *cf.* 535-545.
[2] To which are now joined the old sees of Byblos (Gebail) and
Botrys (Batrūn).
[3] Charon gives a very complete list of all these bishops (in 1911)
with portraits, the career of each and statistics of his diocese (*op. cit.*,
iii, 284-324). A " diocese," by the way, in the Byzantine rite is an
" Eparchy," Ἐπαρχία, Ar. *abrashiyeh*.
[4] See " Orth. Eastern Church," pp. 350-351.
[5] It looks as if its source were rather Latin " metropolitanus."
[6] In the " Collectio Lacensis," ii, 579.

Ḥomṣ and Beirut are Metropolitan sees without suffragans.[1]
It may be that the new synod, the fourth of 'Ain-Trāz (1909),
has made some legislation to this effect. The ordinary bishops,
as well as the Patriarch, have certain civil rights over their
flocks; each receives a berat from the state to this effect.[2]

When a see is vacant, the Patriarch proposes three candidates; of these the diocesan clergy should choose one. As a
matter of fact, the laity, the " Notables of the Nation,"[3] play
a considerable part in the election. Only at Aleppo is there a
special rule, approved by Rome. Here the clergy and notables
have absolutely free choice.[4] The Holy See has no voice nor
part in the election of Melkite bishops.[5] They are ordained by
the Patriarch, with two assistants. Besides the diocesan
Ordinaries there are a certain number of *titular bishops*, either
Patriarchal Vicars or Ordinaries who have retired. The
Patriarch may name and ordain any titular bishops he pleases.
They are called *Synkelloi*.[6] Their titles are those of ancient
sees in the country which no longer have Ordinaries.

A curious right of the Ordinary is that no one may marry
without his consent.[7]

The *lower clergy* is either secular or regular. Till the time
of Maximos III the Melkite clergy consisted almost entirely
of monks of the two Congregations.[8] One of that Patriarch's

---

[1] Charon explains and defends his system, iii, 251-258. He
follows it in his list (284-324) and in the table at p. 329. There are
Arabic words which distinguish. A bishop is *Uskuf*, an archbishop
Ra'īs usākifeh. But one rarely hears them, except in solemn pro-
clamations. In ordinary speech everyone calls every bishop *Mutrān*.

[2] Charon gives an example of a berat—for Dimitri 'Antākī of
Aleppo, in 1846.

[3] These " Notables of the Nation " (ἄρχοντες τοῦ γένους,
arkhanḍūs atTā'ifeh) play a great part in all Eastern Churches in the
Ottoman Empire. In theory they are the chiefs of tribes and leaders
of the people. But the term is vague, and is given easily to any rich
man.

[4] Pius VII approved this by his Brief, *Tristis quidem* of June 3,
1816. See the text in Charon, iii, p. 551.

[5] Charon quotes examples showing that sometimes at Rome they
did not even know of the existence of certain Melkite Ordinaries
(iii, 557).

[6] Σύγκελλος (σύν and *cella*), Ar. *mutrānu-lkillāyeh*. Originally
this was an ecclesiastic who lived with the bishop or abbot, never
quitting him, to be witness of his conduct and morals.

[7] The priest has to apply for a faculty for every marriage.

[8] Not entirely. It is sometimes said that Maximos III founded
the Melkite secular clergy. This is an exaggeration; he greatly
fortified and extended it; but there were secular priests before his
time.

chief works was to organize a normal diocesan clergy. Even now, by far the greater number of churches are served by monks. There are no organized parishes with a rector and his curates. Where several priests live together, they stand all on the same level, each having a district. There is the curious custom that a family will choose one priest to be its director. This family then supports him, and, in return, he administers all sacraments to its members. There will be more to say about the clergy when we come to Uniate Canon Law in general.[1] Here it will be enough to note that the diocesan clergy increases very much in modern times, and that the practice of celibacy becomes more and more common among secular priests. All the modern colleges and seminaries encourage celibacy.[2] The priests are poor. They live from stole fees and small collections. The usual stipend for a liturgy is two or three piastres (4d. or 6d.). But they need little to live. They eat a handful of rice, a cucumber, an olive or two, a little *laban*, and an onion. The title *Chorepiskopos*[3] is now given to many priests as an honour. The Melkite chorepiskopos is never ordained bishop. The real *Archimandrite* is head of a monastery. But there are many titular Archimandrites, again merely an honour given to any deserving priest. The *Protopapas* is a rural dean. The secular priest wears a dark cassock[4] with no buttons, a cloth belt, a cloak, and the kalimaukion black. Monks and dignitaries wear a veil (epanokalimaukion) over this, and a leather belt. Some priests now begin to wear the French douillette, thinking that more European. It is ugly, hot, and inconvenient in their climate. All priests let the hair grow long. When not officiating in church they gather it up, just as a woman does. All, of course, must wear the beard.

The chief *religious orders* are the three Congregations of Salvatorians, Shuwairites, and Alepins (Ḥalibi).[5] These monks claim certain districts as belonging to their orders.

---

[1] See p. 216, n. 1.

[2] Of 172 secular priests in 1911, 92 were celibate (Charon, iii, 340).

[3] Ar. *Ūskufu-lKaryeh*.

[4] Of any dark colour, often blue, brown, grey. Only monks must wear black.

[5] For these see pp. 205-208. Salvatorians write after their name the letters *bā* and *mīm* (= bāsilī mukhallasī), Shuwairites and Alepins *bā* and *ḳāf* (= bāsilī ḳānūnī, " regular Basilian "). All monks by law are subject to the Ordinary. The Melkite Church has no *stauropegia*. For Melkite monastic Canon Law see Charon, *op. cit.*, iii, pp. 383 387.

They serve by far the greater number of churches.[1] As an example, in the diocese of Sidon of forty-six priests, thirty are Salvatorian monks, the other sixteen are married. In Ba'albek, of fifteen priests ten are Shuwairites, one Alepin, four secular. Most bishops are monks;[2] though this is not a rule.

Besides these three monastic Congregations there is a Congregation of priests, on the lines of those we know in the West, which must be mentioned with special honour. Lord Germanos Mu'akkad was Metropolitan of Ba'albek from 1887 to 1894. He had difficulties there and resigned. So the Patriarch gave him the title of Laodicea (Ladakiyeh), and he went to live in the Lebanon. Here, in 1896, with the encouragement and blessing of Pope Leo XIII, he founded the *Congregation of Missionaries of St Paul*. They are trained and have their convent in his house, at Harissa near Bkerki, close to the great statue of our Lady of the Lebanon. His idea was to train priests who should go out to give missions, in the same manner as the Latin Redemptorists. The Congregation is still small; but it has done, and is doing most noble work. Under the guidance and with the example of their saintly founder, the missioners reach perhaps the highest level of zeal, piety, and sound learning that you will find in the Melkite Church. Already they have done untold good in raising the level of religion in the country parishes. Lord Germanos of Laodicea was the chief influence in the late Synod of 'Ain-Trāz.[3] He died the death of the righteous on February 11, 1912. May he rest in peace; *cuius memoria in benedictione erit*.[4] His work has not died with him. As a legacy to his Church he leaves his missioners of St Paul; in their admirable work he still lives.

There are nuns of each Congregation. Dair alBishārah (Convent of the Annunciation) close to the monastery of St Saviour, is Salvatorian; Dair anNiyāḥ (Convent of Rest) at Kafar Taiy near Beirut is Alepin; Dair anNiyāḥ near Mār Sim'ān and Dair alBishārah at Zūk-Mīkā'īl are Shuwairite.

The Melkites are now well provided with *colleges* for the education of their clergy. The chief, most important, and meritorious of these is the *College of St Anne* at Jerusalem, under the direction of Cardinal Lavigerie's White Fathers.

---

[1] As a result, of 315 Melkite monks alive in 1911, 220 lived not in monasteries, but serving parish churches (Charon, iii, 599).

[2] Two-thirds at present.

[3] July, 1909. See *Echos d'Orient*, 1912, p. 356 *seq.*

[4] I have rarely met any man who gave the impression of being a saint as did Germanos Mu'akkad.

There was an old church of St Anne, built by the Crusaders, by the Bāb Sitti Mariam, opposite the north side of the Ḥaram ashSharīf. It is a most beautiful example of French twelfth-century Romanesque, with the arches just pointed; but it had long been desecrated and was used as a stable. Mgr. Lavigerie, supported by the French Government, bought this in 1877. In 1882 he opened here a seminary for the Melkite clergy. Under the wise direction of the White Fathers it has prospered exceedingly. It is now, without question, the most important and useful establishment of its kind. The French professors keep their Roman rite;[1] but all the students are Melkites; the Byzantine rite dominates the whole house. All the ceremonies carried out in the church are Byzantine; the prayers and devotions of the students are scrupulously formed on Byzantine models. They are taught their rite by the Fathers who have become experts in its history and rules. Perhaps nowhere in the East will you see the Byzantine liturgy carried out so carefully and with such reverence as at St Anne's Church, or when the students go to serve and sing at the Patriarchal Church. Nor does any Melkite priest or bishop know half as much about his own rite as do the Latin professors of St Anne.[2] It is only modestly in the early morning that you may see one of them say his own Roman Low Mass. The students all know how to serve this strange liturgy—which does them no harm. But they themselves are loyal and enthusiastic Byzantines. Cardinal Lavigerie made a rule that none of them may enter his Congregation,[3] so that danger of possible latinization is removed. The seminarists of St Anne have by far the best education of any Melkites. Not only among the Melkites, among all Eastern clergy they are a real aristocracy. They all know French thoroughly. If you wish it, they will explain the Canon Law, rites, and practices of their Church to you in beautiful French. They learn Greek really,

[1] It was not till 1897 that Leo XIII allowed the Benedictines in charge of the Greek College at Rome to use the Byzantine rite during their office there (p. 159). Before that a temporary change of rite was supposed to be impossible in Canon Law (see p. 34). The White Fathers at Jerusalem have never applied for the same privilege.

[2] The only sound modern textbooks of the Byzantine rite as used by Uniates are written by professors of St Anne (A. Couturier, "Cours de Liturgie grecque-melkite," Jerusalem and Paris, 1912; J. B. Rebours, " Traité de Psaltique," Paris, 1906).

[3] Except for this college, the White Fathers have only missions in Africa, where all is Roman. So they could do nothing with Byzantine subjects.

not the mere smattering of letters one so often finds, and they learn Latin—an almost unique phenomenon in their Church. Many of the old-fashioned priests at first did not like students of their rite to know Latin, thinking this to be the beginning of latinization. But it does no one any harm to know another language, and you cannot go far in Catholic theology without Latin. From St Anne, of which Germanos of Laodicea was a warm friend, his Congregation of missioners has been formed exclusively. It is the proud boast of the college that every one of their students has kept celibacy. So from St Anne at Jerusalem, year by year, young priests, trained in all a priest should know, with a formation of sound piety, go out to serve the Melkite Church. St Anne is, more than any other institution, the source from which all good for Melkites may be expected.[1]

The Salvatorian monks have their house of studies at St Saviour, and they send a few students to St Anne and the Greek College at Rome. The monks of Shuwair have theirs at Beirut, whence the students frequent the courses of philosophy and theology at the Jesuit University of St Joseph. The Alepins have rather rudimentary studies in their monasteries. The old seminary of 'Ain-Trāz, after many vicissitudes, was closed finally in 1899. It is now only a country house of the Patriarch.

Except at St Anne, in these colleges what is best taught is Arabic grammar, language, style, and literature. To the Moslem these, with fine writing, form pretty well the sum total of human knowledge; they are still almost the only things that can be acquired thoroughly in the country, at least among natives. The students of Melkite colleges learn a little, a very little, Greek and some French. As textbooks of theology they have Gury's " Moral Theology " and Perrone's " Dogmatic Theology " translated into Arabic. A good number of Melkite students attend the admirable University of St Joseph, conducted by the Jesuits at Beirut. Here a complete course of European education in general and Catholic theology is given. Here, too, the students have the advantage of learning Latin, and so being able to read the usual Catholic theological literature. The Jesuits have students of all Uniate Churches, who hear the same lectures, and then have each their own liturgical practices.[2]

---

[1] The history of the college is told at length by Cyril Charon in the *Echos d'Orient*, xii (1909), pp. 234-241, 298-308.

[2] In their big church every Sunday morning various liturgies, Byzantine, Maronite, perhaps Armenian, Coptic, and Syrian, may be seen celebrated in various chapels, attended by groups of students.

There are a few Melkite students at the Greek College at Rome, at St Sulpice and at Propaganda.

Concerning Melkite Canon Law there will be more to say later.[1]   Meanwhile, we may note that, so far, except for the old law, not easy to define in the case of Uniates, they have only one synod approved by the Pope—namely, the third of 'Ain-Trāz in 1835 (p. 211).   Strictly speaking, the twenty-five canons of this synod are the only special Melkite Canon Law. But they quote and refer to their other synods as well.   When the Acts of the fourth synod of 'Ain-Trāz (p. 227) have been approved, this will, of course, be another authentic source.

Of their rite there is little to say here.   It is simply the Byzantine rite; almost entirely in Arabic.   There is hardly any difference in rite between Byzantine Uniates and the Orthodox, only such points as, naturally, the insertion of the Pope's name in their Diptychs, and certain local differences in the use of special troparia and kontakia, such as occur between the various Orthodox Churches also.   As regards language, the Melkites may use either Arabic or Greek.   In practice, nearly all is Arabic.   Only a few exclamations and Ekphoneseis, sometimes on great occasions the lessons, are sung in Greek.   In these the practice varies according to the competence of the celebrant or deacon, or the solemnity of the occasion.   I have assisted at Melkite liturgies in which not one word of Greek was used.   At others, in the larger towns, the celebrant will sing: Ἄνω σχῶμεν τὰς καρδίας, Εὐχαριστήσωμεν τῷ κυρίῳ, Λάβετε φάγετε . . ., Πίετε ἐξ αὐτοῦ πάντες. . . . Τὰ ἅγια τοῖς ἁγίοις · Εἰρήνη πᾶσιν, and so on (roughly the Ekphoneseis) in Greek.   The μυστικῶς prayers are almost always said in Arabic.[2]

In Syria most of the Melkites live in the towns.   Their chief centre is Zaḥleh in the Lebanon, then Aleppo, Damascus,

---

Yet it is impossible, where all rites are together, to educate the theological students, each in the atmosphere of his own.   The Melkite priest from Beirut knows more about Molinism, but less about his own rite than the student of St Anne's.   [1] See p. 216, n. 1.

[2] The liturgy book published by Michael Abraham Rahmeh (kitāb alLītúrǵiyāt alilahiyyeh), Beirut, 18° 1899, 12° 1900, gives a good idea of the usual mixture of languages (on this edition see Charon, " Hist. Melk.," iii, 84-96).   On the other hand, the Great Euchologion of Jerusalem (kitāb alAfkhūlūgiyūn alkabīr, Franciscan Press, 1865; see Charon, ibid., iii, 122-124) is all Arabic.   Charon has compiled a most laborious and exact bibliography of all Melkite liturgical books (and Orthodox Arabic books) with critical notes, from the earliest times to now (" Hist. Melk.," iii, chap. ii, pp. 23-134).

Beirut. Most of them are merchants and shopkeepers; on the whole they are a prosperous community, except that everything in Syria now gives way to the competition of Western imports. In Egypt they are perhaps the most prosperous Christian community. There they hold important offices under the Government; many become extremely rich, even millionaires, in commerce. But the community suffers from the curse of all Christians in the Near East, constant emigration, chiefly to America and Australia. There are many Melkites in the States, South America, Australia, some in South Africa. When they have made their fortune, they generally come home again and build themselves a house in their native village. But they are nearly always spoiled by their voyage. It is among these returned travellers that one finds detestable imitation of the worst vulgarities of the West, horrid ready-made European clothes, houses furnished with pretentious vulgarity and cheap showy furniture; women in appalling French modes, men who talk to you in Yankee English with an impertinence they think a sign of fine breeding. The semi-Europeanized Levantine is a horrid creature.

In the Antiochene Patriarchate the proportion of Melkites to Orthodox is one to two; it is less in Palestine and Egypt. Charon calculates that there are about 150,000 Melkites altogether, of whom 7,000 are in the West.[1]

Summary.

The Melkite Church, meaning thereby Byzantine Uniates of Arab tongue in Syria, Palestine, and Egypt, dates from the Patriarch Cyril VI in the eighteenth century, who, after tentative reunions of his predecessors, finally came back to Catholic unity. Cyril VI and his Catholic successors represent the old line of Antioch, now reunited to Rome. The greatest Patriarch of this line was Maximos III, during the end of the eighteenth and beginning of the nineteenth centuries. He organized the Church, obtained its civil autonomy, and founded many institutions that still remain. At his time there was a Gallican movement among them, which has long since disappeared. Two Congregations of monks, those of St Saviour and Shuwair, eventually three, by the division of Shuwair into Baladites and Alepins, have played a great part in the story. The Melkites use the Byzantine rite, almost entirely in Arabic. They are certainly one of the most prosperous and advanced communities in the Near East.

[1] See his table, " Hist. Melk.," iii, 354-355.

INDEX

ABBREVIATIONS

Alex. =Alexandria.
Ant. =Antioch.
Archbp. Archbpric =Archbishop, Archbishopric.
Bp. =Bishop.
Byz. =Byzantine.
Cple =Constantinople.
Emp. =Emperor.
I-G. =Italo-Greek.
It. =Italy.
Ptr. Ptrchate =Patriarch, Patriarchate.
Kg. =King.
Sic. =Sicily.

ABDULLAH al Ma'mūn (Khalif), 55
Abdullah Zakher, 207
Abyssinian Catholics, 9
Acquaformosa, 161
Acts of martyrs, for S. It. and Sic.,
    68-69
Ādam, Germanos, 208; his Galli-
    canism, 209; at Synod of Ḳarḳa-
    fah, *ibid.;* other heretical views,
    208-209; his smaller catechism,
    210
Adrian, Archimandrite, companion
    of St Theodore of Canterbury, 73
Adrian IV, Pope (1154–1159), 148
Adrian, St, college of, at San
    Demetrio Corone, 162; monas-
    tery of, 147
Agapios III, Ptr. Ant., 203
Agapios Ri' ashī, 219-220
Agatha, St, 68; monastery of, 147
Agatho, Pope, (678-681), 78
Agrigentum, 55
'Ain Trāz, synod of (1811), 203;
    synod (1835), 211-212, 232; synod
    (1909), 223, 227; country-house
    of Ptr. Ant., 204, 225; seminary
    of, 204
Ajaccio, Greeks at, 171
Albania, in Italy, as opp. to Grecia
    in It., 119, n. 2
Albanians: take refuge in It. and
    Sic. 115 *seq.;* Uniates before
    arrival in It., 116, 120; revive
    Byz. rite in It., 120; Latin
    accusations against, 121; statistics
    of, 168, n. 1
Alberich, Count of Tusculum, 148
Alepin Basilians, 208, 231

Aleppo: rivalry with Damascus,
    197; jealousy of Tyre, 209, n. 1,
    212, 229; Shuwairites at, 208
Alessano, 114
Alessio (Lissus, Alise), 117, n. 2
Alexander III, Pope (1159-1181),
    95, 99, 195
Alexander VII, Pope (1655-1667),
    104
Alexandria, Ptrs. of, in union with
    Rome, 194-197; Patriarchate of,
    joined to that of Antioch, 197,
    203
Alldrīsī, the geographer, 65
Allatæ sunt, Encyclical of Benedict
    XIV (1755), 35-37
Allatius, Leo (Allacci), Life and
    works, 153 *seq.;* works recom-
    mended by Benedict XIV, 36
Alphonsus I. Emp. (1442–1458),
    130
Altamura, 99, 105
Amalfi, Prefects of, 60; Patritius
    of, *ibid.* Great power in 10th
    and 11th cent., *ibid.*
Ambrosian rite, 3
Anastasius Bibliothecarius, 82
Ancona, Greek colony at, 142 *seq.;*
    now Orthodox, 143
Anglicans, and the affair of Totūnḡī,
    214; and the Roman Patriarchate
    76-77
Anne, St, church of, at Ancona, 143;
    college of, at Jerusalem, 222,
    229-230
Antioch, Ptrs. of, in union with
    Rome, 191-194
Apocrisarius (Papal legate), 13, 14

Apulia, attached to Ptrchate. of Cple., 83; less Greek than Calabria, 84, 85, 87

'Araktingi, Basil, 211

Arcudius, Peter, his book on the sacraments, 107; Life and works, 154 seq.

Arichis II, duke of Beneventum, 53

Armenian, Uniates, 9; college at Rome, 41

— Patriarch, all Uniates placed under civil authority of, 204, 217

Arsenios II (Pellegrini) Archimandrite of Grottaferrata, 151

Asad ibn Furat (Kadi of Kairowan), 55

Aspren, St, first Bp. of Naples, 67

Assumptionists (French): mission to Chalcedon, 41

Athanasius III, Ptr. Alex., 195

Athanasius III, Ptr. Ant., 192

Athanasius IV, Ptr. Ant., 194; appoints Silvester as successor, 197

Athanasius V, Ptr. Ant. appointment quashed, 202; re-elected, 203

Athanasius VI, Ptr. Ant., 204.

Athanasius, St. " Greek " church of, at Rome, 152

Athanasius 'Ubaid, Bp. of Beirut, 213; Bp. of Ba'albek, 212, n. 2

Athens, Greek Catholic Lyceum at, 41

Aufidus (Ofanto), river, 57

Augustus, Emp., colonizes Sic., 50

Auspicia rerum secunda, Motu proprio of Leo XIII (1896), 41

Azales, Josaphat, 155

Azyme bread, use of, in Eucharist lawful, 30, 31-32; use of, among I-G., 103, 180, and n. 4; now abolished, 182-183

Bacon, Roger, on the Greeks of S. It., 101

Bahūs, Michael, 175

Balamand, monastery of, 206

Balsamon, Theodore, see Theodore IV

Baptism at Epiphany in S. It. and Sic., 71

Barbarigo, Ptr. of Venice, 139

Barlaam, anti-Hesychast, 108 and n. 4

Bartholomew, Bp. of Grosseto, 32

Bartholomew, St (of Rossanum), his Life of St Neilos, 148 and n.

Basil I, Emp. (867–886), 55

Basil II, Emp. (976–1025), 57

Basil, St, rule of, introduced into Italy, 125

Basilians, 128 seq., preservers of Byz. rite in It., 129; decadence of, in 13th cent., ibid.; in 16th cent., 131; attempts at reform of, 130; in Spain, 131-132 and n. 1; formed into one congregation, 132; first general of, 133; strict rules of, 133, n. 2

Basilian nuns, in Calabria and Sic., 134; in Syria, 229

Basilicata, 59

Basilicus, Kg. of Lodomeria, 31

Beard worn by I-G., 182-183; by Melkites, 228

Beirut, college of Shuwairites at, 231; Patriarchal school at, 222

Benedetto (San) d'Ullano, 123, 161

Benedict, Albanian Bp., 118, 121

Benedict IX, Pope (1033–1048), 148

Benedict XIII, Pope (1724–1730), 32, 201

Benedict XIV, Pope (1740–1758), and the Eastern rites, 33-37; on the I-G., 123

Benedictines in charge of Greek college at Rome, 153, 159

Benediction of the Bl. Sacrament among Uniates, 172, 181

Bernard of Valence, 19

Bessarion, Cardinal, Commendatory Archimandrite of St Saviour, 130; his translation of rule of St Basil, ibid.; Protector of O.S. Bas. in Italy, 130, n. 7; his work for Grottaferrata, 148

Bessarione, the review, 40, n. 1

Bibbona, Greek colony at, 143; now all Latin, 144

Bishops, Byz., in Italy, 177 seq.

Bisignano, 160, 161

Blasius, St, church of, at Venice, 136

Boccaccio, on Barlaam, 108, n. 4

Boitylos (Oitylos), 169 and n. 2

Bosra-and-Hauran, diocese of, 226

Bova, 98, 109

Branch theory, existence of Uniate damaging to, 27

Brindisi, 104

Bruttii, Πρωτοσπαθάριος of, 60

Bucali, Maria, 112

Bulgars, colleges for, 41

Buonincontro, Mgr., Bp. of Girganti, 122

Byzantine Uniates, correspond to Orthodox Church, 8

Byzantine rite, Latin infiltrations into, 150. See also Rite.

Caetani, the, 148

Calabria, change of name of, 57; Strabo on the people of, 51; attached to Byz. Patrchate, 83; Albanian colonies in, at present time, 159 *seq.*; their poverty, 163-164

Calendar, Gregorian, adopted by I-G., 181; by Melkites, 221; by Maronites, *ibid.*; by all Uniates, *ibid.* n. 2

Camodeca (Pietro) dei nobili Coronei, 118, 161, 177

Candida, St, 67

Canon Law, of Uniates, *see* p. 216, n. 1; of I-G., 176 *seq.*; Melkite, 232

Capitanata, province of, 57

Carella, Laurence, Archdeacon of Ascoli, 130

Cargese (Carghese), Greeks at, 171-173; Greek dialect at, 173

Cassano al Ionio, 160, 161

Castoreggio, 160

Castrogiovanni, 63 and n. 2

Catanzaro, 101

Catanzariti (Catumsyritus), J. B., enemy of Byz. rite, 107 and nn. 2 and 3

Catapan, vicegerent of Emp. in Italy, 58; subordinate to Exarch. at Ravenna, 59; his difficult task, 60

Celibacy of Roman clergy, 97

Cerularius, intolerant of Roman rite, 30; effect of his schism in S. It. and Sic., 82 *seq.*, 92 *seq.*

Chaldees, 9, Chaldean Ptr., 17

Charles the Great, 53

Chimara (Cimarra), 117

Christianity in S. It. and Sic. in 2nd cent., 69

Churches, sense in which we may speak of various, 2

Cicero on the provincialisms of Sicily, 50

Civita, 161

Clement Bahuth, Ptr. Ant., 221-222; imposes Greg. Calendar on Melkites, 221

Clement IV, Pope (1265-1268), 109

Clement VII, Pope (1523-1574), 32, 143

Clement VIII, Pope (1592-1605), and the Ruthenians, 32

Clement XI, Pope (1700-1721), 140, 194, 196

Clement XII, Pope (1730-1741), and the I-G., 123

Clement XIII, Pope (1758-1769), 141, 174

College, Armenian, at Rome, 41

— Uniate Coptic, at Cairo, *ibid.*

— Bulgarian, at Philoppopolis and at Adrianople, *ibid.*

— Ruthenian, at Rome, 41-42

— Greek, at Rome, 151 *seq.*

Colleges for Melkite clergy, 229-231

Commendatory Archimandrites (Abbots), 125 and n. 6, 126 and n. 1, 149; abolished, 132

Conferences for Union of Churches at Vatican, 39

Congregation of the Oratory of the Greek rite, 123-124

Congregation of the Missionaries of St Paul, 229

Congregation for Eastern rites, 38 and n. 2

Constance, daughter of Roger II, 127

Constans II, Emp. (641–668), 56; his new division of the Empire, 58

Constantinople: policy towards Greeks in It. and Sic., 56, 85; intolerance of Ptrs. of, 14; list of Italian and Sicilian sees subject to, 88

Contessa Entelina, 122, 167

Convents, Melkite, 229; I-G., 125

Copts, Uniate, college for, 41

Corigliano d'Otranto, 112

Corsica, Greeks in, 169 *seq.*; feuds with Greeks, 170, 171

Cosimo I, Grand Duke of Tuscany, 173

Cosimo III, Grand Duke of Tuscany (1670-1723), 143

Crati, river, 160

Crescentius, family of, 147

Croia, 116

Cumæ, 48

Cyril V, Ptr. Ant., 193-194

Cyril VI (Seraphim Tanas), Ptr. Ant., 34, 186, 190; brings about reunion of Melkites with Rome, 197 *seq.*; strife with rival Silvester, 198; validity of his election, 199-200; receives pallium, 201; abdicates, 202; death, *ibid.*

Cyril VIII, Ptr. Melk., 42, 222, 224

Cyril, St, and St Methodius, cult extended to whole church, 39

d'Afflitto, Hannibal, enemy of Byz. rite, 106 and n. 4

Dair al Mukhallis. *See* Saviour, St, monastery of.

Dalmatia, Italian language in, 135

Damascus, Synod of, 192

de Hauteville, family of, 62; Tancred, *ibid.;* William, *ibid.;* Drogo, Humphrey, Robert, Roger, 63
Delfau, Francis, O.S.B., on Commendatory Abbots, 125, n. 6
della Porta, James, architect of the Greek college at Rome, 152
del Pozzo, Joseph, 133
Demandatam cœlitus, decree of Benedict XIV (1743), 34, 202
Demetrius, St, of Thessalonica, church of, at Piana dei Greci, 166
Demetrio (San) Corone, 119, 162
Denny, E., on the limits of the jurisdiction of the Roman Bp., 76, n. 2
Desiderius, last Lombard King, 53
Di Giovanni, John, 73, n. 1
Ditereo (δευτερεύων), 106, n. 1
Domenichino, frescoes by, in church at Grottaferrata, 149
Dominic, Ptr. of Gradus and Aquileia, 30
Dominicans in charge of Greek college at Rome, 152
Dorotheus I, Ptr. Ant., 192
Doxopatres (Doxapatres, etc.). *See* Neilos.
Dress of I-G. clergy, 183

Eastern liturgical practices introduced into the West, 36
— rites, congregation for, 38; reverence due to, 33
Ecclesiology of S. It. in first seven centuries, difficulties concerning, 70, 71
Education, lack of, among Eastern schismatics 24; Western, advantages of in the East, 25, n. 2; of Melkites, 230-231
Egypt, Melkites of, subject to Ptr. Ant., 203, 215
Epigonation, 175
Etshmiadzin, 15
Etsi Pastoralis, Bull of Bened. XIV, 33
Euchologion, 179
Eugene IV, Pope (1431-1447), 130
Euplius, St, Acts of, 65
Euthymios, Bp. of Tyre, 193, 194, 197; introduces changes into Melkite liturgy, 201; founds Salvatorians, 205
Euthymios II, Ptr. Ant., 192
Eutychios, Ptr. Ant., 193
Ex quo primum, Bull of Benedict XIV (1754), 179

Facéa, George, Byz. Bp. of Venice, 140-142
Farneta, 160
Feasts, Roman, observed by I-G., 181
Felix, St, Acts of, 65
Fertorius (Fortore), river, 57
Fi la e t' in' Zoti, Albanian periodical, 165
Filioque, Uniates say, in the Creed, 32; *ibid.,* n. 2
Finān, Basil, Bp. of Baïas, 198
Firman, 201
Firmo, 161
Florence, Council of, on the Byzantine rite, 32, 109, 192
Frascineto, 161
Frederick II, Emp. 65, n. 3, 148

Gaeta, 60
Gaetano, Cardinal, Archbp. of Taranto, 122
Galatina, 112
Galatone, 114
Gallipoli, 98, 100, 112
Garibaldi, Albanians enthusiastic for, 163
Gastalds, 54
Gazir, Jesuit college at, 222
Gelasius I, St, Pope (492-496); letter to Bps. of S. It. and Sic., 71
Gennadios II, Ptr. Cple., 192
George, St, church of, at Venice, 136
Gerace, 97, 98; diocese of, united with Oppido, 108
Gerasimos, 206, 207
Gerasimos Phocas, 140
Germanos Ādam. *See* Ādam.
Germanos. Muᶜakkad, 229
Gibarra, 221-222
Giustiniani, Cardinal, Protector of Greek college at Rome, 152
Goths, invasion of, 51; effects on Greeks of S. It., 52; on ecclesiastical situation, 75
Gradus and Aquileia, Patriarchate of, merged into that of Venice, 30, n. 4
Grafeo, S Maria del, church of, 110 and n. 2
Grande Munus, Encycl. of Leo XIII (1880), 39
Greater Greece, 48-49
Greco-Ruthenum, college in Rome, 152
Greek, college in Rome, 151-159; constant changes in direction, 152; closed at time of Revolution, reopened 1845, 153; great men produced by, 153-155; anomalies

of rite at, 157-158; Byz. ordaining
Bp. at, 159; costume of students,
159
Greek colonies, their relation to the
motherland, 43
Greek dialect at Cargese, 173; in the
Terra d'Otranto, 105
Greek influence, revived in It. and
Sic. 7th-9th cent., 56; at its height
in 10th cent., 57
— islands, Latin Catholics in, 135
— language spoken in most of Im-
perial Themes, 61; the liturgical
language in S. It. and Sic. from
2nd cent., 69
" Greek " rites, 20
Greek writers of S. It. and Sic.,
49-51
Gregory I, St, Pope (590–604); his
zeal for Church in S. It. and Sic,
71-72; letter to Peter Bp. of
Otranto, 77; letter to Southern
Bps. on details of rite, 78-79
Gregory V, Pope (996–999), 147
Gregory VI, Ptr. of Cple, 216
Gregory VII, Pope (1073–1085),
Hildebrand, 95
Gregory IX, Pope (1227–1241), 148
Gregory XIII, Pope (1572–1585),
32, 132; founds Greek college at
Rome, 151
Gregory of Akragas, 72
Gregory Asbestas of, Syracuse, 73, 83
Gregory the Hymnograph, 72
Gregory Yusûf, Melkite Ptr., 222
Grimani, Dominic, Cardinal, Pro-
tector of Basilians, 131
Grottaferrata, monastery of, 128,
134, 146-151; its vicissitudes, 148;
rebuilt, 149; the church, *ibid.;*
school of hymn-writers at, 150;
college for I-G. at, 150; works
on, 151, n. 2
Guiscard. *See* Robert.
Guzzetta, George Fr., founder of
Congr. of Oratory of Greek rite,
and Institution of Holy Family,
124 and n. 3, 164, 165

Hāmud, Emir, 63
Harissa, convent at, 229
Harnack on early Christianity in
Sic., 68
Hats of Melkite clergy, dispute
concerning, 216-217
Haurān, district of, 212 and n. 5
Henry I, Kg. of Cyprus, 31
Hesychasm, 108 and n. 3
Hildebrand. *See* Gregory VII.

Holy See, properties of, in S. It. and
Sic., 81, n. 3
Honorius III, Pope (1216–1227),
31, 130

Iconoclasts, aggression of, in Roman
province, 80
Ignatius IV, Ptr. Ant., 204
Ignatius V, Ptr. Ant., 174, 204
Ignatius Ephrem II, Syrian Catholic
Ptr., 42
Ignatius Gauhăr. *See* Athanasius
V.
Ignatius Sarrûf. *See* Ignatius IV.
Ignorance of some Protestants con-
cerning Uniates, 21
Ikonostasion, not usual in I-G.
churches, 181; at Grottaferrata,
149; at Cargese, 172
Illyricum, Byzantine depredations
in, 82
Innocent III, Pope (1198–1216), 127,
148
Institution of the Holy Family, 166
In suprema, Encycl. of Pius IX, 37
and nn. 3 and 4
Inter cætera, letter of Benedict XIV
to Cyril VI, 202
Intolerance of Orthodox Church, 19
Ioannikios II, Ptr. of Cple, 141,
158, n. 2
Isidore of Kiev, Cardinal, 136
Italo-Albanian seminary at San
Demetrio Corone, now a lay-
college, 162
Itelgrimus, Bp. of Cosenza, 75, n. 1

Jacobites, 9
James, St, " in Acquaviva," church
of, at Leghorn, 173
January, St, 69 and n. 3
Jerusalem, Melkite synod of, 219;
college of St Anne at, 222, 229-
230
Jesuits, in charge of the Greek
college, 152, 153; difficulties, 157;
missions in the Levant, 193
John IV, Ptr. Ant., 191
John V, Pope (685–686), 56
John XIX, Pope (1024–1033), 148
John Chrysostom, St, 13th cen-
tenary of, 42
John Maro, St, 202
Julius II, Pope (1503–1513), 131
Julian della Rovere, Cardinal, and
Grottaferrata, 149. *See* also
Julius II, Pope.
Jurisdiction of Latin and Byz. Bps.,
questions concerning, 120, 121

Kabasilas, Samuel, Ptr. Alex., 196
Kalkeophilos, Athanasius, 109
Kalymaukion (Kamilaukion, etc.), 159, 183, 216
Karkafah, synod of, 203, 209; acts of, condemned, 210
Karlowitz, Peace of, 135
Komnenos, Isaac, Emp. (1057–1059), 191
Korone, Albanian settlement at, 118
Kyriakos, Demetrios Phalereus, 155

Ladislaus, Kg. of Naples (1400–1414), 148
Langénieux, Cardinal, 39
Langobardia, 58, 89; to be distinguished from our " Lombardy," 89, n. 5
Language has little to do with determining rite, 19
Lascaris, Constantine, 110, n. 2, 131
Lateran Council IV, 31
Latin influence on Church of S. It. and Sic. before Norman conquest, 70
Latin names of Bps. in S. It., 75
Lavigerie, Cardinal, 230
Lazii-Albani, family of, 119
Lebanon, Shuwairite monks in, 208
Lectionaries of Naples, Latin, in 6th cent., 74
Leghorn, I-G. at, 173-175
Leo I, St, Pope (440–461), letter to Sicilian Bps., 71, 72, n. 1; insists on attendance of Sicilian Bps. at Roman synods, 78
Leo III, the Isaurian Emp., 60; tries to enforce Iconoclasm in Italy, 81
Leo VI, the Wise, Emp. (886–911), 84
Leo X, Pope (1513–1521), 32
Leo XIII, Pope (1878–1903), and the Eastern Churches, 38-42; and the Byz. rite at Grottaferrata, 150
Leo, St, Bp. of Catana, 90, n. 1
Ligarides, Pantaleon, 156
Liturgikon, 179
Liturgy of St Peter, 180
Lombard. Duchy of Beneventum, 53
Lombard laws and customs, 54
Lombard rites, 75
Lombards invade Italy, 52; Roman hatred of, 53; completely latinized, ibid.; influence in S. It., 54
Louis II, Emp. (855–875), 55
Loyalty of Uniates, 22-23
Lucy, St, 68

Luitprand of Cremona, 84 and n. 1
Lungro, 160

Macchia, 163
Maina, 143
Maine, 169
Makarios III, Ptr. Ant., 193
Makarios IV, Ptr. Ant., 204
Makarios of Diyárbakr, 213
Makarios Sammán, 213
Makrine, St, sister of St Basil, 134
Malabar Uniates, 9
Malta, Byzantines in, 168
Maniakes, George, Greek general against Saracens, 55
Manuel I, Emp. (1143–1180), 195
Marcian, St, Bp. of Sicily, 67
Margunios, Maximos, 137, n. 2
Mar-Hanna, monastery of, 206
Maria, S. dell'Isodia, church of, at Bova, 109
Maria, S. del Patire, monastery of, 101, 127; founded by St Neilos, 127; Archimandrite of, ibid.; origin of name, 128
Maria, S. della Navicella, church of Shuwairites at Rome, 207
Maria, S. Hodegetria, church of, at Rossano, 127, 128, n. 1; at Messina, 128
Mark of Calabria, Bp., present at Council of Nicea, 68
Maronite, Church, 9; Patriarch, 17
Maronites and Melkites, 34-35, 202
Marseilles, Melkite church at, 211
Martin V, Pope (1417–1431), 130
Maximos III (Mazlūm), Ptr. Ant. (1833-1855)   ; early life, 210; elected Ptr., 211; holds synod at 'Ain Tráz, 211-212; ordains too many Bps., 212-213; zeal for Byz. rite, 215; obtains civil emancipation for Melkites, 218; his title, 219; holds synod of Jerusalem, 219; his death, 220; character, ibid.
Maximos, St, the Confessor, 72
Mazlūm. See Maximos III.
Melchitarum catholicorum synodus, Bull of Gregory XVI, 211
Melfi, synod of, 96
Melkites, origin of name, 185-186; ethnological origin of, 187; ecclesiastical origin of, 188 seq.; civil emancipation of, 217-218; persecution of, by Orthodox, 204; government, 223-227; sees, 226; clergy, 227-228; religious orders at present day, 228; chief centres of, 232; rites and customs of, 34; present state of, 233; statistics,

233; at Leghorn, 174; called Χαλεπίδες 200, n. 4; quarrels with Maronites, 34-35, 202

Menniti, Peter, 133

Messagne, 104

Messina, monastery of S Maria de Latina at, 96; church of S Maria del Grafeo at, 110 and n. 2; Archimandrite of, 125; his quarrels with Archbp., 126; at present day, 168

Methodius I, Ptr. Cple. (842-846), 83

Metropolitan (Mutrān), title of Melkite Bps., 226

Metropolitical authority of Pope over Bps. of S. It. and Sic., 76-80

Mezzoiuso (Mezzoiusso), 166 and n. 3

Michael III, Ptr. Ant., 192

Missionaries, Latin, in the East, rules for, 35, 40

Mixed marriages, between different rites, 35

Monasticism (Byzantine) in It. and Sic., 124 seq.; in Syria, 205-208

Monreale, 166, 167

Monte Cassino, 147

Morals of Uniate clergy, 26

Mozarabic rite, 3, 19

Murad II, (1421–1451), 116

Musa (Moses) ibn Nusair, Emir, 54

Mutrān. See Metropolitan.

Naples, chief Greek city in Italy, 59; Duke of, ibid.; last Duke of 60, n. 1; added to kingdom of Normans, 60; six Byz. churches at, in 13th cent., 99; St Peter believed to have founded church at, 67; Latin and Roman in feeling, 85; rebels against Iconoclast edict, 86; immigration of Albanians, 118, 119; Uniates here now all Albanians, 145

Nardò, 112

Nasri, Neophytos, Bp. of Saidnaia, 197, 198, 207 and n. 3

"Nation," in Turkish sense, 15, 187

Naxos, 48

Nazarios, St, monastery of, 147

Neilos, St (Nicholas), the younger, 109; life, 147 seq.; statue of, 151

Neilos, St, the Elder, 147, n. 2

Neilos Doxopatres, Greek Archimandrite at Palermo, 88; his writings, 93

Nicastro, 101

Nicholas I, Pope (858-867), 30, 78

Nicholas II, Pope (1058-1061), 97

Nicholas III, Pope, and the Byz. rite, 32

Nicholas. See Neilos, St.

Nicholas, St, church of, at Palermo, 165

Nikephoras Phocas, Emp. (963-969), 84

Nikon, Ptr. of Moscow, 156

Nikon, St, 69

Nilo, St. See Neilos, St.

Niphon, Ptr. Alex., 195

Norman invasion of It. and Sic., 61 seq.; prevents schism in It. and Sic., 85, 92; alliance with Papacy, 95

Norman attitude towards religion, 64, 94

Nuns, Greek, convents of, 125; —Melkite, 229

Odriscol, Denis, 104

Oppido, 98, 108

Ordaining-Bps. for I-G., 123, 163, 177

Ordinaries, none among the Italo-Greeks now, 176

Ordination of Bps. of S. It. and Sic. by the Pope, 78

Orientalium dignitas, Const. of Leo XIII (1894), 40-41

Orsini, 148

Otranto, 98; diocese of, 111; Terra di, 100, 105

Otto III, Emp. (993-1002), 147

Pachomios, Bp. of Zakynthos and Kephallenia, 137

Paisios, Orth. Ptr. of Jerusalem, 156

Palaiologos, Thomas, 118, 144

Palazzo Adriano, 167, 168

Palermo, I-G., college at, 164; colony of Albanians at, 165

Pancras, St, Bp. of Tauromenium, 67

Pandulf V, Duke of Capua, 62

Pandulf, Iron - Head, Lombard prince, 54

Paomia, 169, 170

"Paradise" of trees, 149

Parasceve, St (Veneranda), 69

Parthenois II, Ptr. of Cple, 138, n. 2

Parthenois Kalkandes, 169

Pascal II, Pope (1099–1118), 95

Passarowitz, Peace of, 135

Patriarchate, Roman, growth of, 5; Byzantine, beginning of, 76

Patriarchates, concept of, 12; relation of, to rite, 12-14; Uniate, involved system of, 16; number of, 3

Patriarchs, Melkite, election of, 223, 227; residence of, at Cairo and Damascus, 225
Patrimony of Holy See, agreement with Norman Kings concerning, 95
Paul I, Pope (757–767), 112
Paul III, Pope (1534–1549), and the Albanians, 121
Paul V, Pope (1605–1621), and the Ruthenians, 32
Paul, Bp. of Naples, 86
Paul, St, in Lower Italy, 66–67
Peter III, Ptr. Ant., 191
Peter IV, Ptr. Ant., 190, 222
Peter Mogilas, Confession of, 193
Peter, St, in Lower Italy, 67
Petri et Pauli Acta, 68
Philagathos, John, Antipope, 147
Philaret, St, monastery of, 133
Philip II, of Spain (1556–1598), 131
Philotheos I, Ptr. Alex., 195
Philotheos II, Ptr. Alex., 196
Phlangineion, School at Venice, 139
Photius, schism of, its effect on It. and Sic., 82, 92
Piana dei Greci, 102 and n. 1, 165, 166; Oratorian house at, 124
Pieri Dom Oderisio Maria, 144
Pius II, Pope (1458–1464), 148
Pius IV, Pope (1555–1559), 32
Pius VI, Pope (1775–1799), 37, 162
Piu VII, Pope (1800–1823), 174
Pius IX, Pope (1846–1878), and the Uniates, 37–39
Pius X, Pope (1903–1914), and the Uniates, 42–43
Place, its relation to rite, 20
Plataci, 161
Policastro, 104
Political history of S. It. and Sic., 48 seq.
Popes and the Uniates, 29–43
Popes of Eastern origin, 56
Porcile, 161
Præclara gratulationis, Encycl. of Leo XIII (1894), 42
Precedence of churches, quarrels concerning, 104
Prejudices against Uniates, 21 seq.
Promiscuity of rite forbidden, 35
Propaganda, University of, 153
Protopapa, 106, n. 1
Provinces, Latin, founded in S. It. and Sic., 91, 96
Pulcheria, Empress (450–457), 127

Rainulf, Count of Aversa, 61
Rason, 159
Ravenna lost to the Empire, 81

Reggio (Rhegium), 98; tenacious of Byz. rite, 99; church of S Maria della Cattolica at, 105, n. 3
Reres, George and Basil, 118
Resurrectionists, in charge of Greek college at Rome, 153
Reunion of Melkites under Cyril VI, 197
Reunion of schismatical Churches, Leo XIII and, 42; reviews for, 40, n. 1; conferences for, at the Vatican, 39
Rhodinos, Neophytos, 155
Ricci, Scipio, Bp. of Pistois, 209
Richard, Count of Aversa, 97
Rite, distinct from religion, 11; how determined, 18; same in various languages, ibid.; rules concerning change of, 41
Rite, Byzantine, spread of, in S. It. and Sic. in 8th cent., 80; decadence of, in 14th cent., 101 seq.; maintenance of, by the Popes, 104; restored in pure form at Grottaferrata, 182
Rite of Italo-Greeks, 178-183; Latin infiltrations into, 180
Rite of Melkites, 232
Rites in Magna Græcia and Sic. until 8th cent., controversy concerning, 73, n. 1, 74
Robert Guiscard (de Hauteville), 63
Rodotà, Felix Samuel, first Byz. ordaining-Bp. for I-G., 123, 161-162
Rodotà, Pietro Pompilio, nephew of the above, 123; historian of the Byz. rite in Italy; life and works, 155; quoted, passim
Roger I, Kg. of Sicily, 63, 96, 97
Roger II, Kg. of Sicily, 64
Romanus Pontifex, Const. of Pius IV, concerning Albanians and I-G., 121-122
Romuald of Salerno, 95 and n. 5
Rossano (Rossanum), 97, 109; centre of Byz. monasticism, 127
Ruffo, Nicholas Anthony, first General of O.S. Bas., in Italy, 133
Ruthenian college at Rome, 41-42
Ruthenians, admitted to Greek college at Rome, 152; protected by Pope Benedict XIII, 32-33
Rutski, Joseph Velamin, 155

Sacraments outside Orth. Church considered invalid by schismatics, 213
Sā'ïgh, Nicholas, 207

Salernum, Στρατηγός of, 60
San Basile, 161
San Benedetto d'Ullano, 123, 161
San Cosimo, 163
San Constantino, 160
San Demetrio Corone, 119, 162
San Giorgio Albanese, 163
Sannà (Osanna), church of, at Brindisi, 104; at Reggio, 106
San Paolo, 160
Santa Cristina Gela, 166
Santa Sofia d'Epiro, 162
Santoro, Cardinal, 98, n. 1; on the state of Basilians in his time, 131; Life of, 131, n. 2; letter to Archbp. of Messina, 110; interest of, in the Greek college at Rome, 152
Saraceni, Matthew, Archbp. of Rossano, 109, 127
Saracens invade Italy, 54-55
Saviour, St, monastery of, at Messina, 110, 125; Philanthropos (Filatropo), convent of, at Palermo, 134
Saviour, St, Melkite monks of, 205-206
Scanderbeg (George Alexander Castriota), 116 and n. 2
Schirò, Joseph, 102, 117, n. 3
Schisms of Photius and Cerularius: effect on It. and Sic., 82 seq., 92, seq.; on Syrians, 189
Schools of Mary, 124, 165, 166
Seberos, Gabriel, 137 and n. 2, 138 and n. 1
Seraphim Tānās. See Cyril VI.
Sergius, Bp. of Naples, 86
Serperi, 147
Severina, St, diocese of, in Calabria, 89, 90, 97; Canons of, 98, n. 1
Shalhūb, Joseph, 175
Shuwair, monks of, 206 seq.; divided into two Congregations, 208
Sicily, earliest evidence of Christianity in, 68; latinization of, under Normans, 96 seq.; Albanian colonies in, 164
Sidi-Meruan, 172
Silvester, rival claimant against Cyril VI of Ant., 197-201
Simeoni, Cardinal, 172
Sirlet (Sirletus, Sirleto), Cardinal William, prefect of Congregation for Eastern rites, 105; Life, 113, n. 2; relations with Greek college in Rome, 152
Solicitude of Popes for Eastern rites, 34
Sophronius II, Ptr. Alex., 195
Sophronius V, Ptr. of Jerusalem, 197

Spiridon, St, 172
Squillace (Scyllatium), 98
Stauropegia (independent monasteries), 96; abolished in Italy after Norman conquest, 127
Stephanopulos, family, 169
Stephen II, Maronite Ptr., 193
Stephen, Duke of Naples and Bp. (767-799), 86
Stephen, St, Bp. of Rhegium, 67
Strabo, on the people of S. It., 51
Sulaimān, 206
Συλλειτουργός, 83
Superiority of Uniates over schismatics, 24-25
Superstitious ideas among Melkites, 34
Synkelloi, 227 and n. 6
Syracuse, siege of, 48; Latin colony at, 50; made Archbpric. by Emperor, 83; Byz. clergy at, in 11th cent., 100
Syria, " The Church of," 214, 215
Syrian Uniates, 9

Τακτικά, 87
Taranto (Tarentum), 55, n. 1; Byzantine in the 16th cent., 114
Tarasios, Ptr. of Cple. (784-806), 83 and n. 2
Tauromenium (Taormina), colonized by Augustus, 50, n. 1; made Archbpric. by the Emperor, 83
Themes, division of Empire into, 57 seq.
Theodore I, Pope (642-649), 56
Theodore IV, Ptr. Ant., 191
Theodore V, Ptr. Ant., 192
Theodore, St, of Canterbury, 73
Theodoric, Kg. of the Goths, 51, 52
Theodosius V, Ptr. Ant., 191
Theophanes Kerameus, 65, n. 1
Theophanes, Ptr. of Jerusalem, 197
Theotiles of Chalkis, 48
Titles of Melkite Ptrs., 223-224
Titular Bps., Melkite, 227
" Titular sees " substituted for the term " in partibus infidelium," 39
Toleration of diversity of rite within the Catholic Church, 11
Totūngī, Athanasius, history, 213-215
Traina, 100
Tropea, 98, 100
Turkish Government and the Uniates, 217-218; Leo XIII intervenes with, 42
Turks and the Albanians, 115
Turmarchs, 59

Typaldos, Meletios, Byz. Bp. of
  Venice (1681–1718), 139; charac-
  ter of, 139-140
Typikon of Grottaferrata, 179
Tyre, 209, n. 1, 212, 229
Tzigalas, Hilarion, 156-157
Tzigalas, John, 155

Ughelli, Ferdinand, Abbot, 133
Uniate Copts, 9
Uniates, meaning of the term, 1;
  reason of the distinction from
  Latins, 4; importance of, to
  concept of the Catholic Church,
  27; statistics of, 21
Urban II, Pope (1088-1099), 112
Urban VIII, Pope (1623–1644), and
  the Greek college in Rome, 158

Vaccarizzo Albanese, 163
Vallelucio, 147
Valletta, Uniates at, 168

Venice, Greek colony at, 135-137;
  whole community of Greeks now
  Orthodox, 142
Vicars General, appointed by Latin
  ordinaries for Byzantine Uniates,
  13, n. 3, 177
Vicars Patriarchal, 225
Villehardouin, family of, 191
Vitus, St, 69

White Fathers, at St Anne's, Jerusalem, 230
William I, Kg. of Sicily (1154–1166),
  148
William II, Kg. of Sicily (1166–1189),
  95
Wiscard. See Robert Guiscard.

Zachary, Pope (741–752), 85
Zaḥleh, diocese of, 212, 222
Zamoisk, synod of, 32
Ziyādatullah ibn Aġlab, Emir, 55
Ẓuḳ Mīkhā'īl, 204